The Culture of Fengshui in Korea

The Culture of Fengshui in Korea

An Exploration of East Asian Geomancy

Hong-key Yoon

LEXINGTON BOOKS

A Division of
ROWMAN & LITTLEFIELD PUBLISHERS, INC.
Lanham • Boulder • New York • Toronto • Plymouth, UK

LEXINGTON BOOKS

A division of Rowman & Littlefield Publishers, Inc.
A wholly owned subsidary of The Rowman & Littlefield Publishing Group, Inc.
4501 Forbes Boulevard, Suite 200
Lanham, MD 20706

Estover Road
Plymouth PL6 7PY
United Kingdom

British Library Cataloguing in Publication Information Available

Library of Congress Cataloging-in-Publication Data

The hardback edition of this book was previously cataloged by the Library of Congress as
follows:

Yoon, Hong-key.
  The culture of fengshui in Korea : an exploration of East Asian geomancy / Hong-key
Yoon.
     p. cm.
  Includes bibliographical references and index.
  1. Feng shui—Korea—History. 2. Feng shui—Social aspects—Korea (South) 3.
  Korea—Social life and customs. 4. Feng shui—East Asia. I. Title.
  BF1779.F4Y66 2006
  133.3'33709519—dc22   2006024929

ISBN-13: 978-0-7391-1348-6 (cloth : alk. paper)
ISBN-10: 0-7391-1348-8 (cloth : alk. paper)
ISBN-13: 978-0-7391-1349-3 (pbk. : alk. paper)
ISBN-10: 0-7391-1349-6 (pbk. : alk. paper)

Printed in the United States of America

 ∞™ The paper used in this publication meets the minimum requirements of American
National Standard for Information Sciences—Permanence of Paper for Printed Library
Materials, ANSI/NISO Z39.48–1992.

To
my wife, Inshil
and
my children,
Albert Sokhon, Caroline Sokyong, Frances Soka,
Annabelle Sokjong and ReneeMarie Sokwoo

Contents

Figures

Tables

Preface

This book explores the nature of geomantic principles and their applications in Korean culture. The importance of geomancy in understanding the East Asian cultural landscape and cultural ecology is difficult to overemphasize. This book represents my attempt to understand geomancy over the last thirty years.

When Edgar Anderson started to write his highly admired scientific book, *Plants, Man and Life*, he was advised not to write a book for an imaginary public, but to think of some actual audience.[1] He decided to write his book for a person with a "deep-seated curiosity; good, disciplined mind; broad interests; but little technical understanding of plants." He chose the prime minister of India, Pandit Nehru, as such a person and kept him in his thoughts throughout the writing of his book.

This story inspired me. I tried to think of a person for whom I wanted to write this book, because geomancy employs vague and strange terminologies and mystic ideas, and can be a confusing and difficult subject to comprehend by Western readers. I failed. I couldn't think of an actual person to serve as my reader. Instead, contrary to Anderson's advice, I came up with an "imaginary" group of Western people as my readers: the students and scholars who want to know more about geomancy but do not yet know much about it. For such westerners, I wrote this book. My goal is to convey a balanced picture of the principles of geomancy and their impact on Korean society and culture.

It might be helpful to state at the outset my personal attitudes toward geomancy as a belief system. I am interested in studying geomantic principles and how they have fashioned the Korean cultural landscape, but I neither believe in nor practice geomancy. I am thus like a person who enjoys watching a football game, without actually playing the game. I am not a professional geomancer who chooses auspicious sites for a fee, but I am an observer of the geomancy 'game'.

A football player may not be a suitable person to write a credible review of a football game, as he does not have a chance to view the game as a whole. In the same way, professional geomancers who choose auspicious sites for their clients may not be the best analysts of geomancy. Scholars typically have a broader perspective and are better able to explain the theory and practice of geomancy. Just as a theologian of Christianity does not need to be a believer or a practicing Christian, a geomancy researcher does not need to believe in the art of geomancy and practice it.

I was born and raised in a small South Korean village, Haepyong, of Sonsan County, North Kyongsang Province. There were about 120 households in the district. There were hills in the background and rice paddies in front. The highest peak behind the village was called *chusan,* which literally means the main mountain of the village in geomantic terms. The village, which sat by the Nakdong River and had a long history of prosperity, was full of geomantic ideas. It was considered an auspicious settlement. Some families changed the locations of their house gates or laid earth-packed fences around their houses according to a geomancer's advice. Geomancy was a part of village life. As I grew up, it was natural to accept the notion that some places were better than others, and that to avoid misfortune one had to be careful not to disturb the geomantic harmony of the site when repairing or modifying one's house and fence. It was considered desirable, if one could afford it, to consult a knowledgeable person or geomancer about any project. When I was a boy, I recall my father commenting that you couldn't take these kinds of superstitious customs seriously. I did not fully understand geomancy, but I grew up with it.

My intellectual journey to the study of geomancy started in 1971 upon meeting Professor Clarence J. Glacken at Berkeley. I became acquainted with the Berkeley geography department through learning about Carl O. Sauer and his geographic tradition. I was fascinated by his studies, especially his works on cultural diffusion. When I wanted to study cultural geography in 1971, he had long since retired from teaching and was a professor emeritus of geography at Berkeley. But Professor Glacken was still active and I had heard of his work *Traces on the Rhodian Shore.*[2] This study of ideas about culture and nature first sparked my desire to study at Berkeley. As soon as I arrived, I called on Professor Glacken. During my visit I noticed a geomancy chart (compass) on the wall of his office. Astonished to find it in this most unlikely place, I exclaimed (as I recall), "This is a geomancy chart! What is it doing here?" Professor Glacken expressed much interest in geomancy and encouraged me to study the art, leading me to write my Ph.D. dissertation on geomancy in Korea. So my study "Fengshui: The Impact of Chinese Geomancy on Korean Culture" began.

While studying at Berkeley, I had the good fortune to learn and discuss cultural geography in person with Professor Sauer and to learn folklore, sociological theories, and Chinese culture from Professor Wolfram Eberhard of the Sociology Department. When I completed my dissertation in 1976, Professor Eberhard arranged that it, along with an appendix on the origin and diffusion of geomancy, be published.[3] Since then I have studied the cultural geography of the Maori people in New Zealand[4], but geomancy has always captivated me. This book was originally meant to be a simple revision of my 1976 work, but it grew to incorporate all of my research on geomancy over the last thirty years.

In Ole Bruun's recently published book, *Fengshui in China,* I found the following perceptive comment on my academic identity:

> Despite being produced by a Korean, Yoon's work has nevertheless become prominent among the 'Western' works on fengshui cited in the recent wave of Chinese works on the subject. Thus regarded as an Eastern writer in the West and as a Western writer in China, Yoon has had a considerable impact not only in conveying ideas between East and West, but as much in adapting Chinese philosophy to a Western mindset and later bringing new inspiration to Chinese writers: his work is commonly cited along with those of Needham, Eberhard and Rossbach.[5]

Indeed, I might be considered an Eastern writer in the West but a Western writer in the East. Although I live in the West and wrote my works in the West, I am a Korean from the East. Thank you, Ole for pointing out an interesting dual identity of myself and my work. Readers may notice the intellectual heritages that I have gained from both Eastern and Western traditions.

My research in this book represents a learning and understanding of geomancy in Korea by a cultural geographer who is a native of Korea, has inherited aspects of the Berkeley academic tradition and is practicing geography in New Zealand by studying the Maori culture and teaching geography from a cross-cultural perspective.[6]

I am indebted to numerous people. First, I would like to acknowledge my three teachers at Berkeley who have since passed away: Clarence J. Glacken, Carl O. Sauer, and Wolfram Eberhard. I am also much indebted to Korean geomancers and others who were willing to share their knowledge or experiences of geomancy. Dr Choi, Won-Suk, a scholar of Korean geomancy led me a field trip to Kyonggi Province and lent me his personal copies of Korean scholars' recent works on geomancy. I am grateful as well to my three brothers and two sisters, especially my elder brother, "Chagun hyongnim," who supported my research into geomancy and led several of my field trips to different rural areas of Korea. And thank you to the School of Geography and Environmental Science at the University of Auckland (Dr Willie Smith, the Director), which encouraged and supported my research and publication of this book in many ways.

A number of people read my manuscript, corrected my grammatical errors, or made other editorial suggestions: June Logie, Linda Cassels, and Tom Wells helped me by reading and offering valuable editorial advice. I would like to extend my thanks to Jan Kelly and Igor Drecki for their professional help with cartographic diagrams and to Beryl Jack for typesetting of the manuscript.

To my beloved family I dedicate this book. My children, Albert, Caroline, Frances, Annabelle, and Renee, all contributed to my research and writing of this manuscript in one way or another by teaching me good New Zealand English and accompanying me on many of my trips to Korea. Annabelle read an early draft of the entire manuscript and caught many of my unidiomatic expressions. She pointed out that I translated the title of a Chinese geomantic textbook in four different ways throughout the manuscript and urged me to adopt one of them. I express my love and gratitude to my wife, Inshil, for sharing the joy and suffering of my research endeavors for this book. She knows how much of my "soul" was put into this book and witnessed many headaches I had while preparing it.

I am grateful to the following publishers of my earlier works who gave me permission to incorporate them into this book: Springer Science and Business Media for my 6 articles in GeoJournal, vol. 4(4) 341–348; vol. 8(1) 77–80; vol. 10(2) 211–212; vol. 21 (1&2) 95–102; vol. 25(4) 387–392; vol. 33(4) 471–477: The British Cartographic Society for my article in The Cartographical Journal, vol. 28(1) 12–15: International Research Centre for Japanese Studies for my paper in *Urban Morphology and the History of Civilization in East Asia*, 385—409: Academy of Korean Studies for permission to reproduce five illustrations of wood block prints from *Oryunyhaengsildo* in the Changseo-gak Library collection and my paper in *Proceedings of the 1ˢᵗ World Congress of Korean Studies*, 554–564.

Finally, I wish to acknowledge with thanks the Korea Foundation's grant to support my publication of this research. However, the opinions, findings, and conclusions expressed in this book are mine and do not necessarily reflect the views of the Korea Foundation.

Notes

1. Edgar Anderson, *Plants, Man and Life* (Berkeley and Los Angeles: University of California Press, 1969), vii.

2. Clarence J. Glacken, *Traces on the Rhodian Shore* (Berkeley, University of California Press, 1967).

3. Hong-key Yoon, *Geomantic Relationships Between Culture and Nature in Korea* (Taipei: The Orient Culture Service, 1976).

4. Hong-key Yoon, *Maori Mind, Maori Land*, Berne: Peter Lang, 1986.

5. Ole Bruun, Fengshui in China: Geomantic Divination Between State Orthodoxy and Popular Religion (Copenhagen: NIAS Press, 2003), 240.

6. In the Romanisation of Korean words, I follow the McCune-Reischauer system without breves (the half-moons over Korean 'o' and 'u'), while for the transliteration of Chinese words, I follow the Pinyin system (with exceptions in the case of some terms and names), and for Japanese words, the Hepburn system.

PART I:
THE NATURE AND HISTORICAL
BACKGROUND OF GEOMANCY

Chapter 1
Introduction

The question of where to live both in this world and the next one has long been one of humanity's fundamental concerns. Where and how to build a home that promises "happiness" has been a common concern in East Asia and Western Europe. However, when it comes to considering life after this world, Europeans seem to have been mainly worried about the destination of their soul in "paradise" and have had relatively minor concerns about where they were buried. East Asians, on the other hand, take their place of burial seriously and in many cases give it greater consideration than where to live in this world.

In East Asia, the process of selecting a favorable house or gravesite and the proper constructions of them gradually developed into a system called "geomancy." As used here, the term refers to the ancient Chinese art of selecting an auspicious site. This art is known as fengshui in China, which literally means "wind and water." Although the English word "geomancy" originally meant "divination by random figures formed when a handful of earth is cast on the ground,"[1] and it does not have the same connotations as the Chinese word fengshui, it is used here because it has been widely accepted by Western scholars. This certainly was the case until the mid-1980s, judging from the titles of publications in English. However, the Chinese term fengshui has rapidly grown in popular usage in the Western world since the 1980s. A search of Bowker's Global Books in Print in 2003 produced 1,202 results for the keyword fengshui while "geomancy" produced only 41 results. This clearly supports the view that fengshui is superseding "geomancy" in the Western world. But despite the current trend I believe that "geomancy" should be used instead of fengshui when referring to the whole East Asian region. Fengshui is the term for geomancy used by the Chinese, while geomancy as practiced in Korea is called pungsu by Koreans, and in Japan it is called fusui. Therefore, "geomancy" is a more neutral English term to denote the age-old Chinese art as practiced in various parts of China, Vietnam, Singapore, Japan, and Korea.

There are probably few ideas in the world more closely related to the natural environment than geomancy. Its premise is that certain locales are more auspicious as sites for dwellings or graves than others. It teaches that people should not cause disorder in the geomantic harmony of nature by indiscriminately

3

modifying either natural or cultural landscapes. Moreover, for the attainment of one's prosperity, the selection of an auspicious site for a house or grave must be made according to geomantic principles. It is difficult to place geomancy in a Western category such as religion, superstition, or science, as it includes all three elements.[2] Therefore, geomancy is best defined as the unique and highly systemized ancient Chinese art of selecting auspicious sites and arranging harmonious structures such as graves, houses, and cities on them by evaluating the surrounding landscape and cosmological directions.[3] Geomancy has had a deep and extensive impact on Chinese and Korean culture; the use of land can hardly be understood apart from it. The missionary Ernest J. Eitel observed that foreigners with no knowledge of geomancy would certainly have difficulty in understanding Chinese attitudes toward the land:

> What is Feng-shui? Ever since foreigners were allowed to settle down on the confines of this strange empire of China, this same question has been cropping up continually here and there. When purchasing a site, when building a house, when pulling down a wall, or raising a flagstaff, residents in the Treaty Ports have encountered innumerable difficulties, and all on account of Feng-shui. When it was proposed to erect a few telegraph poles, when the construction of a railway was urged upon the Chinese Government, when a mere tramway was suggested to utilize the coal mines of the interior, Chinese officials would invariably make a polite bow and declare the thing impossible on account of Feng-shui. When thirty years ago, the leading merchants of the Colony of Hong Kong endeavoured to place the business part of the town in the so-called Happy Valley, and to make that part of the island the centre of the whole town, they ignominiously failed on account of Feng-shui. When the Hong Kong Government cut a road, now known as the Gap, to the Happy Valley, the Chinese community was thrown into a state of abject terror and fright, on account of the disturbance which this amputation of the dragon's limbs would cause to the Feng-shui of Hong Kong; and when many of the engineers, employed at the cutting, died of Hong Kong fever, and the foreign houses already built in the Happy Valley had to be deserted on account of malaria, the Chinese triumphantly declared, it was an act of retributory justice on the part of Feng-shui. When Senhor Amaral, the Governor of Macao, who combined with a great passion for constructing roads an unlimited contempt for Feng-shui, interfered with the situation and aspects of Chinese tombs, he was waylaid by Chinese, his head cut off, and the Chinese called this dastardly deed the revenge of Feng-shui.[4]

Koreans have been no less serious than the Chinese in practicing geomancy. In fact, geomancy has been one of the most important elements regulating the cultural behavior of Koreans. Because the impact of geomancy on Korean culture has not been entirely favorable due to people's fanatical interest in the art, its practice has been criticized by rationalistic Korean scholars. The following statement by Chong Yakyong, a Korean scholar of the eighteenth century, is a good example:

> Presently, litigation in the courts for grave sites has become a troubling problem. About half of the [recent] fighting and assaults resulting in death are due to this

[conflict for grave sites]. Since it is said that the unfortunate acts of excavating graves [to move them to better places] are considered within the practice of filial piety by the people, it is necessary to clarify [the nature of geomancy in order to avoid such negative results].[5]

The impact of geomancy on Korean culture has not been limited to fighting over gravesites but has extended to presidential election campaigns. It is a well-known fact that Kim Daejung moved his family cemetery in 1995 to a supposedly auspicious site that would produce the president of Korea. The site is said to have been chosen by the best-known geomancer of the time, Son Soku, and the place is known to be the geomantic landscape of the 'Heavenly Supernatural Sage descending to the land (Chonson haganghyong).'[6] Kim Daejung's successful bid for the presidency in 1997 has often been attributed to the moving of his family cemetery to this auspicious site, which is near Seoul. Before the presidential election in 2002, several candidates, such as Han Hwagap and Kim Dukryong, are said to have secretly shifted their ancestral graves to auspicious sites before beginning campaigning.[7] It is not known whether these politicians moved their ancestral graves out of genuine faith in geomancy or simply to gain public support.

During any major election campaign in South Korea, people often hear about candidates' ancestral graves in auspicious sites. When the President Rho Muhyun was elected in 2002, some journalists and geomancers claimed that Rho became the successful candidate due to his parents' graves and his childhood home being on auspicious sites.[8] It is said that people frequently came to view the geomantic conditions of Rho's house and his parents' gravesites. Geomancy in Korean society is indeed alive and well.

As a communist state, North Korea would seem to be an unlikely place for geomantic ideas to be accepted and practiced. Many believe that geomancy has been dismissed as superstition and the remains of an undesirable feudal heritage in North Korean society. However, it seems that the state is not free of geomantic ideology. A recent collection of legends relating to the late Kim Il-sung's mausoleum exposes an interesting North Korean attitude toward geomancy. In a legend entitled "The land vein of Kumsusan," the mausoleum site is described as the geomantic landscape of the "golden turtle emerging from the mud," which is an auspicious site of first-class quality, superior to all other sites in the world.[9] In the legend, Kim Il-sung is described as the great sage and leader who knew all about the worldly phenomena—including astro-geomancy—and it comments on the land vein of Mount Kumsu where the mausoleum is located.[10] The legend argues that the mausoleum site is naturally endowed with extraordinary auspiciousness. However, the geomantic quality of the site was enhanced even more by having Kim Il-sung's body laid there.[11] This legend reverses the traditional geomantic belief that nature can influence people to be great by suggesting that Kim Il-sung can influence nature to be great, because he is the great sage. The legend seems to implicitly deify Kim Il-sung by attributing to him the divine power of remaking the geomantic quality of the land around his mausoleum. The story shows that North Koreans have a positive attitude toward the traditional ideology of geomancy, in that they are actively utilizing it to glorify their leader, Kim Il-sung, and his mausoleum. Evidently, geomantic ideology is still alive in the North.

An expert on geomancy is called a geomancer (*chigwan* or *pungsu* in Korean). They are usually professionals who evaluate the geomantic qualities of a site and charge fees to their clients. Although the power of geomancers is at present relatively weak, they once had a great deal of influence. Geomancers were important technicians who belonged to the middle class, or *Chung'in,* just below the noble class, or *Yangban.* The middle class included medicine men, local county counselors, translators, and geomancers. Knowledge of geomancy, however, was not restricted to professional geomancers. People from all classes had some knowledge of it. Many Confucian scholars of the noble class during the Choson dynasty knew about geomancy in depth as part of their shared tradition, and some scholars were actually expert geomancers (Figure 1.1).

Figure 1.1 A traditional scholarly Korean geomancer, Mr Choi Taesok with a geomantic map that he drew. He was 91 years old in 2002 and lived in a village in Kyonggi Province.

Traditionally, the education of the geomancer was largely a matter of apprenticeship. Often an apprentice lived with or near a senior geomancer and accompanied him on geomantic trips, providing servant-like service to his teacher (see Figure 1.2). During the learning period, the apprentice did not normally pay tuition but had to work for his teacher. Apparently, this system still persists to some degree. During a field trip about thirty years ago, when I asked a local geomancer in Sangju County to introduce me to a master who could teach me the art, I was advised to see a certain master and appeal to him to let me become his apprentice.[12] The local geomancer also told me that I should attempt to live in the master's house and do servant-like work for him, such as sweeping the courtyard.

Figure 1.2 The geomancer lectures on geomantic principles at his study room with a geomantic compass on the floor.

An apprenticeship may require mastering several geomantic textbooks written in Chinese and learning to operate the geomantic compass. The education of scholarly geomancers has not been very common in Korea because of the limited number of qualified teachers and students. On the contrary, many geomancers have acquired their knowledge through field study with senior masters without reading important geomantic literature. Nonscholarly geomancers usually do not read geomantic texts but are able to point out auspicious places through experience or knowledge acquired on geomantic field trips. These folk geomancers have been called *Chaktaegi pungsu* (the stake geomancers) by a scholarly geomancer.[13] Whether they know much about the principles of geomancy or not, such folk and scholarly geomancers have guided Koreans to auspicious places and have been leaders and advisers in creating a peculiar relationship between culture and environment through geomancy.

The idea of geomancy reflects a deep association between culture and the environment in East Asia. Geomancy has had an ecologically favorable impact on the environment and has been one of the most important elements controlling Koreans' relationship with the environment. But it has left an unfortunate cultural legacy in Korean society. For example, while it has encouraged people to carefully consider alterations to the environment (such as removing trees, building roads, etc.), its practice has been responsible for numerous crimes and litigations due to people's obsession with auspicious sites for graves and houses. While writing this book, one thought preoccupied me: The impact of geomancy on Chinese and Korean culture has been so large for so long that it is almost impossible to understand East Asian culture without it. Much of the Chinese and Korean landscapes are a product of the implementation of geomantic ideas and thus reflect the geomantic heritage of Chinese and Korean culture. Applying J. and N. Duncan's approach to landscape as text, one can say that the Chinese and Korean landscapes are in fact the physical transformation of geomantic ideas and a text to be read for their culture and society.[14]

Manipulating the cultural landscape as a means of influencing people to accept new ideology and new dynastic power or as a means of challenging to such processes, 'reading landscape as text' has been an integral part of and ingenious reflection of the turbulent socio-political process of Korea and elsewhere in East Asia. A meaningful reading, or interpretation, of the landscape is only possible with a good understanding of geomantic principles and East Asian attitudes toward the idea. Despite its importance, geomancy has been poorly understood and flippantly treated by academics in the West in the study of East Asian culture or cultural geography.

In recent years, more than one thousand books have been published in Western languages on *fengshui* or geomancy. Almost all of them are popular geomantic guides and manuals for curious westerners who want to learn and practice this exotic art of place divination. Very few academic works on *fengshui* are available. In the mid-1980s Sara Rossbach published a book on *fengshui* that was circulated widely.[15] But her book, on an eclectic version of the Tibetan Tantric Black Hat Sect *fengshui* tradition, is a journalistic report rather than a serious academic discourse.

Two contemporary academic books on geomancy by Western anthropologists are worthy of special note. Stephan Feuchtwang's well-known *An Anthropological Analysis of Chinese Geomancy*, first published in 1974 and revised in 2002, was the first major contemporary work in English on the subject and was much sought after by westerners who wanted to learn about geomancy.[16] It aspires to provide a serious academic discourse on *fengshui*, emphasizing geomancy as the indigenous Chinese cosmological model. However, it does not provide a comprehensive picture of geomantic principles. Ole Bruun's *Fengshui in China: Geomantic Divination Between State Orthodoxy and Popular Religion* is based on his fieldwork in China.[17] It is the first work to shed light on the

current revival of the practice of geomancy in China after its severe discourage-
ment by the communist government. Bruun's study demonstrates the difficulty
of defining geomancy. The art of geomancy he observed in his fieldwork is a
somewhat shamanistic practice, but it shows that geomancy as practiced in
China today deviates significantly from the *fengshui* practiced during the nineteenth century.[18] In Korea, geomancy is still practiced more or less separately
from shamanism, although a shaman may sometimes issue geomantic prescrip-
tions. Bruun's book did not aim to document and explain the nature of the
geomantic principles practiced by geomancers, however. It leaves the reader
with unanswered questions about the nature of geomancy.

Two nineteenth-century works by Western missionaries to China still provide valuable insights into geomancy: Ernest J. Eitel's *FENG-SHUI: The Rudiments of Natural Science in China*, first published in 1873, and J. J. M. de
Groot's *The Religious Systems of China,* which was published in 1897 and
contains a section on *fengshui*.[19] Although these two books are outdated and
ingrained with missionary predispositions, they are much more readable and
informative on the nature of geomancy than most recent book-length studies.

Several shorter academic publications also provide insights into geomancy.
"An Appreciation of Chinese Geomancy" by Andrew March, a geographer,
criticizes earlier Western authors such as de Groot and Eitel for their missionary
bias and attempts to explain the nature and basic principles of *fengshui*.[20] An
anthropologist, Maurice Freedman wrote two articles on geomancy in which he
shows good understanding of the Chinese practice; he highlights the fact that the
practice of grave geomancy by the Chinese was for the benefit of the descendants, who expected to extract auspiciousness from the grave.[21]

Some other academic works on geomancy by Western scholars exist in English, but it is not easy to acquire a clear understanding of the nature and practice
of geomancy from them. As I am sometimes told, to Western scholars who
desire to learn about geomancy as a means of understanding East Asian culture,
geomancy may still remain an enigma. This unique East Asian art is complex
and secretive and uses terms and expressions that can seem vague to anyone, not
only Western scholars. Geomantic principles are not always consistent and
different masters emphasize different methods or aspects of geomancy. Many
Western studies do not convey the full picture of geomantic principles, and
instead concentrate on particular aspects or particular traditions. The result is
that geomancy remains a confusing subject to contemporary Western scholars.

My study is centered on interpretation and explanation rather than surveying
data on geomancy as practiced in Korea. My special interest has been interpreting the fundamental meanings behind the principles and practice of geomancy in
Korean culture. Folklore has provided a prime source of material for analyzing
the impact of geomancy on Korean culture and society. Folklore materials,
including myths, legends, folktales, and proverbs, can be invaluable treasures
from which one can learn people's unedited wishes, thoughts, beliefs, and
attitudes.

Following this introduction, my exploration of geomancy starts with a review of the existing theories, after which I present my views on the origin of ancient Chinese geomancy. Important theories on geomancy argue that grave geomancy developed earlier than house geomancy. Previous theorists seem to have deduced the past from the present. Choosing auspicious gravesites has recently become much more popular than choosing house sites. But all important geomantic principles are related to the conditions for choosing a person's residence rather than choosing gravesites. My analysis of geomantic principles suggests that the ancient art was most likely engendered by early cave dwellers of the Loess Plateau of China.

I then look at the development of geomancy in Korea. The art of geomancy was probably introduced to Korea through an early spreading of Chinese culture to Korea, much earlier than some Korean scholars believe. Based on the fact that Silla's royal court removed a Buddhist temple to prepare a tomb for the deceased king on the site, some scholars argue that geomancy probably spread during the eighth century. However, some geomantic legends, Koguryo tomb murals, and even the practice of geomancy in Japan during the eighth century indicate an early introduction of geomancy into the Korean peninsula. Rather than dividing the history of geomancy in Korea into the Korean dynastic cycles (since its developmental pattern does not coincide with them), it was divided into six periods based on the characteristics of the impact of geomancy on Korean culture.

Following my discussion of the origins, evolution, and spread of geomancy, I examine Chinese geomantic principles. These chapters of the book explore different aspects of geomantic principles and their applications for the building of graves and houses: Yin-Yang theory and geomancy, geomantic principles of auspicious sites, the principles of house geomancy, and grave geomancy and grave landscape.

The concept of the Yin-Yang and Five Elements Theory provide a metaphysical basis for geomancy and a conceptual framework for various levels of cosmological directions used in geomancy. The chapter that follows on key geomantic principles used in choosing an auspicious site is the longest and most technical part of the book, as I have introduced traditional geomantic terms and concepts that are alien to Western culture and often difficult to explain adequately in a Western language. Three factors go into choosing an auspicious site: mountains, water, and cosmic directions. An auspicious site requires a piece of flat land surrounded by horseshoe-shaped hills, available water, and maximum sunlight as a result of facing south.

I then discuss house geomancy, which shares the same geomantic principles as grave geomancy, although the former has developed a complicated set of rules for design and construction. In the geomantic examination of a house within a built-up settlement, it is difficult to consider the surrounding hills and watercourses. The most emphasized aspects in house geomancy are the direction the house faces, its floor plan, and its position relative to neighboring houses and roads.

In the next chapter I discuss techniques applicable only to grave geomancy, as well as the fanatical behavior that takes place in Korea when seeking auspicious gravesites and grave landscape.

I then provide an interpretation of geomantic principles. Although the important principles are self-evident in classical geomantic manuals and literature, they are complicated and not always consistent. This chapter discusses the meanings, icons, and symbolisms behind the principles and practices of geomancy in Korea. Three key images of nature in geomancy are explored: the magical image, the personified image, and the vulnerable image. I also discuss the key geomantic principles governing an auspicious landscape. An auspicious place requires a landscape that is harmonious, balanced, and symmetrical. Chinese geomantic principles represent an early Chinese idea of a dynamic environmental cycle and are comparable with environmental determinism in Western environmental ideas.

The chapter on geomantic cartography draws on my initial inquiry into cartographic techniques used in geomancy in my 1992 article in *Cartographical Journal*, and on four other articles on geomantic maps elsewhere. Here I have interpreted the landform expressions in the geomantic maps created by geomancers and concluded that these geomantic maps had a significant impact on traditional Korean cartography.

In the chapters on the relationships between Korean religions and geomancy, I begin with the observation that Buddhism, Confucianism, and geomancy were practiced by Koreans by blending aspects of their religious values. The basic doctrines of Buddhism and the principles of geomancy developed separately without influencing each other, because Buddhism developed from the Indian subcontinent and later spread to China. However, it seems that the two belief systems adapted to each other at the level of consumers, and formed a symbiotic relationship. These relationships are best reflected in geomancy tales, which are examined in terms of the geomancer monk, the ethical values of charity, and the locations of Buddhist temples and pagodas. Confucianism also developed close relationships with geomancy, as represented in the geomancy tales that reflect Confucian ethics and in the locations of Confucian shrines and schools.

In the chapters discussing the influence of geomancy on capital cities, I concentrate on two Korean capital cities, Seoul and Kaesong. The story of the choice of Seoul as the capital in 1395 through applying geomantic ideas is one of the best documented cases of such influence among all East Asian cities, including Beijing, Nanjing, Kyoto and Nara. And Kaesong is one of the most talked about geomantic cities, with more geomantic tales than any other city in Korea. To read the city's landscape is to read an allegorical folktale of "an old mouse."

Iconographic warfare, the subject of the next chapter, reflects the new trend in cultural geography. Here I have documented and interpreted the fierce battle between Japanese colonialism and Korean nationalism over the landscape icon of Korean sovereignty. Kyongbok Palace, the main palace of the Choson dynasty, was constructed in 1395 on the most geomantically auspicious spot in

Seoul and has been the symbol of Korean government authority ever since. When Japan colonized Korea, the Japanese colonial government mutilated the palace by destroying many of its buildings and by constructing the Japanese icon of colonial rule, the Government-General Building, on the palace ground. The act was an attempt to justify and naturalize the icon of Japanese colonial rule at the expense of the Korean one. For the same reason, after liberation from Japanese colonial rule, the Korean government demolished the Japanese colonial building to reconstruct the icon of Korean sovereignty, Kyongbok Palace, to its former glory. When Koreans demolished the Japanese colonial Government-General Building in 1996, its steeple (head) was cut off and placed at the lowest spot of the display park on the Korean Independence Hall ground. Thus, it became the subject of ridicule, reflecting the principle of "an eye for an eye and a tooth for a tooth" in landscape form. One may call this iconographical struggle "the landscape of getting even." Behind this war of icons between Japanese colonialism and Korean nationalism lies age-old Korean geomancy.

Subsequent chapters are the result of my inquiry, representing much of my academic energy into the principles of geomancy and its impact on Korean culture and society.

Notes

1. Webster's New World Dictionary of the American Language (1966), 605.

2. Hong-key Yoon, *Geomantic Relationships Between Culture and Nature in Korea* (Taipei: The Orient Culture Service, 1976), 234.

3. I have previously defined geomancy as a comprehensive system of conceptualizing the physical environment that regulates human ecology by influencing man to select auspicious environments and build harmonious structures (e.g., graves, gardens, houses, and cities) on them. See Yoon, *Geomantic Relationships,* 1. Compare this definition of geomancy with that of J. J. M. de Groot: "Fungshui means a quasi-scientific system, supposed to teach men where and how to build graves, temples and dwellings in order that the dead, the gods and the living may be located therein exclusively, or as far as possible, under the auspicious influences of nature." For further information on this, see J. J. M. de Groot, *The Religious System of China,* vol. 3, 935. The definition quoted here is from my 1976 PhD dissertation: *Geomantic Relationships Between Culture and Nature in Korea* (University of California, Berkeley, 1976), 1.

4. E.J. Eitel, *Fengshui: Or the Rudiments of Natural Science in China* (Hong Kong: Lane, Crawford & Co., 1873), 1–2.

5. Chong Yakyong, *Kukyok Mokmin-simso* [Criticisms and Advice on Governing the People, A Modern Korean Translation] (Seoul: Minjok Munhwa Chujinhoe, 1969), vol. 2, 628.

6. Kim Dukyu and An Yongbae, "Myongdang chja Nammolle Ijanghago Taekwon tojon" [Running for the Presidency after Secretly Moving Their Ancestral Graves to Auspicious Sites]. *Shindonga* [New East Asia], vol. 45–2, February 2002, 183–184.

7. Kim Dukyu and An Yongbae, "Myongdang chja Nammolle Ijanghago", 181–184.

8. For an example of such a journalist's report, see An Yongbae, An Yongbae (2002), "Rho Muhyon dangson Ddak machotta" [Correctly Predicted the Successful

Election of Rho Muhyon], *Chugandonga* [Weekly Donga], vol. 365, December 2002, cover story.

9. Kim Ugyong, Tong Kichun and Kim Chongsok, *Kumsusan Kinyom Kungjon Chonsoljip (1)* [Legends of Kumsusan Memorial Palace] (1) (Pyongyang: Munhak Yesul Chonghap Chulpansa, 1999), 12 & 14.

10. Kim Ugyong, Tong Kichun and Kim Chongsok , *Kumsusan Kinyom Kungjon*, 15.

11. Kim Ugyong, Tong Kichun and Kim Chongsok, *Kumsusan Kinyom Kungjon*, 14.

12. Conversation with Chong Chang-sup at Mikimi, Modong-myon, Sangju-kun, North Kyongsang Province, 23 November 1973.

13. Conversation with Chong Chang-sup, 23 November 1973.

14. For Duncan's approaches to landscape interpretation, see J. and N. Duncan, "(Re) reading the landscape", *Environment and Planning D: Society and Space*, vol.9 (1988): 117–126; J. Duncan, *The City as Text: The Politics of Landscape Interpretation in Nineteenth Century Kandy* (Cambridge: Cambridge University, 1990).

15. Sarah Rossbach, *Feng Shui: The Chinese Art of Placement* (New York: E.P. Dutton, 1983), 169.

16. Stephan D. R. Feuchtwang, *An Anthropological Analysis of Chinese Geomancy.* (Vientianne: Editions Vithangna, 1974); the revised second edition (Bangkok: White Lotus, 2002).

17. Ole Bruun, Fengshui in China: Geomantic Divination Between State Orthodoxy and Popular Religion (Copenhagen: NIAS Press, 2003).

18. Ole Bruun, *Fengshui in China*, 2.

19. Ernest J. Eitel, *Fengshui: Or the Rudiments of Natural Science in China* (Hong Kong: Lane, Crawford & Co., 1873); J. J. M. de Groot , *The Religious System of China.* vol.3 (Leiden: Librairie et Imprimerie, 1897).

20. Andrew March, "An Appreciation of Chinese Geomancy," *Journal of Asian Studies*, vol. 27, no. 2, (1968): 252–267.

21. Maurice Freedman, *The Study of Chinese Society* (Stanford, CA: Stanford University Press, 1979), 5–15.

Chapter 2
The Origin and Evolution of Geomancy[1]

The art of selecting a comfortable place to live has probably existed wherever there have been human settlements, although the criteria for a favorable habitat could have varied greatly depending on the environment. Chinese geomancy can be considered a specific Chinese system that developed from the art of selecting a favorable habitat; it must have developed from early people's ecological relationship with the mountainous environment of China. This geomantic art of site selection seems to have evolved from early human learning about the environment in choosing comfortable places to live and therefore includes some rational elements.

Korean geomancy obviously came from China. Its principles of selecting auspicious sites are the same as the Chinese ones, with only minor differences in interpretation and emphasis; most traditional geomantic textbooks used in Korea were either Chinese geomantic manuals or Korean reproductions. The translated versions of these Chinese texts started appearing only recently. It is important to understand the origin of Chinese geomancy and its diffusion to Korea in order to appreciate geomancy in Korea.

The aim of this chapter is to present a new view on the origin of geomancy and to suggest that Chinese geomancy was probably started by cave dwellers in their searches for ideal cave sites in the Loess Plateau. Since the origin of geomancy has been previously discussed by Western and Eastern scholars, I introduce some important earlier theories before discussing my own views.

A Review of Theories on the Origin of Chinese Geomancy

No plausible written historical records have been found on the date and place of the beginnings of Chinese geomancy, although some theories have been presented. One was proposed by the Dutch scholar and missionary to China J. J. M. de Groot toward the end of the nineteenth century:

Our exposition of the Fung-shui system has shown that its leading principles have their origin in remote antiquity. Its first embryo, indeed, grew out of the worship of the dead, which already in the mist of ages was the religion proper of the Chinese. The deceased ancestors were then their principal patron divinities, who influenced the fate and fortunes of their descendants in every way.[2]

De Groot argued that Chinese geomancy developed from the worship of the dead—that is, that the first form of geomancy was grave geomancy. The following quotation clarifies his ideas about its evolution:

But souls do not dwell in graves only. They also resided in tablets exposed for worship on the domestic altars, and in temples specially erected to shelter them. There, too, precisely for the same reasons, they ought to be made to live under the favourable influences of nature. Consequently, Fung-shui is firmly entwined with house-building and the construction of ancestral temples.[3]

At first glance, de Groot's theory seems plausible enough, but in fact this outdated theory is somewhat illogical and poorly informed as to the nature and principles of Chinese geomancy. This bold theory might have grown out of observing the way geomancy was practiced in China during his time, but failed to examine the nature of key geomantic principles. Most importantly he failed to give attention to the fact that key geomantic principles regarding the gravesites and house or settlement sites are identical and the fact that they are more relevant to the conditions of living people's ideal residences. Unless we can assume that life after death was conjectured from the life of the living and thus the geomantic principles of the living people's residences were developed first and subsequently applied to the selection of gravesites, we cannot explain why the key principles regarding the selection of gravesites are identical to those regarding the houses and settlements of the living. This is why we cannot accept de Groot's theory. Moreover, he provided no evidence in support of his theory. De Groot's argument could be seen as having strong elements of "presentism" which interprets the past by imposing 'present' values to explain and justify the 'present' situation.

A Chinese scholar, Chen Huaizhen, presented a theory on the origin of geomancy seemingly echoing the main points that 'Chinese geomancy grew out of ancestor worship' suggested by J.J.M. de Groot. Chen asserts that the Chinese concept of ancestor worship is responsible for the genesis of geomantic art in China. He writes:

The concept of geomancy [fengshui] has a very long history in China. The concept originated in the system of ancestor worship. The Chinese have always emphasized the importance of filial piety. Therefore, when parents are alive, the children must express their filial devotion by serving them properly; after their death, they should bury them and offer sacrificial services for them in the proper way. Besides the concept of filial piety, Chinese also believe that after their death, their spirits remain in this world. The children then must somehow make the spirits of the dead comfortable by using all kinds of methods. It is believed that if the spirits of the parents do not rest comfortably the children will not be prosperous. In short, most Chinese believe that deceased parents could determine the prosperity of their children. This belief has been very popular since the middle ancient times; the concept of burial arose in that period to meet the beliefs of the time . . . Not until after the custom of burial had already been established did the art of geomancy become popular.[4]

The above statement indicates that the Chinese system of ancestor worship, which rests on the concept of filial piety and the belief in man's life after death, brought about the origin of Chinese geomancy. This idea is basically the same as that of de Groot. My criticism of de Groot's theory can also be applied to Chen's theory, since both made the same mistake. Chen's mistake is a misconception of the origins of geomancy, and probably is due to his failure to properly interpret its principles. An analysis of the basic principles of geomancy strongly suggests that geomancy derived from people's knowledge about their environment and that house geomancy developed earlier than grave geomancy (more discussion to follow in the next section of this chapter). Chen also argues that there was no concept of geomancy in China before the middle ancient times (Han dynasty?). Archaeological evidence and historical documents, however, support the idea that Chinese geomancy existed in China before the Han dynasty. We must notice also that Chen does not present any evidence in support of his speculations. His idea is important, however, in explaining the evolution of Chinese geomancy.

Another valuable speculation has been advanced by a Japanese scholar, Murayama Chijun:

From a remote time in China, people had to give their attention to wind and water conditions to get along in life. The cold northerly wind was a great threat to the people in north China, and the southerly winds accompanied by rain caused much flooding in south China. The protection [of themselves] from [the cold] northerly winds, and the control of water flow, were both very important aspects of people's life during the ancient times. The first condition for providing a comfortable dwelling and happy life was to choose a house site which would be free from disasters caused from wind and water. Thus, they developed the habit of observing the wind and the waters which were indispensable conditions for the selection of a site. It was thus that divination in selecting a [good] site came to be considered as an "art of wind and water", and observing landforms [for the selection of auspicious sites] was called "the practice of fengshui [wind and water];" consequently, whether the selection concerned a house site or a grave site, any activity of observing landforms for the selection of a site became known as fengshui [geomancy].[5]

Although Murayama's concept is deterministic and he is only concerned with possible negative impacts of the natural environment on human life, he does point out the importance of wind and water in ancient times. When we consider the indispensability of water for human life, and the importance of weather to human beings that the impact of the natural environment might have been a factor in the development of Chinese geomancy. In spite of the importance of the earliest forms of Chinese geomancy, Murayama was not interested in relations between house and grave geomancy in the earlier development of fengshui. His theory was rudimentary, and he failed to present supporting evidence.

Another important theory of the origin of geomancy is presented by Yi Pyongdo. Yi Pyongdo states in one of his major works, *Koryo Sidae ui Yongu (The Study of the Koryo Period)* that:

> Geomancy seemed to have systematised its principles by absorbing a number of different theories and thought. In my opinion, geomancy developed from the landscape principles regarding the selection of Capital cities and then acquired metaphysical ideas through adoption of the Yin-Yang and Five Elements Theory. The art of geomancy accelerated its development through the adoption of the ideas regarding astrology and directions, as well as by combining with Confucian ethics (filial piety, ancestor worship, etc.).

> Because the first systematized part of geomancy was the burial art of Yin-Yang (grave geomancy), the name fengshui (geomancy) was exclusively used in the early stage to indicate grave geomancy. Moreover, one can not help but view that due to the influence of grave geomancy, the principles of house geomancy were formed by the adoption and literal application of the principles of grave geomancy. However, as to the origin of the idea of selecting a site, the idea may be derived from practices of selecting settlements for living person. Because the living conditions were the prime concern in the selection of human habitat, the art (geomancy) would have practiced as a practical thought and method of examining livable conditions of a place in terms of economy, military operations and transportation. Therefore, a selection of place through divination with mystic thought and method must have existed during the ancient time of humankind, but this type of geomancy must have been less important (secondary in order) and developed from the earlier mentioned "practical" type of geomancy.[6]

Yi Pyongdo suggests that the idea of selecting sites may have developed from an art of selecting settlements. It implies that the art of site selection (geomantic art) might have developed from the selection of dwelling sites for the living. I am in basic agreement with his theory. Yi, however, does not present any evidence to support it. He also states that geomancy may have originated from the art of selecting sites for cities. That may not be true since the art of geomancy must have developed long before the development of cities.

Yi Pyongdo's theory that the principles of house geomancy derived from the geomantic principles of the gravesite is a misconception. On the contrary, according to my interpretation of geomantic laws, the principles of grave geomancy came from the application of the principles of house geomancy. Yi Pyongdo's conclusion is that although the art of site selection developed from the art of selecting a settlement site, grave geomancy developed earlier than house geomancy. However, since it can be shown that many key principles of grave geomancy are applications of house geomancy, it is my conviction that house geomancy developed earlier than grave geomancy.

There may also be a misconception in Yi Pyongdo's conclusion that the term *fengshui* (wind and water) was first exclusively used to indicate grave geomancy since it developed earlier than house geomancy. Considering the origin and connotations of *fengshui,* its first use in the art of selecting sites must have been associated with the selection of residences, not gravesites. That's because both wind and water are critical elements that must be considered in the selection of a living man's residence; a comfortable sleeping space must be sheltered from winds, and a residence must have water available for daily use. These environmental needs indicate that the elements of *fengshui* are more closely linked with the residence sites of the living than with gravesites. Unless we assume that the principles of grave geomancy were carried over from dwelling site selection, we cannot explain why a grave needs to be examined in terms of wind and water. Thus, I think that the term *fengshui* as well as the art of *fengshui* was first applied to house geomancy and later to the selection of gravesites.

Andrew March in his 1968 article argued that "burial geomancy seems to have arisen later than the geomancy city and building sites."[7] His view is apparently based on a statement he quoted from the eighteenth-century *Ssuk'u ch'uan shut sung mu*: "In the Chou kuan, under the duties both of Tombs Officer and of Graves Administrator, it is stated that burials are to be [situated] according to kinship. This is clear proof that down through the Chou dynasty gravesites were not geomantically selected."[8] This statement may not necessarily support the non-existence of grave geomancy during the Chou dynasty, for the Imperial Tombs of the Ming dynasty near Beijing are concentrated in one valley, although people obviously applied geomancy in the selection of those burial sites. March did not present further evidence to support his view. Although it seems that geomancy existed before the development of cities, his view on the origin of geomancy points in the right direction, and I basically agree with his view that geomancy related to living settlements must have predated that of graves.

Still another theory has been proposed by a Korean, Yi Chonghang (Lee, Jeung Hang), who writes that Chinese geomancy developed out of a combination of earth worship and Yin-Yang theory.[9] However, he has not explained why earth worship and Yin-Yang combined to produce geomancy. For this reason, I cannot accept his theory.

One common and major fault of the previous theories on the origin and evolution of Chinese geomancy is that they fail to explain why the basic principles of house and grave geomancy were the same, and whether they were more relevant to house geomancy or grave geomancy. Therefore, I think that any theory on the origin of geomancy should start with an evaluation of the geomantic principles regarding auspicious site selections.

General Premises Regarding the Origin and Evolution of Chinese Geomancy

Examination of an auspicious site involves complex geomantic principles regarding various landforms, diverse water features, and preferences for cosmic directions. These complex geomantic principles enable us to present the following basic premises on the origin and development of Chinese geomancy:

(1) Chinese geomancy was developed by people who lived in foothill areas where there were various types of landforms

Chinese geomancy would not have developed on plains. This premise is supported by the importance of mountain locations in geomancy; ideal auspicious places must be well surrounded by mountains. Plains along large rivers were not suitable places for primitive people to live, since the rivers were too powerful for them to control.[10] Foothill areas with small streams nearby were probably the most favorable places for the development of centers of early human culture. Geomancy may be evidence of an early Chinese belief in the advantages of dwelling in a mountainous or hilly environment with a variety of landforms.

(2) Chinese geomancy developed in an area with varied climatic conditions

As the Chinese name for geomancy, *fengshui,* which means "wind and water," indicates, it was developed by people who were very much interested in changing weather conditions, especially wind. This could mean that Chinese geomancy was developed in an area where winds were a prominent feature of weather conditions and certain types of strong wind affected their living conditions. The developers of the early geomantic principles must have learned by observation what kind of wind pattern proved most favorable for their habitat.

(3) Chinese geomancy represents an instinctive response to the environment

Human beings prefer to dwell in comfortable and dry places protected from cold, heat, wind, and rain. They also prefer dwelling sites that have drinking water, game, and vegetables nearby. The leading principles of Chinese geomancy may well reflect these particular conditions for the habitat of early humans. Therefore, Chinese geomancy may primarily have existed as simple knowledge about the way the environment affects people's residences. This knowledge was probably handed down from generation to generation by elders and over a period of time came to be more formal and important in the selection of dwelling sites.

Considering that favorable weather conditions and water availability were basic prerequisites for the location of primitive habitations, it is not hard to accept Murayama's theory that emphasizes the negative impact of China's natural environment on the formation of Chinese geomancy. When we learn about the early use of the Chinese word *feng* (wind) from the Yin Oracle Bone Inscriptions, it seems true that, in many cases, the word represented God's disfavor, while the word *yu* (rain) represented God's favor.[11] This may be evidence that ancient people were often threatened by tempest-like winds. Chinese geomancy, however, might not be merely a product of the negative impact of the natural environment but of other factors as well. The positive impact of nature and the desire of man to achieve greater comfort and security may have been more important. The main purpose of the practice of geomancy is to actively seek an auspicious place rather than to passively avoid a bad one. Wind and water were not only threatening elements to ancient people but also elements for which they were most grateful. Water was important for drinking and fishing, besides bringing the threat of floods. Wind was presumably important not only because it threatened to bring cold weather or typhoon-like storms, but because it brought more opportunities to get food and a pleasant feeling when warm winds blew through cold areas. The Chinese character dictionary *Shuo-wen* (about A.D. 100) states that *feng* (風), which means wind, is a combination of Ch'ung (crawling and wiggling creatures) and fan (all, or a sail). According to the *Shuo-wen*, the character *feng* was interpreted this way: "When the winds blow, then the crawling and wiggling creatures are engendered."[12] According to this etymological derivation, the Chinese character "wind" is strongly associated with the favorable impact of wind on the biosphere. We can conclude that the alternating favorable and unfavorable aspects of the natural environment probably made the ancient Chinese respond by formulating theories on the proper selection of sites.

Another reason that I think Chinese geomancy may have been derived from a simple study of the natural environment is the importance given to cosmic magical directions. The perception of the East-West direction may be the result of early people learning from nature by observing natural phenomena such as the sunrise and sunset. Even the concept of the North-South axis may have come from a simple reflection of the amount of sunshine received during wintertime. During winter, only southward-facing houses could receive the maximum amount of sunshine, which served to keep them warm. Direction has been a very important and integral part of Chinese geomancy. However, knowledge of it may have begun with observation of the environment, knowledge that later was colored by religious ideas and myths that came to have magical power.

A New View: Chinese Geomancy First Started as House Geomancy

Further examination and appreciation of geomantic principles suggests that geomancy *(fengshui)* may have started as a simple folk science used in choosing auspicious cave dwelling sites for people living in the Loess Plateau. My theory is based on questions that previous researchers did not pursue: why are the basic principles of grave site selection the same as those of house site selection, and are they more relevant for one than the other? An analysis of the geomantic criteria for an auspicious site suggests the following two important aspects of the origin of geomancy in China:

1. Chinese geomancy first started as house geomancy (the art of selecting a house site), which later came to be applied to grave geomancy (grave site selection).

2. Chinese geomancy was started by cave dwellers in the Loess Plateau.

Although grave geomancy has recently been more popular than house geomancy, house geomancy must have begun first. An appreciation of geomantic
principles shows that the basic principles of selecting house sites and grave sites
are the same, and that they are all critically important for ideal house conditions.
My theory that the principles of grave geomancy derived from those of house
geomancy was developed by exploring why the basic principles are the same
and why they are more relevant to the conditions of an ideal house site. My
hypothesis is that the first form of Chinese geomancy was concerned with house
selection only; later this idea was influenced by Chinese ideas of ancestor
worship and filial piety. Subsequently it began to deal with the selection of
grave sites.

The following are some examples of basic principles of grave geomancy that
may have originated in house geomancy:

Acquiring water, the most important factor

Wind and water, as indicated by the word fengshui, are the two most important elements of nature in Chinese geomancy, and they are both more relevant to
the residences of the living than to those of the dead. De Groot said that the
word *fengshui* indicates that the first task in selecting a site for a grave, house,
temple, or village is learning about wind or air, *feng*.[13] However, I have not been
able to find a textbook of classical geomancy that says wind is the important
factor. *Zangshu*, a standard textbook of Chinese geomancy, says that the
principle of *fengshui* is first of all to acquire water and then to have a calm
wind.[14] This statement may indicate that, since remote antiquity, water was the
most important factor in Chinese geomancy. Whatever factor was more
important, acquiring water and having a calm wind are more closely related to
the residences of the living than to those of the dead. A comfortable sleeping
place protected from cold wind or rain and the availability of water were, of
course, indispensable for ancient Chinese living conditions. The principles of
wind and water in geomancy are very much related to these living conditions,
and the idea obviously derived from people's residences.

The importance of having a watercourse near an auspicious place also supports the earlier development of house geomancy. The watercourse is a vital
element in the selection of both grave and house sites; no site can be auspicious
without it. It is noteworthy that the principle concerning the watercourse applies
not only to the selection of the grave but also to the house.

De Groot indicated in *The Religious System of China* that in the Amoy
region, if there was not a watercourse near the grave or house, the defect could
often be remedied by constructing a water tank in front of it.[15] He added that the
Chinese would often make a shallow water tank without any intention of filling
it with water. I question why they made such a water tank in front of the grave if
there was no watercourse in the area. Why was water so critically important for
a grave? If the ancient Chinese thought that water was as necessary for a dead
person lying in a grave as it was for living person, it is obviously knowledge
derived from residences of the living. If house geomancy had developed out of

grave geomancy, it would be impossible to explain the necessity for the same kind of watercourse at the gravesite. It is even possible that the watercourse was never important for the gravesite, although it is also possible that the geomantic requirements of watercourses near graves were not the same as those for watercourses near house sites.

The fact that an auspicious house site or gravesite should be dry but with water nearby might be the most obvious evidence that the idea of house selection developed earlier than gravesite selection. It is understandable that a living person's residence needs to have water for daily consumption, but also a dry sleeping quarter. But why should a gravesite (the residence of the dead) require water and a dry sleeping quarter? If the ancient people thought that the deceased needed to have the same "living" conditions as they did before they died, it is only logical to assume that the idea of life after death was conjectured from life in this world. Thus, I conclude that the requirement of the watercourse in the selection of the gravesite is a carryover.

The necessity of a calm wind at a gravesite as well as at a house site

According to geomancy, a gravesite generally should not have winds blowing from any direction. One has to ask why a dead person buried under the ground would need such atmospheric conditions. It is understandable that a good house site in windy areas such as the Loess Plateau in northern China needs to be sheltered from winds, especially the cold northwesterlies. But why do the dead require the same calm air conditions? Unless one assumes that the principle of a calm wind is a carryover from the geomantic requirement of the residence, the requirement that a grave be placed in such a location does not make much sense. If people thought that a dead person's residence should have the same wind conditions as a living man's residence, this idea would have to be drawn from the living person's residence. Thus, I assume that the idea of an ideal gravesite was derived from the ideal conditions of a living person's house.

A gravesite should be dry where the coffin is to be placed

Why should a grave be located in a dry place but with a watercourse nearby? Such a location is obviously good for the living, and the idea thus obviously derived from people's residences.

An auspicious grave or house site needs to be located in a place with lush vegetation, so a rocky mountain is not a good location

In grave geomancy, stone mountains and mountains with poor vegetation are considered inauspicious. According to the *Zangshu*, such mountains are inauspicious locations to bury the dead.[16] They could not have been a good place for early man to live, since stone mountains and poorly vegetated areas cannot provide much food or other daily necessities. Such areas are not suitable for supporting either plant or animal life; neither hunters and gatherers nor early farmers could collect much plant or animal food from these areas. Since lush forest was an important source of food for early humans, it is understandable that a house needed to be located in such a site. This principle of geomancy probably reflects qualifications that pertained to habitats of the living; unless the idea was derived from living person's residences it would not make sense that stone mountains and mountains with poor vegetation were bad for graves.

The Chinese word for 'geomancy cave': Xue (穴)

This Chinese character originally meant a cave dwelling (earthen room) but not a hole; its contemporary meaning is still primarily a cave, especially one in a mountain rather than an ordinary hole. The purpose of practicing the art of geomancy is to find an auspicious site (cave) backing up against a hill (a foot-hill). Why have auspicious sites been called "caves"? A cave in a foothill area (the normal location for an auspicious site) is obviously related more to the residences of the living than to graves. In the loess soil areas of northern China, many people have been living in cave dwellings that are known as *Lyodong*. In geomancy, "selecting a *Xue*" means "selecting a geomantically auspicious place." The use of the Chinese word *Xue* to represent the auspicious site could signify that early geomancy was originally used for selecting a favorable cave dwelling site for human residence: a dry cave that was protected from strong winds, rain, and outside temperature due to the storage-heater effect of cave dwellings.[17] When such a cave dwelling was located in a place that had plenty of food resources and drinking water nearby, it was an ideal place to live for the early humans of the Loess Plateau, with its long and cold winter. It is my conjecture that the principle of "finding an auspicious cave" for the residence of a living man was later applied to "finding an auspicious gravesite."

The above discussion demonstrates that grave geomancy principles may have been derived from the selection principles for dwellings. I conclude that dwelling-site geomancy developed earlier than grave geomancy and that the principles of house geomancy were applied to gravesite selection, which became important due to the influence of the newly adopted ideas of ancestor worship and filial piety. Inferring the nature of life after death from the life of the living, the ancient Chinese tried to provide comfortable quarters for their deceased ancestors, and in the selection of such locations they applied the same principles of selecting a house for the living to selecting a house for the dead.

Chinese Geomancy was First Started by the Cave Dwellers in the Loess Plateau

The key geomantic principles for the selection of an auspicious site suggest that Chinese geomancy was first started by the cave dwellers in the Loess Plateau in their search for an ideal cave site. Subsequently, the principles for cave dwelling came to be applied to choosing an ideal gravesite, and even later they were used in choosing auspicious city sites, especially for capital cities. The following analysis and interpretation of geomantic principles and Chinese cosmology are the basis of my hypothesis that the art of geomancy originated from the early Chinese attempt to prepare an ideal cave dwelling in the Loess Plateau:

(1) Backing up to a hill

Certain landform conditions, especially backing up to a hill, are critically important for an ideal cave dwelling site. Loess cave dwellings had been the main dwelling form before the development of free-standing houses in the Loess Plateau, the hearth of ancient Chinese culture. And the geomantic principle that an auspicious site needed to back up against a hill is of much more critical and practical importance for cave dwellings than for free-standing houses.

One of the poems included in an ancient Chinese classic, *The Book of Poetry* or *Sijing (The She King)* suggests that Loess cave dwellings were probably the earliest and most common form of dwelling for the ancient Chinese in the Loess Plateau. The poem reads:[18]

In long trains ever increasing grow the gourds.
When [our] people first sprang,
From the country about the Tseu and the tseih,
The ancient duke Tan-foo,
Made for them kiln-like cave dwellings,
Ere they had yet any house.[19]

The plain of Chow looked beautiful and rich,
With its violets and sowthistles [sweet] as dumplings.
There he began with consulting [his followers];
There he singed the tortoise-shell, [and divined].
The responses were – there to stay, and then;
And they proceeded there to build their houses.

(Translated by James Legge, modified)

This poem suggests that the cave dwelling was an earlier form of dwelling than free-standing houses. Cave dwellings were probably the most ecologically suitable adaptation to the environment for the ancient Chinese. They are easy to construct, with a minimum of tools and building material, and they are better insulated and warmer than free-standing houses during winter due to the storage-heater effect of the cave.[20] Loess is a better insulator than rocks, for it has more trapped air than rock. For these reasons, many millions of people are still using cave dwellings.

The landform conditions required for an auspicious site—protective hills on three sides in a horseshoe shape, especially with its back toward a hill—reflect ideal conditions for cave dwellings. A free-standing house can be built without its back facing a hill, but a cave dwelling cannot be made that way. Having its back toward a hill is much more critical for cave dwellings than for free-standing houses with brick walls and tile roofs (a house style common in other parts of China).

Cave-dwelling builders would often dig out Loess hill slopes in order to make a cliff wall to hollow out a cave. Cutting out a square from the hill slope formed a small flat platform with cliff walls on three sides. Protective walls were automatically created on either side of the prospective cave dwelling, forming the azure dragon and white tiger. The key geomantic principle of "backing onto a hill" is the most critical condition for an ideal cave dwelling.

(2) The most auspicious site in geomancy is named "Xue," or Cave (cave dwelling)

Nowadays in geomancy the word "xue" is metaphorically used to indicate any auspicious site, but originally it meant an earthen room (i.e., cave dwelling). The term "cave" in geomancy most likely came from the ancient practice of finding an auspicious cave dwelling (a comfortable cave that was protected from the cold northwesterlies and enjoyed the sun by facing south). Unlike today, the purpose of geomancy for ancient cave dwellers of the Loess Plateau was probably to find a naturally existing cave or an ideal site to hollow out a cave dwelling; therefore, "finding a cave" literally meant finding a cave or a cave site to dig in. Today in geomancy, finding an auspicious site may well be a carryover from this ancient practice.

(3) Age-old Chinese cosmology supports the hypothesis that geomantic principles were developed from the Loess Plateau[21]

In Chinese cosmology of the five colors and the five elements, the south is represented by red and fire; the north by black and water; the east by azure and wood; the west by white and metal; and the center by yellow and earth (soil). Each direction is also associated with a season: the east is spring; the west is autumn; the north is winter; and the south is summer. The center represents no season. Table 2.1 gives the five elements and five cardinal directions with their cosmological and other iconographical values (based on generally known knowledge in Korea):

Table 2.1 Cosmological Attributes of the Five Elements

Five elements	Direc- tions	Colors	Geomantic landforms	Seasons	5 chi (energy)	Tastes	Yin- Yang
Water	North	Black	Black turtle	Winter	Cold	Salty	Yin
Fire	South	Red	Red bird	Summer	Hot(heat)	Bitter	Yang
Wood	East	Azure (green)	Azure dragon	Spring	Wind	Sour	Yang
Metal	West	white	White tiger	Autumn	Dry	Hot (pepper)	Yin
Earth	Center	yellow	Geomancy cave	Neutral	Moist	Sweet	Neutral

It is not exactly known how those colors and elements came to represent their specific directions. However, one can easily notice that the attributes of the five colors and the five elements are closely associated with the environmental conditions of the four directions in northern China. Incorporating the traditional explanations, I suggest that the attributes of the four directions in terms of color symbolism and the five elements represent the ancient Chinese observations of natural phenomena as follows:

(a) In northern China the winds from the south are normally warm, and a house facing the south enjoys maximum sunshine. Therefore, assigning the fire element and the color red to the south is logical. The north represents water, and its color is black, as a house that is facing the north in northern China is shaded and cold. Black is the opposite of sunlight, while water is the opposite of fire since water extinguishes fire. Therefore, it is appropriate that the north is represented by black and water.

(b) The east is associated with the Chinese word *qing*(青), which refers to both green and azure. The east is the direction of the sunrise, which represents vitality and life; the green color also symbolizes life. When the sun rises and brings a warm atmosphere, trees grow and the wood turns green. The east is assigned to the season of new life, the spring. The sun is the most critical factor in keeping the trees green. Therefore, assigning green or azure to the direction of the sunrise, the east is justified and appropriately represents the environmental conditions of northern China.

(c) The fact that the west is represented by white and metal is more difficult to justify. However, one can argue that white might represent the silvery white sand of western China, the perpetual snows of the high mountains, or the white stones and rock salt found on the surface of the Qinghai Plateau in the west.[22] Logically, the attributes of the west should be the opposite of those of the east. The west is the direction of the sunset, which represents the end of a day. West is the direction representing the final stage in the completion of a cycle. It is then logical for west to represent autumn, the season of yielding and harvesting the seeds. Weathered dead wood in an arid region is indeed white in color, and a pale face is the sign of sickness or lack of vitality. Therefore, it may be appropriate for the west to be represented by white. As for metal, perhaps it may be related to the fact that autumn seeds are often found in a hard shell. In this sense, the seed (fruits) and rock share the quality of hardness. Rocks were considered to be metal or the source of metal in traditional China. Therefore, it may be appropriate for the west to be represented by white.

(d) The characteristics of the center, yellow and earth (soil) cannot be explained in the way the four directions are explained by citing the natural phenomena, other than the loess, the yellow earth of North China.[23] Unlike the European color of yellow, the Chinese yellow is an earthy yellow, the color of loess soil. When the Chinese word for yellow, *huang*, and that for soil, *tu*, are combined, they form the Chinese term for loess, *huangtu*.[24] This is one reason I believe that the Chinese symbolisms for the center in geomancy originated from the Loess Plateau.

(4) The Shape-of-the-Earth-Mountain supports the hypothesis that Chinese geomancy originated from the Loess Plateau

In geomancy, mountains are classified into five types corresponding to Five Elements Theory: earth, fire, water, wood (tree), and metal. Aside from the earth type (hill), they have traditionally been explained through their shapes. A fire mountain is a mountain with a sharp pointed peak that is shaped like a tongue of flame; a water mountain is one of rolling hills shaped like rolling waves; a wood mountain is a highly projected mountain that is like a tall tree (like an Italian cypress); the metal mountain is a dome-shaped mountain that is like a metal bell. We can observe these four types of mountains frequently in China, Japan, and Korea.

The earth type of mountain has steep slopes and a flat top, and its shape cannot be explained by analogy the way the other four types of mountains are explained, unless we relate it to landforms in the Loess Plateau. The typical earth-type mountain cannot be easily observed in China except in the Loess Plateau. Its shape cannot be related to the features of earth (soil), although a well-known traditional geomantic textbook, *Dili-Renzixuezhi* (*The Fact that All Humanity Must Know*), argues that the shapes of the all five mountain types in geomancy are reflections of natural phenomena, not the result of artificially or whimsically assigned names.[25] The book explains the shapes of the other four types of mountains by comparing them with the relevant natural features. But it does not describe the shape of an earth mountain by comparing it with the earth. Rather, it describes the earth mountain as having steep slopes with a broad flat top, like a storage house, a free-standing screen, or the Chinese writing character *ji* (study table).[26]

The shape of the earth-type mountain, which is common in the Loess Plateau, can be explained better by relating it to the landform in the Loess Plateau. Loess is created by wind deposits, and the fine particles of loess soil are extremely susceptible to soil erosion when it rains. The summer rain often causes serious landslides and soil erosion. Therefore, the originally flat Loess Plateau was eroded and formed steep slopes with broad, flat tops. Those who visit this area will realize that the typical earth-type mountain is not an imaginary mountain shape but a common type of landform in the region. There are plenty of hills (mountains) with steep slopes and broad, flat tops made of fine earthy yellow soil that is like soybean flour. Here we can see why yellow and earth are assigned to the center, and why the earth mountain has steep slopes with a broad, flat top: these may reflect the environmental conditions of the Loess Plateau.

(5) The most desired soil condition

In geomancy the most desired soil condition at auspicious sites is well compacted and fine soybean-flour-like soil. Pure loess earth is indeed such an ideal soil in geomancy. During my 1988 field trip to cave dwelling areas of the Loess Plateau, I confirmed that the most desired soil condition for a cave dwelling is such yellow loessial soil. This was confirmed in Myrdal's report on cave dwelling: "The earth caves are dug into the hillside. The first thing to do is to find a place with the right kind of soil, hard yellow loessial soil. You cannot build a cave where the soil is sandy."[27] This soil is critically important in preparing a cave dwelling but not in building a free-standing house or a grave. I learned in my fieldwork that cave builders avoid a site with gravel or large grains of soil, or where the soil has blackish spots or lines that indicate water seepage.[28] Cave-dwelling people learned that if water seeped through, it normally left black marks or lines, for the organic matter dissolved in it decayed. They also found that gravel and other large grains of soil are signs of unstable soil conditions. It is reasonable to conjecture that the well compacted and fine soybean-flour-like soil represents the pure loessial soil of North China that provided ideal conditions for cave-dwelling construction.

In sum, we can reasonably hypothesize that the art of geomancy was first developed by cave dwellers in the Loess Plateau, and that the main principles of geomancy were developed from their experiences searching for ideal cave-dwelling sites. This art then came to be gradually evolved to be a complex system of auspicious site selection technique and applied in the selection of city sites as well as gravesites, and was diffused to other parts of China and other nations in East Asia.

The Development of Chinese Geomancy into Two Schools

The two important aspects of the early form of geomancy were consideration of surrounding landforms and cardinal facing directions. However, landform consideration is of prime importance and is summarized in what is probably the oldest and the most important work of geomancy literature, *Zangshu (Book of Burial)*, which is thought to be written by Guo Pu (276–324).[29] Scholars of geomancy often say that the art of geomancy later developed into two distinct schools: the method of landforms that is known as the Jiangxi School and the method of constellations and cosmological directions that is known as the Fujian School. These two schools seem to have developed as geomancy spread to flat areas from the Loess Plateau and houses were examined within an urban environment. The landform school was applied more extensively to grave geomancy in mountainous areas while the constellation and cosmological direction school seemed to specialize in house geomancy. The origin of these two schools can be traced back to the Han dynasty (B.C. 206–220), though they seem to have developed more during the Song dynasty (960–1279). The most prominent geomancer of the landform school was Wang Junsong. He was known as the master who saved humankind from poverty, as he found auspicious gravesites that made descendants rich. The most prominent figure in the cosmological direction school was Wang Ji, who wrote *The Cannon of the Core or Centre*.[30] Wang Ji's Fujian School defined the method of house geomancy and involved more compass use than landform examination.[31]

During the Qing dynasty (1662–1912) a scholar of geomancy belonging to the Fujian School is said to have commented that one does not need to examine landforms to find an auspicious site, as the quality of auspiciousness can be determined solely with a compass.[32] Some geomancers belonging to each school seemed to have indulged in their main doctrines and did not communicate much with geomancers in the other school. However, my understanding is that both schools never ignored the other aspect of geomancy and only gave more importance to their own specialization within geomantic principles as a whole. The division of these two schools seems to have resulted from the practical applicability of geomancy in different environmental conditions, whether the examination of a house in a built-up urban environment with little room for the consideration of surrounding landforms, or the examination of a gravesite in a hilly open area with ample room for considering surrounding landforms. However, I have never met any geomancer who completely rejects either the doctrines of landforms or those of compass directions, although some empha- sized either side. The nineteenth-century missionary-scholar J.J.M. de Groot clearly stated the then-current state of *fengshui* practice in China:

> Professors of geomancy unanimously assert that there still exists a distinct line of demarcation between the two schools, but that they are in so far fused together that no good expert in either ever neglects to practice the methods of the other school as well as his own. In the mountainous southern provinces, the School of Forms obviously predominates. Even in Fuhkien [Fujian] no geomancers are so highly esteemed as those who pretend to exercise their vocation in strict accordance with the Kiangsi [Jiangxi] method, and in every town of that province there are houses with sign-boards to decoy patrons by stating that the inmate is an adept of that school, or has improved his talents by the teaching of a genuine Kan-cheu profes- sor.[33]

It is my belief that no credible geomancers have ever ignored either the cos- mological directions or the quality of landforms completely, and whenever possible the consideration of landforms was of basic and prime importance. The so-called two schools of geomancy have never been completely separated. In any case, the division of the two is not important today (although it may have been at some stage in the history of geomancy). Now, the landscape, including the surrounding landforms and buildings, would be examined first, then the cardinal direction of the site.

Concluding Remarks

One can conclude that geomancy must have been developed by the early cave dwellers who had to dig out caves on the slopes of hills made of fine loess soil. In the cold Loess Plateau, a warm cave that was protected from the cold was essential for people's survival.

The early Chinese culture grew from the area of this yellow loess earth and spread to areas beyond the Loess Plateau. It is reasonable to assume that the early loess cave dwellers from the Loess Plateau migrated outwards to find that the soil in new places was not yellow anymore and that the mountain shapes were not earth types. Therefore I propose that the assigning of yellow soil and earth mountain shapes to the center is related to the early home of people from the Loess Plateau. The home signifies the center of one's environment or world. The center in Chinese cosmology represents absolute neutrality, tranquility, and stillness—the characteristics of an ideal home. Perhaps the ancient Chinese thought the Loess Plateau was the real center of the world.

The idea that people can artificially remedy shortcomings of a geomantic landscape was a later development of geomancy. Though this idea was not significant in the formation of the Chinese landscape, it is very important in the study of people's modifications of the earth. The considerations of surrounding landforms and cosmological directions have always been fundamental elements of the practice of geomancy, and the so-called schools of landforms and cosmological directions never completely ignored either of the two key principles.

Notes

1. The discussion in this chapter is based on and has developed from my earlier work: Hong-key Yoon, *Geomantic Relationships Between Culture and Nature in Korea.* (Taipei: The Orient Culture Service, 1976), 245-259.

2. J.J.M. de Groot, *The Religious System of China.* vol.3 (Leiden: Librairie et Imprimerie, 1897), 982.

3. J.J.M. de Groot, The Religious System of China, 937.

4. Chen Huaizhen, "Fengshui yu zhangmai" [Geomancy and Burial], *Shehui Yenjiu,* [Studies on Society], vol.1, no. 3 (1937): 1–12.

5. Murayama Chijun, *Chosen no Fusui* [Korean Geomancy] (Seoul: Chosen Shotofu, 1931), 5.

6. Yi Pyongdo, *Koryo Sidaeui Yongu,* 25–26.

7. Andrew March, "An Appreciation of Chinese Geomancy," 260.

8. This statement is from a quotation in Andrew March, "An Appreciation of Chinese Geomancy," 260.

9. Yi Chonghang (Lee, Joung Hang), "Pungsu Chirisol ui Songhaenggwa Kugosi uri Minjoksonge Michin Ak-yonghyange Kwanhan Ilkochal [A Study of the Practice of Geomancy and its Adverse Impact on Korean Characteristics]," *Kyongbuk Taehakkyo Nonmunijip,* vol. 5 (1962): 489.

10. Carl O. Sauer, *Agricultural Origins and Dispersals,* (New York: The American Geographical Society, 1952), 21.

11. Chen Mengjia, *Yinxu buci zongshu* [Comprehensive Discourse on the Divinational Phrases from Yin Ruins] (Beijing: Kexue Chubanshe, 1956), 571.

12. Xu Shen, Shuowen Jiezi [Etymology of Chinese Characters] (Beijing: Zhonghua Shuju, 1963), 284.

13. J.J.M. de Groot, The Religious System of China, 946.

14. Guo Pu, Zangshu, in *Dili zhengzong* [The Cardinal Principles of Geomancy] commentary by Jiang Guo, (Shinchu: Chulin shuchu, 1967), vol. 3, 1

15. J.J.M. de Groot, The Religious System of China, 946.

16. Guo Pu, Zangshu, in *Dili zhengzong,* vol. 3, 1.

17. For a discussion of the storage-heater effect of cave dwellings in Loessland, see Hong-key Yoon, "Loess Cave-Dwellings in Shaanxi Province, China," *GeoJournal,* vol. 21, no. 1& (1990): 100–101.

18. Legge (trans.), The She King, "Book I. Decade of King Wan, Ode III Meen," (Hong Kong: Hong Kong University Press, 1960), 437.

19. The italicization is my own. Legge translated the Chinese word 'taoxue (陶穴)' as kiln-like huts and caves. I think that the word should be translated as kiln-like cave dwellings, for the caves in the Loess Plateau used as dwelling are shaped like the traditional kilns in East Asia.

20. Hong-key Yoon, "Loess Cave-Dwellings in Shaanxi Province," 100.

21. The discussion in this section is based on my earlier works: Hong-key Yoon, "The Nature and Origin of Chinese Geomancy," *Eratosthene-Sphragide*, vol. 1 (1986), 96; Hong-key Yoon, "Towards a Theory on the Origin of Geomancy," Environment and Quality of Life in Central Europe: Problems of Transition: Proceedings, International Geographical Union, Regional Conference (CD-ROM, ISBN 80–7184–153–6), Prague, 22–26 August 1994.

22. Hong-key Yoon, "The Nature and Origin of Chinese Geomancy," 96; Hong-key Yoon, "Towards a Theory on the Origin of Geomancy".

23. Hong-key Yoon, "The Nature and Origin of Chinese Geomancy," 96; Hong-key Yoon, "Towards a Theory on the Origin of Geomancy".

24. Hong-key Yoon, "The Nature and Origin of Chinese Geomancy," 96; Hong-key Yoon, "Towards a Theory on the Origin of Geomancy".

25. Xu Shanji and Xu Shanshu, *Dili-Renzixuezhi* [The Fact that All Humanity Must Know] (Hsin-chu: Chulin Shu-chu, 1969), vol. 3, part 12, 1.

26. Xu Shanji and Xu Shanshu, *Dili-Renzixuezhi*, vol. 3, part 1, 3–4.

27. Jan Myrdal, *Report from a Chinese Village* (London: Heinemann, 1965), 12.

28. Hong-key Yoon, "Loess Cave-Dwellings in Shaanxi Province," 97.

29. Guo Pu is considered to be the patriarch of Chinese geomancy and lived in China during the Jin dynasty. He is famous not only as a geomancer but also as a writer of literary works and commentaries.

30. J.J.M. de Groot, *The Religious System of China*, vol. 3, 1007–1008.

31. J.J.M. de Groot, *The Religious System of China*, vol. 3, 1008.

32. Choi Changjo, "Palmun," in *Hosunsin ui Chiri Shinpop* [The New Geomantic Principles by Hosunsin], translated by Kim Dukyu (Seoul: Changnak, 2001), 5–6.

33. J.J.M. de Groot, *The Religious System of China*, vol. 3, 1008–9.

Chapter 3
The Introduction and Development of
Geomancy in Korea

The geomantic principle, developed in the Loess Plateau, spread to outlying districts as the Chinese people and their culture spread. The art of geomancy has always been such an important part of the Chinese way of life that any non-Chinese people brought into contact with Chinese culture would have been exposed to geomancy at an early stage. The non-Chinese who adopted geomantic ideas would have considered the characteristics of the local culture and environment as they applied those ideas locally. Koreans maintained the basic principles of original Chinese geomancy even after geomancy spread to Korea. The foundation of the Korean geomantic belief system, these principles have not changed. However, they were interpreted and applied to the Korean situation differently and led to the development of Korea's own style of geomancy, which reflected particular cultural, political, and physical aspects of Korea. The Korean culture and environment are different from those of the Loess Plateau in China, and the developmental pattern of Korean history is different from that of China. Thus, Korean geomancy differs somewhat from Chinese geomancy.

The diffusion and development of Chinese geomancy in Korea can be compared with Christianity in Korea. The pattern of diffusion and adoption of Christianity in Korea was quite different than it was in northern Europe or the islands of the Pacific Ocean. The Bible and Christian doctrines were interpreted differently depending on the local culture, and the levels of emphasis varied. Korean Buddhism and Confucianism can be understood in similar ways.

Even though the interpretation, application, and emphasis of certain geomantic principles changed through time in Korea, they continuously had an important impact on Korean culture. The essence of Korean geomantic traditions is often best reflected in Korean folklore and Korean geomantic prophecies, for they are the unedited records of people's lives and thoughts. Thus, analyzing and interpreting Korean folklore and folk life is an effective way of identifying the characteristics of Korean geomancy.

The development of Korean geomancy has often been examined by adopting the standard periodization of Korean history, namely the sequence of dynastic successions from the Ancient Period through the Three Kingdoms Period and the Koryo dynasty to the Choson dynasty and the present. Yi Mong-il's recent study on the history of Korean geomantic thought, which adopted such periodization, may well be the first systematic attempt to survey Korean geomancy through all the periods of Korean history.[1] However, the history of Korean geomancy can be more meaningfully described and understood if it is periodized according to the characteristics of the applications of geomancy and its impact on Korean culture and society. The following is an initial attempt to identify meaningful periods of the development of Korean geomantic thought, based on the way geomantic principles were interpreted, emphasized, and applied to the Korean situation:

1) From the time of its introduction to the time before Master Toson, the geomancer-monk (eighth century).

2) From the time of Master Toson to the Fourth King of Choson, Sejong (eighth century to 1450).

3) From the time of King Sejo to the development of Sirhak thought (Practical Learning) (1455–1670).

4) From Sirhak time to the end of the Choson dynasty (1670–1910).

5) During the Japanese colonial occupation (1910–1945).

6) From the time of liberation to the present (1945–).

Let's take each period in turn.

From the Time of Introduction to the Time
Before Master Toson

The question of when geomancy first spread from China to Korea has briefly been considered by several scholars. Some say that it spread to Korea during the middle of the end of the Silla dynasty (57 B.C. [?]–A.D. 935).[2] Yi Pyongdo in his earlier work argued that the introduction of geomancy to Korea occurred after Silla's unification of Korea in 667, when Korea had frequent contacts with China.[3] Later Yi Pyongdo speculated that the ancient Chinese symbols of four directions painted on the walls inside Koguryo tombs could be a sign of the introduction of geomancy to the Koguryo dynasty (38 B.C.–A.D. 667).[4]

Yi Chonghang (Lee, Jeung Hang) has speculated that Chinese geomancy may have been introduced during the Koguryo dynasty along with the spread of Chinese literature (including the writing system), although he states that it is not known when Chinese literature was first introduced.[5] It is my belief, however, that geomancy may have been introduced to Korea even before the Koguryo dynasty along with the initial wave of Chinese culture to Korea.

In tracing the introduction of geomancy to Korea, it is important to examine two stories contained in the early historical sources of China and Korea:

(1) Qizhi (Kija)'s migration to Korea.

(2) The way King Talhae of Silla acquired an auspicious house site.

It is also important to consider four pieces of historical evidence on the introduction of geomancy to Korea:

(1) The formation of the Han Chinese commentaries (108 B.C.–313) in the Korean Peninsula.

(2) The tomb paintings of four animal symbols that represent the four cardinal directions of Chinese geomancy in Koguryo tombs.

(3) The city walls of Koguryo (Kungnaesong and Hwandosong).

(4) The building of King Wonsong's tomb (789) of the Sills dynasty at an auspicious site by removing the Koksa Temple that was already there (Choi Chiwon).

Here I'll explore these two stories and four pieces of historical evidence in chronological order.

1. Qizhi's (Kija's) migration to Korea

The origin and evolution of Chinese geomancy may be traced back to prehistoric times. The idea that geomantic art played a very important role in ancient Chinese life in the selection of sites is shown in the "Zhaogao" section of *Shujing,* or *The Book of History.* If this is so, it is possible that the diffusion of Chinese geomancy to Korea is as old as the introduction of Chinese culture to Korea. Initial cultural contacts between Korea and China began long before the Three Kingdom period (57 B.C.–A.D. 667), as indicated by archaeological evidence from the Chinese period of the Warring States (B.C. 403–221 B.C.).[6] In tracing the origins of the diffusion of Chinese culture to Korea, the story of Qizhi's exile to Korea becomes very important. This story appears in three places in old Chinese historical writings: Shangshu Dazhuan, Shiji, and Hanshu. According to *Shangshu Dazhuan,* the story of Qizhi (Kija in Korean) is as follows:

> After Wenwang [of Zhou] conquered Yin [about 1050 B.C.] . . . he released Qizhi, one of the prisoners. Qizhi fled to Choson [Korea], because he did not like the Zhou regime. When Wen-wang heard about it, he ceded Choson to Qizhi. Since Qizhi was thus appointed [by the Zhou regime as the ruler of Choson], he felt constrained to pay homage [to Wen-wang]. Thus, he appeared at the court [of Zhou] in the 13th year [of Wenwang's reign].[7]

Other documents show a slightly different version from the Shangshu Dazhuan, but are essentially the same concerning Qizhi's flight to Korea. Some versions of the story state that Qizhi, a famous sage at the end of the Yin dynasty (the beginning of Zhou), taught Wen-wang about the "Great Plan with its Nine Divisions."[8] Other versions tell us that Qizhi civilized his people by teaching morality, farming methods, and weaving. The important events about Qizhi in these stories can be summarized this way: a great Chinese sage, Qizhi, fled to Korea in order to preserve his loyalty to the Yin dynasty, and in doing so he brought the Chinese culture to the Koreans. Whether or not it is based on historical facts, the Qizhi story indicates an important aspect of early Chinese influence on Korean culture.

Many Korean historians believe, however, that Qizhi may not have gone to Korea. The significance of the story lies in its symbolic meaning rather than the truth or falsity of Qizhi's flight to Choson.[9] The story may signify that since ancient times many civilized Chinese not in agreement with the political situation in their own country fled to Choson and brought much cultural knowledge with them. If some civilized Chinese had actually moved to Choson during ancient times, it is very possible that they took Chinese geomancy with them into Korea. This is only speculation. But since archaeological evidence suggests that there was some Chinese influence on Korea during ancient times (especially since the Zhou dynasty), it is my belief that one should not simply dismiss the story as meaningless and false, whether or not one can disprove Qizhi's travel to Korea during the early part of the Zhou dynasty. The story serves to indicate the approximate beginning and ways in which the ancient Chinese culture influenced Korea. Therefore, it is my hypothesis that geomancy, as an important part of Chinese culture, diffused along with the initial flows of Chinese culture to Korea. The newly introduced geomantic art may have been incorporated with some native Korean ideas in the beginning, but it probably was continually influenced by Chinese geomancy.

2. Talhae (Silla) and the auspicious site: perhaps the oldest geomancy tale in Korea

Besides the story of Qizhi, there are other stories and several tomb paintings that can support the theory of an ancient diffusion of Chinese geomancy into Korea before the middle of the Sills dynasty. These stories, however, do not suggest that this diffusion was as old as the Qizhi period. The story of *Talhae and the Auspicious Place* appears to be most clearly identifiable as the oldest geomancy tale in Korea. Some may argue that the Tan'gun myth is the first one, because the illegitimate son of god in heaven, Hwan'ung, before descending to the world, looked around the world for a livable place and settled on Korea. However, the Tan'gun myth does not mention specific geomantically auspicious sites as does the legend of Talhae (57–79), the fourth king of the Sills dynasty, and thus it may not be considered a geomancy tale.

Memorabilia of the Three Kingdoms (Sam uk yusa) of the thirteenth century, one of the two most ancient extant Korean historical writings, records the story of Talhae and how he finds an auspicious place. When he was a young boy, Talhae acquired a house in a crescent-shaped place, an auspicious site in geomancy, by tricking the resident of the house, Hokong:

A boy [young Talhae before he became king] hiked up Toham Mountain with a walking stick and two servants, and made a stone tomb. He stayed on the mountain for seven days looking down over the [capital] city hoping to find a favourable place to live. Looking down on the city, he saw a place shaped like a crescent which he decided was a worthy place in which to live. He went down to that place and found that it was owned by a person whose name was Hogong. Young Talhae decided to trick Hogong by burying charcoal in the garden and telling him that the locale belonged to Talhae's ancestor. Hogong knew the claim was false and insisted that the land belonged to him, completely rejecting Talhae's claim. The argument, however, could not be settled without going to court. The court officer asked Talhae how he could prove that the place was his ancestor's. Talhae answered as follows: "My ancestors were blacksmiths. When they temporarily moved to a neighbouring area, this stranger took our house site. If you [the officer] dig the soil in the garden, it will be proved." The officer did so and found charcoal which he took as evidence of the previous existence of a blacksmith shop. Talhae was thus able to obtain the place and live there.[10]

Thanks to its auspiciousness, Talhae became a king of the early Silla dynasty.

In this tale, there are two important geomantic aspects: Talhae had the desire to live in a favorable place, and the place was shaped like a crescent, which represents an auspicious site. The place was obviously described in geomantic terms, since a place surrounded by mountains (like a horseshoe) is usually an auspicious place. Thus, the legend supports the existence of geomantic concepts in the early Sills period. That Talhae took the house site by tricking the former owner clearly reflects the ancient idea of Koreans fighting over auspicious sites through various means. The story was collected and recorded by the Buddhist monk Ilyon during the thirteenth century based on oral history and folklore and might not be regarded as an accurate historical record. But it nevertheless supports the view that geomancy already existed in Korea at that time.

3. The formation of the Han Chinese Commentaries (108 B.C.–313)

Geomancy must have been introduced to Korea from China at the time of the initial wave of diffusion of Chinese culture to Korea. By the first century B.C., China had established the so-called four commentaries of the Han dynasty (BC.108–AD.313)" in the area that included the north-western part of the Korean Peninsula. During that time Chinese culture must have been introduced to Korea. This period came before the *Book of Burial,* or *Zangjing,* the key classic in geomancy that was written by Kuo Pu. However, the basic idea of geomancy already existed in China and in the Han dynasty period there is clear evidence of the practice of geomancy.

4. The tomb paintings at the Koguryo Tombs of four animal symbols representing the four cardinal directions of Chinese geomancy

The Koguryo tomb paintings show four animal symbols that represent the four cardinal directions of Chinese geomancy: the turtle, the bird, the tiger, and the dragon. Yi Pyongdo comments that the poses in the animal pictures suggest that Chinese geomancy may have arrived in Korea during the middle period of the Koguryo dynasty. The basis of his speculation is that the postures of the four guardian animals in the Koguryo tomb paintings match the geomantic principles stated in classical geomantic literature, Zangshu (Zangjing). He wrote:

I wonder whether those [the symbol paintings of four directions] on the walls [inside the tombs] were the results of the influence of geomantic ideas. —Commenting on the Great Tomb and the Middle Tomb in Kangso County that are most clear in colour, the dancing pose of the red bird on the Southern wall, the undulating pose of the azure dragon with powerful feet on the Eastern wall, the pose of stretching out and putting the heads of the turtle and snake together in the painting of the black warrior, and others are in accordance with the expressions of [the geomantic principles in] Zangshu [the book of Burial], such as the red bird must bounce and dance; the azure dragon must be undulating and the black warrior must stretch and bend its head.[11]

Yi Pyongdo made a perceptive assessment. The red bird, azure dragon, and black warrior in the Koguryo tomb paintings match the geomantic principles in terms of the directions indicated as well as their poses. In particular, the red bird in the painting appears to be dancing in the air by stretching out both its wings upward as if flying. This picture literally matches the geomantic principle stated in Zangshu, that the red bird must bounce and dance.[12] However, Yi Pyongdo does not mention the pose of the white tiger in the Koguryo paintings. Why didn't he comment on it? Perhaps its pose was as powerful as that of the azure dragon and he thought it did not agree with geomantic principles. Indeed, the pose of the white tiger *was* as powerful as that of the azure dragon. The tiger's pose, similar to the dragon's, is a geomantically desirable one in accordance with geomantic principles. This is because Zangshu states that both the azure dragon and the white tiger are the two outstretched arms of the Main Mountain. Zangshu said that the azure dragon should be undulating and the white tiger should be sitting low (in a straddling position).[13] This statement metaphorically describes both of the parallel protective hills' undulating landforms.

For these reasons I support Yi Pyongdo's view. The postures of all four animal icons in the Koguryo tomb painting match well with the geomantic principles expressed in the ancient geomantic manual, Zangshu, and support the view that geomancy was introduced to Korea from China at least during the middle part of the Koguryo dynasty (B.C. 37–668). It is interesting that although they evidently used geomantic concepts on the inside of tombs, there is no clear evidence to show geomantic harmony of landforms outside some Koguryo tombs. However, the general locations of Koguryo tombs near Hwandosong (Hwando Fortress in Manchuria) are located in geomantically desirable land with background hills and water in front.

Taking into account the above examples, we can speculate that geomancy may have diffused to Korea long before the middle of the Three Kingdoms period. It probably occurred along with the initial flows of Chinese culture to Korea.

5. The city walls of Koguryo (Kungnaesong and Hwandosong)

According to the *History of the Three Kingdoms (Samguksagi)*, the early kings of Koguryo and Paekje examined the landscape to select sites for the capitals of their kingdoms.[14] Their selections met the important requirements of a geomantically auspicious place, although Samguksagi did not say those places were selected according to geomantic principles (see Figure 3.1). We can speculate that geomancy played an important role in the selections of the capitals. The location and the surrounding hills of the Hwandosong provided a textbook example of a geomantically auspicious site.

Figure 3.1 A distant view of Hwandosong, the mountain fortress of Koguryo's capital city, Kungnaesong. Note the surrounding hills in a horseshoe shape, a geomantic condition necessary for a site to be considered auspicious.

6. King Wonsong's tomb (789) at the Koksa Temple Site (Choi Chiwon's stele inscription)

Chinese geomancy was clearly being practiced seriously in Korea by the eighth century at the latest. By this time, if not much earlier, the art of geomancy had penetrated deeply into the Korean mentality. In particular, it was adopted by the royal and aristocratic societies as well as the Buddhist communities. In the inscription made by the famous scholar of Silla, Choi Chiwon, on the Stele of Sungbok temple (Sungboksa bimun), it is recorded that in 798 when King Wonsong died the court built his tomb at the Buddhist Temple, Koksa, by forcefully removing the existing temple building.[15] That this was done in spite of strong opposition clearly demonstrates how seriously geomancy was taken by the royal families and Buddhists who had already located temples in auspicious sites. Since geomancy was taken so seriously and had become so popular, it must have been introduced into Korea much earlier, perhaps centuries earlier.

During the unified Silla period, many Buddhist temples were built in geomantically auspicious sites. In the later parts of the unified Silla period, the practice of geomancy became increasingly popular and Korean society in general took the art seriously. This is supported by Koryo Taejo's warnings that constructing the numerous temples all over Korea at the end of the Silla dynasty caused the fall of that dynasty.[16]

Having considered the two legends and the four historical events, I would like to summaries my views on the introduction and development of geomancy in Korea up to the time of Master Toson. In the study of the early diffusion of Chinese culture to Korea, the story of the Chinese sage Qizhi's migration to Korea is important, even though it is not historically reliable. It has symbolic and metaphorical value signifying the time and method of Chinese cultural diffusion to Korea. The practice of geomancy in Korea must have been reinforced by the Chinese who brought their culture with them to the Han Chinese commentaries (108 B.C.–313) in the north-western part of the Korean Peninsula. After that the practice of geomancy spread widely in Korea. By the A.D. 700s the practice of geomancy was so popular and so seriously undertaken among the Korean people that even a well-established Buddhist temple in a geomantically auspicious site had to be removed to make way for a royal tomb. In such sociocultural environments Master Toson gained his prominence as a geomancer-monk with the introduction of the geomantic art of reinforcing landscape.

From the Time of Master Toson to the Fourth King of Choson, Sejong

This period spans the time of the geomancer-monk and zen master Toson (827–898) of the Silla dynasty to the fourth king of the Choson dynasty, Sejong (r.1418–1450). The time from the last period of the Silla dynasty through the entire period of the Koryo dynasty and the early period of the Choson dynasty is characterized by the strong influence of geomancy on Korean politics. Geomantic issues were often among the top political agendas and exercised a stronger influence over Korean politics and society than during any other period of Korean history. Geomancy exercised enormous power in building palaces, planning cities, and moving national capitals. And geomantic issues spawned serious political disputes.

Master Toson is certainly the best known geomancer-monk throughout the history of Korea and is often considered to be the founding father of Korean geomancy. He was born in Yongam County, South Cholla Province, in 827 and is thought to have died in 898. He is considered to be the person responsible for introducing the art of reinforcing the geomantic conditions through artificial means. He played an important role in locating Buddhist temples in geomantically auspicious sites throughout Korea. In article 2 of the Koryo Taejo's Ten Injunctions (Hunyosipjo), it states: "All Buddhist temples are built by considering the auspicious and inauspicious sites according to Monk Toson's evaluations." Taejo, the first king of the Koryo dynasty, took geomancy seriously and his strong faith in Buddhism and geomancy had a significant impact on politics throughout the Koryo dynasty. Based on different geomantic prophecies and different interpretations of geomantic theories, the Koryo government was often embroiled in political debates and disputes over building new palaces or even shifting entire capital cities to other places that were seen as more auspicious. These politically charged geomantic disputes, which drained government resources, were based on the geomantic theory of waxing and waning vital energy in a place or the theory of reinforcing geomantic conditions through artificial means.

The geomantic theory of waxing and waning vital energy in a place argues that the fortunes of places change as time passes due to the changing availability of vital energy in the place. This happens no matter how auspicious the place may be. The main aim of the Geomantic Theory of Waxing and Waning Vital Energy (chigisoewangsol) was to predict the current and future state of the fortunes of well-known auspicious sites (myongdang), especially those of the capital cities. The theory encouraged the Koryo government to build separate palaces in Seoul, Pyongyang, and elsewhere. Mainly due to the influence of this theory during the Koryo dynasty, political disputes and struggles erupted among different factions over the plan to shift the capital from Kaekyong (present-day Kaesong) to Soyong (present-day Pyongyang). Eventually these events fueled the Revolt of Myochong (?–1135). The influential Monk Myochong attempted to sway King Injong to abandon Kaekyong and move the capital to Pyongyang, arguing that the vital energy at Kaekyong was waning and that of Pyongyang waxing. He also petitioned the king to declare himself emperor and to assert equality with Sung-China. When this plan failed, he decided to achieve his goal by force and revolted against the central government in Kaekyong. He declared his newly formed state Taewikuk (the Nation of Great Achievement), but his nationalistic and geomantic revolt was short-lived, lasting less than a year.

During the Choson dynasty from Taejo, the first king (r.1392–1398), to Sejong, the fourth king (1418–1450), the geomantic issues relating to the moving of the capital to Seoul and the subsequent city planning there were some of the main political issues. After Taejo searched seriously for an auspicious capital site by consulting well-known geomancers and geomantic literature, he moved the capital from Kaekyong to Seoul. However, Chongjong, the second king (r.1398–1400), shifted the capital back to Kaekyong, the capital of the previous dynasty. Taejong, the third king (r.1400–1418), then moved the capital back to Seoul, which remains the capital of Korea today.

Although Sejong did not consider moving the capital city elsewhere, he was deeply interested in geomancy and consequently geomancy continued to have a strong influence over politics at this time. For instance, the following became political issues: whether the site of Kyongbok Palace was correctly located in an auspicious site; whether the geomantic veins from Paekak Mountain to the palace site flowed soundly; and whether Inwang Mountain, the highest peak surrounding Seoul, was the main mountain of the city. King Sejong himself carried out fieldwork by climbing up Paekak Mountain to examine the geomantic conditions of Seoul and evaluate conflicting opinions on this issue. It seemed that King Sejong's private life and daily behavior was seriously influenced by geomancy. According to Sejong Sillok, Sejong often stayed in his relatives' private homes for months at a time rather than in the Kyongbok Palace. Sejong eventually died at the private residence of Yong'ong Taegun in 1452.[17] King Sejong's behavior was probably mainly due to his belief in geomancy and suspicion about the auspiciousness of the Kyongbok Palace.[18]

This early part of the Choson dynasty was very similar to the Koryo dynasty in terms of geomantic thought and its influence on the sociopolitical issues of the time. Therefore, this period can be considered an extension of the Koryo period.

From King Sejo (r.1455–1468) to the Time Before the Rise of the Practical Learning School, or Sirhak (1670)

The period after King Sejong until the rise of Sirhak was marked by relative quiet in terms of geomantic issues in Korean politics and society in general. The

main geomantic issues were auspicious tomb sites for royal families and auspicious gravesites for commoners. Even Confucian scholars tended to accept the
practice of geomancy in the search for auspicious gravesites as a way of expressing filial piety to deceased ancestors. That is why they embraced geomancy
without being critical about this seemingly superstitious art. The attitudes of
Korean Confucian scholars may also reflect Zhu Xi (1130–1200), the great Neo-
Confucian scholar of the Southern Song dynasty of China, who used geomancy
for locating his family graves in auspicious sites.[19] However, that endeavor may
have been an expression of his desire to extract benefits (auspiciousness) from
the gravesites for the living or for future generations of descendants, rather than
an expression of concern for the welfare of deceased ancestors.

From the Rise of the Practical Learning School to
the Japanese annexation of Korea (1910)

This period is characterized by strong criticism, particularly by the Confucian
scholars who belonged to the Sirhak, or Practical Learning School, of the art of
geomancy and the way it was practiced in Korea. For instance, the Sirhak
scholars of the later period of the Choson dynasty, such as Yi lk (1681–1763) in
his masterpiece work, *Songhosasol (Fragmental Discourses by Songho, the
Star-Lake)* severely criticised the practice of geomancy. Chong Yakyong (1762–
1836), another distinguished Sirhak scholar, recorded in his book *Mokmin Simso
(Book of Advice on Governing the People)* that litigation in the courts for gravesites has become a troubling problem and about half of the fighting and assaults
resulting in death are due to conflict for graves. [20]

Chong listed examples of the adverse impact of geomancy on people and argued that local magistrates should handle each court case relating to geomancy
fairly and rationally after studying the situation carefully.[21] To demonstrate the
extreme and desperate Korean behavior of attempting to acquire an auspicious
gravesite, Chong Yakyong cited Chong Sun's words:

> People who desire to bury their parents in auspicious places are violating private
> property rights by [illegally] occupying grave sites in hills belonging to others and
> sometimes digging out the bones of others' ancestors in [an auspicious grave site].
> This kind of behaviour causes great resentment among the people and leads to
> court litigation where all parties want to win the court case at any cost. In this
> manner people waste all the wealth they have and ruin their lives, and may not
> succeed in acquiring an auspicious grave site in the end. This kind of disastrous
> behaviour brings misfortune instead of blessings. Why has people's behaviour
> come to this level of foolishness?[22]

Indeed, people's eager search for auspicious gravesites by any available
means was a major social problem during the later period of the Choson dynasty. Sirkahk scholars' criticism of the art of geomancy became stronger. A

quote from one such Shirhak scholar, Pak Chega, summarizes geomantic behavior of the time:

> The idea of geomancy has had a more adverse influence [on Korean society] than Buddhism or Taoism. Even the noble class followed the idea and made it a custom. It is said that moving an ancestor's grave to a better location expresses filial piety. Since the noble class considered the making of its ancestors' graves as important, the common people imitated their behaviour. . . . Generally, it is bad to expect [depend upon] one's fortune through one's dead parents. Moreover, occupying others' mountains illegally and destroying others' funeral biers are not right things to do. To have more splendid worship ceremonies at graves than at home during special seasons is against proper principles. There is no need to list all the stories about people who perform deeds against such principles by wasting all of their wealth [in finding auspicious places], do not take care of their ancestral bones, and yet expect things to turn out well [in their lives].[23]

The Period of Japanese Colonial Rule
(1910–1945)

This period saw the introduction of the public cemetery system in designated areas and the Japanese government's systematic interference with Korean palaces in Seoul and local government offices in other cities—key geomantic landscapes—to implant Japanese colonial icons. New Japanese colonial government buildings were constructed on the Korean palace ground in Seoul and many Japanese Shinto shrines were built in major Korean cities. This policy can be interpreted as a Japanese attempt to control the Korean mind and get it to accept Japanese colonial rule in the name of modernization and development.

After Japan annexed Korea as a colony the Japanese colonial government adopted a cemetery system where graves were allowed to be made only within the confinement of a designated section, a system new to Korea. Formerly, Koreans could make a grave anywhere they considered auspicious, as long as they had access to the spot. As a result of this policy, the application of geomancy in gravesite selection became somewhat restricted. However, grave geomancy was deeply seated in Korean hearts and this new colonial policy could not be strictly enforced in many parts of rural Korea. Therefore, social problems and crimes relating to grave geomancy continued to occur.

The Japanese colonial government manipulated for its political purpose the deeply rooted Korean belief in geomancy in order to legitimize and promote colonial rule while suppressing Korean resistance to the Japanese colonial government. For example, the Japanese colonial government mutilated the Kyongbok Palace by sandwiching it between the new colonial government office building and the Governor General's Residence to the front and rear of the Korean palace. By doing so, it effectively disrupted the flow of vital energy and auspiciousness of the Korean palace. Anyone who knows anything about geomancy and Seoul's geomantic conditions would understand that Korea's fortunes were finished and that the new Japanese colonial government would replace the Korean monarchy. By contrasting the majestic Western-style Japanese colonial government office building with the old and relatively smaller and shabby wooden building of the Korean palace, the Japanese government seemed to have attempted to justify and legitimize its colonial rule over Korea. It appeared to be suggesting that Japan came to Korea to modernize Korea and that the Koreans should accept Japanese rule and leave its shabby Korean heritage behind.

In provincial districts, the Japanese built Shinto shrines in geomantically important places, sometimes by forcefully removing the existing Korean building of significance. By doing so the Japanese government might have been attempting to give the impression to Koreans that the Japanese colonial government had become the legitimate beneficiary of all of Korea's important vital energy.

Yi Mongil suggested that this Japanese colonial period in the history of Korean geomantic thought is characterized by Japan's disconnecting of the veins of Korea's vital energy.[24] His argument is based on the fact that the Japanese government established railways and highways by cutting off some important Korean geomantic arteries of vital energy as well as on the public belief that the Japanese drove iron piles into geomantically critical points; Koreans thought they were attempting to disrupt the flow of vital energy and thus ruin the geomantically auspicious Korean landscape. However, when we examine geomantic thought and practice during this period, it might be more accurate to describe it as the time of Japanese manipulation of Korean geomancy to legitimize Japan's colonial rule and get Koreans to submit to Japan's colonial authority, as well as the time of the introduction of the cemetery system to control Koreans' practice of grave geomancy.

From the Time of Liberation (1945)
to the Present

Since Korea's liberation from Japanese colonial rule in 1945, the practice of geomancy has not been officially recognized by the government, but many Koreans have continued to engage in it, especially in gravesite selection. The practice of geomancy did not cause many social problems during the Korean War (1950–1953) or during the 1960s and 1970s when Korea was relatively poor economically. Traditional Korean culture was pushed aside during the fast-track modernization drive by the Korean government. At that time Koreans did not have the luxury of considering values of their cultural heritage that were not essential to the urgent task of improving the standard of living. Since the 1980s, however, as they have accumulated wealth through rapid industrialization and modernization, they have come to have nostalgic feelings toward traditional cultural values, and they can afford to look at nonessential aspects of life. In my view, this economic development awakened the traditional value of filial piety and enabled many Koreans to hire geomancers to search for auspicious gravesites or to face-lift grave decorations with stone works. They could not afford to do such things when they were poor and preoccupied with economic development and the modernization of their society. For these reasons there seems to have been a popularization of geomancy in Korea since the 1980s. In the 1970s I was able to find only a few books (fewer than ten titles) on the principles and practice of geomancy written by professional geomancers. In the late 1980s, however, I was able to find more than two dozen such books, filling several book shelves of Kyobo Books, the largest bookstore in Seoul. On 23 October 2004 in the same bookstore, I was astonished to find that the geomancy section had expanded greatly: I counted 183 different books on geomancy filling a six-tier bookshelf, and 29 different titles of "overflow" geomancy books were shelved on the bottom tier in the next bookshelf marked "divination." In total, 212 different geomancy books were available for sale in the bookstore that day. When I typed in the key word "pungsu (geomancy)" into the bookstore computer, 184 book titles were retrieved, and with the key word "myongdang (auspicious land)," another commonly used Korean term to connote geomancy, I retrieved another 47 book titles. Hence, 231 book titles were being sold in the bookstore.

Today, Korea's politics are influenced by geomancy. As mentioned, Kim Dae-Jung shifted his family graves to an auspicious site in Yong-in near Seoul, after which he was elected president. The graves were moved by Son Sok-u, who was then the best-known geomancer in Korea. There were widespread rumors in 2002 that several candidates for the Korean presidency shifted their ancestral graves to auspicious sites. In every major parliamentary or presidential election in Korea, we often hear that someone has shifted his or her ancestor's grave to an auspicious site by hiring a well-known geomancer. Although some such stories may be exaggerated or groundless, others are true. They may well demonstrate that geomancy is still being used to influence and sway public opinion. Kim Dukyu perceptively commented:

> When Chun Duhwan was the president of the fifth republic, many thoughtless geomancers visited and examined the graves of his ancestors, for it was thought that he became the president due to the auspiciousness manifested from those grave sites. It may be natural for Koreans who are soaked in geomantic ideas to talk about the [auspicious] grave sites of the successful candidates in the elections or the person in charge of the government. However, such phenomena may not be such a simple matter, because these rumours were intentionally spread by the people in power or election candidates to manipulate public psychology [relating to geomancy] in their favour. They fabricate [or sway] public opinion by hiring influential fortune tellers and geomancers. They attempt to spread rumours that so-and-so will become a king this time or such-and-such a person is destined to be elected as the president, in order to influence the people to accept a particular candidate as the one who has a heavenly mandate to become the ruler of the country.[25]

During my field trips in South Korea since the 1970s, I found that the practice of geomancy still persisted despite the inroads of Western culture. Geomantic ideas are more important to older generations in rural areas than to younger generations in urban areas, although even in cities the geomancer is not yet neglected. Since the 1980s, the practice of geomancy in Korea, aided by the improving economy and living standards, has been popularized and a number of geomantic manuals and works of literature have been published. Today geomancers in Korea are still important as gravesite and house site consultants, although their role in society has significantly faded. Most Korean intellectuals regard them as superstitious sorcerers, although some view geomancy as a traditional ecological idea with relevance for modern environmental planning. Geomancers are still persuasive authorities in selecting gravesites and house sites.

The following case, recorded during my last field trip, illustrates the contemporary attitude toward geomancers.[26] I met a young man, a Mr Kim, who was in his thirties, at Modong-myon, Sangju County, in North Kyongsang Province. A farmer with more than six years of modern school education, he said that when his father died he ignored the geomancer's advice in selecting the gravesite because he did not believe in geomancy. After the burial, however, many untoward events occurred in his family, and the village elders advised him to check his father's gravesite. Despite his skepticism, he hired a geomancer and they went together to see the grave. When Mr Kim pointed out his father's grave on a distant mountain slope, the geomancer said that he did not even need to go there for he already knew that the gravesite was bad. The geomancer told Mr Kim that the coffin had been floating on water inside the grave. When Mr Kim opened the grave he found that it was true. Therefore, he moved his father's grave according to the geomancer's advice. Since then, Mr Kim has believed in the art of geomancy. He told me that he did not even suspect water would be in a grave located on a well-drained mountain slope.

Some young Koreans, then, are not completely free from the influence of geomancers. I also met a middle-aged man, an ex-congressman who probably had more modern education than the farmer. He was a very firm believer in geomancy and gave much respect to geomancers.[27] He told me that he wished to rebury his father in a more auspicious place as part of his filial piety, and that he had even carried a seventy-year-old geomancer on his back during a trip to the mountains in search of an auspicious gravesite. He eventually acquired such a site and moved the grave.

Geomancy is still deeply rooted in parts of Korean society, and geomancers are still able to collect fees for selecting house sites and gravesites. People's belief in geomancy is problematic for the South Korean government as far as national environmental planning is concerned, since encouraging cremation and limiting the expansion of graves and cemeteries are important social issues for the government.

It is said that there are still significant numbers of geomancers in Seoul alone. A weekly magazine in 1974 even introduced the leading Seoul geomancers of the time.[28]

According to the magazine, a Mr Chi selected the tomb sites of the late Korean president Syngman Ree, the late Korean army general Kim Chong-o, the late Vice-Prime Minister Kim Hak-yol, and the late Korean first lady Mrs. Pak (Yuk Yongsu), who was assassinated on 15 August 1974. In addition, it reported that due to the number of requests by the people, a Mr Chang once examined more than fifty gravesites in a single day during March 1974.

Yet geomancers are no longer important to most of the younger generation who have received a modern education. The role of the geomancer is much more limited in cities than in rural areas, probably due to the limited space in the city and the greater degree of modern education available. Today most city dwellers use purpose-built cemeteries or crematoriums.

Three Types of Korean Geomantic Thought

An examination of the history of Korean geomantic thought will find that it can be classified into one (or more) of three types. The first type is the basic geomantic belief that an auspicious site provides benefits to people. Out of this belief, people have at times been so eager to find an auspicious site that they were willing to lose their lives. This belief often led government authorities, at the time of constructing royal tombs or government offices, to take over private property (land), and people were often forced to concede their property to the government.

The second type of Korean geomantic thought involves the improvement of geomantic conditions in a place through artificial means. People modify the landscape slightly to make up for shortcomings and to remove excessive aspects of any geomantic conditions. Planting trees, building pagodas or temples in critically important places, reinforcing an existing hill, or even creating an artificial hill by piling up dirt to make up for a weakness are examples. These means of modifying geomantic conditions were practiced widely in cities as well as rural areas throughout the Koryo and Choson dynasties. Many governmental and private resources were used to carry out this geomantic reinforcement work, or Pibo.

The third type of Korean geomantic thought, which we have come across already, involves the idea that vital energy can wax and wane in an auspicious site. According to this theory, the vital energy of an auspicious site, such as a capital city, will not be constant over time. The length of the waxing and waning phases could either last several centuries or be shorter depending on the geomantic landscape characteristics of an auspicious site. This means that the fortunes of a dynasty that has its capital city in an auspicious site could dwindle or improve depending on the phase of vital energy. Therefore this idea came to be associated with geomantic prophecies and divination to determine whether a place is in its waxing or waning phase. This idea was especially influential during the Koryo dynasty. This type of geomantic thought is not seen in the classical geomantic textbooks, and I have not heard any geomancer or other believers in geomancy comment on its validity today.

A Review of Modern Research into Geomantic
Thought in Korea

We have to honor two book-length monumental works, one by a Korean, the
other by a Japanese, which were written prior to my own 1976 book-length
study of Korean geomancy. Yi Pyongdo's *Koryo Sidae ui Yongu (A Study of the
Koryo Period),* published in 1948, is a study of the impact of geomancy and
geomantic prophecy on the government of the Koryo dynasty (A.D. 918–1392)
and the early Choson dynasty (1392–1450's). Murayama Chijun's *Chosen no
Fusui (Korean Geomancy),* published in 1931 as one of thirty-one volumes of a
survey series by the Japanese government general of Korea, provides the most
comprehensive study of Korean geomancy. As for key monographic works, the
first modern scholar to study Korean geomancy may have been Murayama
Chijun, a Japanese researcher who was employed by the Japanese colonial
government of Korea. He documented and explained the principles and practice
of geomancy in Korea in his book *Geomancy of Korea (Chosen no fusui)*.[29] The
Japanese colonial government extensively surveyed and documented traditional
Korean customs, lifestyles, and belief systems for the effective colonial rule of
Korea. Murayama Chijun was employed as a temporary researcher for this
purpose and was involved in the research projects on geomancy and other belief
systems. The Japanese colonial government must have thought that understanding geomancy was critically important for effective colonial rule, and they
carried out extensive surveys and research on this subject. Murayama Chijun's
Geomancy of Korea is the result of the Colonial Government's research project.
It is fair to say that Murayama's work was at least partly intended to serve the
Japanese colonial rule of Korea. However, this book compiles perhaps the
richest and most extensive folkloristic and anthropological information on
geomancy as practiced at that time. It is said that the former Korean court
geomancer, Chon Kiung, and other well-known geomancers of the time were
consultants for the research project for the book and are assumed to have provided valuable information. Murayam's *Geomancy of Korea,* written in Japanese, has become an important milestone in the history of research into Korean
geomancy.

   Yi Pyongdo, a prominent Korean historian, turned his attention to the importance of geomancy in understanding Korean history. During Japanese colonial rule he started studying the impact of geomancy on Korean capital city site
selections and on planning at the beginning of the Choson dynasty.[30] However,
his most significant work on Korean geomancy was his book *A Study of the
Koryo Period (Koryo sidae ui yongu),*[31] where he carefully examines in detail
the impact of geomantic beliefs on the politics and society during the Koryo
dynasty. His book, even after fifty years, is still considered a reliable and
authoritative study. Professor Yi shows how much the Korean elite was influenced in the selection and maintenance of capitals and how important geomantic
prophesies have been in Korean society.

After Yi Pyongdo's work in 1975, another historian, Choi Pyonghon, examined the social function of geomancy and its historical significance through the study of Monk Toson (827–898).[32] In his article, Choi evaluated the significance of geomantic ideas in the history of Korean thought.

In the 1970s research on geomancy in Korea increased, especially in the fields of geography, anthropology, and folk literature. In cultural geography, my book *Geomantic Relationships Between Culture and Nature in Korea* was printed in English in Taiwan in 1976.[33] I also published several articles on Chinese and Korean geomancy, especially on the image of nature in geomancy and on the origin of geomancy in China and its spread to Korea. Most of my works were written in English and naturally were read more widely outside Korea.

Perhaps the most popular and influential work on geomancy in Korea by a modern scholar is *Geomantic Thought of Korea (Hankuk ui pungsu sasang)* by Choi Chang jo, which was published in Korea in 1984.[34] This book, written in Korean, became a key book introducing geomancy to scholars as well as to the general Korean public. Choi wrote a number of books and articles on geomancy in Korea and translated the classical Chinese geomantic textbooks such as *Chingujing and Jangjing (jingnang-jing)* into modern Korean. His writing and lecturing through public broadcasts have heightened the public's interest in geomancy. His activities have drawn public interest in the geomantic belief system, leading some scholars to present more critical views on geomancy.

Park Sea-ik might be the first contemporary architect to enter into serious geomancy research and to attempt to apply geomantic principles to the design of modern homes and buildings. In his Ph.D. dissertation, *A Study of the Background and Origin of Feng shui Theory*, he advocated the possible Korean origin of Chinese geomantic theory. He also wrote another book on geomancy and architecture.[35]

In 1987 David J. Nemeth published a monograph entitled *The Architecture of Ideology: Neo-Confucian Imprinting on Cheju Island, Korea*.[36] Based on his Ph.D. thesis, it discusses geomancy as a key ideology in the formation and understanding of the cultural landscape on Cheju Island. He also wrote several articles on geomantic maps of Cheju Island.[37] His works must be some of the most substantive introductions to geomancy and the landscape of Cheju Island, Korea.

Kim Dukyu is an active researcher and prolific writer about geomancy in Korea. His sympathetic views are similar to those of Choi Chang jo. He has perceptively examined the positive and negative aspects of grave geomancy as practiced in modern Korean society. He has translated two classics of Chinese geomantic discourse, *Chiri shinpop (New Principles of Geomancy)* by Hu Shunshin of the Song dynasty, and *Myongsanron (Discourses on the Auspicious Mountains)*. His book *Choson Pungsuhakinui Saeng'aewa nonjaneg (The Life and Discourses of Choson Dynasty Geomancers)* is the result of his sound research into famous geomancers during the Choson dynasty based on the annals of the Choson dynasty.

Since the 1990s, several young Korean cultural geographers have completed their Ph.D. theses on geomancy in Korea. Lee Mong-il studied the history of Korean geomantic thought; his PhD dissertation was published subsequently.[38] Sung Dong Hwan studied the Zen Buddhist temple locations of geomantic significance during the late Silla dynasty in Korea.[39] Choi Won-Suk studied "bibo," or the geomantic ideas of reinforcing or moderating the deficiencies of a geomantic landscape in an auspicious site by artificial means.[40] His work is a milestone in the study of geomantic thought in Korea.

A Korean Philosopher, Yun Chonkun, wrote *Pungsuui Cholhak (Philosophy of Geomancy).*[41] In this book Yun presented the rather complicated and ambiguous geomantic concepts and terms in plain modern Korean for an easy-to-comprehend summary of the metaphysical aspects of geomantic thought. He pointed out that classical Chinese geomantic thought clearly reflects the Chinese cultural and philosophical tradition. However, he did not consult any of a number of well-known works written in Western languages on the subjects.

There have also been many academic articles and journalistic essays on Korean geomancy. Most of these works have been published since the mid-1980s.

To determine the general trend of research into Korean geomancy, in September 2001 I looked at the website of the National Institute of Korean History (Kuksa Pyonchan wuiwonhoe). All articles, books, and other publications on Korean history were listed from April 1973 to February 1999. In this database, 74 out of 25,201 articles on Korean history in academic periodicals were related to geomancy. Many were written by scholars in the fields of geography, folklore, architecture, and literature rather than history.

The Electronic Library of the Korean National Assembly had a database of articles from Korean academic periodicals from May 1977 to the early part of 2001. From this database, I identified 140 articles on geomancy in Korea, broken down as follows:

Geography — 38
Architecture (landscape architecture and planning) — 35
Korean literature (folklore) — 30
Anthropology (including folk customs and belief systems) — 12
History — 7
Other subjects (philosophy, fine arts, and philology) — 18

My classification of subjects may be rudimentary, but it should be sufficient to get a feel for the general trend of academic research into Korean geomancy—in other words, what academic fields are studying what aspects of Korean geomancy.

In examining the research themes of these articles, it became clear that geographers' research on geomancy was mainly on geomantic location analysis and settlements, while research in Korean literature on geomancy was mainly on geomancy tales as a form of oral literature; many of those works classified the types of Korean geomancy tales. Research in architecture was mainly on the application of geomantic principles to architectural design, or the use of geomantic theories in the explanation of the traditional Korean architectural heritage. Research from landscape architecture was on traditional Korean gardens and royal tomb landscapes. Anthropologists investigated geomancy and ancestral worship in prominent Korean families, as well as the religiosity of geomancy. Historians mainly investigated issues relating to the selection and construction of new capitals during the Koryo and Choson dynasties.

More than 50 percent (73 out of 140) of academic journal articles published in Korea were authored by scholars in the fields of geography, architecture, landscape architecture, and city planning. This may demonstrate that the theory and practice of geomancy in Korea has been closely related to the academic fields dealing with environmental and spatial issues. In these fields, research interests in geomancy lie mainly in landscape planning, building design, and settlement and gravesite selections. Articles on geomancy by scholars of Korean literature demonstrate the importance of geomancy in Korean literature. Geomancy has been an important theme not only in Korean folklore (oral literature) but also in poetry and the novels. On the other hand, there is not much research into geomancy by contemporary historians, although a prominent historian, Yi Pyongdo produced a monumental research work in geomancy in the 1940s. Scholarship in Korea today emphasizes the spatial dimensions of geomancy, not its time dimension.

Notes

1. Lee Mong-il, "Kyongbokgungkwa Choson chongdokbu chognsaui Pungsuchirijok kwanke" [The P'ungsu Relationship between the Kyongpok Palace and the Old Government-General Building in Seoul, Korea], *Chong kwan Yi Pyongkon Kyosu Hwagap Kinyum Nonmunjip* [Festschrift, in Honour of Professor Yi Pyongkon on his 60th Birthday] (1992), 333–363.

2. Immannishi Ryu, *Shiragi shi Kenkyu* [A Study of Silla History] (Seoul: Chikasawa shoten, 1933), 137.

3. Yi Pyongdo, *Koryo Sidaeui Yongu* [A Study of the Koryo Period], revised edition. (Seoul: Asea Munhwasa, 1980), 28–29.

4. Yi Pyongdo, *Hankuk Kodae Sahoewa ku Munhwa* [The Society of Ancient Korea and Its Culture] (Seoul: Somundang, 1973), 304-307.

5. Yi Chonghang (Lee, Joung Hang), "Pungsu Chirisol ui Songhaenggwa Kugosi uri Minjoksonge Michin Ak-yonghyange Kwanhan Ilkochal [A Study of the Practice of Geomancy and its Adverse Impact on Korean Characteristics]," *Kyongbuk Taehakkyo Nonmunijip*, vol. 5 (1962), 491.

6. For example, Chinese sword-money during the Warring States is found in Korea. For further information, see Chindan-hakhoe, ed., *Hankuk-sa* [History of Korea] (Seoul: Ulyu Munhwa-sa, 1959), 48-64.

7. Fu Sheng, *Shangshu dachuan* (Shanghai: Shangwu Yinshuguan, 1937), 59.

8. It is an ancient concept of Chinese cosmology. According to Shuching or the Book of History (Records), it is Chi-tzu's explanation of the principle of the universe.

9. For discussion on the truth or falsity of Chi-tsu's flight to Choson, see Chon Kwan-u, "Kijago [A Study of Qizhi]," *Tongbang Hakji*, vol. 15 (1974): 1–72.

10. Ilyon, *Samguk yusa* [Memorabilia of the Three Kingdoms], Translated into modern Korean by Yi Cheho (Seoul: Kwangmunchulpansa, 1969), vol. l, 15-16. In the story, it is interesting that even though Talhae obtained the land through cheating Hogong, the auspiciousness of the land was manifested to him. This aspect of the story supports the idea that playing tricks and cheating were accepted to some degree in traditional Korean society. For the discussion on this, see chapter 8 of this book. However, considering that although he obtained the land through dishonest means, the auspiciousness was yet manifested to him, this factor contradicts some later stories which emphasized the importance of being virtuous in order to obtain an auspicious place. Such contradictory concepts are often found in geomancy.

11. Yi Pyongdo, Hankuk Kodae Sahoewa ku Munhwa, 307-311.

12. Guo Pu, Zangshu, in *Dili zhengzong* [The Cardinal Principles of Geomancy] commentary by Jiang Guo (Shinchu: Chulin shuchu, 1967), part 2, 3b.

13. Guo Pu, Zangshu, in *Dili zhengzong* , part 2, 3b.

14. Kim Pusik , *Samkuk sagi* [history of the Three Kingdoms]. Translated into modern Korean by Yi Pyongdo (Seoul: Eul-yoo Publishing, 1960), 249 and 393.

15. Lee Ki-baek (Yi Kibaek), "Han'guk pungsuchirisol ui kiwon" [The Origin of Korean Geomancy]. *Han'guksa siminkangchoa,* vol. 14 (1994) 1–17; Yi Pyongdo, *Koryo Sidaeui Yongu,* 29

16. The second article of the Ten Injunctions decreed by the first king (Taejo) of the Koryo dynasty includes the following statement: "During the last period of the Silla Dynasty many temples were built and damaged the land energy of the nation. For such activities caused the dynasty to collapse eventually, how can we afford not to guard against this affair?" The Korean text for this translation is from Chong Inji and others, trans. by Pak Sihyong and Hong Hwoiyu, *Pukyok Koryosa*, vol. 1, Sega 2, Taejo 2, (Seoul: Sinsowon,1992), 115.

17. Yi Sungnyong, "Sejong Taewang ui Kaesong ui kochal" [A Study of King Sejong's Personality]. *Taedong Munhwa Yongu* [Studies in Great Eastern Culture] vol. 3 (1966): 57–59.

18. Yi Sungnyong, "Sejong Taewang ui Kaesong ui kochal," 57–59.

19. Kim Dukyu, *Uri Ttang, Uri Pungsu* [Our Land, Our Geomancy] (Seoul: Tonghaksa, 1998), 17–18.

20. Chong Yakyong, *Kukyok Mokmin-simso* [Criticisms and Advice on Governing the People, A Modern Korean Translation] (Seoul: Minjok Munhwa Chujinhoe, 1969), 390.

21. Chong Yakyong, *Kukyok Mokmin-simso*, 390–399.

22. Chong Yakyong, *Kukyok Mokmin-Simso*, Chapter 'Hyongjon 1,' Section 'Chongsong, ha': Yi Hwa, *Choson Sidae Myoji Pungsu Sinang Yongu*, MA Thesis (Seoul National University, 1999), 22.

23. Pak Chega, *Pukhakui* [Discourse on Northern Studies], Translated into modern Korean by Yi Sokho (Seoul: Taeyang Sojok, 1972), 402.

24. Lee Mong-il, "Kyongbokgungkwa Choson chongdokbu," 208.

25. Kim Dukyu, *Hankuk Pungsu ui ho wa sil* [Truth and False of Korean Geomancy] (Seoul: Tonghaksa, 1995), 268.

26. Interview at Chungmo Market place, Modong-myon, Sangju-kun, North Kyongsang Province, 24 November 1973. Informant's name withheld.

27. Interview with Mr Shim Pongsop at Chollong-dong, Tongdaemun-ku, Seoul, 8 February 1974.

28. *Chugan chung-ang* [Weekly Chung-ang](Seoul), 17 March 1974, 28. The four names of famous geomancers given are Chi Chong-o (age 54), Chang Yongduk (age 50), Choi Musan (age 57), and Choi Donhon (age 76).

29. Murayama Chijun, *Chosen no Fusui* [Korean Geomancy] (Seoul: Chosen Sho-tofu, 1931).

30. Yi Pyongdo, "Yijo chogiui kondo munjae" [Issues Relating to the New Capital during the Early the Choson Dynasty]. *Jindan Hakpo*, vol 9 (1938) 30–85.

31. Yi Pyongdo, *Koryo Sidae ui Yongu* [A Study of the Koryo Period] (Seoul: Ulyu munhwa-sa, 1948).

32. Choi Byong-hon, "Tosonui Saengaewa Rmalyochoui Pungsuchirisol" [The Life of Toson and Geomancy during the Period of the End of Silla and the Beginning of Koryo], in *Hankuksa Yongu [A Study of Korean History]*, vol. 11 (1975) 101–146.

33. Yoon Hong-key, *Geomantic Relationships Between Culture and Nature in Korea* (Taipei: The Orient Culture Service, 1976).

34. Choi Changjo, *Hankuk ui Pungsusasang* [Geomantic Thought of Korea] (Seoul: Minumsa, 1984).

35. Park Sea-ik, *"Pungsuchirisol Palsaeng Paekuyong e kwanhan punsok yon'gu"* [A Study on the Background and Origin of Fengshui Theory], PhD dissertation, Korea University, 1987; Park Sea-ik, Pungsuschriri wa konchuk [Geomancy and Architecture] (Seoul: Kyonghyang Shinmunsa, 1997).

36. David J. Nemeth, *The Architecture of Ideology: Neo-Confucian Imprinting on Cheju Island, Korea*, University of California Publications, Geography, vol. 26, (Berkeley, University of California Press, 1987).

37. David J. Nemeth, "Bright Yard, Maps from Cheju Island, *Landscape*, vol. 25, no. 2 (1981): 20–21; David Nemeth "Fengshui as Terrestrial Astrology in Traditional China and Korea", in *The Power of Place: Sacred Ground in Natural and Human Environments*, ed. James A. Swan (Wheaton, Ill: Quest Books, 1991), 215–234; David Nemeth "A Cross-Cultural Cosmographic Interpretation of Some Korean Geomancy Maps," *Cartographica*, vol.30, no.1, (1993): 85–97.

38. Lee Mong il, "Kyongbokgungkwa Choson chongdokbu"

39. Sung Dong Hwan, "*Ramalyocho Sonjongkeyol sachalui ilji yongu*" [A Study on the location of Zen Buddhist temples during the Late Silla dynasty in Korea]," PhD dissertation, Taegu Hyosong Catholic University, 1999.

40. Choi Won-Suk (2000), "Yongnamui Bibo [Bibo of the Yongnam Region]," PhD dissertation, Korea University, 2000.

41. Yun Chonkun (2001), *Pungsu ui cholhak* [Philosophy of Geomancy] (Seoul: Norumto, 2001).

PART II:
GEOMANTIC PRINCIPLES INTO PRACTICE

Chapter 4
Yin-Yang Theory and Geomancy[1]

The concept of Yin-Yang has expressed a basic Chinese attitude toward the world since remote times. This world view has influenced all aspects of Chinese culture, including medicine, philosophy, political thought, legal thought, divination, religion, music, and geomancy.

The basic doctrine of the theory is simple enough: all things and events of the world are the products of two elements: yin and yang. The doctrine in its sophisticated form is perhaps best summarized by Zhou Duni, one of the greatest neo-Confucian scholars, in his book *An Explanation of the Diagram of the Great Ultimate (T'aijitushuo)*:

> The Ultimate of Non-being and also the Great Ultimate (*T'ai-chi*)! The Great Ultimate through movement generates yang. When its activity reaches its limit, it becomes tranquil. Through tranquillity the Great Ultimate generates yin. When tranquillity reaches its limit, activity begins again. So movement and tranquillity alternate and become the root of each other, giving rise to the distinction of yin and yang, and the two modes are thus established.
>
> By the transformation of yang and its union with yin, the Five Agents of Water, Fire, Wood, Metal, and Earth arise. When these five material forces (*ch'i*) are distributed in harmonious order, the four seasons run their course.
>
> The Five Agents constitute one system of yin and yang, and yin and yang constitute one Great Ultimate. The Great Ultimate is fundamentally the Non-ultimate. The Five Agents arise, each with its specific nature.
>
> When the reality of the Ultimate of Non-being and the essence of yin, yang, and the Five Agents come into mysterious union, integration ensues. *Ch'ien* (Heaven) constitutes the male element, and *k'un* (Earth) constitutes the female element. The interaction of these two material forces engenders and transforms the myriad things. The myriad things produce and reproduce, resulting in an unending transformation.[2]

These yin and yang forces and five agents (elements) produce everything and every event in the world (see Figure 4.1). All things and events can be

classified as either yin or yang forces and as any one of the five elements—
wood, fire, earth, metal, and water. This is the central doctrine of the yin and
yang theory.

Yang represents the sky, the male, the father, positivity, strength, hardness,
brightness, and constructiveness. Yin represents the earth, the female, the
mother, negativity, weakness, softness, darkness, wetness, and destructiveness.[3]
The interaction of these two opposing elements produces the five elements,
which transform and elaborate further characteristics of yin and yang.

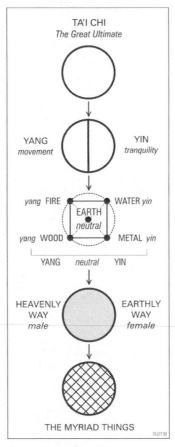

Figure 4.1 Diagram of Zhou Duni's Yin-Yang and Five Elements Theory

The origins of the concepts of yin and yang and the five elements are obscure. We do not even know if they have the same origin. If the concept of the
five elements does have a different origin than that of yin and yang, we still do
not know when the Yin-Yang theory adopted the five elements concept. If the
five elements concept was later adopted by the Yin-Yang theory, the five

elements concept must have brought significant meaning to it by adding the concepts of cycle and succession, as the five elements succeed one another.[4]

Theoretically speaking, the yin and yang concept is the foundation or trunk of a system with many branches: the five elements become the upper structure or branches of the system. Epistemologically speaking, however, the five elements concept allows for a more concrete and detailed way of observing things than does the Yin-Yang duality. Hence, it is my opinion that the five elements concept became more important and fundamental in geomancy and other cosmological systems. One of the earliest Chinese texts that describes the five elements is the *Shujing*:

> The first category is the Five Agents [Elements] namely, Water, Fire, Wood, Metal, and Earth. The nature of Water is to moisten and descend; of Fire, to burn and ascend; of Wood, to be bend and to [grow] straight; of Metal to yield and to be modified; of Earth, to be provided for sowing and reaping. That which moistens and descends produces saltiness; that which burns and ascends produces bitterness; that which is crooked and straight produces acridity; that which provides for sowing and reaping produces sweetness.[5]

These five elements (*Wuxing* in Chinese) should not be considered static but rather dynamic and interacting forces.[6] According to the Yin-Yang and Five Elements Theories, these five interacting forces (elements) can either give birth to one another or destroy one another, depending on how they occur in the cycle of the five elements. This cycle has two principles: the principle of five elements producing one another and the principle of five elements destroying one another.

The principle of five elements producing one another stipulates that metal produces water, water produces wood, wood produces fire, fire produces earth, and earth produces metal. It is not clearly known how this order or series was formulated and why the order shows a sequential birth relationship among the five elements. There is some rational basis in the principle, however: water (or nutrients in liquid form) nourishes wood; wood becomes fuel for fire; the remains of fire become ash or earth; and metal is deposited under earth.[7] The idea that metal produces water is somewhat more difficult to rationalize, but metal and rock, which are solid and hard, share basically the same substance and belong to the same category. Water surfaces between rocks (through the cracks).

The principle of five elements destroying one another stipulates that metal destroys wood, wood destroys earth, earth destroys water, water destroys fire, and fire destroys metal. The origin of this order is also obscure. But, again, it is not difficult to find a rational basis in the order, since metal (an axe) can cut trees; seeds of plants (wood) break the earth and sprout; earth can fill water wells or change watercourses; water can extinguish fire; and fire can melt metal.

The order of the five elements is important for establishing harmony among geomantic elements in an area. It is particularly important in determining the auspicious positional relationships between the four principal mountains of an auspicious site, namely the main mountain, azure dragon, white tiger, and peace mountain. It is also critical in the evaluation of the dragon range behind the mountain. If the mountain peaks of the range are positioned in the order of "five elements producing one another," they are auspicious, while "five elements destroying one another" is inauspicious.

Certain characteristics are associated with each of the five elements:[8]

Wood. Of the four seasons, the element of wood represents spring; chia/yi in Ten Stems; east in Five Directions; and green in Five Colors.[9]

The element of wood is also an activity of the yang force, the symbol of childhood and of the activities of birth, growth, and unification.[10]

Fire. Of the four seasons, the element of fire represents summer; ping/ting in Ten Stems; south in Five Directions; and red in Five Colors.[11]

The element of fire is also an activity of the yang force, the symbol of youth in human life and of the activities of fighting, dispersion, growth, and prosperity.[12]

Earth. No season is represented by the element of earth; the force represents wu/chi in Ten Stems; center in Five Directions; and yellow in Five Colors.[13]

The element of earth belongs to the activity of neither yang or yin, but is an "absolute neutral force." It is a symbol of mature age (transition between youth and middle age) in human life and of neutrality, roundness, a mean (between the two extremes), and fullness.[14]

Metal. Of the four seasons, the element of metal represents autumn; keng/hsin in Ten Stems; west in Five Directions; and white in Five Colors.[15]

This element is an activity of the yin force and is a symbol of fruit, harvest, hardness, sharpness, or resolute decision. In human life, it represents middle age.[16]

Water. Of the four seasons, the element of water represents winter; jen/kuei in Ten Stems; north in Five Directions; and black in Five Colors.[17] This element is an activity of the yin force and is a symbol of old age in human life, solidification, wisdom, cleverness, and seeds (fruit).[18]

The above is a simple description of some important characteristics of the five elements. Since all things and events may be classified into any of the five elements, numerous attributes of each element could be elaborated upon.

Because the five elements have been the basic mode of analyzing geomantic features, in the examination of both directions and landforms, we will now further investigate the relationship between the five elements and the directions used in geomancy.

a) The five elements represent five directions

In geomancy, the center, which is represented by the element, earth, is invariable; hence it is omitted in the analysis of geomantic directions. The principal directions represented by the five elements are north (water), south (fire), east (wood), west (metal) and center (earth).

b) The four directions

North, south, east, and west can be subdivided into eight directions according to the eight trigrams that appear in the *Yijing (I-Ching)*, or the *Book of Changes*. According to the *Yijing*, there are two different systems in the arrangement of these eight directions: the Earlier Heaven arrangement of Eight Trigrams and the Later Heaven arrangement of Eight Trigrams. The directions and characteristics of these eight trigrams according to the Earlier Arrangement of Eight Trigrams are as follows: [19]

K'un, symbolized by earth, is north
Chen, symbolized by thunder, is northeast
Li, symbolized by lightning and flames, is east
Tui, symbolized by a marsh or lake, is southeast
Ch'en, symbolized by heaven, is south
Sun, symbolized by wind, is southwest
K'an, symbolized by rain or water, is west
Ken, symbolized by a mountain, is northwest.

The eight trigrams in the Later Heaven Arrangement are exactly the same as those in the Earlier Heaven Arrangement, except that each trigram does not represent the same direction. The different directions represented by the eight trigrams in the two arrangements are shown in Table 4.1.[20]

Table 4.1 Directions represented by the eight trigrams in the Earlier and Later Heaven Arrangements.

Term	Directions	
	Earlier Heaven Arrangement	*Later Heaven Arrangement*
Kon (K'un)	North	Southwest
Chin (Chen)	Northeast	East
Ri (Li)	East	South
Tae (Tui)	Southeast	West
Kon (Ch'ien)	South	Northwest
Son (Sun)	Southwest	Southeast
Kam (K'an)	West	North
Kan (Ken)	Northwest	Northeast

The terms are in Korean (Chinese are given inside parentheses in the Wade-Giles system)

It is not known why and when the earlier arrangement was superseded by the later system. Geomancy, however, largely followed the Later Heaven Arrangement, which is critically important in house geomancy. The relationship between the Earlier and the Later Arrangements of Eight Trigrams is shown in Figure 4.2.

Table 4.2 The twelve zodiacal symbols and their associated directions

Korean (Chinese) term	English translation	Direction
Cha (Zhi)	Rat	North
Chuk (Chuo)	Ox	North-north-east
In (Ren)	Tiger	East-north-east
Myo (Mao)	Hare	East
Chin (Chen)	Dragon	East-south-east
Sa (Si)	Serpent	South-south-east
O (Wu)	Horse	South
Mi (Wei)	Sheep	South-south-west
Sin (Shen)	Monkey	West-south-west
Yu (You)	Cock	West
Sul (Xu)	Dog	West-north-west
He (Hai)	Boar	North-north-west

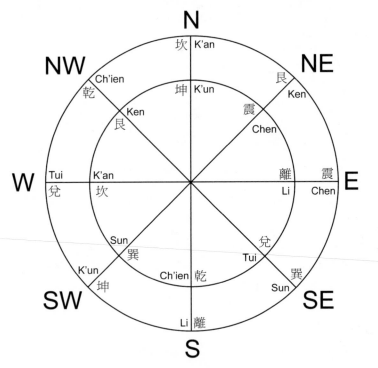

Figure 4.2 The relationship between the Earlier and Later Arrangements of Eight Tri-grams (outer circle = Later Heaven Arrangement; inner circle = Earlier Heaven Arrangement)

The four directions can also be divided into twelve according to the twelve zodiacal symbols. These symbols are called the Twelve Branches or the Earthly Branches. Joseph Needham wrote of the ancient use of these symbols:

The twelve Chih were already in very ancient times applied to the lunations [months] of the tropical year, but also served in other ways, particularly as azimuth direction points [compass points] and as names for the double-hours of each sidereal day. Some think that the twelve cyclical signs derive from rites proper for each lunation.[21]

These twelve animal symbols have been especially important in East Asia, providing names to the system of a sexagesimal cycle, which is the original way of counting days and years in China. The sexagesimal cycle is the alternating combination of the twelve zodiacal symbols with the system of the Ten Stems (Shigan). The Ten Stems are also called the Heavenly Stems (Tiengan) and were probably originally, as Shinjo stated, the names of the days of Hsun, the Chinese system of the ten-day period of a month.[22]

These twelve animal symbols are still used in East Asia to indicate directions, hours, and years. The twelve directions assigned according to the twelve zodiacal symbols are given in Table 4.2.

The directions and the corresponding agents are shown in Figure 4.3.

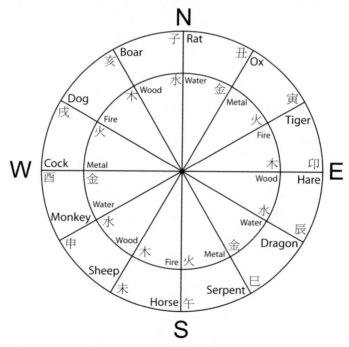

Figure 4.3 The twelve zodiacal symbols and the corresponding five agents

The twenty-four directions are the most commonly used and the most important, and they are standard directions in geomancy. They are based on the Yin-Yang and five agents theory. This system of directions can be considered a subdivision of the system of the twelve directions according to the twelve zodiacal symbols. One reason for such a conjecture is that the names of the directions are combinations of the twelve zodiacal symbols (all twelve names were kept) that have been added to the Ten Stems (eight were chosen from the Ten Stems) and eight trigrams (only four were chosen from the eight names) in the *Yijing*. The names of the directions chosen from the three different sources are as follows:

a) Twelve words from the twelve zodiacal symbols:
   Zhi, Chuo, Ren, Mao, Chen, Si, Wu, wei, Shen, You, Xu, Hai

b) Eight words from the Ten Stems:
   Chia, Yi, Ping, Ting, Keng, Hsin, Jen, Kuei.

c) Four words from the eight trigrams:
   Ch'ien, K'un, Sun, Ken.

The second reason this system of directions can be considered a subdivision of the system of twelve directions is that the symbols from the Ten Stems and eight trigrams are evenly distributed among the twelve zodiacal symbols (twelve branches). The arrangement of the directions is shown in Figure 4.4.

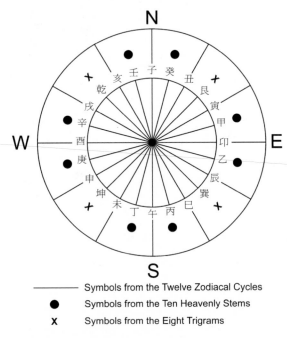

Figure 4.4 The composition of twenty-four directions

The Yin-Yang and Five Elements theories, which probably originated from early Chinese observation of the natural environment, are an essential part of geomancy. Geomancy cannot be separated from Yin-Yang, because geomancy adopted the theory as the means of identifying and categorizing geomantic landscape elements such as mountains, watercourses, and directions.

Notes

1. This chapter is based on and has developed from Hong-key Yoon, *Geomantic Relationships Between Culture and Nature in Korea* (Taipei: The Orient Culture Service, 1976), 10–23.

2. Wing-Tsit Chan, Chan, A *Source Book in Chinese Philosophy* (Princeton: Princeton University Press, 1973), 463.

3. This is a generalized explanation of the characteristics of yin and yang.

4. Wing-tsit Chan said, "The two concepts of the Yin-Yang and the Five Agents (Elements) go far back to antiquity and to quite independent origins." See Wing-tsit Chan, A *Source Book in Chinese Philosophy*, 244.

5. Wing-tsit Chan, Chan, A Source Book in Chinese Philosophy, 249

6. Fung, Yu-lan, *A Short History of Chinese Philosophy* (New York: The Macmillan Co., 1948), 131.

7. This explanation is a generalised idea and is based on my personal understanding of the principle, taught by an elderly Korean during my boyhood.

8. Qi (ki in Korean) can be translated into English in many ways according to the context; namely, agent, force, pneuma (breath), spirit, energy, matter, or element.

9. This information is based on Alfred Forke, The World Conception of the Chinese: Their Astronomical, Cosmological and Physico-philosophical Speculations (London: Arthur Probsthain, 1925), 253–259.

10. Kim Myongjin, "Umyang Ohaengnonkwa Tongyang Jongchi Sasang," *Konkuk Haksul-ji* [Konkuk University Collection of Academic Essays] vol. 12 (1971), 253–259.

11. Alfred Forke, The World Conception of the Chinese, 253–259.

12. Alfred Forke, The World Conception of the Chinese, 253–259.

13. Alfred Forke, The World Conception of the Chinese, 253–259.

14. Kim Myongjin, "Umyang Ohaengnonkwa Tongyang Jongchi Sasang," 253-259.

15. Alfred Forke, The World Conception of the Chinese, 253–259.

16. Kim Myongjin, "Umyang Ohaengnonkwa Tongyang Jongchi Sasang," 253-259.

17. Alfred Forke, The World Conception of the Chinese, 253–259.

18. Kim Myongjin, "Umyang Ohaengnonkwa Tongyang Jongchi Sasang," 253-259.

19. Richard Wilhelm, trans.into German, rendered into English by Cary F. Baynes, I-ching. (Princeton: Princeton University Press, 1967), 266.

20. Richard Wilhelm, trans.into German, rendered into English by Cary F. Baynes, *I-ching*, 266 and 268.

21. Joseph Needham, *Science and Civilisation in China*, (Cambridge: Cambridge University Press, 1959), 398.

22. Shinjo Shinzo, *Zhongguo shanggu tianwen*. Chinese translation by Shen Xuan (Shanghai: Shangwu Yinshuguan, 1936), 7.

Chapter 5
The Geomantic Principles for
an Auspicious Site[1]

According to *Zangshu*, probably the most important geomantic textbook, the first principle of geomancy is the acquiring of water and the second is the calming of wind.[2] But why are these principles so important in geomancy? What is their significance to geomancers and believers? How are they applied in the selection of gravesites and house sites? And are these principles more important for house geomancy or grave geomancy? To answer these questions, this chapter discusses the nature of geomantic principles in terms of both the underlying philosophy and the practical application of the art.

Two Fundamental Questions in Geomancy

The application of geomantic principles in site selection and the construction of structures (either graves or houses) can be divided into two main categories depending on usage: (1) grave geomancy that is practiced for the selection of an auspicious site on which to make an appropriate grave, and (2) house geomancy that is practiced for the selection of an auspicious site on which to build a suitable house. Grave geomancy can be further divided into geomancy for royal tombs and for commoners' graves. House geomancy can also be divided into two types: geomancy for settlements including villages, towns, and capital cities; and geomancy for individual houses within a given settlement. Grave geomancy and house geomancy employ the same principles in the selection of sites. Only their scale may be different, for the site of a city is incomparably bigger than that of a grave. The construction of a grave is relatively simple work, while that of a house is much more complex. Therefore, house geomancy has a rather complex set of construction rules compared with those of grave geomancy. All of these forms of geomancy are based on common geomantic principles, but those principles are interpreted and applied differently.

All geomantic principles and ideas may well be based on the three following premises:

(1) A certain locale is more auspicious than others for a grave or home.

(2) An auspicious place can be acquired only through the examination of local landscape according to geomantic principles.

(3) Once it is acquired and occupied, people who have lived on the site or the descendants of ancestors buried on the site can be blessed by the auspiciousness of the locale.

If these three premises were not accepted by those who practice geomancy, the art would be meaningless. Therefore, almost all geomantic textbooks have addressed these points. Such discussions are usually carried out on a metaphysical plane through the adoption of the Yin-Yang and Five Elements Theories.

Now let us look at how classical writers of geomantic discourses and contemporary professional geomancers address such issues. Actual geomantic principles will be discussed in a later section. For our discussion here, we can look to both *Zangshu* and living geomancers. The following is the philosophical basis of geomancy as discussed in *Zangshu* and in oral explanations by contemporary Korean geomancers.

1. What is vital energy and why is one place more auspicious than another?

If one asks a geomancer why some places are auspicious while others are inauspicious and thus to be avoided, he may answer that it is because of the availability of vital energy in a place. In *Zangshu*, also known as *Zangjing*, we read:

> The buried corpse is beneficially influenced by the vital energy. The energy of Yin-Yang belches and becomes wind; ascends and becomes cloud; descends and becomes rain; flows underground and becomes vital energy. When the vital energy flows underground and is manifested, myriad things are born. . . . The canon states that as the vital energy emerges to the wind, it disperses.[3]

According to *Zangshu*, vital energy is one phase of the cycle of Yin-Yang energy, which is being continually and dynamically transformed into such manifestations as wind, cloud, rain, and vital energy. Vital energy transforms itself into various environmental elements depending on its situation and motion. Importantly, when Yin-Yang energy descends it becomes rain and when it seeps into the ground (where it remains) it becomes vital energy. According to *Zangshu*, vital energy is the moisture that is contained in the soil below ground level.

The function of vital energy (*shengqi:* 生氣, *senggi* in Korean) is well described in *Zangshu*: "The five energies (a vital energy in the form of the five elements) flow under ground, and manifest and give birth to all."[4] Geomancers believe that the moisture in soil is vital energy and supports all living things. But what is the moist element in the soil that supports life? If we were to use a contemporary term,[5] we could say that it is a form of nutrient. Yet it is not equivalent to a nutrient. It only has some similarities to plant nutrients. Nutrients in the soil cannot be identified by the naked eye, but we can recognize that a soil is rich in nutrients by looking at plant growth. Likewise, one can argue that vital energy is not seen by the human eye, but one can tell by looking at the prosperity of living things, especially humans, that certain places conserve vital energy. However, vital energy is much more than nutrients; it is a mystic metaphysical concept of invigorating and engendering power that flows underground. What is even more mystical and hard to explain is the claim that human bones buried in the right place can absorb this energy and mysteriously deliver it to the living descendants of the buried person.

Human beings can utilize this vital energy by either burying their ancestors or residing in a place where such energy accumulates. Vital energy only accumulates in places that meet geomantic requirements. This is why professional geomancers carefully examine sites for certain geomantic conditions, including their surrounding landforms, watercourses, and the cardinal directions they face.

2. Why and how can a person acquire the benefits of vital energy (shengqi)?

Most geomancers in modern Korea do not adequately explain how descendants receive auspiciousness from their ancestors' graves. They say "it simply works somehow." A few educated geomancers, however, will explain this concept by using geomantic statements, usually based on *Zangshu*, which has several relevant discussions such as the following:

> The buried corpse can be influenced by the vital energy. . . . Every living body is a concentration of [vital] energy. The energy condenses and forms bones. When a person dies, only the bones remain [underground]. Therefore, it is a principle that a buried corpse can latently influence its descendants by returning the energy from its bones.[6]

Thus it is evident that the mediator between the vital energy beneath the ground and living descendants is the bones of buried ancestors. The geomancer reasons that a dead person's bones can auspiciously influence descendants when they rest where there is available vital energy. The book *Zangshu* explains this reasoning in a metaphysical way:

> People received their body from their parents. When the main body [dead body] acquires the energy [a vital energy], the remaining body [living descendants] receives auspiciousness from the energy. The scripture said that the energy induces spirit, and then the auspiciousness is delivered to people [living descendants]. This is as if when a copper mountain collapses in the west, the spiritual bell [made from the copper from the mine] rings in the east, or when trees bloom in spring, chestnuts bud in the room.[7]

Parents are considered to be the main body (root) of their children. They are, in effect, the root or trunk of a tree with many branches. When the dead bodies of the parents or ancestors are suffused with vital energy, the remaining living branches—the descendants—may also receive benefits from the energy.

But this fails to explain the mechanism whereby auspiciousness is delivered to descendants. That mechanism is very ambiguous; only mysterious statements are offered about the absorption of vital energy by the living. *Zangshu* explains that the induction is similar to the relationship between a copper mine (the parents) and a spiritual bell made of copper from the mine (the child), or to the relationship between blooming trees in spring (timing, the environment, the parents) and chestnuts (children) inside a room sprouting. Zheng Mi writes of "a vital energy that passes from the main body to prosperous branches."[8] Geomantic textbooks do not discuss the mechanism of the flow of auspicious energy, so I asked a learned geomancer in Seoul, Korea, about it. He answered that he did not know the mechanism itself and that his knowledge came from observing the relationship between descendants and graves.[9] Geomancers accept the idea of delivering auspiciousness to descendants on faith.

Books considered to be geomantic classics have addressed the question of how an auspicious gravesite mysteriously transmits blessings to living descendants through the bones of ancestors. However, I have not seen discussions in them on how auspicious house sites transmit their auspiciousness to living residents. We can explain the direct transmission from an auspicious site (a house or town) to a resident of the house or the people inhabiting a settlement only by considering the characteristics of the energy. The bones of ancestors (uncovered by flesh) in a grave are more readily and safely influenced by vital energy without being disturbed by wind. Once the vital energy escapes and surfaces on the ground, it is easily dispersed by wind and is not available for humanity. Once the ancestral bones have absorbed the vital energy, they can safely transmit the energy to the living descendants without interruption, because the ancestral bones and the bones of the living descendants share the same energy as a tree trunk with many branches. In contrast, transmitting vital energy from an auspicious house site to the residents (descendants) was considered to be less efficient and riskier, because the vital energy has to surface on the ground as well as go through the flesh of the descendants to influence the bones. As stated in the classical geomantic texts, when the energy ascends, it becomes wind, and it is only when it flows under the ground that it remains vital energy. Therefore, obtaining vital energy from under the ground is much more secure than obtaining it from above ground. Apparently, it is also believed by geomancers that bones (condensed vital energy) covered by flesh are not as efficient in absorbing vital energy as bones under the ground without flesh.[10] For these reasons, the selection of gravesites has probably been more important and favored by Korean people than the selection of house sites.

This concludes the key mystic and metaphysical discourse on the fundamental reasons for the practice of geomantic ideas. In the evaluation of landscape in geomancy, the three important landscape elements are landforms (mountains), waters and cosmic directions.

Geomantic Principles Concerning Landforms: Mountains (or Hills) and Their Attributes

The key aim of practicing geomancy is to locate an auspicious place that accumulates vital energy and to benefit from it by building a house or grave on it. Therefore all geomantic principles are about identifying an auspicious place and the appropriate use of it. Classical geomantic textbooks laid down the three key principles of identifying an auspicious place. These principles consider landforms, watercourses, and cosmological directions. Of these three basic elements that determine the quality of a place, landforms, especially surrounding hills (mountains), have been considered the most important.[11] Although *Zangshu* and some other geomantic textbooks state that watercourses are more important than mountains, the conditions of the surrounding hills of a place have attracted more attention from geomancers than anything else, because the characteristics of watercourses are, by and large, dependent on the configurations of mountains. Classical geomantic textbooks usually assign the most serious and detailed discussion to the conditions of surrounding hills or mountains.

The two important functions of mountains in geomancy are delivering vital energy to an auspicious place and calming the wind (storing the energy) in it. The transmission of vital energy is entirely dependent upon the shape of the mountain ranges that connect to the main mountain.[12] Such mountain ranges were commonly called dragons by geomancers, because their undulating shapes resembled the Chinese dragon. The business of calming wind is largely determined by the shapes and locations of the four mountains, the so-called Sasinsa, which encircle the auspicious place.

The Nature of the 'Dragon' in Geomancy

The term 'dragon' is very widely and commonly used by geomancers to indicate mountain ranges, the identification of which is one of the basic tasks of geomancy. Why do they refer to mountains as a 'dragon'? In order to grasp this, one has to understand that the East Asian concept of the dragon originated from China and differs from that of Europe. Both the dragons of the East and West are imaginary forms of an animal that can be classified as a reptile with scales that often lives in swampy places.

As shown in Figures 5.1 and 5.2, the East Asian dragon, which is more serpent-like than the Western dragon, has a body like a snake with four short feet, and its head resembles a magical horse. Europeans think the dragon is a dreadful and undesirable imaginary animal while the Chinese consider it to be an attractive and good imaginary creature. In brief, the Westerner would attempt to kill a dragon, while the East Asians would admire and respect it. This attitude is probably why geomancers perceived auspicious mountain ranges as undulating dragons and eventually adopted the term 'dragon' for a mountain range. If not, geomancers at least tried to compare the various configurations of mountain ranges with those of an undulating dragon. *Dili-Renzixuezhi (The Fact that All*

Humanity Must Know), a popular geomantic textbook both in Korea and China written by the twin brothers Xu Shanji and Xu Shanshu during the Ming dynasty, asks:

> Why do geomancers refer to mountains as a 'dragon'? The forms of a mountain range are various. Some of them are big while others are small, some rise up while others crawl, some are concurrent while others are anti-current, and some are hidden while others are revealed. The body of branch mountains is not constant; even within a short distance; it turns and makes many changes. Observing the object, it reminds one of a dragon; therefore, they [geomancers] refer to them as dragons.[13]

But not all mountain ranges are called dragons. An old handwritten geomantic textbook, *Chiri Chongjong*, which I found in a second-hand bookstore in Korea, argues:

> Bury [the dead] in a dragon, not in a mountain, because a mountain is a difficult place to acquire water; "mountain" has dead energy. However, a "dragon" is an easy place to acquire water. Thus, one can find vital energy in some places of the dragon. Therefore, bury in a dragon, not in a mountain. [14]

A geomancer I spoke with in Korea simply stated that a mountain that has possible gravesites or house sites is called a dragon and that a mountain that does not have such sites is merely called a mountain.[15] A mountain range worthy of delivering and accumulating vital energy is a dragon, but rocky hills that are not covered with soil and cannot deliver vital energy are just a mountain. *Chiri Chongjong* says that a dragon has branches, while hills, which do not deliver vital energy, do not have branches.

Burial in a hill is not as good as burial in the branch of the dragon; a hill is the bone of a dragon and a branch is its flesh. Hills with exposed bedrocks are considered inauspicious, while hills covered with soil (thus having lush vegetation) are called the branches of the dragon, which are auspicious. Therefore, burying in a bone (rock) of a dragon is not as good as burying in the flesh (soil).[16] Human bones can concentrate vital energy, but the bones (rocks) of mountains cannot, and since vital energy can only flow through soil, rocks do not easily transmit the energy to the dead. The bone of a dragon means bedrock or the exposed boulders in a mountain. An analysis of the meaning of the Chinese characters for branch and hill makes it safe to say that the difference between the branch and the hill is that a branch is a continuing line of hills or mountain ranges leading off from the main body of a dragon, while a hill is not necessarily a branch of a dragon but any place higher than its surrounding landforms. Thus, it is clear that a mountain with soil or a hill that is also a branch of a mountain range is a good place to bury the dead or build a house (settlement). This idea reflects the age-old geomantic principle stated in *Zangshu:* 'a treeless rocky mountain is a bad mountain.'[17]

We can conclude that a dragon in geomancy as practiced in Korea refers to a mountain range covered with soil that is connected to a mountain system facilitating the flow of vital energy.

Figure 5.1 A Chinese dragon in a Japanese painting of a Chinese dragon dance. From Kaura Kunio, comp., *Nagasaki Kohnga*.

Figure 5.2 An image of a Western dragon that lived in a swamp and harassed nearby people. For the purpose of comparison with the Chinese dragon, the background elements of the original drawing have been modified and partly redrawn. Adapted from Archibald Marshall, *The Dragon*, p.1.

Types of Dragons

Dragons have been classified into many categories according to geomantic criteria. Classification was necessary so that geomancers could describe the geomantic harmony of a place from various aspects. The kinds of dragons discussed by geomancers are as follows:

1. The live dragon and the dead dragon

Not all dragons are qualified to provide gravesites; only living dragons are. A live dragon refers to mountain ranges with rolling relief, many folds, and many changes both in direction and form. Such an appearance resembles a live snake.[18] A dead dragon indicates a static and straight mountain range without a change in its direction or relief formation, and thus it resembles a dead snake. Determining whether dragons are alive or dead is one of the basic tasks of geomancers.

2. The trunk dragon and the branch dragon

All dragons can be classified into these two categories according to their origin. The major distinction between the trunk and the branch dragon is that the former is the highest mountain range that forms the backbone of other smaller mountains in an area, while the latter is a small range that is an off-shoot of the main mountain. According to a geomantic textbook:

> Kun-l'un Mt. is the backbone of the world. It sits right in the middle of the world, as if [it is] the backbone of a human being or the central beam [of a house]. From this central mass, four Branch Dragons [four mountain ranges which are comparable to four legs of a beast] stretch out into the world. The north, south, east and west become the four parts. The north and west [branch] is Kong Tung which is big and long. The east [branch] continues far away into Korea. Only the south dragon came into China. [19]

Geomancers believe that the source of all geomantic dragons is Kun-lu'n Mountain, from which four main branch dragons originate, one of which runs into Korea and forms the patriarchal mountain of Korea, Mount Paektu. From this mountain, the main dragon of Korea runs southward and generates many further branch dragons throughout Korea. However, a trunk dragon and a branch dragon are relative terms. In a geomancer's survey of an auspicious site in a district, the main mountain range of the district is labeled the trunk dragon of the district, while the branching-out ranges of the main range are called branch dragons.

3. The yin dragon and the yang dragon

If a dragon runs to the left side from its starting point, while bending in a clockwise direction (like the run of the azure dragon from the main mountain), it is called a yang dragon.[20] If a dragon runs opposite to the yang dragon (like the run of the white tiger from the main mountain), it is called a yin dragon. Both yang and yin dragons, however, commonly make small left or right turns while they run. Therefore, there are usually small yin and yang elements in both yin and yang dragons.

4. The concurrent dragon and the anti-current dragon

Some parts of a main dragon or its branch dragons occasionally run in an opposite direction from the main dragon. This is called an anti-current dragon (Yok'yong).[21] Naturally, a concurrent dragon (Sunyong) is one that runs in the same direction as a main dragon. An auspicious place is usually located where there is a balance of concurrent and anti-current dragons. If there are only concurrent dragons, it is understood that the mountain does want to accumulate vital energy in a particular place.

Four Important Mountains Surrounding an Auspicious Site

As mentioned, dragons are analogous to plants having roots, a trunk, branches, and flowers. In geomancy, the interrelationships of dragons or a network of the mountain system are often compared with the network of blood vessels in the human body. A dragon in geomancy is treated as a living organism that has a channel which conveys vital energy to a geomancy cave, the symbolic term for an auspicious spot where people can extract the energy. Geomancy caves are usually located at the end of a branch dragon as if they were flowers blossoming in a tree. The auspicious spots (geomancy caves), however, are found only in a location surrounded by hills that block any inbound winds, and where water is present near the cave to retain the vital energy (see Figure 5.3). These landform conditions reflect the cardinal geomantic principle that calming wind and acquiring water are the two most important conditions for an auspicious site.[22] The surrounding hills of an auspicious site, then, are usually parts of dragons (mountain ranges). Geomancers believe that natural forces created such surrounding mountains in order to form geomancy caves.[23]

The quality of surrounding mountains is critically important in examining the characteristics of a geomancy cave; their shapes and locations determine the amount of available vital energy and are an indication of the quality of the auspicious place. All mountains surrounding the geomancy cave that hold vital energy are called "sands" in geomancy.[24] The different parts of sands have been given different names; for instance, the peak of a hill is called "the head of sand," and the middle slope of a hill is called "the body of sand."[25]

The so-called Sands of the Four Spirits (spirits meaning directions) of an auspicious site, or "sashinsa" in Korean, are the most important of these surrounding mountains. They are the azure dragon in the east, the white tiger in the west, the red bird in the south, and the black turtle in the north. These should be located in the four directions of the geomancy cave. The following discussion of the Sands of the Four Spirits is derived primarily from *Zangshu*.

AUSPICIOUS MONUTAINS AND WATERCOURSES IN GEOMANCY
(based or traditional geomatic maps)

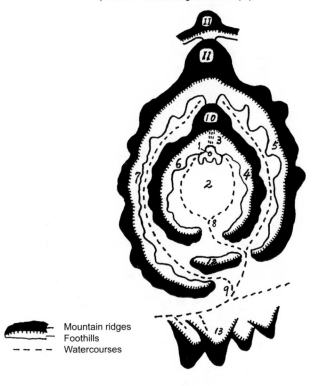

1.	Geomancy Cave	혈	穴
2.	Bright Yard	명당	明堂
3.	Entrance Slope	입수	入首
4.	Inner Azure Dragon	내청룡	內青龍
5.	Outer Azure Dragon	외청룡	外青龍
6.	Inner White Tiger	내빅호	內白虎
7.	Outer White Tiger	외백호	外白虎
8.	Inner Water Discharge	내수구	內水口
9.	Outer Water Discharge	외수구	外水口
10.	Main Mountain	주산	主山
11.	Oncoming Dragon	내룡	來龍
12.	Peace Mountain	안산	安山
13.	Homage Mountain	조산	朝山

Figure 5.3 Auspicious mountains and watercourses in geomancy

1. The black turtle, or somber warrior (Hyunmu)

The black turtle is symbolized by the entangled bodies of a turtle and snake, and indicates the mountain located at the end of a dragon where a geomancy cave is formed; it is also called the main mountain (Chusan). According to *Zangshu*, an auspicious black turtle should be shaped as if bending its head toward the geomancy cave.[26] This bending of the head, or inclining slope from the peak of the main mountain, was interpreted by Zheng Mi, in his commentary on *Zhangshu*, as its desire to embrace the auspicious site (e.g., a house or burial site).[27] *Zangshu* states that if the black turtle does not bend its head toward the geomancy cave, this signifies its refusal to accept the auspicious site or the burial in it. This statement was interpreted by Zheng Mi to mean that a main mountain was high but lacked a gentle slope toward the geomancy cave.[28] This kind of main mountain is not considered to have the desire to embrace the buried dead or a house or town, and therefore such a main mountain (black turtle) is inauspicious.

Since a black turtle is the end of a dragon, vital energy comes through the dragon to the end of the mountain where the geomancy cave is located. Thus the shape of the mountain represents the quality of the available energy. Geomancers recommend that a mountain be beautiful and majestic in addition to bending its head toward the geomancy cave.[29] Such a mountain is the master among its surrounding mountains.

2. The red bird (Chujak)

The red bird refers to the mountains located in front of a geomancy cave; it is symbolized by a bird. According to *Zangshu*, the mountains of a red bird should be shaped as if flying and dancing in the air in order to be auspicious.[30] Zheng Mi's interpretation of this statement is that mountains and watercourses that are positioned before the geomancy cave are to roll beautifully and meander gently: If they are so shaped, these landforms are considered to have affection for the geomancy cave.[31] *Zangshu* stated that a red bird that does not dance would fly away from the site.[32] Zheng Mi interprets this to mean that a red bird is inauspicious if it faces away from and shows no desire to embrace the geomancy cave.[33] Since these mountain ranges are like guests or officers to the main mountain, they should be subservient to the auspicious site and thus must appear to bow to the geomancy cave (main mountain).

There are two important mountains in the red bird: the peace mountain, or Ansan, and the homage paying mountain, or Chosan. Geomantic principles require that Ansan should be smaller than Chosan and closer to the geomancy cave. In order to form geomantic harmony between Chosan and Ansan, it is required that Chosan appear more dignified than Ansan. The peace mountain is considered to act as a daily need of the main mountain.[34]

3. The azure dragon (Chongyong)

The azure dragon is the name given to the mountain range on the left side of the geomancy cave; it is symbolized by the undulating dragon as shown in Figure 5.1. *Zangshu* says that in order to be an auspicious azure dragon, the mountain should be shaped as if undulating with the desire to embrace the geomancy cave.[35] In this interpretation, the mountain range should be shaped as encircling the auspicious site, with its end bending toward the auspicious place. Also, it is said that the tail of the azure dragon should be lower than its head, as if the dragon has landed from the sky and is undulating with its end bending inward to watch the geomancy cave.[36]

An azure dragon that has a high and projecting end bending outward is an inauspicious one.[37] Such a shape is considered to show no desire to hold the geomancy cave and be jealous of the main mountain. Therefore, with this kind of azure dragon, a place cannot be auspicious.

In some cases, several branch dragons run out from the oncoming dragon or the main mountain to both sides of its left (the azure dragon direction) and right (the white tiger direction), and so encircle the auspicious site several times. In this situation, the azure dragon closest to the auspicious site is called the inner azure dragon and all other branches are called the outer azure dragons.

The main task of both the azure dragon and the white tiger is to protect the auspicious site from any inbound wind by encircling it. Since the calming of wind is one of the two important geomantic concerns in the acquisition of a favorable location, the figures of both the azure dragon and the white tiger have attracted great attention from all geomancers. These two hills or mountains act as auxiliaries in forming an auspicious place, when compared to the main mountain, which is the key mountain for conveying vital energy to the auspicious site (geomancy cave). No matter how well an azure dragon or white tiger is shaped, the area is not auspicious if they are disconnected from the main mountain, because vital energy is not available.

4. The white tiger (Paekho)

The white tiger refers to the mountain range on the right side of the geomancy cave; it is symbolized by a tiger. According to *Zangshu,* the mountain must be shaped as if it were well tamed, with its head bowed, for it to be an auspicious white tiger.[38] One commentary on *Zangshu* interprets this to mean that the tiger should be well tamed like a well-trained dog whose master does not have to worry about being bitten.[39] In addition, the tiger should bend its end toward the ground and be reclining. This means that the end of the white tiger should be lower than its other parts, and that its end should curve inward like the end of the azure dragon. If the tiger was shaped as if crouching and ready to pounce, it was considered to be an inauspicious place, as the tiger would have the desire to devour the auspicious site (and the burial or house in the geomancy cave).[40] This principle of the white tiger has been very controversial among geomancers. As Zheng Mi noted, there is a theory completely opposite to it: that the crouching figure is the auspicious white tiger, while the tamed one is the inauspicious tiger.[41] Apparently, many Korean geomancers followed the latter theory, which does not seem to be the original principle.

The white tiger and the azure dragon of an auspicious site are considered a pair and should be comparable and harmonious in their shapes and sizes.

However, they have opposite characteristics in the Yin-Yang theory: the azure dragon signifies the yang, male, son, honor, fame, and civil officers, while the white tiger represents the yin, female, daughter, material wealth, and military officers.[42] For these reasons, if a place is endowed with a good azure dragon but a poorly shaped white tiger, the site is more favorable for the male descendants, bringing honor and fame to the family.

The Geomancy Cave (Hyol)

The important geomantic principles concerning mountains, watercourses, wind, and directions are all clues to finding a geomancy cave where auspiciousness can be extracted through the influence of vital energy. In spite of the help of such complicated clues in the search for the geomancy cave, apparently it is not easy for even a good geomancer to find such a site. A geomancer in Sangju County, Korea, said that it is not very difficult for an ordinary geomancer to indicate an area that has a geomancy cave, but it is very difficult for even a skillful geomancer to point out its exact location. This is mainly because the size of the cave is not much bigger than a coffin.[43] This geomancer further explained by using a geomantic proverb: "To see the house is easy, but to see the woman in the house is difficult." It must be explained that upper-class women usually resided deep within the Korean house in places that were seldom seen from the outside. During my field trips in rural South Korea, I heard from some geomancers that many good gravesites were not properly located in the geomancy cave, but only near it. Apparently, many geomancers were able to approach the general area of the geomancy cave by observing the surrounding mountains and watercourses, but failed to pinpoint it. It is said that gravesites in such situations cannot manifest as much auspiciousness as they should, because the vital energy that flows beneath the ground is only available through the cave.[44] If one fails to find the cave, of course, all efforts at observing the mountains and watercourses will have been in vain.

Now let us see what these geomancy caves look like and where they might be.

The types of geomancy caves

Geomancy caves are classified into four categories according to their shapes. This classification is apparently accepted by all geomancers and is basic knowledge to even an uneducated country geomancer (see Figure 5.4). The four basic categories are:[45]

a) Wa type, or grotto type

This type, as shown in the Figure 5.4, is shaped like an open mouth. If the shape of the auspicious site suggests two arms embracing something, it is considered to be a good shape. Such a cave can be found in either high mountains or low hills.[46]

b) Kyom type, or tweezer type
   This type is shaped like two widespread legs.

c) Yu type, or breast type
   This type is shaped like a breast.

d) Tol type, or projecting type
   This type is shaped like an upside-down pan.

These four types may connote sexually important human organs (groin, mouth, and breast).

Geomancers believe that the geomancy cave is located where all the power of the land is concentrated.[47] This idea may have originated from the location and function of the human sexual organs. Furthermore, the outflow of auspiciousness from a geomancy cave is considered comparable to a woman giving birth.

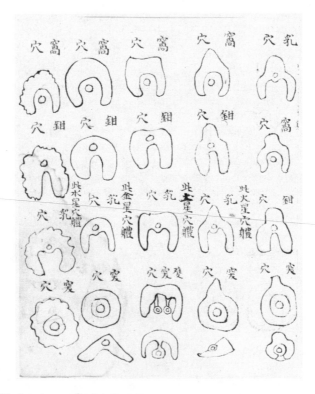

Figure 5.4 Various types of geomancy caves

The process of finding a geomancy cave

How does a geomancer approach an area to find a place that is auspicious according to geomantic principles? Although not all geomancers follow the same procedures, there is a standard set of procedures upon which most geomancers will agree:

a) Go to the top of a rather high hill or mountain and look over the area to see if there are any good "dragons." If there is one, follow the dragon to the place where it ends.

b) Look at the mountains to see if they surround the place at the end of the dragon.

c) If mountains surround the place, examine the "four sands" and watercourses in terms of the geomantic principles.

d) Then go down to the location of the geomancy cave (end of the main mountain) and examine the directions of the "entrance slope" and the protective hills and pinpoint the grave site.

e) Then examine the soil conditions of the geomancy cave.

Geomancer Chang Yongdu'k compared the entire procedure to finding fruit on a melon vine: the examination begins from the root, then goes on to the tendrils, next to the branches, and eventually reaches a precious melon.[48]

Types of Mountain Forms

Because the location and shapes of mountains have been very important in determining the auspiciousness of a place, the art of observing mountains is well developed. A mountain classification system was probably necessary for geomancers to observe mountains carefully. Whether this speculation is true or not, there are some well-developed classification systems of mountains in geomancy. The following are some examples:

Classification of Mountains According to the Five Agents

All mountains can be classified into any one of the five elements (wood, fire, earth, metal, and water) depending on their shape (see Figure 5.5). Some have said that these categories may be an imitation of the five stars of Jupiter, Mars, Saturn, Venus, and Mercury, while others have said that the five may represent attributes of the five agents in the five agents theory.[49] The geomantic work *Mandu Osong Kusong Cheyong Kyol* states that the five constellations are also the five elements and thus the elements formed stars in the sky and mountains on earth.[50] Although the origin of the names of the five categories of mountains is obscure, it is clear that the five categories certainly represent the attributes of the five elements. The shapes of the five elements are as follows:[51]

Wood type:

The mountain is round in shape, projecting straight into the sky. The shape may represent the figure of a trunk of a tree.

Fire type:

The mountain is shaped like powerful flames of fire. Such a mountain is often called the mountain of the writing brush because it looks like one.

Earth type:

This mountain is shaped like a flat roof,[52] or the Chinese character chi meaning a desk or a plate having a flat top with a supporting base that was used in sacrificial rituals.[53] In other words, it is a projecting figure with a flat top and sharp slopes on the sides.

Metal type:

This mountain is high and rounded on top without any sharp edges. It is shaped like a big bell on the floor.

Water type:

This mountain is shaped like water waves or a living snake. A mountain with many gently rolling hills belongs to this type.

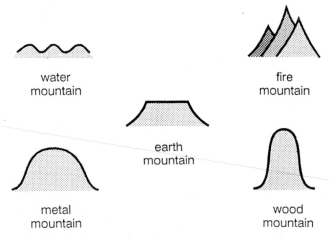

water
mountain

fire
mountain

earth
mountain

metal
mountain

wood
mountain

Figure 5.5 The ideal shapes of the five mountain types

Perceiving mountains in terms of the five elements theory is one of the basic geomantic means of evaluation. This classification is important not only because a certain type of mountain connotes a certain type of auspiciousness but also because the combination of the types of mountains in a range (dragon) must follow the sequence of the five agents producing one another. For instance, it is said that the beautiful fire-type mountains, the so-called writing brush mountains, are effective in producing good scholars, while a wood-type mountain produces high government officers.[54] The types of mountains in a dragon should be arranged according to the principle of the five elements producing one another.[55] No matter how beautiful an individual mountain in a dragon is, if the parts of the dragon do not run in this order, the dragon is inauspicious. According to this principle of the five agents producing one another, when a dragon starts from a fire-type mountain in the south, it should be followed by an earth type, then a metal, water, and wood type. If a dragon runs in this order, the auspiciousness will be quickly available to the people. However, properly arranged mountains in a dragon still must be beautiful in order to bring good fortune to men.[56]

The reverse order of mountain arrangement according to the five elements producing one another—wood, water, metal, earth, and fire instead of fire, earth, metal, water, and wood—is acceptable and will also bring good fortune to distant descendants.[57] This order, however, will not bring good fortune quickly, but only after several generations of dormancy.

If a dragon (mountain range) is arranged according to the principle of five elements destroying one another, the dragon is considered to be especially inauspicious and to bring all kinds of misfortune.[58] For instance, if a metal-type mountain is followed by a fire type and then a water, earth, and wood type, the mountain range would be arranged according to the principle of the five elements destroying one another. In such a case, no matter how beautiful a particular mountain range may be, the dragon would not be considered auspicious. Even if the mountain were to produce some good fortune due to its beauty, the good fortune would not last long; it may pass through briefly to future generations, but it would soon dwindle and eventually desert the people. For these reasons, geomancers emphasize the importance of observing mountains in terms of the five elements theory.

Classification of mountains into nine categories

Although all mountains can be classified into the five categories according to the five elements theory, not all mountains completely exemplify one of the five categories.[59] When a geomancer evaluates the available fortune in a mountain, the descriptive tool of the five categories may not be specific enough. Thus, the five categories are divided into nine more specific types. By using the nine categories in addition to the five main categories, geomancers believe, one is better able to measure mountains' auspiciousness. The nine categories are:[60]

1. Greedy Wolf: *T'an-lang* in Chinese and *Tamnang* in Korean
                          A variant of a wood-type mountain
2. Great Gate: *Chu'-mun* in Chinese and *Komun* in Korean
                          A variant of an earth-type mountain
3. Blessings Preserved: *Lu-ts'un* in Chinese and *Nokjon* in Korean
                          A variant of an earth-type mountain
4. Purity and Chastity: *Lien-cheng* in Chinese and *Yomjong* in Korean
                          A variant of a fire-type mountain

5. The Song of Literati: *Wen-ch'u"* in Chinese and *Munkok* in Korean
                            A variant of a water-type mountain
6. The Military Ditty: *Wu-ch'u"* in Chinese and *Choapo* in Korean
                            A variant of a metal-type mountain
7. Left Reinforcement: *Tso-fu* in Chinese and *Wupil* in Korean
                            A variant of a wood-type mountain
8. Right Assistant: *Yu-pi* in Chinese and *Wupil* in Korean
                            A variant of a metal-type mountain
                            [In a diagram of Pakok it is described as a water-
                            type mountain.]
9. Destroying Army: *P'o-chun* in Chinese and *Pakun* in Korean
                            A variant of a metal-type mountain

For the shapes of these nine categories, see Figure 5.6.

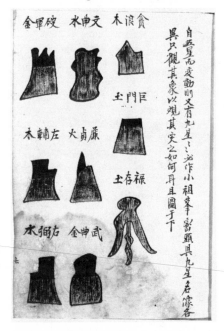

Figure 5.6 Configurations of the Nine Types of Mountains. From Pakok, Anon.

Classification of mountains according to the auspiciousness manifested

Mr Chang, a geomancer in Seoul, has classified mountains into two main groups: good mountains and bad mountains.[61] A good mountain, according to him, is one with a thick layer of good soil that supports dense vegetation and plenty of wildlife. A mountain exposed to bedrock without dense vegetation indicates a lack of the vital energy that supports all creatures; it is a bad mountain. A simple method to tell the auspiciousness of a mountain, according to Mr Chang, is to observe the conditions of the vegetation on it. A mountain with good soil and dense vegetation is considered auspicious, while a rocky mountain without good vegetation is considered inauspicious. His classification has some rational justification; dense vegetation on a mountain can indicate that it has good soil conditions and sufficient water to support the vegetation, while poor vegetation may indicate the opposite. A densely vegetated area is certainly more favorable for the necessities of life than a poorly vegetated one. Mr Chang's classification of mountains is, without a doubt, based on *Zangshu*, which lists the five inauspicious mountains for burying the dead as follows:[62]

a. *Tongsan* (child mountain). A *tongsan* is a poorly vegetated mountain. *Zangshu* says that this mountain is not a good place to bury the dead, because the five energies are neutralized.

b. *Tansan* (disconnected mountain). Since the energy flows through the mountain ridges, any disconnected mountain ridges result in the flow of vital energy being blocked; therefore, this mountain is also not a good place to bury people.

c. *Soksan* (stone mountain). A stone mountain with exposed bedrock or boulders is generally a poorly vegetated mountain, and therefore can be considered a subcategory of *tongsan* (child mountain). The vital energy of the land that can be compared with the blood of the human body can only flow through soil; it cannot pass through rocks, which are the equivalent of the bones of the human body. A stone mountain is not a good place to bury the dead or build a house, because the vital energy flows through the flesh, not the bones of the land.

d. *Kwasan* (passing through mountain). An auspicious place is located at the end of a dragon where the vital energy stops flowing. If a mountain passes through a gravesite, the spot cannot be good because vital energy would pass through the hole instead of remaining on the site.

e. *Toksan* (independent mountain). Vital energy stays where many dragons meet (a site encircled by many mountains). Therefore an independent mountain has no available vital energy and is not a good place for burial.

These are some of the important ways of classifying mountains in geomancy. There is no question about the prime importance of the quality of mountains in the geomantic harmony of an area. The mountain is important because it plays a main role in conserving the auspiciousness in an area by keeping out winds and delivering vital energy to the geomancy cave. The shapes of mountains reflect the types of available auspiciousness.

Geomantic Principles Concerning Soil Conditions

The condition of the soil is another important factor in geomancy. Soil conditions are dependent on the mountain types and are especially important at the gravesite or house site (the geomancy cave). This is why soil conditions are discussed in the landforms section. The soil conditions relate directly to the preservation of human bones in a grave. The condition of the bones is very critical in geomancy, because descendants are theoretically influenced by the vital energy that passes through the bones.[63] Geomancers believe that if the bones turn yellow and are preserved well, the soil is auspicious, but when the bones turn black or decay the soil is bad.[64] Firm and fine yellow soil like well compacted soybean flour is considered auspicious.[65] This idea is obviously based on the following statement in *Zangshu* "Generally, [auspicious] soil must be fine and firm, rich and shine brightly [as if] cut fat or cut jade, it should also have a luster reflecting the entire range of primary colors [literally, the five colors]."[66] Soil at the geomancy cave should be neither too soft nor too hard. Thus, it should be very fine, very well compacted, and very well nourished so that its appearance is like cut fat, and so fresh, tender, and smooth that it shines brightly like cut jade. In explaining the five colors, Zheng Mi states:

> The five energies flow under the ground. The energy of metal condenses and becomes white; the energy of wood condenses and becomes azure; that of fire becomes red; the earth becomes yellow. All of these are auspicious colours. The energy of water, which forms black, is considered to be inauspicious. Of the five elements, yellow is considered to be the most auspicious [it comes from earth, the centre]. Thus, pure colour is auspicious. Also, alternating colours of yellow and red makes [the soil] even more beautiful [auspicious].[67]

Zangshu states that the soil is bad if it is "dry as millet in a cave, wet as cut [decayed] meat, or coarse as sand or gravel."[68] We can infer that soil that is like a pile of dried kernels of millet or a piece of decayed meat is very bad, because its structure is not firm. We can also infer that soil as coarse as sand or gravel along a shoreline is inauspicious.

Only well-compacted natural soil with a fine texture can contain auspicious vital energy and therefore preserve bones in a good condition by protecting them from the outside interferences of temperature and moisture. If the soil is soft, coarse, or wet, it is believed that auspicious energy cannot stay there but will be dispersed or flow away. A gravesite with wet soil and underground water was considered the worst of all possible gravesites, because vital energy can be neither transmitted through nor stored in water. Such soil would turn human bones black or cause them to decay quickly.

These geomantic principles of soil from *Zangshu* have been the foundation for geomancers' discussions of soil. According to a present-day Korean book, *Essential Points of Geomancy* by Hwang Ilsun, soil can be divided into two groups: living soil, which is auspicious, and dead soil, which is bad.[69] The book states that living soil is virgin soil that has never been disturbed.[70] This means that even soil deposited by wind or water is not considered living soil. This idea is also based on the concept of auspicious soil in *Zangshu*. According to Hwang, dead soil is any soil deposited by any agents or any soil that has once been dug. Living soil maintains a constant temperature at a certain depth from the surface, meaning it is not influenced by surface temperatures. However, geomancers believe that dead soil is influenced by surface temperatures no matter how far below the earth's surface, and that it is easily penetrated by water. Therefore, such sites will be very wet in the rainy season, hot in the summer, dry in the arid period, and cold in winter. Such soil conditions obviously accelerate the decay of bones in a grave. As discussed, the decay of the flesh of the dead is desirable but not the decay of the bones. They should be preserved in good condition to deliver auspiciousness to the descendants. Thus, a fine, firm soil and moisture are required.

Geomantic Principles Concerning Wind

According to geomancers, wind conditions are the reflections of, and are controlled by, surrounding hills and mountains and are controlled by them, as sheltered areas are protected from unwanted winds. This is why geomantic conditions concerning winds are discussed in the section on landforms that are mainly concerned with mountains. As the Chinese name for geomancy, *fengshui,* indicates, wind as well as water conditions are important in the selection of a site. *Zangshu,* the classic geomancy text, states that a calming wind is the most important condition in geomancy.[71] But in spite of its importance, most geomantic textbooks rarely mention wind. *Zangshu* does not list mountains as one of the two most important geomantic principles, yet they are discussed in most geomantic textbooks more fully than any of the other geomantic elements.

In order to explain the emphasis on mountains in geomancy, it is important to know the geomancer's concept of energy as discussed in *Zangshu.* The book states that when the energy of Yin-Yang flows underground, it becomes vital energy, but when it belches out it becomes wind.[72] To a geomancer, then, wind and vital energy are different forms of the same substance, Yin-Yang energy. Therefore, in geomantic logic, when vital energy emerges from the ground and ascends into the air, it becomes wind and can then be dispersed and blown away, thus being unavailable for extraction. It is necessary to prevent the energy from being blown away in order to maintain vital energy (auspiciousness) in an area. Keeping out wind, however, can only be done by mountains surrounding an auspicious place. This is the reason an auspicious place is usually a basin that is encircled by mountain ranges. Thus, theoretically speaking, if winds blow into an auspicious place, it is not worthy of being occupied, as even vital energy acquired from an auspicious range (dragon) would not be available to people.

Jiri Palsippalhyang Chinkyol grouped winds into eight types:[73]

a) Hollowed wind (valley wind) from the front of a geomancy cave, which is an indication of a sloping ground (bright yard) in front of it. It can also be a sign that there is a poor-quality, low-lying peace mountain. Such a place cannot conserve vital energy. The wind in the front of an auspicious site is a bad omen, which will result in poverty and a discontinuance of the family line.

b) Hollowed wind (valley wind) from the back of a geomancy cave, which indicates the lack of a main mountain. This wind is bad and will result in poverty, a short life, and few descendants.

c) Hollowed wind (valley wind) from the left of a geomancy cave, which is an indication of a weak and dispirited azure dragon, one bad enough to cause widowhood.

d) Hollowed wind (valley wind) from the right of a geomancy cave, which indicates a disconnected white tiger. This is also bad and will result in a discontinuance of the family line.

e) Hollowed wind (valley wind) from both eyebrows. These are winds from the junction of the main mountain and the azure dragon and of the main mountain and the white tiger.[74] These two bad winds will result in a discontinuance of the family line.

f) Hollowed winds from both feet. These are winds from the ends of the azure dragon and the white tiger.[75] (Feet refer to the ends of the two embracing mountain ranges, the white tiger and the azure dragon.) These two winds are so inauspicious that they will cause both bankruptcy and a termination of the family line. If these winds blow from the *Kan* direction (northeast), they are considered to be the worst of all.

All eight winds, then, are inauspicious. The Korean word for eight winds, *Palpung*, is an abridgement of the word *Palbang-pung*, which means "winds from eight directions." There is no convex wind in geomancy but only hollowed wind, because winds can only blow into an auspicious area that is surrounded by hills and mountains when there is a valley among the mountains.[76] If an auspicious place is well surrounded by continuous hills or mountains when the wind blows, the wind will pass over the place and not blow into it.[77] Thus, wind in an auspicious place reflects the quality of the hills or mountains around it. Here we can see why the mountain is the most important element in geomancy and is emphasized more than wind.

Considering the nature of wind in an auspicious place, a geomancer believes there should not be any wind blowing from any direction in a geomantic cave. However, in a few exceptional cases, a place with wind blowing from many directions can be auspicious.

Wind can also be classified into two categories according to yin and yang concepts. If wind blows down to an area from the top of the mountains, it is called a yang wind (*Yangpung* in Korean), while wind blowing up from a valley is called a yin wind (*Umpung* in Korean).[78] This is a very general classification system for wind.

A Geomancer's Attitude Toward Mountains and Water

A geomancer in Seoul who taught me the art of geomancy said that the principles behind the formation of mountains and watercourses are the same as those in the formation of a plant. A plant has roots, a stem (branches), leaves, and flowers, and a mountain has comparable parts. All parts of a plant are linked together in the production of fruit; similarly, all components of mountains and watercourses form a system that produces auspicious places. It is the geomancer's task to search for the auspicious places of mountains. Therefore, a good geomancer should be able to tell, when he is in the field, which components of the mountain are comparable to the roots, stem, or flowers of a plant. *Myong-dang-ron* by Chang Yongduk advises:

> Let us consider the shapes of mountains and watercourses as a vine of a melon. First, let us think about mountains. The highest peak of a mountain range is analogous to the root of a melon tendril. In our country [Korea], Paektu Mountain is the root of our mountains. Trunks sprouting from the root of a plant are analogous to the distribution of major mountain ranges flanking the highest peak. The many branches developing from the trunk are analogous to the existence of many big and small mountains near the main peak of a mountain range. The many attached leaves on branches are analogous to the basins and small plains between mountains.[79]

Here a particular landscape is treated as a living organism with vital energy flowing in the veins. In the geomancer's view, a local landscape is part of the greater national landscape as a whole. And a national landscape is part of the world landscape system as a result of the flow of vital energy through the mountain ranges. No place stands alone, and all landscapes are interconnected and part of a greater landscape system. This is a fundamental geomantic attitude toward the environment and why, when they are in search of an auspicious site, geomancers relentlessly journey to distant places to observe relationships between various landscapes to see how vital energy might flow. To a geomancer, the configuration of a mountain reflects the quality of a mountain, just as the appearance of a plant reflects its quality.

Geomantic Principles Concerning Water

As we see in *Zangshu*, acquiring water is more important than calming wind. However, watercourses have attracted less attention than mountains in geomancy, because the characteristics of watercourses are largely dependent on those of mountains.

It is essential to have water in front of an auspicious place. Ideally, a slow, winding watercourse should flow some distance from the front of the auspicious location, and there should be a small watercourse both to the right and left of the auspicious place. These watercourses were so critical in geomancy that, as J. J.

M. de Groot noticed, people in the Amoy region of China would often build a water tank in front of an auspiciously located grave to compensate for a lack of water.[80] Why is water so important in grave geomancy? Let's turn to *Zangshu* again: "The scripture states that when [vital] energy is influenced by wind, it is dispersed, but when the energy meets water, its flow is stopped," because the energy cannot penetrate water.[81] Thus, water located in front of an auspicious place can help retain vital energy in a geomancy cave that flew to it from the main mountain. If there is no water available in front of the place, the vital energy that is the source of auspiciousness will flow away from the auspicious site. This is the reason for the geomantic requirement of having water in front of a propitious site and the reason that the people of Amoy built water tanks when no such water was available.

Professional geomancers apply certain principles about water.[82] They believe that good watercourses should not flow in a direction parallel to the course of mountain ranges because such watercourses cannot contain vital energy. In order to keep vital energy in a place, watercourses must cross the mountain ranges; therefore, when watercourses and mountains run in the same direction, the area is inauspicious. A desirable watercourse flows in a curve as if embracing the auspicious place from an angle perpendicular to the mountain ranges. Watercourses, in any case, should not flow in a straight line through the field. If they do, they are considered to have no desire to hold vital energy. Good watercourses in geomancy, then, gently meander, with many curves. If the curves are too sharp or are tortuous, the watercourse is considered to be very bad. A watercourse is considered auspicious when it meanders as if constantly looking back to the auspicious site (geomancy cave), as if it is reluctant to leave the place. The most desirable characteristics of all geomantic objects, such as mountains and watercourses, are gentleness of form and beauty of shape. Any sharp figure or form that appears to attack the geomancy cave renders the place inauspicious. If watercourses near the auspicious place flow gracefully and slowly, then the water is considered to express its affection for the site and have no desire to leave it.

The direction of water flow is also critically important: a good watercourse should flow from an auspicious to an inauspicious direction.[83] Then the residents of the place will enjoy long-lasting auspiciousness.

Now, why have good watercourses been important to geomancers? Hu Shunshen, who lived during the Sung dynasty in China, writes in *Dili xinfa*:

> The mountain, a static material, belongs to Yin. Water a dynamic material, belongs to Yang. The characteristic of Yin is constancy, and that of Yang is primarily change. Now, the matter of auspiciousness or inauspiciousness is fundamentally related to the observation of water. Generally, the mountain is comparable to the body [flesh and bones], and the watercourse to the blood vessels in the human body. The matter of the growing or perishing of human bodies depends on the condition of the blood vessels. When blood is circulated around the body and the flow is orderly, the person is healthy and strong. However, in the opposite case of the above, everyone is subject to disease or death. No one is an exception to this

natural principle. This principle then requires the correct flow of water and a right location of mountains in order to form an auspicious place. Each of the five mountains has their own locations [directions] of auspiciousness or inauspiciousness.

Generally, water should flow from the auspicious direction to the inauspicious direction; then the place can be auspicious. If water flows from the inauspicious direction to the auspicious direction, the place cannot be auspicious, because it destroys all the vitality and prosperity of the place.[84]

It is also important for a geomancer to examine the junction of watercourses in front of the geomancy cave: watercourses from both the white tiger and the azure dragon should meet at the center of the bright yard, a name for the area in front of the geomancy cave.[85] The junction should be close and equidistant from each of the two embracing mountains. It is said that the white tiger and the azure dragon are in balance when the junction is an equal distance from both mountains. Balance, or symmetry of landscape, is a basic principle of geomancy.

Water can connote wealth. It is necessary for water to collect in front of a geomancy cave to bring wealth to it. Hwang Ilsun has said that junctures of watercourses cause streams to flow slowly.[86] Slow-moving water is a required condition in geomancy.

It is also important to examine the directions of "obtaining water"—the entry of water flow—and those of "destroying water"—the discharge of water. The direction of a watercourse is more important than any other condition of water. Generally, the direction of the entry of water flow (*Tuksu,* which literally means "obtaining water") should be an auspicious one and the outgoing direction of water (*Pasu,* which literally means "destroying water") should be inauspicious. This means that water should flow from an auspicious direction (e.g., eastern) toward an inauspicious direction (e.g., western). In particular, the watercourses from either the azure dragon or the white tiger that meet in the front of the geomancy cave should flow from a vital and therefore good direction to a perishing and therefore bad direction.[87]

A yang water is a watercourse that flows from the left to the right of the geomancy cave (clockwise in the modern sense). Water flowing from the azure dragon belongs to this category. A watercourse that flows from right to left (counter-clockwise) is called a yin water.[88] This is water that flows from the white tiger. Of the several systems of classification, the most popular have categories based on Yin-Yang principles.

Watercourses can also be divided into two categories according to their distances from the geomancy cave. They are inner water, or *Naesu,* which refers to the watercourses near the geomantic cave, and outer water, or *Woisu,* which refers to the watercourses further from the geomantic cave.[89] Watercourses from the black turtle, the azure dragon, and the white tiger belong to inner water, while watercourses from the red bird (peace and homage paying mountain) or those from any area which flows into or through a given geomantic landscape near a geomantic cave, or *Kungnae,* belong to outer water.[90]

In geomancy, after finding a site surrounded by auspicious mountains, the direction and shape of the watercourses are the next most critical elements to observe.

Geomantic Principles Using a Geomantic Compass

The examination of the direction of mountains and watercourses is as important as the observation of their shapes. The examination of cosmic directions has been important since the ancient times when the Chinese compass was apparently invented for geomantic purposes; this compass only later came to be applied to navigating, according to Joseph Needhams's study.[91]

After considering the complex geomantic principles for landforms and water, one may well wonder if there is any place that is auspicious. According to a geomancer in Seoul, however, well-shaped mountains and watercourses are usually located in good directions, because affiliation of phenomena of the same kind is a principle of the universe.[92] This can be interpreted to mean that if the mountains at the beginning are formed to produce a good place, they will be set in good directions. In his experience, badly shaped mountains usually run in directions that are inauspicious.

The importance of the direction of mountains and watercourses is summarized in a well-known geomantic saying, "Mountains from auspicious directions are good mountains and watercourses flowing to inauspicious directions are good watercourses." These "auspicious directions" and "inauspicious directions" can be examined only with a compass (see Figure 5.7). The cosmology of directions in a geomantic compass and their values of being auspicious or inauspicious are based on the age-old Chinese theories of Yin-Yang and the five elements discussed earlier.

There are many forms of geomantic compasses, ranging from simple ones that have only a few rings to complex ones that have many rings.[93] The simplest compass I found had only two rings, while the most complex one had nine. The variations in the number of rings may indicate that each ring is set up for a different purpose, and that certain rings are more important for examining a certain locale. Some rings that are exclusively used in examining a gravesite may not be necessary for examining a house site. This variation can also indicate that folk geomancers do not always need detailed directions to determine the site of a grave or house since many are not familiar with the proper use of the geomantic compass. According to a scholarly geomancer, about six rings are essential for examining a possible gravesite, and each ring is used for a specific purpose. The following is an explanation of the six rings:[94]

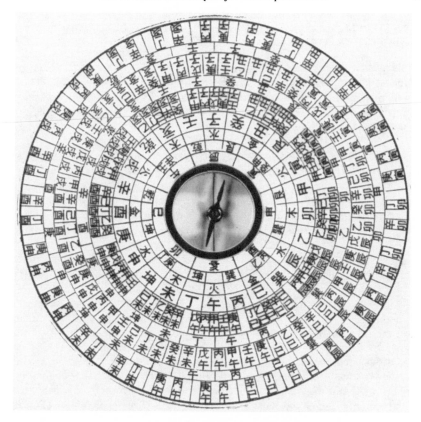

Figure 5.7 A Geomancer's Compass (Obtained in Seoul, December 1973.)

a) The first ring from the center (the ring of the yellow spring water)

This ring is used for measuring the direction of the underground water flow.[95] It has eight characters, which indicate eight directions: Yin, Ch'en, Wu, Szu, Mao, Hai, Yu, and Shen. These eight names are chosen from the twelve zodiacal symbols and represent the eight directions according to the eight trigrams in the *I-Ching*; we do not know why the zodiacal names are substituted for those of the eight trigrams.

The method of measuring underground water (yellow spring water) conditions at a geomancy cave is explained by geomancer Chang Yongdu'k as follows:

For instance, when a geomancy cave is facing due south, that is, the *pyong-o* direction [one reads this in the fourth ring], it is called *pyong-o hyol* or the geomancy cave of *pyong-o* direction. This cave indicates "hae or bore" in the first ring; "hae" in the fourth ring indicates the direction of NNNW. If a gully or valley lies in this direction near the geomancy cave, we can tell that underground water is flowing in the geomancy cave. [This then is not a good place to bury the dead.]. . . . If a hill occupies the direction, "hae" instead of a valley, the place is safe from the influence of underground water.[96]

Since vital energy cannot flow through water, if an underground water vein is located at the geomancy cave, naturally the energy is not available. This is why there should be no water flowing through the very auspicious spot itself; it should flow near the front of the geomancy cave in order to keep the energy at the auspicious site.

b) The second ring from the center (the ring of the eight light winds)

This ring is used for measuring the direction of "the winds of eight lights (Palyopung)" or the "underground wind (Chihapung)" blowing toward an auspicious site.[97] These types of wind are on the ground level and are thought to affect the buried corpse in a grave, for this type of wind affects the soil conditions underground. Measuring wind directions means measuring the conditions of the background (protective) hills of an auspicious site, because it is assumed that wind blows from the direction of any valleys and lowlands in background hills. The background hills disjointed by valleys and flat land are considered inauspicious.

This ring is also used for measuring the direction of "thief peaks," or *kyubong* in Korean. A thief peak is a partially visible mountain that rises slightly above the surrounding mountains of an auspicious site; it is considered inauspicious. The eight main divisions of the first ring are themselves divided into twenty-four subdivisions in the second ring. Every alternate one of the twenty-four subdivisions is left blank. The remaining twelve are filled with the eight words of the eight trigrams of the *I-Ching* and the four combined words of the eight Heavenly Stems in pairing with the Ten Heavenly Stems. (For the arrangement of these words, see Figure 4.4.)

The method of examining wind is the same as for examining water. Here is a summary of the geomancer Chang's lesson on the use of the second ring:

> When the geomancy cave is facing south or *pyong-o* direction [find this in the fourth ring], you look at the second ring above *pyong-o* in the fourth ring and read the *son* direction in the second ring. Then, find the *son*, the SSE direction in the fourth ring, and assume that there is wind blowing from the SSE toward the geomancy cave, unless a mountain range surrounds the cave in that direction. The blowing wind is bad for the cave. If the surrounding mountains are not connected soundly, the place has Yin wind. It is not qualified for an auspicious burial.[98]

In order to be an auspicious site, the direction from which wind blows should be particularly well blocked by a mountain range.

c) The third ring from the center (the ring of five elements with three zodiac characteristics)

This ring measures the characteristics of directions given according to the five agents theory. In other words, it is used for converting the directions indicated by the twelve animals in the Chinese zodiac cycle into the direction indicated by any one of the following four elements: water, wood, fire, and metal. Since the characteristics of earth are absolutely neutral and indicate no direction or center, this element is not used in this ring. The associations of the twelve animals with the five agents are

Water	—	monkey, rat, dragon
Wood	—	boar, hare, sheep
Fire	—	tiger, horse, dog
Metal	—	serpent, cock, ox[99]

This ring is especially useful for examining the relationships of surrounding mountains to the principles of the five agents producing or destroying one another. It is mainly used in determining the facing direction of graves in auspicious sites, but it is also used in predicting the timing of the different types of blessings or misfortunes manifested from the construction of a structure in the site.[100]

d) The fourth ring from the center (the ring of the correct needle for land)

This ring indicates the twenty-four detailed and standard directions in positioning a grave or house in geomancy. Each name of the twenty-four directions has been formulated from a combination of the twelve zodiacal animals, eight names from the Ten Stems, and the names of four cardinal directions from the eight trigrams.[101] This ring is used in measuring and evaluating the conditions of an auspicious site. Four elements constitute the immediate surroundings of a geomancy cave that is an auspicious gravesite or house site and determine its quality: the entrance slope to the auspicious site in front of the main mountain; the two eyebrows, which are two slightly elevated parts of the ground immediately behind the auspicious site; and the auspicious site itself, known as the geomancy cave (a desirable house site or grave site). The conditions and positions of these four elements are examined with this ring. To examine them, you begin by placing the geomancer's compass on the auspicious site, standing toward the main mountain, and reading the direction of the line that passes through the geomancy cave. This is "the direction of looking behind the geomancy cave," or *choa*; the opposite direction is "the direction looking in front of the geomancy cave," or *hyang*. Then you find the direction of the protective "eyebrow rise" (*misa*, literally eyebrow sand), look at each of the two areas of moderately elevated ground behind the auspicious site, and read the directions. Next, you measure the direction of the "entrance slope," or *ipsu*, go up the "entrance slope" from the geomancy cave, place the compass in the center of the entrance slope, and look at the main mountain. Then you read the direction of the entrance slope.

This ring is the most versatile and frequently consulted. The twenty-four directions indicated in it are the standard directions used to describe the facing directions of structures (a grave or a house) in an auspicious site.

e) The fifth ring from the center (the ring of the central needle for humanity)

The division and arrangement of the directions into twenty-four subdivisions in this ring are the same as in the fourth ring, except that they are shifted 7.5 degrees anticlockwise (backward).[102] This ring is used in examining the auspiciousness and inauspiciousness of key landform features surrounding the auspicious site.[103]

The compass with only six rings is also used for the positioning of coffins in geomancy caves. Since vital energy is available to people only through the geomancy cave, it is critically important to set the corpse in the right location and direction. In geomancy, the method of placing the corpse in the right direction at a gravesite is called "the method of dividing metal," or *pun'gumpop*. The essence of the method is to place the dead in a direction harmonious with the characteristic of the dead person, or *mangmyong saenggi*.[104] Every direction has one of the five characteristics of the five agents, and as every year of the calendar has one of the five agents' characteristics every human being has characteristics depending on one's birth year. According to the principle of the five elements producing one another, in the burial of a corpse the characteristics of the dead person and the direction of his grave should be in harmony.[105] For instance, if a dead man's birth year was metal, he should be buried either in the direction of water or earth in order to maintain a harmonious relationship (metal produces water and earth produces metal). However, this dead person should avoid the directions of wood and fire, because they are in a relationship of mutual destruction (fire destroys metal, metal destroys wood). Thus, "the method of dividing metal" is critically important after acquiring the auspicious site.

The fifth ring is divided into twelve distinct portions according to the directions of the twelve zodiacal animals. Each portion is separated by one blank space, and each of those portions is divided into five equal spaces, which are subcategories of a zodiacal direction.

f) The sixth ring from the center (the ring of the needle seaming heaven)

The division and arrangement of the directions into twenty-four subdivisions in this ring are the same as in the fourth ring (the ring of the correct needle for land), except that they are shifted 7.5 degrees clockwise (forward).[106] This is the second most important ring after the fourth ring in a geomantic compass and is used in a variety of ways, including the designation of auspicious directions using the method of star movement, or *unsongpop*.[107]

This ring shows twenty-four directions and is also used in positioning the coffin and in predicting the kind of auspiciousness received from the grave. Each direction connotes a certain kind of auspiciousness. For instance, the directions of *imja* and *pyong-o* represent honor, while the directions of *chongmi* and *shinsul* represent wealth.[108]

g) The seventh ring from the center (the ring of the seventy-two directions of dividing metal, or pungum)

The rings seven, eight, and nine all exclusively deal with *pungumpop*, or "the method of dividing metal," and are used for correctly positioning coffins in harmony with the geomantic characteristics of the gravesite according to the principle of the five elements producing one another.

The seventh ring indicates the seventy-two directions that are the subdivisions of the twenty-four directions in the fourth ring. Each direction in the fourth ring is equally divided into three sub-directions (each direction is allocated with 5 degrees).[109] This suggests that there are seventy-two directions to position a coffin in a gravesite.

h) The eighth ring from the center (the ring of pungum according to the correct needle for land)

In this ring, 120 directions are indicated. Each of the 120 directions is one-fifth of one of the 24 directions on the fourth ring and has only 3 degrees.[110] This suggests that a coffin can be positioned in 120 different directions. This method of positioning a coffin in a gravesite is used after determining the facing direction of a grave according to the eight trigram method.[111]

i) The ninth ring from the center (the ring of pungum according to the needle seaming heaven)

This ring also has 120 fine directions, each direction (only 3 degrees) being one-fifth of one of the 24 directions on the sixth ring.[112] This method of positioning a coffin in a gravesite is used after determining the facing direction of a grave according to the method of star movement, or *Unsongpop*.[113]

The Ideal Conditions of an Auspicious Place

So far we have examined the various geomantic conditions and principles for an auspicious site, grouped into three categories: landforms, water, and cosmological directions. Now by summarizing and synthesizing these geomantic principles, the landscape conditions for an ideal auspicious place can be described as follows (see Figure 5.8 and Figure 5.9):

1) The oncoming dragon (the main range of the background mountain joining the main mountain) must be long and shaped as if alive (i.e., with many folds). It must be continuous, as it runs down to the auspicious site. The mountain range must also be aesthetically pleasing.

2) The main mountain (the mountain behind the auspicious site) must be majestic and appear to be capable of delivering vital energy.

3) The azure dragon and the white tiger should encircle the auspicious place to hold the vital energy.

4) The peace mountain and the homage paying mountain must be shaped as if waiting on and existing for the main mountain.

5) There must be watercourses in and around the auspicious area, and the waters should flow slowly and with many curves.

6) Neither underground nor surface water should be at the auspicious site (grave or house).

7) There should not be any wind blowing into the area of the auspicious site (though there are a few exceptions).

8) It is necessary to have good soil conditions in the auspicious site. The soil should be firm in structure, fine in texture, and beautiful in color.

9) The landforms should be associated with auspicious directions.

10) These principles apply to both houses and graves.

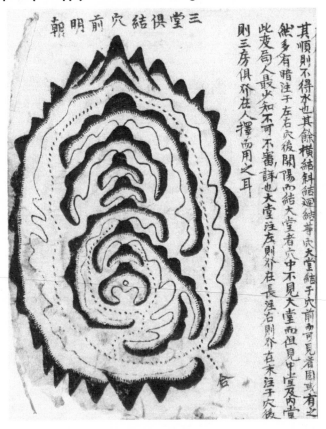

Figure 5.8 A geomantic illustration of an auspicious site (I) (from Sanpop-Chonso, Anon.)

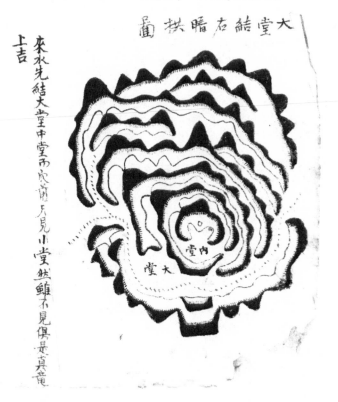

Figure 5.9   A geomantic illustration of an auspicious site (II) (from Sanpop-Chonso, Anon.)

Types of Geomantic Landscapes

The geomantic elements create many kinds of inanimate objects. For instance, the surrounding mountains and watercourses of the geomancy cave can form the geomantic landscape of a sailing boat or a brooding golden hen. All important geomantic landscapes are personified. The term "geomantic landscape" is used here to indicate such personified landscapes of auspicious sites formed by landforms surrounding them.

The landscape that forms an object should be harmonious with its environment. For instance, if there is an ox, there should be food; if there is a general, there should be soldiers.[114] If there is anything lacking in the geomantic setting, people will attempt to compensate for the inadequacy; often artificial objects have been made to complete the harmony of a geomantic landscape.[115] On the other hand, if a geomantic landscape is well harmonized, people are extremely careful not to disturb it.

Geomancers name landscapes after certain animate or inanimate objects depending on how they perceive the landscape. According to a geomancer in Sangju County, North Kyongsang Province, there are innumerable names that can be applied to landscapes.[116] He mentioned as examples the names of birds, mammals, plants, and inanimate man-made objects. Some popular names of personified geomantic landscapes found during my field trips are:[117]

Chamdu-hyong (geomantic landscape of the head of a silkworm)

Changkun Taechoa-hyong (geomantic landscape of a sitting general)

Changkun-hyong (geomantic landscape of a military general)

Chinma-hyong (geomantic landscape of horses in a battle formation).

Chonghak Poran-hyong (geomantic landscape of an azure crane sitting on its nest)

Haengju-hyong (geomantic landscape of a sailing boat)

Hwangryong Togang-hyong (geomantic landscape of a yellow dragon crossing a river)

Inyong-hyong (geomantic landscape of an earthworm-dragon).

Kahak Dunggong-hyong (geomantic landscape of a flying crane)

Kalyong Umsu-hyong (geomantic landscape of a thirsty dragon drinking water)

Kirogi-hyong (geomantic landscape of a flock of wild geese)

Kumban Okbae-hyong (geomantic landscape of a gold dish and a jade cup)

Kumke Poranhyong (geomantic landscape of a golden hen sitting on eggs)

Kumo Taks-hyongi (geomantic landscape of a golden crow pecking a corpse)

Kwoidung-hyong (geomantic landscape of a lantern, or candle)

Maehwa Nakj-hyongi (geomantic landscape of a plum flower lying on the ground)

Noso Hajonhyong (geomantic landscape of an old mouse descending to a field)

Odu-hyong (geomantic landscape of the head of a crow).

Ogong Ipjihyong (geomantic landscape of a centipede entering the soil)

Oknyo Sanbalhyong (geomantic landscape of a jade woman with loose hair)

Oknyo Tangum-hyon (geomantic landscape of a jade woman playing an instrument)

Paek-a Sangchonhyong (geomantic landscape of a white wild duck flying towards the sky)

Pibong Kwiso-hyong (geomantic landscape of a phoenix returning to its nest)

Pibong Poran-hyong (geomantic landscape of a phoenix sitting on eggs)

Piran Koik-hyong (geomantic landscape of a leaping "ran"—mystic bird—looking back over its shoulder)

Piryong Dungchon-hyong (geomantic landscape of a dragon rising to the heavens)

Piryong Nongju-hyong (geomantic landscape of a flying dragon playing with pearls)

Piryong Sangchon-hyong (geomantic landscape of a dragon flying in the sky)

Pokchi-hyong (geomantic landscape of a reclining pheasant)

Pokho-hyong (geomantic landscape of a reclining tiger)

Pyongsa Nakan-hyong (geomantic landscape of a wild goose landing on flat sand)

Sadu-hyong (geomantic landscape of the head of a snake).

Sonin Musu-hyong (geomantic landscape of a dancing supernatural man)

Sujung Ju-hyong (geomantic landscape of a boat in water).

Ungki-hyong (geomantic landscape of a rising bear).

Unjung Chowol-hyong (geomantic landscape of a crescent moon amidst the clouds).

Wau-hyong (geomantic landscape of a reclining ox)

Yacha-hyong (geomantic landscape in the form of a Chinese written character that means "words")

Yonhwa Pusu-hyong (geomantic landscape of a floating lotus)

There are many more names of geomantic landscapes than those listed here. Murayama Chijun listed 174 names.[118] Many of the thirty-nine names that I collected in the field are included in Murayama's book, *Chosen no Fusui* (*Korean Geomancy*). These thirty-nine names are some of those currently popular among folk geomancers of Korea.

Some believe that a certain type of geomantic landscape only yields a certain type of benefit.[119] A scholarly geomancer in a rural village, however, told me that the types of geomantic landscapes do not matter—all are more or less the same in terms of the benefits they give.[120] The kinds of benefits and the times of their manifestations are completely dependent on the scale, beauty, and harmony of all elements in the geomantic landscape. This means that the geomantic landscape of a "reclining ox" in one place does not necessarily manifest the same kind of benefit at the same time as the geomantic landscape of a "reclining ox" in another place. Depending on its scale and beauty, one landscape may manifest better benefits and at an earlier time than another landscape. Also depending on scale and beauty, different types of geomantic landscapes, such as a "reclining ox" and a "flying phoenix," can produce similar benefits at similar times. The benefits yielded by different geomantic landscapes are all more or less concerned with the prosperity of the family, and more specifically with wealth, fame, and having many children.

Although some benefits are available soon after occupying either a gravesite or a house site, they are usually manifested to the descendants after a period of dormancy of several decades or even several generations. I was unable to find any geomantic textbooks that specified the time required for benefits to manifest themselves according to the type of geomantic landscape. The time when benefits can be received is determined by the scale, beauty, and harmony of elements in a landscape rather than the type of landscape.

Individual mountains, other components of a local landscape, and even the entire landscape of an area are also often personified. Depending on the perception of the geomancer, they are named after animate or inanimate objects. For instance, if a mountain is shaped like a writing brush, it is often called *Munpilbong*, or writing brush mountain, which is a fire-type mountain because of its sharp points like a writing brush or tongues of flame.[121] If a mountain is rather small, smooth, and chubby in the shape of a pretty woman, it is called *Oknyo-che*, or jade woman mountain.[122] If a mountain is large, tall, and slender in form, it is called *Shinson-che*, or supernatural person mountain. Other examples include:[123]

Sonnyo-bong (mountain of a fairy girl)
Wau (mountain of a reclining ox)
Pokho (mountain of a tiger lying flat)
Nakta (mountain of a camel)
Kumdae (mountain of a golden belt)
Okchuk (mountain of a jade axle)
Ku'mtong (mountain of a golden pipe)
Ku'msang (mountain of a golden box)

These are some typical geomantic terms that describe individual figures or components of a personified geomantic landscape. Benefits manifested by these mountains are largely dependent on a harmonious relationship with neighboring mountains and waters. The benefits are also determined by the characteristics of a given type of mountain; for example, an auspicious mountain of the writing brush type will produce good scholars.

Notes

1. This chapter is based on and has developed from Hong-key Yoon, *Geomantic Relationships Between Culture and Nature in Korea* (Taipei: The Orient Culture Service, 1976), 24–73.

2. Guo Pu, Zangshu, in *Dili zhengzong* [The Cardinal Principles of Geomancy] commentary by Jiang Guo (Shinchu: Chulin shuchu, 1967), 1.

3. Guo Pu, *Zangjing, neipian* [The Book of Burial, the inner volume], in Chongwen Shuju Heikeshu (Wuhan: Hubei Chongwen Shuju, 1875), 1.

4. Guo Pu, Zangjing, neipian, 1.

5. Hong-key Yoon, "Towards a Theory on the Origin of Geomancy," Environment and Quality of Life in Central Europe: Problems of Transition: Proceedings, International Geographical Union, Regional Conference (CD-ROM, ISBN 80–7184–153–6), (Prague: 1994), 188–189; Hong-key Yoon, "Hankuk pungsuchiri yonguui hoigowa chonmang" [Prospect and Retrospect of Research into Geomancy in Korea]. *Hankuk Sasangsahak* [History of Korean Thought] vol. 17 (2001), 14.

6. Guo Pu, Zangjing, neipian, 1.

7. Guo Pu, Zangjing, neipian, 1.

8. Guo Pu, *Liujiangdong jiacang shanpen Zhangshu* (commentary by Zheng Mi) in Linlang Mishi Chongshu. Case 2. vol. 10, (1888), part 1, 2.

9. Interview with Mr Chang Yongduk at Chollong-dong, Tongdaemun-ku, Seoul, January 1974.

10. Yi Hidok, "Pungsu Chiri" in Yi Sang-il and others, eds., *Hankuk Sasangui Wonchon* [Sources of Korean Thought] (Seoul: Yangyong-gak, 1973), 205.

11. In geomancy any convex or projected landforms are called mountains. The mountains in this sense include hillocks, hills, and, of course, standard mountains.

12. This is basic knowledge in geomancy. Interviews with geomancers during field trip, October 1973 to February 1974.

13. Xu Shanji and Xu Shanshu (Ming dynasty), *Dili-Renzixuezhi* [The Fact that All Humanity Must Know] (Hsin-chu: Chulin Shu-chu, 1969), 5.

14. Anon., Chiri Chongjong, 2.

15. Interview with a geomancer in Sangju, North Kyongsang Province, 24 November 1973.

16. Anon., Chiri Chongjong, 2

17. Guo Pu, Zangshu, in *Dili zhengzong*, 4.

18. Chugan Choson (Seoul), 29 August 1975, 28.

19. Yang I, *Han lung ching*, in *Dili Zhengzhong* [Authentic Collection of Geomantic Principles]. Commentary by Jiang Guo, (Hsin-chu: Chu-lin Shu-chu, 1967), 1.

20. Kim Myongje, *Chiri Palsip Pal-hyang Chinkyol* [True Discourse on Eighty-Eight Geomantic directions] (Seoul: Samsin sojok, 1971), 67.

21. Kim Myongj, *Chiri Palsip Pal-hyang*, 94, and interviews with geomancers during a field trip, October 1973 to February 1974.

22. Guo Pu, Zangshu, in *Dili zhengzong*, 1.

23. Interview during field trip, October 1973 to February 1974.

24. Yi Hidok, "Pungsu Chiri," 193.

25. Kim Myongje, *Chiri Palsip Pal-hyang*, 161.

26. Guo Pu, Liujiangdong jiacang shanpen Zhangshu, part 2, 36.

27. Guo Pu, Liujiangdong jiacang shanpen Zhangshu, part 2, 36.

28. Guo Pu, Liujiangdong jiacang shanpen Zhangshu, part 2, 38.

29. Interviews with geomancers during a field trip, October 1973 to February 1974.

30. Guo Pu, Liujiangdong jiacang shanpen Zhangshu, part 2, 36.

31. Guo Pu, Liujiangdong jiacang shanpen Zhangshu, part 2, 38.

32. Guo Pu, Liujiangdong jiacang shanpen Zhangshu, part 2, 38.

33. Guo Pu, Liujiangdong jiacang shanpen Zhangshu, part 2, 38.

34. Guo Pu, Liujiangdong jiacang shanpen Zhangshu, part 2, 38.

35. Guo Pu, Liujiangdong jiacang shanpen Zhangshu, part 2, 36.

36. Interviews with geomancers during a field trip, October 1973 to February 1974.

37. Guo Pu, Liujiangdong jiacang shanpen Zhangshu, part 2, 37.

38. Guo Pu, Liujiangdong jiacang shanpen Zhangshu, part 2, 36.

39. Guo Pu, Liujiangdong jiacang shanpen Zhangshu, part 2, 36–37.

40. Guo Pu, Liujiangdong jiacang shanpen Zhangshu, part 2, 37.

41. Guo Pu, Liujiangdong jiacang shanpen Zhangshu, part 2, 36–37.

42. Kim Ki-duk, "Koryo sidae Kaegyong ui Pungsuchirijok Kochal" [Examining the Geographical Features of the Koryo Dynasty's Gaegyeong in Fengshui Theoretical Terms]. *Hankuk Sasangsahak* [Studies in Korean Thought] vol. 17 (2001), 96–97.

43. Interview with a geomancer at Mikimi, Modong-myon, Sangju-kun, 23 November 1973.

44. Interview with a geomancer at Mikimi, Modong-myon, Sangju-kun, 23 November 1973.

45. This is a generalized concept in geomancy. See Chong Chisu, *Chiri-yocho* [Geomancy in Brief] (Taegu: Chinmun Chulpansa, 1968), 13–14; Chang Yongduk (1973), 76–80.

46. Chong Chisu (1968), 13.

47. Interview with a geomancer at Mikimi, Modong-myon, Sangju-kun, 23 November 1973.

48. Chang Yongduk, *Myongdang-non* [On Auspicious Sites] (Seoul: Emille Misulk-wan, 1973), 37.

49. Yi Hidok, "Pungsu Chiri," 193.

50. Kim Myongje, *Chiri Palsip Pal-hyang*, 124.

51. The information is largely compiled from interviews from October 1973 to February 1974; Kim Myongje, *Chiri Palsip Pal-hyang*, 158–160; and other geomantic manuscripts.

52. Chang Yongduk, *Myongdang-non*, 52.

53. Anon., Chiri Chongjong, 28.

54. Interview with a geomancer at Mikimi, Modong-myon, Sangju-kun, North Kyongsang Province, on 24 November 1973.

55. Kim Myongje, *Chiri Palsip Pal-hyang*, 125–128.

56. Kim Myongje, Chiri Palsip Pal-hyang, 126.

57. Kim Myongje, *Chiri Palsip Pal-hyang*, 126.

58. Kim Myongje, *Chiri Palsip Pal-hyang*, 126–127.

59. Kim Myongje, *Chiri Palsip Pal-hyang*, 125.

60. Kim Myongje, *Chiri Palsip Pal-hyang*, 125

61. This information is compiled from anon., *Chiri Chongjong*, 14, and anon., *Pakok,* 7.

62. Guo Pu, Liujiangdong jiacang shanpen Zhangshu, part 1, 21–23.

63. Guo Pu, Liujiangdong jiacang shanpen Zhangshu, part 1, 6.

64. Interview with a geomancer at Mikimi, Modong-myon, Sangju-kun, North Kyongsang Province, 23 November 1973. Informant's name withheld.

65. Interview with Mr Chang Yongduk, 8 February 1974.

66. Guo Pu Liujiangdong jiacang shanpen Zhangshu, part 2, 24.

67. Guo Pu Liujiangdong jiacang shanpen Zhangshu, part 2, 24.

68. Guo Pu Liujiangdong jiacang shanpen Zhangshu, part 2, 35.

69. Hwang Ilsun, *Pungsu Chiri-hak Kaeyo* [An Overview of Geomancy] (Seoul: Pakmun-gak, 1968), 28.

70. Hwang Ilsun, *Pungsu Chiri-hak Kaeyo*, 29.

71. Guo Pu, Zangshu, in *Dili zhengzong*, 1.

72. Guo Pu, Zangshu, in *Dili zhengzong*, 1.

73. Kim Myongje, *Chiri Palsip Pal-hyang*, 191–192.

74. Interview with Mr Chong Changsup at Mikimi, Modong-myon, Sangju-kun, North Kyongsang Province, 7 January 1974.

75. Interview with Mr Chong Changsup at Mikimi, Modong-myon, Sangju-kun, North Kyongsang Province, 7 January 1974.

76. Interview with Mr Chong Changsup at Mikimi, Modong-myon, Sangju-kun, North Kyongsang Province, 7 January 1974.

77. Interview with Mr Chong Changsup at Mikimi, Modong-myon, Sangju-kun, North Kyongsang Province, 7 January 1974.

78. Interview with Chang Yongduk, 12 March 1974 and Chang Yongduk, *Myongdang-non*, 6.

79. Chang Yongduk, *Myongdang-non*, 33–34.

80. J.J. M. De Groot , *The Religious System of China*. vol.3 (Leiden: Librairie et Im-primerie, 1897), 946.

81. Guo Pu, Zangshu, in Dili zhengzong, 1.

82. Interviews with geomancers in Korea, October 1973 to February 1974.

83. Interviews with geomancers In Korea, October 1973 to February 1974.

84. Hu Shunshen, *Dili xinfa* [New Principles of Geomancy]. (The edition in the Kyujang-gak Collection at Seoul National University Library), 4–5.

85. Hwang Ilsun, *Pungsu Chiri-hak Kaeyo* [An Overview of Geomancy] (Seoul: Pakmun-gak, 1968), 38.

86. Hwang Ilsun, *Pungsu Chiri-hak Kaeyo*, 42.

87. Interview with a geomancer at Chungmo, Modong-myon, Sangju-kun, North Kyongsang Province, 24 November 1973.

88. Interview with a geomancer at Chungmo, Modong-myon, Sangju-kun, North Kyongsang Province, 24 November 1973.

89. Interview with a geomancer at Chungmo, Modong-myon, Sangju-kun, North Kyongsang Province, 24 November 1973. Also see Murayama, Chijun, *Chosen no Fusui* [Korean Geomancy] (Seoul: Chosen Shotofu, 1931), 93.

90. The term Kungnae refers to a harmonious geomantic landscape of an auspicious place which includes all necessary geomantic objects of a place: a main mountain, azure dragon, white tiger, peace mountain, homage paying mountain, watercourses, etc.

91. According to Joseph Needham, the Chinese were the first to invent the compass for geomantic purposes rather than for navigation. He declared, "There is now no doubt that the magnetic compass was first developed for fengshui purposes." See Joseph Needham, *Science and Civilisation in China*, (Cambridge: Cambridge University Press, 1959), vol. 2, section 14, 361.

92. Interview with Mr Chang Yongduk at Chollong-dong, Tongdaemun-ku, Seoul, January 1974.

93. Feuchtwang considered the geomantic compass to be a concrete model of Chinese cosmology; see Stephan D. R. Feuchtwang, *An Anthropological Analysis of Chinese Geomancy*. (Vientianne: Editions Vithangna, 1974), 18–111.

94. The information is essentially based on my private lessons in geomancy from Mr Chang Yongduk in Seoul and a geomancer in Sangju-kun, North Kyongsang Province.

95. Kim Hangbai, *Silyong Pungsuchiri* [Practical Geomancy], (Seoul: Ilsan Chulpansa, 1997), 362.

96. Chang Yongduk (1974), "Myongdang Chapki" [Essays on Auspicious Sites], *Hankuk I Ibo*, 14 March 1974; Interview with Chang Yongduk, January 1974.

97. Kim Hangbai, Silyong Pungsuchiri.

98. Interview with Mr Chang Yongduk at Chollong-dong, Tongdaemun-ku, Seoul, January 1974. See also Chang Yongduk, "Myongdang Chapki" 14 March 1974.

99. For further discussion, see Chapter Four.

100. Kim Hangbai, *Silyong Pungsuchiri*, 363.

101. Kim Hangbai, *Silyong Pungsuchiri*, 363; Chang Yongduk (1973), 71.

102. Kim Hangbai, *Silyong Pungsuchiri*, 363.

103. Kim Hangbai, *Silyong Pungsuchiri*, 363.

104. Mangmyong saenggi referred to the characteristics of a dead man's birth year that was converted into Yin-Yang and the Five Elements Theory.

105. Personal communication with a geomancer at Mikimi, Modong-myon, Sangju-kun, North Kyongsang Province, 7 January 1975.

106. Kim Hangbai, *Silyong Pungsuchiri*, 364.

107. Kim Hangbai, *Silyong Pungsuchiri*, 364

108. Chang Yongduk, *Myongdangron*, 82–87.

109. Kim Hangbai, *Silyong Pungsuchir*,, 364.

110. Kim Hangbai, *Silyong Pungsuchiri*, 364.

111. Kim Hangbai, *Silyong Pungsuchiri*, 364

112. Kim Hangbai, *Silyong Pungsuchiri*, 365.

113. Kim Hangbai, *Silyong Pungsuchiri*, 365

114. This is evidenced by many geomantic legends, including the "Chongchon Market," "Phoenix Hill in Sonsan County," "Phoenix Terrace and Well in Chestnut Forest," etc. This idea is common sense to geomancers in Korea, as evidenced during interviews, October 1973 to February 1974.

115. Interviews of geomancers, October 1973–February 1974.

116. Personal communication with the geomancer in Sangju County, 7 January 1974.

117. The sources for the names of geomantic landscapes are: interview with Chong Changsop at Mikimi, Modong Myon, Sangju County, 7 January 1974; interview with Kim Kihyon at Kyongno-dang cattle market, Andong City, North Kyongsang Province, 16 February 1974; interview with Mr Kim Songchan at Kyongno-dang cattle market, Andong City, North Kyongsang Province, 16 February 1974; interview with Chang Yongduk, "Myongdang Chapki," 23 February 1974; a selection from handwritten manuscript, Anon., Sanga Yoram, 17; a selection from Chi Chong-o, "Myongdang Chaja Samchonri" [Searching for Auspicious Places over the Three Thousands Ri] *Chugan Chung-ang* [Weekly Chung-ang], 27 October 1974 – 2 March 1975.

118. Murayama Chijun (1931), Chosen no Fusui [Korean Geomancy] (Seoul: Chosen Shotofu, 1931), 265–275.

119. Anon., Sanga Yoram, 17.

120. Personal communication with a geomancer in Sangju-kun, North Kyong-sang Province, 7 January 1975. Informant's name withheld.

121. Interview with a geomancer at Mikimi, Modong-myon, Sangju-kun, North Kyongsang Province, 23 November 1975.

122. Interviews with geomancers in Korea, October 1973–February 1974.

123. Interviews with geomancers in Korea, October 1973–February 1974. Also see Murayama Chijun, *Chosen no Fusui*, 235–238.

Chapter 6
The Principles of House Geomancy[1]

The basic geomantic principles for an auspicious house site are the same as those for a gravesite. However, a house in Korea, unlike a grave, is part of a settlement, whether a village, town, or major city. Therefore, the selection range for a house site is much more limited than for a gravesite, which can be located anywhere with a suitable facing direction and landforms. A house site in a city or an agglomerated village is examined by considering the section size, building arrangement, and road patterns, which are more important than the surrounding landforms and watercourses.

The basic question in house geomancy is: How can one locate an auspicious house site and dwell there in harmony with the natural and cultural environment and thus extract benefits from the location? The following six considerations are the most important in house geomancy: selecting a favorable house location, choosing the direction a house should face, determining the spatial organization or form of a house, completing a surrounding fence, deciding what kind of person should live there and choosing appropriate plants, especially trees for a house section (garden). All five of these considerations are concerned with ways to achieve perfect harmony between humanity and the environment.

Selecting a Favorable Settlement and House Site

Theoretically speaking, the selection of a house site follows the same principles as the selection of a gravesite. As with a gravesite, a good settlement site requires four important mountains (the azure dragon, white tiger, black turtle, and red bird) and nearby watercourses. But a house or settlement site requires much more ground than a grave. When one intends to build a house in a settled area or planned town, the choice of sites is limited. Geomancers, however, still give much attention to the landforms surrounding the site. The geomantic principles to which one should give special attention when choosing a house or settlement site are probably best summarized by Yi Chung-hwan, a geographer during the Choson dynasty (Korea). In his book *Taengni-ji*, he says that geomancy is one of the four important factors that should be considered in the selection of a favorable settlement site along with economic conditions, traits of the people, and natural scenery. In examining a site, six geomantic aspects are especially important, according to Yi Chung-hwan:[2]

> How should the geomantic conditions of a site be examined? First, observe *Sugu*, or the mouth of a watercourse; then *Yase*, or the feature of the field; *Sanhyong*, or the forms of the mountains; *Tosaek*, or the colour of the soil; *Suri*, or the availability of water; and finally observe *Chosan Chosu*, the Homage Paying Mountains and waters.

As for watercourses,

> if *Sugu*, the mouth of the watercourse, is warped, organised loosely, empty, or broad, prosperity cannot be extended to the next generation even if the place has a lot of farm land and big houses on it. Those who live there will naturally disperse and disappear. Therefore, when people search for and observe a house site, they should look for a stream whose water discharge cannot be observed and a field enclosed by mountains. Although it is easy to find such a watercourse in a mountainous area, it is not easy to find it in a plain. . . . Whether it is a high mountain or a low land (yin hill), if water flows nearby in a direction away from the place, it is auspicious.

Yi Chung-hwan says about the features of a field:

> Generally, humanity is engendered through receiving the Yang force. Since the sky is the yang light, a place surrounded by high mountains with only a small part of visible sky is not a good place to live. For this reason, a broad field is a beautiful [good] place to live. Here, the light of the sun, moon, and stars will always shine brightly with mild and moderate various weather conditions; wind, rain, heat, and cold. In such a place there would be many great people born and few diseases. [The place] which should be avoided most [in the selection of a place to live] is an area which has a late sunrise and early sunset due to the obstruction of high mountains in the four directions.

> If the spiritual light of the Big Dipper is not seen [in a place] at night, it always has a small Yin force. Yin force taking the ascendancy would results in many ghosts, inauspicious power [atmosphere] in the mornings and evenings, and people becoming ill easily. For these reasons, living in a narrow valley is worse than living in an open field. Low mountains surrounding a big field should not be called mountains. They are also called fields, because such areas are not cut off from the light of the sky, and the power of water flows distantly. In high mountains, if there is an open field, it is also a good place to live.

As for the forms of mountains,

> generally the best features of mountains are, as geomancers say, a high projection for an Ancestral Mountain and a beautiful, neat, clean, and soft appearance for a

Main Mountain. . . . The feature that one should avoid the most is an Oncoming Dragon [mountain range] which lacks vital energy due to the dragon's weak shape.

And as for the color of the soil,

Generally, in rural settlements, the soil should be firm in structure and fine in texture not only at the bottom but also on the edge of the water. This will result in cool and clean wells. These make the most ideal living conditions for one's livelihood. If the soil is red clay, black sand, gravely soil or fine yellow soil, it is considered "dead", and water from such soil will be unpleasant without exception. Such a place is not suitable for human life.

On the availability of water, Yi Chung-hwan writes,

Generally, humanity cannot live in a place with no available water. A mountain should have streams, then it can engender the mysterious transforming power of auspiciousness. The outlets and inlets of water flow should be in accordance with the principles [of geomancy]. Such a place is auspicious.

And as for homage paying mountains and homage waters,

if a Homage Paying Mountain is a rugged and ugly stone mountain, a tilted lonely hill [a shape caused by landslides], or a spying or thief mountain [suggested by the summit of a mountain partly visible behind a mountain range] . . . it is not a good place to live. If the mountain profile does not have a rugged and hateful appearance, it is an auspicious mountain. Homage Waters are also called Outer [distant] Waters . . . The oncoming waters should flow in the direction to meet the dragons [mountain ranges], to combine Yin and Yang forces and should flow slowly and with many turns; they should never flow in a straight line.

For these reasons, if you desire to build a house and pass it on to your descendants, you should select the location by observing the geomancy [of the place]. The above six factors are the essence [of the geomantic principles].

Thus, geomantic principles for a settlement site require the same landforms, directions, and kinds of water flow nearby as a gravesite requires. But the site needs to be situated in a larger area of flat land.

In choosing a specific site for a house within the confines of a settlement, it is difficult to fully consider the geomantic principles for cosmic directions and landforms. This limitation seems to have forced early practitioners of house geomancy to interpret and adapt the classical geomantic principles in the context of built-up settlements.

A Japanese scholar of architecture has aptly pointed out that a house site is auspicious if a section's front is lower than its back.[3] It is clear that this principle reflects the classical geomantic principle of landform conditions applied to a grave, cave dwelling, or settlement site: an auspicious site should back toward a hill with an open front. If a house section's back is slightly elevated, it acts as the background hills of a house site. If the section's front is lower than its back, it acts as the open front of an auspicious site, or *myongdang,* the bright yard.

In house geomancy, the road is considered to be a type of watercourse, because people and vehicles move through the roads just as water flows through a river channel. On sloping land, a road should be in the front or side of a house section, not behind, as water should flow in front of an auspicious site. If a house section is below the road, it is bound to have the front (road-facing) section higher than the back of the section, which is undesirable. This geomantic principle may reflect universal environmental values held by humanity. Even in the Western world, such as New Zealand, house sections above the road are considered to be better and more valuable than those below the roads.

A house section at a T-junction road intersection is considered to be bad, because its attacking force is equivalent to the eroding bank of a meandering river. In the geomantic evaluation of the land around a meandering river, the sites on the accreting bank side are considered to be auspicious, while the land on the eroding bank side is bad. A house in a T-junction road is in effect the same as a house on a dangerous eroding bank of a river and is inauspicious. Geomancers advise that an ordinary house in such a dangerous T-junction is inauspicious, as it cannot counter the eroding power (traffic flow) of the road. However, a strong government building or other public building with power in such a site would be able to counter adverse influence.

Choosing the Direction a House Should Face

The direction a house should face is probably more important than any other element in house geomancy. In the Northern Hemisphere, the most desired direction for a house to face is south, so it can enjoy maximum sunlight. Accordingly, a manual of house geomancy states that a house section with open space (an empty section) toward the south is auspicious.[4]

As noted, when choosing a house site the opportunities for considering the surrounding landforms are limited compared to choosing a gravesite[5] Therefore, when a house was planned on a section within a built environment, the direction in which the house would face was one of only a few choices open to a house designer (Figure 6.1). In considering the direction, geomancers use the term "sitting and facing directions," which refers to the Chinese term *zuoxiang* (*choahyang* in Korean). The term is composed of two elements, *zuo* and *xiang.* The Chinese character, *zuo,* literally means "to sit" or "sitting." In geomancy as practiced in Korea, it denotes the so-called *choa,* or "sitting direction," which is measured from the front to back of a house or grave. The Chinese character *xiang*, which literally means "to face" or "facing," denotes the Korean term, *hyang,* or the "facing direction"; it is the opposite direction of *choa*, the forward direction of a house or grave.[6] These two words are almost always used in the combined form *Choahyang.*

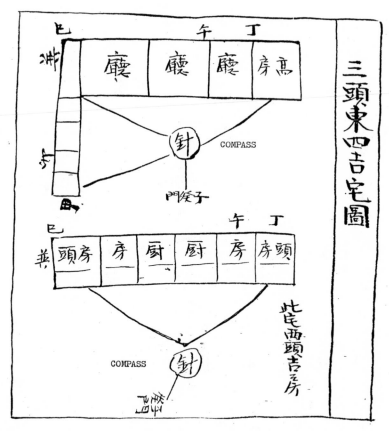

Figure 6.1 A drawing of a house with the various rooms labeled, and showing the location of the compass in the geomantic examination of the house. Adapted from Yangataek, Anon.

All houses are divided into two groups based on the sitting and facing directions: eastern four houses and western four houses. The former are called *Tongsataek* or *Tongsamyong* and the latter are called *Sosataek* or *Sosamyong*.[7] Apparently, for this classification of houses, geomancers used the eight principal directions based on the later heaven arrangement of eight trigrams in the *Yijing (I-Ching)*.

The sitting direction of a house primarily determines its classification. For instance, if a house has a sitting direction of *K'un*, or southwest, it belongs to the western four houses, but if it has a sitting direction of *K'an*, or north, it belongs to the eastern four houses. The grouping of houses into the two categories is as follows:[8]

Eastern four houses (with the Korean transcription)
   a. Chingung — Chen (east)

b. Songung — Sun (southeast)

c. Yigung — Li (south)

d. Kamgung — K'an (north)

Western four houses (with the Korean transcription)

a. Taegung — Tui (west)

b. Kongung — K'un (southwest)

c. Kungung — Ch'ien (northwest)

d. Kangung — Ken (northeast)

This directional classification used in house geomancy is illustrated in the following diagram (Figure 6.2):

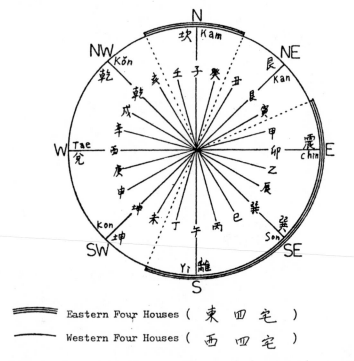

Figure 6.2 Directional classifications in house geomancy

As shown above, the names of the eight principal house groups (or eight principal house directions) are adopted from the later heaven arrangement of eight trigrams. In house geomancy the names and their directions are taken from the *Book of Changes*, or *Yijing.*

Why are the concepts of the eight principal directions of houses and the classification of houses into the eastern and western four houses important in house geomancy? The primary reason is that the facing directions of important house elements, especially the main gate and the main room, should not conflict with the directions of the eastern and western four houses but should be in harmony with them.[9] For instance, if the main gate faces the direction of the eastern four houses, the main room should also face in that direction, and vice versa. If the directions of the eastern and western four houses are confused in a house (that is, if the direction of the main gate is toward the eastern four houses), the house is very inauspicious and could bring harm to its inhabitants or cause bankruptcy.[10] This conflict of the eastern four house directions and the western four house directions in a house is the first situation to avoid in house geomancy.

Applying these principles, a geomancy textbook explains the luck and misfortune that can be caused by the combination of the directions of the main gate and the main room of a house:[11]

a. Northwest main gate and southwest main room—very auspicious. Both the main gate and the main room face two of the directions of the western four houses.

b. Northwest main gate and north main room—unlucky. The main gate belongs to the western four houses while the main room belongs to the eastern four houses.

Numerous other examples of the combinations could be mentioned. But suffice it to say that the direction of the various elements of the house is the most critical factor in determining its auspiciousness.

Determining the Spatial Organization and Forms of a House

According to the *Huangdi Zhaijing (The Book of the Yellow Emperor's Discourse on House Geomancy),* which may be the oldest Chinese textbook on house geomancy, there are five deficiencies and five fulfilling factors in the art. The five deficiencies are:

(1) a big house for few dwellers
(2) a big main gate for a small house
(3) an incomplete house fence
(4) a well in an inappropriate location
(5) a small house with a big garden on a large site[12]

These five deficiencies are related to undesirable qualities of a residence such as the feeling of emptiness, being dominated by size, a modest substance for a grand appearance, incompleteness, and an inappropriate location. These deficiencies may in part represent aspects of a house and section that are against the age-old Chinese ethical principle of humility. Any signs of "showing off" are considered inauspicious. Classical house geomancy recommends avoiding extravagant and overwhelming size and quality of a house or section. *The Book of the Yellow Emperor's Discourse on House Geomancy* states that if people live in a house with any of the above five deficiencies, they will suffer poverty.[13]

The Book of the Yellow Emperor's Discourse on House Geomancy also recommends five desirable qualities of a residence. These auspicious qualities are known as the five fulfilling (fruitful) factors:

(1) a small house for many dwellers
(2) a small main gate for a big house
(3) a completed house fence
(4) many domesticated animals in a small house
(5) a watercourse flow in the direction of southeast[14]

The book states that if a person lives in a house with one or more of these five characteristics, they will enjoy wealth and honor. The general quality of the five desirable features of a residence reflects Chinese virtues and is the opposite of the five undesirable factors. Humbleness, humility, and living as a member of a large family are especially emphasized. The second factor—a small main gate for a big house—may represent the classical Chinese virtue of humility, which discourages arrogance and encourages lowering oneself when presenting oneself in public. The principles recommend full or maximum utilization of a site; thus they encourage crowding. This probably reflects praise for the extended family system.

There are many other rules and restrictions on the spatial organization and design of a house site. As we shall see, for instance, when plants are planted within the boundary of a house, only certain types can be in certain areas of the house.

Once a house structure is decided upon, it should be harmonious with the surrounding houses, structures, and forms. In a built-up urban environment, the surrounding landscape of a house (including other homes) is, in most cases, artificial and human-made. The surrounding houses often act as natural landforms around an auspicious gravesite. For this reason, an auspicious house should not face any form that appears to "attack" the house.[15] If the surrounding environment of a house appears to protect and be in harmony with it, the house is considered auspicious.

Furthermore, when a house is built, it should have a good overall appearance and balanced structure.[16] If a house looks ugly or unbalanced, it is considered inauspicious. Thus, symmetry is very important in house geomancy.[17]

There are restrictions even in the use of construction materials. For example, a stud (or a post) should not be set upside down but according to the position of the living tree, and a beam should be a whole piece of lumber, not spliced.[18]

House geomancy requires maximum utilization of space and a harmonious balance between the house structure and its environment. Its principles probably developed from generations of experience building and living in dwellings.

The Necessity of a Completed House Fence

This geomantic principle may be key to understanding the nature and function of Korean house fences. Traditionally, cities in Korea have city walls, palaces have palace walls, government offices have office walls, and almost all private houses, whether mansions or humble cottages, have fences.

Presently, most houses in the city have high fences built of cement. Such fences may have been installed for the purpose of enhancing privacy and security against intruders. From the Korean War (1950–1953) until the 1970s, before current economic prosperity, most Koreans, including urbanites, lived in single-story houses. At one stage private homes were often surrounded by barbed wire on high cement fences. Although barbed wire on top of house fences has disappeared in South Korea, house fences built of cement block or red brick are still used. Private houses in cities invariably have a completed fence with a front gate. This practice is rooted deeply in classic house geomancy, although to a foreigner it may look strange or overly protective. Nowadays, the majority of Koreans live in high-rise apartment blocks built in the Western style with low-lying Western-type fences, often with hedges.

In rural villages, there are many humble but romantic traditional Korean fences around cottages that were obviously not built to keep out intruders. They are usually built with clay bricks or stone, and are neither high enough nor strong enough to keep intruders out (a person can easily climb them); they usually have no gates and a permanently open entrance. So why were they built? To fulfill a geomantic requirement: an auspicious house should always have a complete fence.

A house fence can be considered an imitation of the mountains surrounding an auspicious area in three directions. The fence acts symbolically as a miniaturized landform around an auspicious spot; namely, as the azure dragon and white tiger with the main mountain in the background. To keep auspicious vital energy inside a house, it is necessary to prepare a surrounding fence with an open entrance, according to the principle of house geomancy. In rural Korea even the mansions of the rich often only have a poor *saripmun*, or simple entrance, instead of a suitably majestic gate. Therefore, we can assume that Korean fences were not originally built for the prevention of theft. Although fences in cities are presently used for such purposes, they originally had a more symbolic and geomantic significance.

Deciding What Kind of Person Should Live in a House

Geomancers say that every person is assigned to one of the eight trigrams according to their birth year.[19] For instance, if a person was born in 1976 (the year of the dragon), they are assigned to *Ch'ien*; if they were born in 1977 (the year of the snake), they are assigned to *K'un*; and so on. In geomancy the name of the trigram representing one's birth year is called his *myongkung*, or fate determination. For example, the *myongkung* of 1976 is *Ch'ien*. This *myongkung* is very important in the selection of a house. The *myongkung* of the patriarch of the family should be harmonious with the sitting and facing direction of the house represented by the eight trigrams.[20] If a person whose *myongkung* is *Ch'ien* lives in a *Ch'ien, Kun, Ken,* or *Tui* house, the family can be in harmony with the house. But if he lives in a *K'an, Chen, Sun,* or *Li* house, disaster will come. This reflects the importance of harmony in house geomancy. The art requires not only harmony between the house structure and its environment but also between the house and its inhabitants.

Choosing Plants for a House Section

Trees and vegetation are also important in house geomancy. In Korea people were very enthusiastic about conserving certain types of vegetation in auspicious places where cities and houses were established. This practice was ecologically sound and contributed to Koreans' harmonious relationship with nature. They also planted trees on mountains that were auspicious but lacked lush vegetation. It is possible that geomancers advised them to reinforce the growth of vegetation in certain areas to make them more auspicious. In the *Koryo-sa* (*History of the Koryo Dynasty*), there is a story about the advice of a geomancer to plant pine trees in the Songak Mountains to reinforce the geomantic harmony of the area by increasing the lushness of the vegetation:

At this time, the Kamgan of the Silla dynasty, Palwon, who was a profound geomancer, reached Puso County [presently Kaesong] and was amazed by the beauty of the northern part of Puso-san in the northern part of the county. He sent his servant to Kang Chung to tell the people, "If you move the county to the southern part of the mountains and plant pine trees there, the rocks of the mountains will be hidden by the trees. If the rocks are thus hidden, a great man who will unify the three Hans [three Korean dynasties] will be born in the county." King Chung and the county people moved the settlement to the south of the mountain and planted pine trees in order to cover the rocks. They also changed the name of the county to "Songak-kun" [pine mountain].[21]

There is no way to either prove or disprove the truthfulness of this story. It is undeniably true, however, that Songak-san was often "reinforced" by planting pines during the Koryo dynasty.[22] Even if the story is not based on a historical event, it illustrates people's attitude about the transformation of an inauspicious, poorly vegetated Tongsan (child mountain) into an auspicious, densely vegetated mountain for a settlement site.

Having suitable plants in a house section is also important in geomancy. This had a significant impact on the selection of plants for homes' yards. According to the principles of house geomancy in *Sanrim Kyongje* by Hong Manson, a certain kind of plant can only be planted in a certain quarter of the house site to create geomantic harmony. The book argues that:

1) Planting *jujubi* (date) trees to the west of the house will be beneficial to cattle. Planting them in the southwestern corner or to the south is good. Planting two *jujubi* trees in front of the main gate is also auspicious.

2) If weeping willows are planted to the east of the house, it will make cattle and the household prosperous. It is forbidden to plant a weeping willow at the gate or west of the house.

3) If an elm tree is planted in the back of the house, it is considered auspicious.

4) It is especially forbidden to plant peach trees around water wells.

5) It is suitable to plant a plum tree to the east of the house, but forbidden to plant one to the west, south, or north of the house.

6) It is forbidden to plant ginkgo trees in the east-southeast, but planting them to the north of the house is suitable.

7) Planting three groves of paulownia trees in the west-northwest and the north-northwest will result in an abundance of slaves, but it is forbidden to plant such trees directly to the north.

8) The lacquer tree is suitable for planting on inauspicious land that is fated to harm people.

9) Planting three groves of leguminous trees at the middle gate can guarantee wealth and respect for generations. It is said that planting this tree in front of the house can bring much auspiciousness. And planting it in the west-southwest direction can help avoid robberies.

10) The large yellow plum tree is suitable for the north of the house.

11) The mulberry tree is suitable for the east-southeast direction, but one should never plant it within the house fence.

12) The mountain mulberry is suitable for the west.

13) The Chinese plum tree is suitable for the south.

14) It is forbidden to plant the rose of Sharon within the house boundary.

15) Planting a pomegranate in the front garden of the house will ensure the birth of a good son.

16) The Chinese hazel is suitable for the north.[23]

The book thus advises choosing some plants for certain locations to suppress inauspiciousness, and planting others to extract the benefits of an auspicious direction or location.

According to house geomancy principles, plants can also compensate or substitute for the lack of auspicious geomantic landforms (such as the white tiger or azure dragon) around a house site. The best example can be found in the *Sanrim Kyongje,* which states that planting peaches and weeping willows to the east of the house, Chinese plums and *jujubis* in the south, pomegranates in the west, and almond and bullace trees (large yellow plum trees) in the north can substitute for the azure dragon, white tiger, red bird, and black turtle.[24]

Notes

1. A portion of this chapter is based on and has developed from Hong-key Yoon, *Geomantic Relationships Between Culture and Nature in Korea* (Taipei: The Orient Culture Service, 1976), 76-86.

2. Yi Chunghwan, *Taengni-ji* [Book of Choosing Settlement] (Seoul: Choson kwangmunhoe, 1912), 42.

3. Kiyoshi Seike, *Kaso no Kagaku* [The Science of House Geomancy], (Tokyo: Kobunsha, 1969), 44.

4. Kiyoshi Seike, *Kaso no Kagaku*, 48.

5. There were no cemeteries in Korea until the early part of the 20th century, the beginning of Western and Japanese influence on Korea. Theoretically speaking, the cemetery system is against the principles of geomancy.

6. Interview with Mr Chang Yongduk at Chollong-dong, Tongdaemun-ku, Seoul, 19 February 1974. Also see Chang Yongduk, *Myongdang-non* [On Auspicious Sites] (Seoul: Emille Misulkwan, 1973), 111.

7. Kim Myongje, *Chiri Palsip Pal-hyang Chinkyol* [True Discourse on Eighty-Eight Geomantic directions] (Seoul: Samsin sojok, 1971), 372.

8. Kim Myongje, *Chiri Palsip Pal-hyang*, 372–376; Chang Yongduk, *Myhongdang-non*, 112-115.

9. Kim Myongje, *Chiri Palsip Pal-hyang*, 372–373.

10. Kim Myongje, *Chiri Palsip Pal-hyang*, 373.

11. Original source was not available. A modern source is Kim Sokyong, ed., Kim So-kyong, ed. *Kasang ui Kwahak* [The Science of House Geomancy]. (Seoul: Hyonamsa, 1972), 262–315.

12. Anonymous, *Huangdi Zhaijing* [The Book of the Yellow Emperor's Discourse on House Geomancy]. 5th case, vol. 49 of Chongwen shuju huikeshu (Wuch'ang City: Hubei Ch'ung-wen Shu-chu, 1887) 3.

13. Anonymous, Huangdi Zhaijing, 3.

14. Anonymous. *Huangdi Zhaijing,* 3.

15. Interview with Mr Chang Yongduk at Chollong-dong, Tongdaemun-ku, Seoul, 8 February 1974.

16. Interview with Mr Chang Yongduk. 8 February 1974

17. Interview with Mr Chang Yongduk 8 February 1974

18. This is a commonly held idea among geomancers. Also see Hong Manson, *Sallim-kyongje*. Handwritten manuscript: copy in the East Asiatic Library, University of California, Berkeley, 6.

19. Interview with geomancers during field trips, October 1973 to February 1974. Also see Chang Yongduk *Myongdang-non*, 116.

20. Interview with geomancers during field trips, October 1973 to February 1974. Also see Chang Yongduk *Myongdang-non*, 116.

21. Chong Inji and others, *Koryosa* [History of Koryo] (Seoul: Yonhi Taehakgyo Chulpanbu, 1955), 2.

22. *Koryosa*, or History of Koryo Dynasty, notes at least four different occasions of planting trees or protecting the existing vegetation in the fourth moon of 1035, the fifth moon of 1036, the second moon of 1041, and the second moon of 1106. See *Koryosa*, vol. 6, 2, 8, and 22, and vol. 12, 20;Hong-key Yoon, *Geomantic Relationships,* 119.

23. Hong Manson, *Sallim-kyongje,* 23–24.

24. Hong Manson, *Sallim-kyongje,* 24.

Chapter 7
Grave Geomancy and Grave Landscape

The impact of geomancy on the Korean grave landscape has been greater than that on houses, settlements, or anything else. For at least the last several centuries, grave geomancy has been more important and popular in Korea than house geomancy. Overcrowded cemeteries and the many new graves over mountains and fields are clear signs of the popularity of grave geomancy in Korea today. The rapidly expanding number of graves has been a serious social and environmental problem for a long time. In response, the Korean government and nongovernmental organizations have recently encouraged the cremation of corpses, and citizens have responded favorably. The city of Seoul reports that 57.1 percent of its deceased were cremated in 2002.[1] This rate has been increasing fast and was estimated to have exceeded 60 percent by 2005, for a gravesite is at such a premium and is hard for an average person to secure. However, even today many insist on the burial of their dead in a mountain slope of their home village or in a cemetery near their cities. In such cases, mourners often hire geomancers to find auspicious gravesites or to direct the correct positioning of the corpse in a grave pit.

Korean Grave Landscape

The Korean grave landscape is a geomantic landscape. Without exception, all royal tombs during the Koryo and Choson dynasties and almost all the graves of the common people then were located through geomancers. The typical grave of a common person, as shown in Figure 7.1, is a dome of grass-covered soil. Often a *sangsok*, an offering table made of stone, is placed before the grave. Many poor people, who of course cannot afford expensive polished stone tables, make their own with soil. In the final stage, they also make a small dirt bank to surround the site except for the front of the grave. This artificial encirclement may represent the important landforms of an auspicious place, such as the main mountain, azure dragon, and white tiger. The bank conforms with the principles of geomancy for the mountain forms required in an auspicious place. A rich noble person's grave may have additional objects before it, such as a stone monument and two guardian pillars, or *mangjusok*. A stele, or *pisok,* is usually a polished black stone with inscriptions of the dead person's biography or memorials to him.

Figure 7.1 A Filial Son of Korea Who Lived in a Thatched Hut Near His Father's Grave. The grave is located at the foot of a mountain: 1. grave, 2. monument, 3. offering table, 4. guardian pillar, 5. incense burner, 6. mourner. From Yi Pyongmo, *Oryun Haengsil-do,* 1859 Woodblock Print Edition, the Jangseo-gak Library Collection, Academy of Korean Studies.

The royal tombs of Korean kings of the Choson dynasty are more elaborate and luxurious. The royal grave mounds are several times larger than those of the commoners. The upper part of the tomb is a dome-shaped earth mound covered with grass, but the lower part is covered with stone slates that are sometimes engraved with auspicious icons. Some examples of such icons are patterns of clouds, the twelve zodiac animals, and wild peonies.[2] Within a properly set up royal tomb complex, there are various buildings such as the main memorial hall, the tomb keeper's office block, and a roofed shelter that houses the stele of the king. There are also stone objects in front of the tomb or the main memorial hall. They consist of a pair of each of the stone statues of the scholar-officer and army general, and a pair of each of the stone images of animals such as an elephant, lion, haetae (an omniscient Korean mythical beast), camel, and horse. These stone objects must have been established to serve the soul of the buried king as well as to guard and protect the tomb.

The Review of the Auspiciousness of a Gravesite After Burial

Geomantic principles for the choice of auspicious gravesites are documented in Chinese geomantic classics. The key geomantic principles and thought that form the backbone of geomantic art are based on the *Book of Burial,* or *Zangshu,* the classic geomantic text also known as *Zangjing,* which is attributed to Guo Pu of the Jin dynasty (263–317). The principles of grave geomancy are fundamental for selecting any auspicious site, not only graves but cities, rural villages, and house sites.

After the burial of a corpse at a geomantically qualified place, the conditions of the corpse after some years may show that the gravesite was not correctly chosen. It may therefore be declared a disastrously evil spot. Often descendants who were suspicious of the auspiciousness of their ancestral gravesite would call in a geomancer to review its auspiciousness. The geomancer would advise the descendants that the current site had some serious defects and recommend moving the grave to a better location. Of course, by dispensing such advice a geomancer could secure more jobs and increase his income. The moving of graves was also practiced by people who experienced family misfortunes, such as untimely deaths or natural disasters.

When graves were opened up for moving, the condition of bones and coffins was a critical measure of the geomantic quality of the site. Geomancers say that an auspicious gravesite will decay flesh but preserve bones in a good earthy yellow condition—that is, turn them to the color of gold.[3] If the bones were found in good condition, the site would be deemed auspicious and the bones would be returned to the same place. If the bones were in a bad condition—they had decayed, turned black, or been disturbed by tree roots—the gravesite was considered inauspicious and to be avoided. Some modern Korean geomancy textbooks discuss the signs of an appallingly bad gravesite. Two such works are *Myongdangron (A Discourse on Auspicious sites)* by Chang Yongduk and *Pungsu Chirihak Kaeyo (Introduction to Geomancy)* by Hwang Ilsun. Drawing on them, I have assembled the following most common signs of ominous grave conditions. If a grave showed any one of these signs, it was an inauspicious site to be avoided, and therefore the deceased merited reburial in a more auspicious site.

a. *Saengsi*, or living corpse

Saengsi refers to a corpse whose bones and flesh are preserved like a living body without decay.[4] A geomancer commented that this phenomenon, which is considered a mystery of land energy in Korean geomancy, occurs rarely, but does exist. *Saengsi* happens when the corpse is buried in soil of a permafrost state or cool ground with a constantly low temperature, producing a refrigeration effect.[5] This was probably considered inauspicious because undecayed flesh would prevent direct induction of vital energy to the bones, which are the medium for delivering auspiciousness to descendants.

b. *Pungyom,* or wind disaster

This term refers to a corpse that has "turned itself over" in the gravesite or a corpse that has "moved itself" away from the original grave pit. When a gravesite is located in a mountain that is shaped as if twisted by wind, a buried corpse can turn over by itself (this is called *Poksi)*; a contemporary geomancy master commented that when winds travel through a gravesite, the corpse moves away from the original gravesite (this is called *Tosi,* or escaped corpse*).*[6] Both conditions are inauspicious and would cause either an early death for the descendants or family members to run away from home, or even convicted family member on the run to avoid being caught.[7]

Poksi and *Tosi* are considered geomantic mysteries in Korea. A geomancer commented that such cases are rare but more frequently occur in soil fills or dead soil, (a landfill that is easily influenced by water), or on slopes.[8] He logically conjectured that soil movement below ground level at a gravesite might cause this phenomenon. It is a basic geomantic belief in Korea that landfill sites are bad and that making a grave in such a site with dead soil (deposited soil) is inauspicious.

c. *Suryom*, or water disaster

This refers to a buried corpse immersed in water.[9] This disaster could happen when a corpse is buried in a water table. Such a burial is considered so inauspicious that it will cause *Puwhang-pyong,* or disease among descendants.[10] *Puwhang-pyong* is known in Korea as a disease caused by malnutrition and starvation, and its symptoms are swelling and turning skin "yellow." It implies that descendants will suffer from chronic starvation for generations.

d. *Mokyom,* or wood disaster

This refers to a corpse being disturbed by the roots of plants. This kind of gravesite is inauspicious and will cause bankruptcy among descendants.[11] *Mokyom* can be divided into two categories. *Moryom,* or hair disaster, is a state in which the buried corpse is covered with hair-like plant roots.[12] *Mokgun,* or tree root disaster, is a state in which the corpse is covered with tree roots.[13] A geomancer insists that both *moryom* and *mokgun* are not products of roots that grow from surface vegetation, but of independent underground plants.[14] Although I had no chance to observe either such plants or such corpses, I assume that the roots are probably of surface vegetation around the grave. At any rate, any kind of vegetational invasion of a buried corpse is inauspicious. This is probably one of the reasons that people clear all vegetation around a grave except for grass.

e. *Chungyom,* or insects and worms disaster

This is a state in which the corpse is invaded by insects, worms, snakes, mice, or other animals. It occurs when a gravesite is dominated by yin energy that has coagulated in the gravesite.[15]

The invasion of *chachi-bolle* (a kind of bug) is a very common insects and worms disaster. I did not have a chance to observe the bug, but according to geomancers it is a very small parasite that feeds on the corpse.[16] It is said that geomancers often see the bugs when graves are opened to be moved to a better location. This kind of grave is so inauspicious that it is believed to cause leprosy or tuberculosis among descendants.[17]

f. *Hwayom,* or fire disaster

This refers to a state in which the buried bones turn black, as if burned in a fire.[18] I was told that in such cases the burial site is as black as the inside of a chimney. This kind of place is so inauspicious that it is said to cause mental illness among descendants.

These six types of signs are important indications of extremely bad gravesites that are to be avoided. However, they can only be seen when descendants open graves in order to move them to another location.

Grave Geomancy and Vegetation

The impact on vegetation of the practice of geomancy has been significant for grave areas as well as houses. As *Zangshu* instructs, a mountain poor in vegetation cannot be an auspicious mountain no matter how well shaped it may be.[19] To a geomancer such as Chang Yongduk, the quality and quantity of vegetation in an area is important for determining the quality of a mountain: one with thick vegetation is auspicious because the land has enough vital energy to support it.[20] Healthy vegetation around a cemetery is a geomantic requirement.

A Small Grove of Trees Around a Grave

By the later part of the nineteenth century, mountains near settlements in Korea had been fairly well cleared of trees by the woodcutters of commercial enterprises and peasants who collected firewood for cooking and heating. Since the turn of the twentieth century, the cutting of trees had accelerated to meet the increasing demand for firewood and lumber. In such denuded mountains and hills, small groves of big trees (mainly pines) can be found. These groves usually have one or more gravesites in the center. Several square feet around the graves are usually cleared and covered with grass; beyond the grass the area is surrounded by trees (usually tall pines) that have survived denudation. Most of these trees are preserved due to two geomantic considerations:

(1) People have tried to preserve trees around grave areas to keep gravesites from being barren and thus inauspicious.

(2) Trees surrounding a gravesite may act as a fence for the grave and keep out the wind. As noted, calm wind with surrounding hills is of prime importance in geomancy. In a denuded area, the trees surrounding a grave can protect it from winds and may help keep the grave calm. (These trees thus represent the miniature main mountain, the white tiger, and the azure dragon.) Theoretically, an auspicious gravesite should be located in a geomancy cave that is well surrounded by mountains with flourishing vegetation. Practically speaking, however, obtaining such a place in generally denuded areas has been very hard for common people. Even if one could find such a place, it would not have been possible to keep the whole geomantic landscape covered with forest, because the demand for wood was so great. Therefore, most grave owners tried to preserve some trees around the grave as a final effort to save its auspiciousness. We can say that these small graves with nearby trees are monuments of the common people's efforts to keep the land auspicious.

Royal Graves and Trees

Powerful people, such as the royal family, were able to maintain large tracts of forested areas around their tombs. Just like the capital of the nation, the king's tomb was always placed in an auspicious place and carefully managed so as not to disturb the vital energy of the area. In the *Annals of the Choson Dynasty,* we can read of many efforts to keep vegetation undisturbed in the area of the king's tomb. For example, on the nineteenth day of the second moon of the twenty-ninth year of King Sejong (1447 A.D.), the king gave an order to reopen mountain passes near the royal tombs of Konwonnung, Chenung, and Honnung, because the closing of these roads had caused much inconvenience to the peasants who had farms in the vicinity.[21] The area of the royal tombs had been made sacred and was protected from disturbance by common people who would have liked to walk along the tract. This was done, of course, to keep the vegetation healthy through prohibiting the entrance of woodcutters, and by closing roads that interfered with the geomantic harmony of the tomb. Also, if a certain place with poor vegetation was chosen as a tomb site, this geomantic deficiency was corrected by planting more trees.

When a royal tomb was made, all cultural objects of people within the designated area, such as commoners' houses, graves, and cultivated farmland, were evacuated and no people were allowed to live there. The tomb guarding officer enforced the prohibition of farming and grazing within the royal tomb area. Anyone who disturbed the area (for example, with tilling or grazing) could be punished by up to 100 strokes of caning, and the local governor of the county or province of the tomb was liable for dismissal.[22] This relocation of people and the confiscation of their property were carried out to avoid disturbing the geomantic harmony of the tomb and to keep the tomb site auspicious by fostering the vegetation in a natural state. We mention here three instances of royal management of a tomb area as documented in the *Annals of the Choson Dynasty:*

1. In the second moon of 1444 (the twenty-sixth year of King Sejong), according to a geomancer's advice all graves in the geomantic area of a king's tomb, Hon-rung, were removed and the road to the west of the main mountain was closed.[23]

2. In the sixth moon of 1470 (the first year of King Songjong), farmlands in the outlying areas of a king's tomb, Yongrung, were returned to the people for cultivation.[24]

3. In the fourth moon of 1497 (the third year of King Yonsankun), the king allowed farmers to cultivate their lands in the area between the two peace mountains of the king's tomb, Son-rung.[25]

The compounds of a royal tomb, which were often comprised of several valleys covering hundreds of hectares, were acquired by the kings through the government requisition of land. The relocated peasants who had been evacuated from their home area sometimes appealed to the government for permission to till the land when it was not a very important part of the geomantic landscape of the royal tomb. This must be the reason, as some dynastic annals record, that the government returned some marginal lands to the people for cultivation. The following are two examples:

1. On the day of kehe in the sixth moon of 1400 . . . Ku Chikwan returned from Yongrung [the tomb of King Sejong] and reported [to the king] that the abandoned farmland of the outlying foothills of the western mountains of the tomb, the northern foothills of the Main Mountain, the outlying foothills of the Azure Dragon and the outside of the Peace Mountain could be returned to the people for cultivation.[26]

2. On the day of kapo in the fourth moon of 1497, [the king] issued a decree allowing people to cultivate the rice paddies located in the area between the Inner and Outer Peace Mountain of Son-rung [a king's tomb] and to pile up earth [soil] and plant trees at the outside of the Inner Peace Mountain foothills in order to prevent [the farmers'] invasion of the land by [future] cultivation.[27]

In the second case, farming was allowed in an area distant from the royal tomb, the field between the inner and outer peace mountain. However, the extensive core area of the tomb compound, which was the inside of the inner peace mountain, was protected from the encroachment of farming. This was done by planting trees and marking the area with raised ground. We can infer that they were greatly concerned with conserving vegetation.

The Obsession With Grave Geomancy as Reflected in Koreans' Behavior

The interest of people in obtaining and occupying an auspicious gravesite has traditionally been very strong, since it was considered to be the most efficient means of extracting benefits through the bones of ancestors. Because preserving an ancestor's bones in an auspicious place was of such importance to Koreans, many unscrupulous people took advantage of this concern to collect ransom and carry out revenge, as in the following example:

> On 12 August 1916, some people reported to the police that the grave of the late Pak Yangnae in Chang-kudong Mountain, Nubong-ri, Kosong County, South Cholla Province was dug up. The lid of the coffin was broken, the skeleton was stolen, and the upper part of the coffin was filled with soil. It was also reported that a threatening letter was found near the grave. The letter said, "On the evening of August 18 bring 500 *won* to Kuji Mountain, Namwon County and then the skeleton will be exchanged for the money. If you call the police, the skeleton will be broken and thrown away." On that day, the police waited for the criminals, but they did not appear.[28]

Cases like this have been common in Korean history. *Chosen Bosei Ippan (An Overview of the Korean Burial System)* lists four similar cases.[29] However, there have been no recent reports of such crimes of digging up buried corpses from a grave and mutilating them.

The eagerness of people to acquire a gravesite is far beyond Western imagination. Throughout Korean history, there have been numerous conflicts and feuds among people over auspicious gravesites. As Chong Yakyong, a scholar of the late Choson dynasty, pointed out, about half of court litigations in Korea during the Choson dynasty were a result of the often fatal fights and assaults that had arisen out of disputes over geomantically auspicious gravesites.[30] A French Catholic missionary to Korea, C. H. Dallet, vividly recorded one bloody conflict over a gravesite:

> The law forbids anyone to dig up a corpse belonging to another family. Only the relatives [especially direct descendants] of the dead are allowed to dig up a grave. Some years ago, behind the mountain where a missionary was living, a rich merchant who had just lost his father found a burial place that he liked. Nearby were some tombs of a nobleman. The distance between the graves was legally adequate and the merchant would have been within his rights to bury there. But in Korea, the powerful usually have their way and the nobleman opposed anyone choosing a

site near his. But the merchant persisted in his effort [to bury his father's corpse there]. He secretly hired about a hundred resolute men to fight any resistance on the part of the guards, proceeded with the burial according to the rules and then left with his men around six o'clock in the evening.

The nobleman lived ten miles from the grave site and had already been there once in the morning [in order to prevent the burial]. When the nobleman heard about the "invasion" of his burial territory, he set out with 200–300 men, to put a stop to the burial, but he arrived a half hour too late. The mountain had been taken away from the nobleman. [His ancestor's grave had been invaded by the grave of the merchant.] However, he dared not touch the corpse which had just been buried. He set off in an attack on the merchant, beat up his followers, tied him by his hands and feet, and brought him to the grave of his father, while shouting as loud as possible. The poor man, half dead from fright and fear, started digging up [the grave]. Then, the others dug up the body, which was done in a matter of minutes. The merchant had to look for another burial place.[31]

This account exemplifies the Korean attitude toward grave geomancy: people tried to occupy an auspicious gravesite through every possible means and were ready to protect it at any price from outside interference. It was obviously more difficult for the common people to protect their graves than it was for the nobility, but the commoners used every means since it could well have been the only precious property they had. They may have thought that such a gravesite might rescue them from poverty in the future. Father Dallet also recorded the following two events:

One day, some local county councillors wanted to bury one of their relatives in a place which was owned by a poor family. The head of the poor family, seeing that all his claims were useless, quietly attended the councillor's burial ceremony and even offered wine to the grave diggers who accepted it. Then, with great composure he cut flesh from his own thighs and offered bloody vessels [flesh] to finish up the meal. Upon learning about these facts and hearing the complaints of the poor families of the area against these county councillors, the local magistrate severely punished these councillors and made them dig up the body and return the grave area to the first owners.

Another time, a butcher who dealt in beef was deprived of his father's burial place by a very powerful nobleman who buried his mother in the same place, very near. The poor man [who was from the lowest class] did not resist, but helped with the ceremony and he asked to be the guardian of the tomb as a reward of his good will. After some days, he planted a hedge between the two corpses. The noble man, while paying his usual visit to his mother's grave, asked [the butcher] for some explanation. "I had to act this way, but it is impossible to tell you the reason, even if I must die," answered the guard. The noble man was very much intrigued and flattered him, assuring him that nothing would happen. "How can I speak about such things," said the butcher. "Some nights ago, I saw the body of my father rise up and walk straight to the tomb of your mother—I dare not finish; but the next morning I planted this hedge to prevent such scandalous behaviour." The nobleman, half dead from shame, did not answer but the same night had his mother's casket removed and taken to another burial site.[32]

In the first of these two stories, the grave owner expressed his deepest resentment to the grave invader, the councilor, and his grave diggers by offering them the most sincere expression of one's filial piety to one's parents: one's own flesh. Of course, this was to be done discreetly without letting the parents know. People used to say that such sincere filial piety impresses heaven and cures sick parents. For the poor and powerless man, this self-mutilating form of passive resistance to the oppressor must have been a last resort in his attempt to protect his parents' grave.

In Korea people often moved their ancestral graves to new sites when they could find more auspicious places. But they seldom moved their homes for geomantic reasons. Their stronger interest in grave geomancy may have been largely for the following four reasons:

(1) The buried bones of ancestors without flesh were believed to absorb and induct vital energy more effectively from an auspicious site than the bones of a living man.

(2) The structure of a grave is simpler than a house, and it can be dug almost anywhere. Therefore, changing one's residence is more difficult than moving a grave. And, unlike grave geomancy, house geomancy is more concerned with the proper direction and construction than with the surrounding landforms. When a house is deficient geomantically, geomancers instruct that the short-comings be remedied by remodeling the house structure, floor plan, or interior design. Poor house geomancy can also be improved by rearranging the house's garden, changing the location of the gate, or reinforcing fences. On the other hand, as the structure of a grave is a simple earth mound, there is not much to change to compensate for geomantic shortcomings. Thus, people move it to a better place.

(3) Popular practices of grave geomancy may have been accelerated by so-cial pressures from neighbors. If the grave of a family's ancestor was located in an inauspicious place, the neighbors of the descendants would often exert pressure to have the grave moved to a better location. Such pressure was expressed through various forms of criticism. If the descendants did not move the grave, people would reproach them for "unfilial behavior." When the Western-influenced mining boom was at its peak and mining shafts had destroyed the geomantic harmony of many gravesites, a saying was created: "Because of a miner's hole, I came to be called a son of a bitch."[33] In other words, if descendants of a gravesite destroyed geomantically by a miner's hole did not move the grave to a more auspicious location, they were as low as a son of a bitch.

(4) Koreans consider filial piety one of the most important ethical principles. Most filial descendants would have buried the corpse of a deceased ancestor in an auspicious place without expecting to benefit from it (see Figures 7.2 to 7.5). Even the desires of those who expected benefits for themselves and their descendants may have been motivated by honest filial feelings, since having prosperous descendants was also considered a great blessing to deceased ancestors; if descendants are prosperous, they can offer good ancestral worship services for their ancestors.

Figure 7.2 Digging a Grave Pit. The grave is for a Korean woman who killed herself when her husband died. From Yi Pyongmo, *Oryun Hanegsil-do,* 1859 Woodblock Print Edition, the Jangseo-gak Library Collection, Academy of Korean Studies.

Figure 7.3 A Korean Mourner and Grave. A Korean illustration of a filial Chinese son who is digging a grave for a deer near his father's grave. From Yi Pyongmo, *Oryun Hanegsil-do*, 1859 Woodblock Print Edition, the Jangseo-gak Library Collection, Academy of Korean Studies.

Figure 7.4 A Korean Illustration of a Filial Son of China Crying in Front of His Mother's Grave. From Yi Pyongmo, *Oryun Hanegsil-do,* 1859 Woodblock Print Edition, the Jangseo-gak Library Collection, Academy of Korean Studies.

殷保感烏本朝

Figure 7.5 A Korean Grave and Landscape. The drawing is from a story of a filial son of Korea who was helped by a bird in finding a lost incense burner. From Yi Pyongmo, *Oryun Hanegsil-do,* 1859 Woodblock Print Edition, the Jangseo-gak Library Collection, Academy of Korean Studies.

Criticism of the Fanatic Exercise of Grave Geomancy

The obsession of Koreans with finding an auspicious gravesite was often expressed to an alarming degree Scholars belonging to Sirhak, or the Practical Learning School, in the seventeenth century criticized and refuted such fanatical practice and its lamentable consequences. Yi Ik (1681–1763), a major figure in Sirhak, wrote:

> The art of geomancy has constant additions and increasing complexities. People came to think that their fortune and misfortune depend on (the quality of their ancestral) graves. People who are obsessed with geomancy sometimes move their ancestral graves two or three times, because they fear that luck or bad luck are caused by the gravesites.

> Recently when Government minister so-and-so was the Mayor of Chonju city, he pleaded (to the king) to remove the crowded graves of commoners in the hills around Kyonggijon (The birth place of the royal family of the Choson dynasty), for those places have been people's favored burial sites for a long time. Then the central government granted the request. The mayor through his officers visited every opening of the graves before moving them and examined the degree of auspiciousness and inauspiciousness of the burial sites and the prosperity of their descendants. The result of the examination is that the gravesites belonging to the rich descendants are not necessarily propitious, while those belonging to the poor and suffering descendants are not necessarily inferior. Someone came to me and told me this fact in detail.[34]

Yi Ik showed that there was no relationship between geomantically auspicious gravesites and the prosperity of living descendants. His refutation of grave geomancy using survey evidence was almost as rigorous as contemporary scientific research.

Yi Ik also refuted another key geomantic principle: that vital energy is transferred from ancestors in graves to their living descendants. *Zangshu,* it will be recalled, explained this principle with an analogy: when a copper mine collapses in the west, the spiritual bell (made from copper from the mine) rings in the east, and when chestnut trees bloom in spring, chestnuts bud in the room.[35] Yi Ik wrote:

> If chestnut trees in the mountain are not affected by the spring time, wouldn't chestnuts in the room sprout [in the Spring season]? Even if the chestnut trees [parents] are cut down by axe or burned to roots by fire, wouldn't the chestnuts [children] stored in the room sprout, when the spring season arrives? [The fallacy of] the logic behind the relationships between the copper mine and copper bell is as the chestnut tree and chestnut.[36]

Hong Taeyong (1731–1783), another Sirhak scholar, also refuted the idea that vital energy is conveyed from deceased parents to living descendants, saying it was illogical and groundless by saying that I have never heard that when a criminal in a jail is suffering from unbearable pain (from torturing), the children at home suffered from corresponding pain from a bad disease.[37]

But despite the refutation of geomantic principles by Korean intellectuals, the fanatical practice of grave geomancy persisted, as did the resultant social problems. And now graves are scattered all over Korean mountains and forests.

Notes

1. <http://www.hani.co.kr/section-005000000/2003/03/005000000200303> (12 March 2003).

2. Kim Yongbin, "Pungsu sasang eso pon Choson wangnungwonmyo chosong kipop e kwanhan yongu [A Study from Geomantic Perspectives on the Construction Method of the Royal Tombs during the Choson Dynasty] sang, part 1. *Hankuk Chontong munhwa yongu* [Studies on the traditional Korean culture]. Hyosong Women's University, vol. 4 (1988), 45.

3. Interview with a geomancer at Sangju County, North Kyongsang Province, 23 November 1975.

4. Hwang Ilsun, *Pungsu Chiri-hak Kaeyo* [An Overview of Geomancy] (Seoul: Pakmun-gak, 1968), 34.

5. Hwang Ilsun, Pungsu Chiri-hak Kaeyo, 34.

6. Chang Yongduk, *Myongdang-non* [On Auspicious Sites] (Seoul: Emille Misulk-wan, 1973), 93.

7. Chang Yongduk, *Myongdang-non*, 93.

8. Chang Yongduk, *Myongdang-non*, 93.

9. Chang Yongduk, *Myongdang-non*, 91.

10. Chang Yongduk , *Myongdang-non*, 91.

11. Chang Yongduk, *Myongdang-non*, 92.

12. Hwang Ilsun, *Pungsu Chiri-hak Kaeyo* [An Overview of Geomancy] (Seoul: Pakmun-gak, 1968), 31.

13. Hwang Ilsun Pungsu Chiri-hak Kaeyo, 31

14. Hwang Ilsun, *Pungsu Chiri-hak Kaeyo* 31-32.

15. Chang Yongduk, *Myongdang-non*, 92.

16. Hwang Ilsun, *Pungsu Chiri-hak Kaeyo*, 32.

17. Chang Yongduk, *Myongdang-non*, 92.

18. Chang Yongduk *Myongdang-non*, 92.

19. Guo Pu, *Liujiangdong jiacang shanpen Zhangshu* (commentary by Zheng Mi) in Linlang Mishi Chongshu. Case 2. vol. 10, n.p. (1888) part 1, 21-23.

20. From an interview with Mr Chang Yongduk at Chollong-dong, Tongdaemun-ku, Seoul, 19 February 1974.

21. Sejong Sillok, vol. 115, 14.

22. Kim Yongbin, "Pungsu sasang eso pon Choson wangnungwonmyo," 4.

23. Sejong Sillok, vol. 105, 7.

24. Songjong Sillok, vol. 6, 14.

25. Yonsankun Ilgi, vol. 22, 32.

26. Songjong Sillok, vol. 6, 14.

27. Yonsankun Ilgi, vol. 22, 32.

28. Aono Yoshio and Kim Song-yol (1924), *Chosen Bosei Ippan* [Burial Systems in Korea] (Seoul: Iwa Matsudo Shoten, 1924), 80-81.

29. Aono Yoshio and Kim Song-yol, *Chosen Bosei Ippan*, 81-84.

30. Chong Yakyong, *Kukyok Mokmin-simso* [Criticisms and Advice on Governing the People, A Modern Korean Translation] (Seoul: Minjok Munhwa Chujinhoe. 1969), vol 2, 628.

31. Ch. Dallet, *Histoire de L'église de Corée* (Paris: Librairie Victor Palme', E'diteur, 1874), "Introduction," 141–142.

32. Ch. Dallet, Histoire de L'église de Corée, 142–143.

33. Yi Kyutae, *Kaehwa Paekkyong* [Hundred Scenes of the Enlightenment Period] (Seoul: Shintaeyang-sa, 1969), vol. 5, 44. It is assumed that this proverb was circulated in the southern part of South Korea around the last decade of the nineteenth century and the early part of the twentieth century. According to Yi Kyutae, people used to say that only after moving his ancestral graves three times to better gravesites that a filial son had done his duty.

34. Yi Ik, Songhosasol, vol. 9, "Insamun, Kamyojo (the section of geomancy)," from Choi Changjo, "Choson hugi sirhakja turui pungsusasang" [Geomantic thought of Sirhak Scholars during the later Choson Dynasty], *Hankuk Munhwa* [Korean Culture], Seoul National University, vol. 11 (1992), 495.

35. Guo Pu (1875), *Zangjing, neipian* [The Book of Burial, the inner volume], in Chongwen Shuju Heikeshu (Wuhan: Hubei Chongwen Shuju, 1875), 1.

36. Yi Ik, Songhosasol, vol. 12, "Insamun, Kamyosoljo (section on geomantic theory)", from Choi Changjo, "Choson hugi sirhakja turui pungsusasang," 496.

37. Hong Taeyong, Tamhunso, Naepyon (inner volume), vol. 1, "Poyu." From Choi Changjo, "Choson hugi sirhakja turui pungsusasang," 497.

Chapter 8
An Interpretation of Geomantic Principles

By analyzing geomantic principles and observing the practice of the art, we can determine some fundamental meanings of geomancy. Here I present my own interpretation of geomantic principles.

The Three Images of Nature in Geomancy

My discussion here endeavors to clarify the three basic concepts of nature in geomancy: magical, personified, and vulnerable. These three concepts embody the essence of people's geomantic interpretation and evaluation of their natural environment. Because geomancy is such an influential East Asian way of relating to the environment, the geomantic belief system underlies the East Asian image of nature, and the geomantic image of nature is the essence of the East Asian image of nature.

The Magical Image

In geomancy nature is perceived as a magical and mysterious being that can influence humanity either favorably or adversely. If people select auspicious sites and occupy them properly, they will enjoy good fortune. If they select and occupy inauspicious places, they will suffer misfortune. In geomancy this is the most fundamental way of interpreting nature in comparison with the concepts of personified and vulnerable nature. This magical image of nature is the foundation of the practice of geomancy and the reason for seeking propitious sites. In China, an example of this magical image was noted by the Western scholar J. J. M. de Groot. The city site of Chü-jung near Nanking was considered so auspicious that the town would produce an emperor and all its inhabitants would become mandarins.[1] A Chinese example of this image was applied to a gravesite at San-kang, Ch'ang-shan County in Che-kiang Province; it was so auspicious that a descendant of the buried person became a minister of justice.[2]

It is possible to document numerous Korean examples of the magical image of nature in geomancy. To take two: the site of Hyongok-ri village in Tanyang County in North Chungchong Province was seemingly so auspicious that many great men, including a prime minister of the Chosen dynasty, were born there;[3] and a place near Keryong Mountain in South Chungchong Province is deemed by geomancers an extraordinarily auspicious site that will eventually serve as the capital of the nation.[4]

Geomancers in Korea have evaluated almost all parts of their land for magical qualities. These evaluations are reflected in geomantic legends (oral tradition), geomantic textbooks, and manuals.

Why do people recognize nature as having magical power? Because of the vital energy that flows underground and influences people in mysterious ways.[5] The current of vital energy under the ground is the key to understanding the magical aspect of nature in geomancy, for places that concentrate and preserve vital energy are, of course, auspicious, while others are inauspicious. The function of the vital energy is to engender and support all living things. But it is not found everywhere under the ground but only beneath those places where geomantic harmony is established.

The Personified Image

The land that can offer magical blessings to humanity is usually perceived as a personified object. An individual component of a landscape, such as a mountain, as well as the entire landscape of an area may be perceived as an animate or inanimate object, such as an ox, a tiger, a dragon, a turtle, a boat, an army general, or a jade woman. They can either be auspicious or inauspicious depending on their pose. Beautiful, erotic, peaceful, majestic, or graceful poses of images usually indicate auspicious geomantic harmony, while indifferent, unloving, inharmonious, or ugly poses indicate inauspicious geomantic landscapes. For instance, the geomantic landscape of a dragon[6] flying into heaven is an auspicious place, but the geomantic landscape of a dead snake hanging on a tree branch is inauspicious.

It is unclear why landscapes are personified in geomancy. But every landscape surrounding an auspicious site is considered a functioning system that produces magical power to influence humanity. This function of geomantic landscapes came to be compared with functions of living organisms around people or artifacts used by them. Such comparisons may well be responsible for the personification. Depending on the personified images of the land, the quality of auspiciousness available to humanity can vary, although all of those blessings are more or less about the prosperity and happiness of the relevant people.

A landscape can be named after any object depending on how a geomancer perceives it. "In naming geomantic landscapes there are no restrictions," a Korean geomancer told me.[7] Innumerable names of birds, plants, or artifacts can be applied to landscapes. The following are some examples of the personified image of land listed in *Dili-Renzixuezhi (The Fact that All Humanity Must Know)*:[8]

(a) The geomantic landscape of a golden turtle descending to a field. This is an auspicious image and is located at the grave of an ancestor of Mr Yang of Chin-an, whose title was Wen Min Kung, at Mount Pai-ho (white crane) just east of the city wall of Chien-ning fu in China's Hunan Province. It is said that not many years after the grave was dug, Mr Yang obtained the degree of an advanced scholar and later became a high government officer. Several officers were produced among his descendants.

(b) The geomantic landscape of a sleeping cow. This is also an auspicious image and is located at the grave of an ancestor of Mr Chiang of Hang-chou, who was a government minister, at a place called Chiang-tou (the head of the river) in Hang-chou of Chekiang Province in China. It is said that after this tomb was built, Minister Chiang was born and several high government officers were produced amongst his descendants.

(c) The geomantic landscape of an ox chasing a cow. This too is an example of an auspicious image and is located at the grave of an ancestor of Mr Chen of Hsiu-ning, who was a government minister, at a place called Ninguan, Hsiuning of Anhwei Province in China. It is said that after the tomb was built, Mr Chen, who became a minister of war, was born and his son became a minister of ceremonies.

The famous *Toson Pikyol (Master Toson's Secret Know-How)* lists 87 different geomantic images of land, and Murayam Jijun tabulated 174 different names of personified images of places from the 1929 Japanese colonial government's survey.[9] The following examples were provided by a rural geomancer from whom I learned some aspects of grave geomancy in Korea:[10]

(a) The geomantic landscape of a golden hen hatching eggs. This is an auspicious image of a place and is located at the grave of an ancestor of the Chong family of Tongnae-kun in South Kyongsang Province. It is said that after the grave was built, the Chong family became prosperous.

(b) The geomantic landscape of a jade woman with unbound hair. This is an auspicious image and is located at the grave of an ancestor of the Song family of Changryong at Nungpau, Naesongmyon, Sangju-kun. It is said that after the grave was built, the Song family became prosperous.

(c) The geomantic landscape of a dead snake hanging on a tree branch. This is an example of an inauspicious place, fated to harm humanity. A geomancer told me the following story, entitled "Master. Nam Sago and His Mother's Grave," in which this inauspicious landscape is mistakenly chosen by a famous geomancer of the Choson dynasty, Master Nam Sago:

> Mr Nam Sago was a famous geomancer during the Yi (Choson) dynasty. When his mother died, he searched and eventually located an auspicious site which was

in the geomantic landscape of "A Dragon Flying into Heaven." He examined the place very carefully, since it was his mother's grave site. When he examined the locale, he saw that the place was certainly a geomantic landscape of "A Dragon Flying into Heaven," an auspicious type. Therefore, he buried the corpse there. After he finished the burial, he noticed some writing in the air; it said, "Why have you chosen an inauspicious site for the grave? This is a geomantic landscape of 'Overhanging Dead Snake on a Tree Branch,' and not a geomantic landscape of 'A Dragon Flying into Heaven.'" He re-examined the locale and realised that the site was indeed a geomantic landscape of "Overhanging Dead Snake on a Tree Branch," which was very inauspicious.

Since the geomantic landscape of "Flying Dragon" and "Overhanging Dead Snake" were similar, it is said that his error in selecting the site was caused by the sins his mother had committed during her lifetime. When his mother was preparing for her wedding, her servant burned the cotton stuffing for her quilt by mistake. His mother beat the servant to death. Such a criminal deed made her unworthy to be buried in an auspicious place.[11]

In geomancy the landscape must constitute a functioning system analogous to the objects that the landscape personifies. For instance, if there is an ox, there must be food in a trough. If the geomantic landscape is incomplete by lacking a certain landscape object, it cannot manifest benefits to humanity. Often people will construct buildings, artificial hills, temples, or a new market to complete the harmony of a geomantic landscape. One Korean legend goes:

There is a market called Chongchon-jang in Chongchon-myon, Kwoisan-kun, North Chungchong Province. This market was first established by Mr Song Chongsu, who was a descendant of a great Confucian scholar Song Siyol. Mr Song Chongsu moved Song Siyol's tomb to this place from Suwon, Hyonggi Province. The new tomb site was located in "the Geomantic Landscape of a Commanding Army General." The site, however, was lacking soldiers for the tomb (i.e., there were no natural figures which could serve as soldiers for the tomb-general). Thus, the geomancer advised Mr Song to provide soldiers in order to receive benefits from the auspicious place. Therefore, Mr Song donated 300 nyang of Korean money to establish a market before the tomb.

After the market was opened, the place served as a periodic market six times a month and the tomb thus had many soldiers whenever a market was organised. Thanks to this arrangement, it is said that the Song family became prosperous.[12]

Vulnerable Images

Animate and inanimate geomantic landscapes are vulnerable systems that can easily be destroyed or recovered by people who modify the natural landscape. By cutting off mountain ridges or changing the direction of watercourses, people can harm the flow of vital energy. Even simple actions like breaking rocks, drilling a tunnel, or creating a pass over a mountain ridge can ruin the smooth flow of energy. If this occurs, the harmony of the geomantic landscape is destroyed and the energy cannot flow and accumulate to benefit people.

The vulnerability of nature in geomancy is mainly based on the following three concepts:

1) Vital energy is vulnerable. As discussed, it is only a phase of Yin-Yang energy, and only when the energy flows under the ground is it vital energy. When it leaks out of the ground and ascends into the air, it becomes something else—a cloud, wind, or rain. Therefore, one should be extremely careful not to disturb the flow of vital energy and lose it. It is believed that the energy does not flow very deep below the surface of the ground; therefore humanity's modifications, such as cutting off mountain ridges or changing the direction of watercourses, can harm its flow.

2) Nature is vulnerable, since the vital energy stays only in a place with auspicious geomantic harmony, which can be disturbed easily by slight human modification of the natural landform.

3) Geomantic landscape is vulnerable, because it is a personified and functioning system that produces magical power. To those who accept nature as personified and functioning, it may well be perceived as vulnerable as a sailing boat in the sea and even a hungry cow in search of food.

Once the geomantic harmony of a place is destroyed by humans, the vital energy there is no longer available. What's worse, the place could be transformed into an inauspicious geomantic landscape that is fated to harm the people who use it. When the land becomes inauspicious, humanity is expected to suffer all sorts of misfortune, including epidemic diseases, fire, flood, and drought. People are thus careful not to disturb the geomantic harmony of an area. If a Westerner who was ignorant of geomancy tried to build a new railroad in the geomantic landscape of an ox by passing though the neck, this design would inevitably result in the destruction of the geomantic harmony of the place. The Westerner would hear serious objections to the project from the local people.

The destruction of geomantic harmony by inharmonious construction is well illustrated in a modern legend recorded by a local elder in Chochiwon, a small Korean town:

> Mr Choi Dalshik's house and its surrounding area at the back of the Chimsan village office in Chochiwon was an extraordinarily auspicious house site. About eight years ago, when a railway line was laid through the town, mountain ranges on the left and the right of the village were cut off. After the cut off area was flattened, the two arms of the auspicious place were broken. Since that time, the village has become poverty-stricken.[13]

Traditionally, a geomantic landscape is believed to be so vulnerable that a small amount of human interference with a mountain ridge, such as driving in an iron pile, can ruin the smooth flow of energy. If such interference occurs, the harmony of the landscape is destroyed. This is well described in the story of *The Mountain Ridge of Sonsan*:

> When Hideyoshi's soldiers of Japan invaded Korea, they set up camp in Sonsan for a time. A Japanese geomancer in the army unit observed the form of the

mountains and realised that the place would produce many great men and that Korea would be prosperous. For this reason, the Japanese geomancer advised the soldiers to burn an important place on the mountain in the back of Sonsan town and to drive in a giant iron piling. In this way he killed the vital energy of the mountain. After that time, strangely, no great men were born in Sonsan or even in the neighbouring counties.[14]

Thus, until a few decades ago people were reportedly roaming around the mountains of Sonsan County to find the iron bar.

A geomantic landscape harmed or destroyed by human interference can also be restored through human action. People believed that putting together broken rocks, pulling out an iron bar, relocating a road, remodeling a house to fit geomantic principles, building temples or pagodas in geomantically significant locations, and even chanting or praying could restore a once harmonized landscape. The story of "The Ancestor's Tomb of the Yi Family of Kosong" goes:

> An ancestor's tomb of the Yi family of Kosong is located in an auspicious place with a geomantic landscape of a "Reclining Cow." Six generations after the tomb was made, its benefits began to be effective for the descendants. For this reason high government officers visited their native town so often that the common people were forced to work to prepare for their visits. Naturally, this obligation caused them to complain.
>
> When a geomancer monk heard their complaints, he advised them to break a geomantically important rock at Ansan (The Peace Mountain). The form of the rock was food for the Cow. When they broke the rock, the Cow lost its food and eventually starved to death. No more of the tomb's benefits were available to the descendants. Therefore, the Yi family could no longer produce high government officials.
>
> Later on, when the Yi family realised what had happened, they put the broken pieces of rock together again and regained their prosperity.[15]

Koreans have attempted to rectify shortcomings in geomantic landscapes by means such as planting trees and modifying the channels of water flow. By doing so, they believed, they could make the landscape better accumulate vital energy in the geomancy cave and manifest benefits to the people. The image of vulnerable nature might have influenced them to establish more stable relationships with the natural environment by abstaining from frequent and drastic changes to it, and to be careful in their management of it.

Only Through Association With People Does an Auspicious Place Manifest Benefits

According to geomancy, the auspiciousness of a place cannot manifest itself to people until a person comes into relationship with the place by digging a grave or building a house on it. Only the person who occupies an auspicious place in a proper geomantic way can receive its benefits. On a larger scale, if a country has an auspicious place suitable for a capital city, the country cannot be prosperous unless that place became the site of the capital city. The benefits cannot be extracted from owning an auspicious place and leaving it idle. For these reasons, Koreans were eager to occupy auspicious places and often willing to pay high prices for doing so, including shedding their blood.

Auspicious Places Are Available Only to Good People: Ethics in Korean Geomancy

This is a particularly important concept of Korean geomancy. I met several geomancers on my field trips who mentioned the importance of being a good person to obtain a good place. They said that if a person had accumulated sins he could not find an auspicious place even if he were to stand on it! People believe that evil persons should not try to find auspicious sites since they will not appear to them. And even if an evil person were able to obtain an auspicious place, it would not only fail to manifest auspiciousness to him but would be ruined by him.[16] Numerous geomantic folk narratives emphasize the importance of being ethical in order to obtain an auspicious site and say that charitable and ethical men somehow can determine the correct geomancy cave in which to be buried.[17] Legends insist that a good person is somehow able to obtain an auspicious place.

Why Are Ethical Values Important in Geomancy?

Although people believe that geomantic principles are objective like scientific laws, their linkage with ethics is still strong. This linkage weakens their objectivity but gives geomancers an opportunity to rationalize incorrect prophecies. In other words, if an auspicious site does not produce benefits, they can say, it is because the person who occupies it is not a good person. The geomancy textbooks rarely mention ethical values in the selection of propitious sites, however, and people's basic attitude toward geomancy has been that its principles are objective. Generally, people have believed that if they occupied an auspicious location, it would manifest its merits to them regardless of their morality. One wonders whether the ethical element in geomancy was introduced and emphasized by professional geomancers to justify and defend their prophecies that turn out to be untrue.

As geomancers like to point out, there are numerous folk narratives about good people attaining auspicious places and receiving benefits from them. This idea is firmly rooted both among geomancers and the people who use their services. Good people are normally referred to as charitable or filial persons. The concept of charity is from Buddhism and the concept of filial piety is the cornerstone of Confucian ethical codes (see chapters ten and eleven on these concepts).

A scholarly geomancer told me that to obtain an auspicious site and receive benefits from it, both the person to be buried and the descendants who bury the corpse should have accumulated no evil deeds during their lives. Even a master of geomancy will not be able to choose an auspicious site for his mother who committed a grave sin when she was young. In the story "Master Nam Sago and His Mother's Grave", the geomancer mistakenly chose the inauspicious landscape of a dead snake hanging on a tree branch for his mother's grave, thinking that it was the auspicious geomantic landscape of a dragon flying into heaven. This mistake was partly due to the similar appearances of the two landscapes, although in a normal situation a geomancy master should be able to tell the difference. However, his mother's sin confused him when inspecting the landscape and led him to choose an inauspicious site for his mother's grave. His mother's sin not only prevented her from being buried in an auspicious place but also deprived her descendants of the opportunity to receive benefits from it.

A geomancer in Andong City recounted the story of "The Master Toson and the Spoiling of an Auspicious Place" in response to my question on the relationship between geomancy and ethics:

> The Master Toson learned the art of geomancy in China. On his return to Korea he met a young man who was tilling a rice paddy. When the exhausted monk rested nearby, the young man stopped tilling the paddy and approached him. When asked if he did not feel well, the monk replied that he was hungry. The young man gave the monk his lunch. The monk ate it all hungrily. After finishing the lunch, the monk asked the young man if his father was dead. He asked that because the young man was wearing a mourning gown. The young man told him that his father had died, but because he could not find an auspicious place to bury him, he buried the body temporarily until a good place could be found. The monk asked if he would be able to bury the body for good that night if he found an auspicious place. The young man said "yes." The Master Toson selected an auspicious place right away and they buried the body that night. Then, the monk predicted that the young man would marry within three days and be a very rich man within three years.

> The prophecy, however, was never fulfilled. When the Master Toson returned to the grave to check out the fulfilment of his prophecy, he found that there was not a single descendant alive to look after the grave. The family line had become extinct. He thought that he had mis-selected the site and was going to destroy his geomancer's compass [to terminate his profession as geomancer]. At that moment, a sage-elder appeared to him and said, "Don't destroy your compass, you selected the correct auspicious place. However, the grave could not manifest its benefits to the descendants because the person who is buried there committed homicide three times while he lived. Thus, you, Master Toson, have ruined only the auspicious place."[18]

In this story as in many other geomantic tales, the charitable young man was given an auspicious place but it could not manifest its benefits because of the deceased's crimes. A geomancer in Sangju told me, "If one has accumulated sinful deeds, it will more adversely influence one's descendants than oneself."

This idea shaped family relations in traditional Korean society. No matter what a person achieved in his life, his destiny (especially social status) could hardly be separated from that of his family. One's glory, failure, prestige, or responsibility to society was not just one's own but affected one's entire extended family. When one achieved something, the entire family shared the glory, while if one committed a crime the entire family (including later generations) felt the consequences. In the traditional Korean society, whenever one did something while away from one's family, the person was a representative of the family. Koreans have traditionally understood themselves not as independent individuals but as members of a family.

What Kinds of Ethical Values Have Been Important in Geomancy?

In geomancy, ethical values can be classified into several categories, some of which are emphasized more than others in tales and by geomancers. The ethical values discussed here are mainly derived from an analysis of Korean geomantic tales. Since geomancers usually cite folk narratives to elaborate on the relationship between geomancy and ethical values, tales become the best source for examining ethical values in geomancy. We can regard all ethical principles that appear in geomantic tales as expressing the real ethical values of Koreans of the time.

According to these folk narratives and sayings, the following are important ethical precepts of geomancy:

i) The Buddhist concept of charity

One of the most common ethical concepts in geomancy tales is charity, which is clearly derived from the Buddhist tradition. Charity to all poor living things, such as suffering animals or traveling monks, is especially emphasized. In many folk narratives, a person who offers help or charity to poor creatures is rewarded with an auspicious place, often by supernatural means.

ii) Confucian ethical codes regarding parent-child relationships

The three aspects of Confucian ethical codes—filial piety, parents' sacrifice for their descendants, and a married woman's attitudes toward her birth family—are important. Confucian teachings of filial piety were the single most important ethical code in traditional Korean society during the Choson dynasty, and continue to be so today. Filial piety, which is a one-way obligation to the parents from the children, functioned as the cardinal code of ethics that maintained Korean society. Despite its importance, it is less well represented in Korean geomancy tales than the other ethical codes.

Confucian teachings do not require that parents sacrifice for their descendants. However, in practice, parents often do so. This is for the benefit of the parents themselves as well as for their children.

A married woman's attitude toward her father's family is that once she is married she becomes an integral part of her husband's family and leaves her own birth family. This attitude is found in geomancy tales in which a woman takes an auspicious site for her husband's family from her own birth family by tricking her mother and brothers.

iii) The principle of repayment in kind, or podap

The ethical principle of *podap* is emphasized in Korean geomancy. When one is helped or benefited by others, the ethic stipulates, he should pay them the correct reward; however, when one is hurt by others, he reserves the right to exact revenge. Geomantic tales about a charitable man's acquisition of an auspicious place through the help of a benefactor are good examples of the former idea, while tales of mistreated monks taking revenge by giving uncharitable people false advice are good examples of the latter. The legend "Returning Reward to the Master by Giving an Auspicious Place" excellently illustrates *podap*:

> Han Kwanggun's grandfather was going to punish a slave who disgraced his master. The slave, however, ran away. Therefore, the grandfather put the slave's wife in jail. The wife, who had with her a seven-day-old baby, cried all night. The daughter-in-law, who had just married Mr Han Kwanggun's father, was so charitable that she secretly released the slave's wife and son.

> After many years, the daughter-in-law became old and died, leaving two sons. The sons were very sad about their mother's death, but they could not acquire an auspicious grave site because of their poverty. In the meantime, a travelling monk visited them and cried for the deceased. He had come to attend his benefactress's funeral.

> He had become a monk and had studied geomancy in order to prepare to repay the benefactress by selecting an auspicious place for her two sons. Thanks to the benefit from the grave, Mr Han Kwanggun passed the government examination and his family became prosperous.[19]

The monk in this story was an extremely ethical person who devoted his entire life to preparing a reward for his benefactress. The concept of *podap* is such an important ethical value in Korean society that anyone who will not pay a reward to a benefactor is looked down upon. And if one does not have a chance to repay a benefactor, one should repay the benefactor's descendants. It is also taught that if one is not able to reward the benefactor, one's descendants should pay the reward to him as soon as possible. The responsibility to pay and the right to receive a reward can pass on and become a responsibility of descendants.

Repayment in kind also operates when one is hurt by others. One then has the right to pay a "reward" to the foe by avenging himself. The story of "Dotgoge (Hill)" is a good example: the monk who was beaten took revenge on his assailant by leading him to destroy the auspiciousness of the grave.[20]

The concept of *podap* certainly corresponds to the concept of *pao,* or payback, in China, and to *on* and *giri* ("being benefited" and "obligations") in Japan. Therefore, we may assume that the Korean concept *podap* and the Japanese concepts *on* and *giri* are derived from the Chinese concept of *pao.*

iv) Cheating and tricks

According to many tales, playing tricks and cheating were not considered as sinful or evil in traditional Korean society as they were in Christian or Confucian societies. Even the story of "The Grave of the Yu Family of Andong,"[21] which reveals a strong Confucian influence, tells of a girl cheating her family and playing tricks by pouring water onto the proposed gravesite for her father to obtain the auspicious place. This girl is not described as a bad woman. In another story, "The Grave of the Crop Keeper Old Lady,"[22] we see Mrs. Ho's trick of committing suicide to obtain an auspicious site. The tricksters, however, are not described as evil. In the following story, "An Auspicious Site on Yondok Mountain in Pukchong," another serious and more complex trick was played:

> There were two geomancers who were also friends named Mr Tong and Mr Chin. One day they found two auspicious grave sites, one of which was better than the other. They decided that the one who died earlier would be buried at the better site.

> Mr Chin was so anxious to obtain the better site that he killed himself and left a will asking his friend to choose the right direction for his burial. Mr Tong was so mad at losing such a good grave site that he tricked Mr Chin's son by asking the son whether he wanted a "direction of playing the flute" or a "direction having a man play the flute." The son told him that he wanted a "direction of playing the flute" and the geomancer determined the direction accordingly. Therefore, the auspiciousness of the grave came to be expressed as the production of many musicians who played musical instruments rather than as great officials who could enjoy the performance of such music.[23]

Each geomancer played a trick. By killing himself, Mr Chin obtained the auspicious place. But by posing a tricky question to the son of his friend, Mr Tong degraded the auspiciousness of the gravesite. However, no punishment for these tricks is suggested in the legend.

If folklore accurately reflects a people's cultural behavior, then playing tricks and cheating were accepted to some degree in traditional Korean society. As Wolfram Eberhard has observed, "both Chinese and Korean folk often played tricks without feeling guilty."[24] When we consider that Confucian ethics taught that people such as merchants were not of a desirable social status because they cheated people, we realize that cheating and trick-playing were certainly not part of virtuous behavior in the Confucian ethical system.

The Impact of Geomancy on Loyalty to One's Hometown

To traditional Koreans, the hometown and the family name were the two basic ways to identify one's social status. Therefore, no matter where one lived, one's family hometown (*kohyang*) hardly could have been separated from one's identity. People's social identity was in the beginning determined by their family line and hometown. When a person lived away from his hometown, his intention of ultimately returning was very strong. Such feeling is well expressed in the proverb "Even a tiger returns home when it is about to die."[25] The proverb has often been used by elders living away from their hometown to express their desire to return home. Why have Koreans been so loyal to their hometown? There are many reasons, including the following most important ones:

a. Villages were usually made up of one or more clans and were the only places where one could be completely accepted by the neighbors (villagers are very exclusive).

b. One's feeling toward ancestors and the importance of the family line, especially an honorable one, played an important role in encouraging one's love for one's hometown, for an individual's identity used to be framed first by their genealogical background.

c. The influence of geomantic ideas also encouraged such feeling. Villagers who lived at an auspicious place were proud of their home village.

Most villages are located in places that are said to be auspicious, but they commonly have some geomantic shortcomings that presumably could be a cause of unfortunate happenings. Since the natural environment of one village differs from that of another, some villages are assumed to be better than others geomantically. Those who live in a village with better geomantic qualifications than others are proud of it and more loyal to it. The story of "The Birth of Yu Soae" illustrates this:

> The mother of Yu Soae gave birth to the son thanks to the buying of an auspicious dream from her sister.[26] When the mother conceived him, she was staying with her father's family who lived in Sachon Village in Uisong County, which was said to be a very auspicious place. Since the village was auspicious enough to produce three great ministers of the nation, the villagers [all of whom belonged to his father's clan, the Kim family of Andong] decided not to allow members of any other clan to give birth in the village [in order not to lose the auspiciousness to another family]. Even daughters of the villagers were not allowed to give birth in the village, and so the pregnant daughters were prohibited from visiting their own birth families. When the mother of Yu So-ae became pregnant, she disguised her pregnancy by fastening her waist belt tightly. Eventually she was able to stay in the village until the time of birth. When she was going to give birth to the baby, the villagers were forcibly taking her out of the village. She, however, gave birth to the baby in the village forest before completely leaving the village.[27]

We can infer from this legend that the villagers of Sachon were proud of their home village and loyal enough to it to prohibit outsiders, including their own daughters who had married into other clans, from giving birth there.

The following story from "Kaehwapaekkyoong (Hundred Sceneries of the Korean Modernisation)," a journalistic essay on the Westernisation of Korea, also illustrates the impact of geomancy on people's loyalty to their hometown:

> Hyongok-ri village in Tanyang County, an auspicious place, is also called *Pumdal-chon* which means "the Village of Honoured people," because many great men were produced there. The great Confucian scholar, Wu Tak, and Yu Chokgi, a prime minister of the Choson dynasty, were born there. The villagers said that there were still auspicious locations in the village for producing such great men, and there were people who moved into the village for that reason. It became also the custom for daughters married to men of other villages to give birth to babies in their home village [at their father's home] with the desire of obtaining the auspi-

ciousness. They were not sure of receiving auspiciousness merely by giving birth there, so couples also visited the village to conceive a baby there. This custom continued until very recently.[28]

An Interpretation of the Geomantic Principles Governing Auspicious Landscapes

The Principle of Balance

We have seen that a harmonious relationship among the geomantic elements of a site is a critical factor in geomancy. No conflict or jealousy between elements of any kind is allowed. For example, there should be no conflict between the azure dragon and the white tiger, or between the black turtle and the red bird. All parts of a landscape should be shaped as if they have a desire to embrace the geomancy cave. Rejection of the cave by any part of the geomantic landscape means that the place cannot be auspicious.

A harmonious relationship implies a balanced and equal relationship, not a threatening and dominating one. Balance among the elements is necessary for harmony. For example, the form, size, and shape of the azure dragon and the white tiger must be proportionate to one another. The balance between Yin and Yang elements is very important. The following legend, "Mr Maeng Sasong and Vagina Mountain," illustrates this principle of harmony and balance:

> When a famous government officer, Maeng Sasong, came to Andong as the governor of the county [during the early Choson dynasty], he recognized many shortcomings in the geomantic harmony of the district. With his knowledge of geomancy, he set out to remedy the geomantic shortcomings of the region.
>
> In order to prevent the women of the county from being promiscuous, he planted many stone monuments of phallic images before a mountain which had a shape of a woman's vagina. The mountain in the back of Yongnam-san has such a form.[29]

Mr Maeng thought that the dominance of the female element of the area would cause immorality among the women of the county. It is a geomantic belief that the shortcomings of a geomantic landscape can be compensated or remedied through artificial means.

The Principle of Symmetry

The principle of symmetry is very much emphasized in geomancy. The symmetry between left and right, or between front and rear, is important in the organization of an auspicious place. So is that between the azure dragon and the white tiger, between the main mountain and the red bird, and between elements in a house structure.

The Principle of Beauty of Mountains and Waters

The principle of beauty of mountains and waters in geomancy reflects the Chinese concept of beauty in human beings. Generally, what Chinese or Koreans most desire in a personality is gentleness and graciousness. Even in conflicts with others, one should persuade with one's virtue rather than with one's power. The Chinese admired the personality traits of compromise and ability to concede in a gentle and gracious way.

The criteria for judging people's appearance are similar to those for judging their personality: to be plump, gentle, and smooth looking are considered better than the opposite characteristics. People prefer things that are smooth and have a round shape to those with sharp angles or corners.

My opinion is that the geomantic principles concerning mountains and waters reflect the Chinese and Korean criteria for a good personality, a beautiful appearance, and the preferred shapes of things. Through my field trips and analysis, I am convinced that auspicious geomantic objects should be gentle, gracious, smooth, and good looking. The appearance of ugly, sharp, and aggressive forms is considered inauspicious. For instance, the basic qualification of an auspicious mountain is beauty; qualities like "gentle" and "gracious" are especially sought (generally, rocky mountains do not qualify). A good watercourse should also be gentle and gracious.

Each Individual Component of a Landscape or the Entire Landscape Can Influence Humanity

As we have seen, geomantic principles clearly state that an individual geomantic component, such as a mountain or a river, as well as an entire landscape can influence humanity.[30] Folk narratives and sayings about these influences can be collected throughout Korea. Examples of such sayings include: if the azure dragon has two peaks, the descendants will pass the government examinations; if the white tiger looks fat, the descendants will be rich.[31] When a grave has a good azure dragon, it is also believed, the descendants of the buried person's sons will be well, but if the place has a good white tiger its daughter's descendants will be well.[32] As for entire geomantic landscapes, "hatching hen," "flying phoenix," and "reclining cow" can manifest benefits to the people who occupy them.

Sexual Connotations Behind Geomantic Principles

Murayama Chijun, in his book *Chosen no Fusui*, describes some kinds of Korean graves and comments on them as follows:

There are many graves in Korea which are considered to be influenced by belief in the reincarnation [of humanity] and by belief that the appearance of natural objects [i.e., a mountain or a landscape] can influence the fortunes of human beings. This is the case for graves which are located in the geomantic landscapes of "Virgin" and "Woman's Sex Organ". Needless to say, the desire to locate grave sites in such places originated from the belief that graves placed in locations which resemble the figure of a "Virgin" or "Woman's Sex Organ", can better guarantee reincarnation to the persons buried there. Generally, Korean graves, especially those located geomantically, are in places which resemble a woman's sex organ. Some are located in places which really have the form of a vagina. . . . Moreover, not only the outward appearance of a grave site, but also the internal structure of a site often has a form said to represent a woman's sex organ. Old tombs of the Koguryo and Paekje both have entrance ways and chambers for the coffin which clearly represent "a mother's sex organ ; the room for the coffin represents a mother's womb while the entrance way to the room represents the vaginal canal.[33]

This interpretation may well be based on sound information and reasonable judgment. It is questionable, however, whether the grave customs originated in the people's belief that the person buried would achieve a better reincarnation. Since almost all Korean graves are located and built under the influence of geomantic ideas, graves must have been made to accord with geomantic requirements. An auspicious site is surrounded by hills in the shape of a horseshoe or an armchair—basically a basin. Such a landscape may well represent the shape of a woman's vagina with thighs stretching outward. In reality, graves were geomantically placed in landforms resembling the shape of a woman's sex organ because such places were believed to be good for producing abundant auspiciousness to the descendants rather than because they were believed to be good for the dead ancestor's reincarnation. There is hardly any evidence to support the belief that the art of geomancy includes the idea of reincarnation.

After analyzing many aspects of geomantic principles, it is my conviction that not only do some Korean graves, as Murayama has commented, represent the shape and location of a woman's sexual organ, but the leading principles of geomancy themselves have sexual connotations. For example:

a) The use of the Yin-Yang principle of male and female in geomancy implies sex. All geomantic objects can be classified into yin or yang elements, and the balance between the male part and the female part is essential,[34] as reflected in the legend "Mr Maeng Sasong and Vagina Mountain."

b) As Wolfram Eberhard has suggested, even the Chinese name for geomancy, *fengshui,* which means "wind and water" in both Chinese and Korean, can indicate sex.[35] The association of the word wind (*feng*) with other words often connotes sexual behavior. *Pungryugaek,* which means a kind of playboy, is an example. A Korean phrase, "he generates wind (Gunom Param Piunda),'' means "he swings with women besides his wife." The Chinese character for the word "water" is often used with other words to describe sexual relations with women. A traditional expression, "a swallow which kicked water (a swallow after taking a shower?),'' was a metaphor for an energetic, beautiful, and erotic woman.

c) The shape of both the azure dragon and the white tiger developed from the main mountain resembles and is comparable to the location of a human groin with slightly spread legs. The location of the geomancy cave is comparable to the location of woman's vagina situated between the legs (see Figure 5.3).

d) As Eberhard has suggested, symbols for the four important landforms that surround an auspicious place—the turtle (warrior), bird, dragon, and tiger—can all connote sex.[36] Each pair—turtle and bird, or dragon and tiger—obviously represent male and female. The turtle is a male symbol, and turtle food is even believed by Koreans to be good for strengthening male sexual ability. The Chinese word for black turtle, the mountain behind an auspicious place in geomancy, is *Hsu'an-wu* (which literally means "black warrior") and suggests a strong male soldier. It is symbolized by the entangled bodies of a turtle and a snake. Perhaps to the ancient Chinese a turtle that has a popped-out head and a hard back shaped like a warrior's shield and a snake that has a penis-like body and head might well have been an important symbol of the strong male.

A bird is a female symbol. In Korea women are often compared with birds. If a group of women talk a lot, they are sometimes referred to as a "flock of sparrows." In geomancy, a good red bird (a mountain in front of an auspicious place) must be shaped as if "dancing in the air." This is comparable to a girl dancing before a strong warrior.

A dragon obviously represents male power. Both in China and Korea the Chinese character for dragon, *Yong (lung:* 龍), is mainly used for a man's name and seldom for a woman's. A tiger sometimes represents femininity, at other times masculinity. In the popular folktale in China and Korea, "Grand-aunt Tiger," the tiger is a woman.[37] In the Korean national foundation myth of "Tan'gun," the tiger is described as a female, for a bear and a tiger in the story both prayed and wished to be women. However, a tiger in China and Korea more often represents maleness for its bravery and strength. These four symbols may well represent the extremely strong sexual powers of male and female.

e) The appearance and location of geomancy caves (a metaphoric expression) are certainly comparable to the form and location of the human sex organs. The shape of a geomancy cave is similar to the mouth, groin, crotched legs, or breasts of a woman (see Figure 5.5). In general, the locations of geomancy caves are junctions of two mountain ranges (concurrent and anticurrent ranges), which are comparable to the location of the human sex organs in the groin of the human body.

f) The names of the four types of geomancy caves can be considered as having sexual connotations: cave (vagina), tweezers (groin), breasts, and projection (penis).

g) The desirable condition of soil in geomancy may well have sexual connotations. As we have seen, a good soil in geomancy must be fine in texture and firm in structure and should neither be soft, deposited soil, nor soil which has been dug by others. These soil conditions are comparable to the characteristics of a virgin. Burying a corpse in such a soil by digging a hole could symbolize the conquest of a virgin or her special attractiveness.

h) People's desire to have many children has been strong and they have often anticipated that the benefits of an auspicious place would include having many prosperous children. This may have sexual connotations. The geomancy cave is supposed to be located where all the power of an area is centered. The location can be comparable to that of the sexual organs of the human body. In comparing the geomancy cave with a woman's sex organ, we find a similarity between the two in terms of their functions. The geomancy cave is the only place where the benefits of underground vital energy can be made available to human beings while a woman's sex organ is the only place where a baby can be born. Both the geomancy cave and a woman's sex organ are places where the results or fruits of a process are produced. And having many prosperous children can, of course, be achieved only through sex.

An Early Chinese Idea of a Dynamic Environmental Cycle[38]

The most important geomantic classic of all time, *Zangshu (Book of Burial)*, presents the concept of an environmental cycle. Its basic tenet is that the Yin-Yang energy that is the essence of all environmental phenomena becomes wind, cloud, rain, and vital energy, and then returns to wind (Figure 8.1). This depiction is significant for two main reasons: it is perhaps the first record of a Chinese concept of an environmental cycle, and it suggests that the Chinese concept evolved from the practice of geomancy.

Zangshu says that "the canon" states that when vital energy emerges from the earth and becomes wind it disperses. The name of this canon is unknown. It may not refer to any specific book, since early Chinese writers often used the expression "the canon states" to lend power to their own ideas or to show humility and politeness. An old printed version of *Qingwujing* says that "the canon" referred to in *Zangshu* is *Qingwujing,* which was supposedly authored by Mater Qingwu (Master Azure Crow) of the Han dynasty and originally written earlier than *Zangshu*.[39] Indeed, *Qingwujing* said that as vital energy emerges into the wind it disperses.[40] However, it is a generally accepted view among scholars that Qingwujing may not date earlier than the twelfth century, and a Chinese scholar, Wang Yude, postulated that it was compiled during the Yuan (1279–1368) or Ming (1368–1662) dynasties.[41]

The author of *Zangshu* apparently did not intend to identify the complete environmental cycle, because the purpose of the statement in the book was to explain the nature of vital energy. That is probably why, having briefly established the evolutionary process up to vital energy, the author moves on to the main point of the introductory discussion: the nature and function of vital energy.

This ancient Chinese concept of vital energy resembles the modern concept of soil nutriment. The Chinese idea of an environmental cycle is somewhat similar to the concepts of a hydraulic cycle or an ecosystem, although it is not as sophisticated as these more modern Western concepts.

We do not know for sure whether the author of *Zangshu* was the first to write of an environmental cycle or whether he was employing an already established thesis. However, we do know that the early Chinese were well aware of the cyclical nature of physical phenomena including seasonal changes and the motions of the sun and the moon. They studied the circulation of blood in the human body more than 2,000 years ago.[42] Indeed, Joseph Needham remarks that, of the ancient cultures known to us, the Chinese were perhaps the most circula-tion minded.[43] Perhaps a further appreciation of geomantic literature may enable us to uncover more about ancient Chinese conceptions of the environmental cycle.

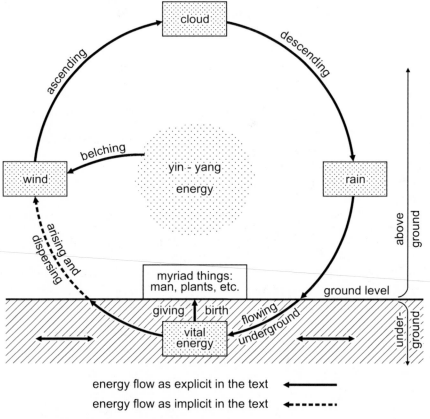

Figure 8.1 Diagrammatic interpretation of the early Chinese idea of an environmental cycle as discussed in *Zangjing (Book of Burial)*. Source, Hong-key Yoon, 1985, p.211.

Geomancy and Environmental Determinism: a Comparison[44]

Among the many ideas explaining the role of the physical environment in shaping human life, the concepts of environmental determinism in European culture and geomancy in Chinese culture highlight particularly well some key underlying issues. Although both concepts place strong emphasis on the role of the environment, they are very different in terms of their origins and development, their roles in their particular societies, and their perspectives on humanity-nature relationships.

In environmental determinism, humanity is largely subordinated to the environment, which is the shaping force. Nature (especially climate and landforms) influences and controls human behavior or culture. Probabilism and possibilism are softened versions of the idea of environmental influence. Griffith Taylor's "Stop-and-Go Determinism," on the other hand, is an example of strict environmental determinism, although it is much more sophisticated than the traditional version.[45] According to Taylor, humanity is not so much a free agent as a follower of the directions rather unalterably set by nature, and human beings, like the traffic controller in a city, are able to accelerate, slow, or stop progression along the "natural" route.[46]

The origins of such deterministic thought go back to travelers' observations of different peoples and environments, to medical theories of natural influences, and to religions that focused on elements in the environment as objects of worship.[47] According to Clarence Glacken, the main stimulus to the emphasis on environmental influence in the Western tradition was originally medicine (the Hippocratic corpus, in particular) and the school of thought developed along two lines, one physiologically based and one stressing geographic position.[48] These involved the empirical observance of health and disease among inhabitants, different psychological and physiological characteristics, and advantages and disadvantages of different environmental qualities for the location of settlement features, such as town sites.

Geomancy in China also evaluates the environment as it affects humanity. However, it involves a much more complicated system of location analysis and environmental planning than does the environmental determinism of the West. There seems to be no precisely equivalent concept of geomancy in European culture, nor can geomancy be subsumed under any one Western "category," because it is not simply a form of divination, superstition, religion, or science.[49] Geomancy is a rather complicated, quasi-scientific, quasi-religious Chinese art built on the concept that humanity can benefit from nature only when humanity chooses an auspicious environment and uses it appropriately. One environment is more conducive to fortune than others, according to geomancy, and nature provides environments ranging from highly auspicious to highly harmful.

Geomancy was probably developed by early humanity's response, especially by the cave dweller of the Loess Plateau, to local environments during the search for comfortable dwelling locations, and gradually evolved into rather complex principles for evaluating and selecting favorable sites.[50]

Both environmental determinism and geomancy focused on nature rather than humanity, and both envisaged the environment as the primary influence on at least certain aspects of human life. Both were based on the view that certain types of environments molded certain types of human destinies. Some places were undesirable, while others were beneficial for health and prosperity. In environmental determinism, however, the environment is conceived as qualitatively alien and external to humanity. Particular environmental qualities are seen as objectively existing quite apart from any human wish to change them. No matter what humanity may or may not do about it, the environment remains, in principle, an external force to which humanity should conform, since the basic patterns and directions set are not fundamentally malleable or reversible by human action.[51]

In geomancy, by contrast, the environment is not a completely autonomous force existing apart from humanity: both humanity and nature are different forms of expression of one underlying spiritual unity—Yin-Yang energy. Environmental influence is therefore responsive, for better or worse, to the way humanity uses the environment.[52] According to Chinese geomancy, the environment involves magical yet vulnerable forces, since the vital energy which manifests itself as "auspiciousness" is a delicate quality that can only be accumulated or flow through localities that have the appropriate geomantic qualifications. This vital energy is supposed to function mysteriously in the birth and sustenance of all living things, and every animate body, including that of humanity, exists as a particular concentration of that energy.[53] This manifestation of vital energy in nature and humanity is but one phase of the mysterious cosmic Yin-Yang energy that is continually and dynamically transformed into the multitudinous forces of nature such as blowing wind, ascending clouds, rolling thunder, descending rain, as well as the vital energy that flows beneath the ground.[54] If humanity disregards this unity, damage to the geomantic harmony of a landscape may result. The construction of a railroad that conforms to Western concepts of adjustment to the environment might be quite out of harmony with geomantic principles. The line might follow its natural route along a valley but destroy the local geomantic harmony. Awareness of geomantic principles may also enable humanity to improve the latent harmony of a local environment by countering any minor deficiencies through the addition of harmonious objects. A less auspicious environment might thus be converted into a more favorable one by a judicious modification of the surrounding landforms. But humanity is not allowed to create an auspicious environment by purely artificial means: the fundamental contours of the setting must be respected.

The dichotomy between humanity and nature inherent in environmental determinism does not therefore exist in the geomantic framework of thought. The Western environmentalist may describe humanity as "a product of the earth's surface,"[55] but humanity and that surface are never interchangeable.

Whatever their origins, they are characteristically presented as two different entities with a clear boundary and dualistic interaction between them.

In geomancy, by contrast, the boundary between humanity and nature is unclear. Since they express a common force, humanity can act as a natural object, complement the shortcomings of a natural landscape, and receive the energies of nature that are transmitted to people. Humanity is one with nature rather than against it.

Geomancy in East Asian culture and environmental determinism in Western culture conceive humanity-nature relationships in distinctly different terms and through different cultural lenses. Basic to Western attitudes toward nature has been the notion that either humanity or nature is passive in the relationship.[56] When humanity is passive, nature is active, and vice versa. For example, in the concept of humanity as a geographic agent, humanity is inherently active while nature is passive. However, in environmental determinism humanity is passive while nature is active. No matter how much Western thought may have softened the degree of determinism, relationships are understood in terms of external influence between two essentially different components. In environmental determinism the relationship is essentially uni-directional, a one-way influence from environment to humanity, whereas geomancy views the relationship as bidirectional and both humanity and the environment as part of a larger whole. Both are recipients of the common vital energy transmitted among materials that share the same quality or substance in their manifold appearances. Environmental influence is part of a system involving the transmission, conservation, and utilization of cosmic vital energy. Evidently, geomantic influences flow both ways, although the influence from environment to humanity may be much greater than the reverse.

Even if geomantic thought in East Asia understands nature as the prime active and determining factor, humanity is not perceived as simply a passive being adversative to the environment and subject to its control. Humanity is an active participant in the realization of latent humanity-nature relationships, correcting the shortcomings of natural landscapes and selecting auspicious sites for its activity. Unless humanity achieves a harmonious association with nature, the latter cannot manifest its latent auspiciousness.[57] Accordingly in geomancy, humanity and nature can both be passive and active at the same time. To obtain good fortune from the land, the selection of a good natural environment is essential. Koreans often believe that the birth of a great person is due to the auspiciousness of the place his parents lived or where his ancestors were buried, and people have been willing to pay very high prices for finding and occupying auspicious places throughout the millennia. In the humanity-nature relationship, according to geomancy, although humanity can select a place, it must adjust to nature first by finding a place that nature has provided and build things that fit into the geomantic harmony of the landscape.

In the analyses of environments, the criteria employed in geomancy are not necessarily the same as those employed by environmental determinism, as the latter has sought to interpret cultural and physiological differences and provide principles to guide the interpretation of data. But environmental determinism was neither institutionalized nor utilized as a guide to environmental planning (and certainly not for gravesites) in European culture. In a sense, the concept was more explanatory than directive.

By contrast, geomancy in China served as a most powerful and highly institutionalized system of environmental planning as well as a means of interpreting the divergence of culture in different places. It has left vivid records on the Chinese landscape, most particularly in the selection and design of tombs, temples, urban and rural settlements (including Beijing and Nanjing), and the graves of royal families and commoners alike. In this sense, geomancy has played a directive and regulatory role.

Naturally enough, both environmental determinism and geomancy are closely linked to the discipline of geography. At least in some times and places, environmental determinism helped shape the pattern of research in Western geography: indeed, the field was sometimes defined in terms of the search for environmental determinants. A well-known geography textbook during the early decades of the twentieth century, *Modern Geography,* written by the then-leading geographers from the Department of Geography at the University of Chicago, begins by contrasting "ancient and modern geography" as follows:

> Geography has been studied since ancient times, for people always have wanted to know about the earth on which they lived. . . . In olden times it was regarded as a description of the earth. It included an account of the countries into which the earth is divided, their physical features, such as rivers, mountains, and plains, and their inhabitants and products. Modern geography is concerned especially with the effects of physical features, such as land forms, water, and climate, on living things.[58]

In this book, published in 1913, "modern" geography was clearly defined as the study of the effects of physical features on living things, including human beings. This environmental deterministic approach dominated geographical research in the first three decades of American geography until Carl O. Sauer's landscape approach was endorsed.[59]

In China, geomancy and geography were also closely related. In fact, there was no clear boundary between them. This fact is well demonstrated by usage of the expression *dili*, which is still the only word for geography but which also serves as one of several terms for geomancy: *dilixiansheng* may mean either professional geomancer or geography teacher.

Environmental determinism and geomancy thus reflect some significant parallels and differences between European and East Asian cultures. Both view the environment as the force shaping human life, but they view the relationship differently. Both also assume a stable relationship between culture and the environment. But they are rooted in different perspectives on humanity, nature, and their relationship. Environmental determinism seeks to analyze the influence of nature on humanity, while geomancy seeks to comprehend the transmission of energy among natural and human phenomena that are essentially the same, despite the diversity of their surface appearances.

Notes

1. J. J. M. De Groot, *The Religious System of China*. vol.3 (Leiden: Librairie et Imprimerie, 1897), 1045.

2. Xu Shanji and Xu Shanshu, *Dili-Renzixuezhi* [The Fact that All Humanity Must Know] (Hsin-chu: Chulin Shu-chu, 1969), vol. 5, 13.

3. Yi Kyutae, *Kaehwa Paekkyong* [Hundred Scenes of the Enlightenment Period] (Seoul: Shintaeyang-sa, 1969), 81.

4. This is a well-known geomantic prophecy in Korea.

5. Guo Pu, Zangshu, in *Dili zhengzong* [The Cardinal Principles of Geomancy] commentary by Jiang Guo, (Shinchu: Chulin shuchu, 1967), 1.

6. The dragon in East Asia is an auspicious imaginary form of animal while in the West it is a dreadful and inauspicious one.

7. It is generalized knowledge among geomancers. Interview with Mr Chong at Sangju County, November 1973.

8. These three examples are from Xu Shanji and Xu Shanshu, *Dili-Renzixuezhi*, vol. 1, 14–15.

9. Murayama, Chijun (1931), *Chosen no Fusui* [Korean Geomancy] (Seoul: Chosen Shotofu, 1931), 260–275.

10. Interview with Mr Chong Changsop at Mikimi, Modong Myon, Sangju County, 23 November 1973.

11. Interview with Mr Chong Changsop, 23 November 1973.

12. Translated and abridged from Chang Yongduk, "Myongdang Chapki" [Essays on Auspicious Sites], *Hankuk I Ibo*, 23 February 1974, 6.

13. Translated and abridged from Maeng Uisop, *"Sabon Sokjokchong Tapsagi"* Handwritten report of a stone-piled tomb in Chochiwon, on the author's personal field survey in the middle of October 1964), written on 15 December 1964, 4–5.

14. Choi Sangsu, *Hankuk Mingan Chonsoljip* [Collection of Korean Legends] (Seoul: Tongmunkwan, 1958), 291.

15. Translated and abridged from Chugan Choson (Seoul), *"Pungsu Sipgang"* [Ten Lectures on Geomancy] 29 August 1971.

16. This information is based on two interviews: one with Mr Kim Songchan at Usijang (cattle market), Andong City, North Kyongsang Province, 16 February 1974, and the other with Mr Chong Changsop at Modong-myon, Sangju County, North Kyongsang Province, 23 November 1973.

17. Kim Myongje, *Chiri Palsip Pal-hyang Chinkyol* [True Discourse on Eighty-Eight Geomantic directions] (Seoul: Samsin sojok, 1971), 290.

18. From an interview with Mr Kim Songchan at Usijang, Andong City, North Kyongsang Province, on 16 February 1974.

19. Original source, Choi Yonghyon, ed., Silsa Chongdam, was not available. The story quoted here is translated from Chang Doksun (Duk-soon), *Hankuk Solhwa Munhak Yongu* [A Study of Korean Folk Narratives] (Seoul: Seoul Taehakgyo Chulpanbu, 1971), 253.

20. For the story of this legend, see page 194.

21. For the story of the legend, see page 202-203.

22. For the story of the legend, see page 204-205.

23. Chugan Choson, *"Pungsu Sipgang"* [Ten Lectures on Geomancy], 12 September 1971.

24. From private discussions with Professor Wolfram Eberhard at the University of California, Berkeley, during the spring of 1972.

25. This is a well-known proverb in Korea. See Choi Kunhak, *Sokdam Sajon* [Dictionary of Proverbs] (Seoul: Kyonghak-sa, 1968), 414.

26. The details of the auspicious dream and the agreement to sell have been omitted here, as that part of the story is rather lengthy and little related to geomancy.

27. From an interview with Yi Hyon (age seventy) at Kyongno-dang, Usijang, Andong City, 16 February 1974.

28. Yi Kyutae, *Kaehwa Paekkyong*, 81.

29. Interview with Mr Kim Kihyon (age seventy-six) at Kyongno-dang, Usinjang (cattle market), Andong City, 16 February 1974.

30. Interview with geomancers in Korea during field trips, October 1973-February 1974. See also Hyon Yongjun (1966), "Ammaejang ui Kaeson," *Chejudo [Cheju Province]*, vol. 27 (October 1966), 85.

31. Anonymous, Sanga Yoram, 11–14.

32. Interview with a Buddhist monk, Mr Choi Wonmyong, at Tae Toson-sa Buddhist Temple, Samgak-san Mountain, Seoul, December 1973.

33. Murayama Chijun, *Chosen no Fusui*, 214–216.

34. Andrew March said, "The sexual connotations of the Yin-Yang theory often become explicit, and the feeling of liveliness and diversity in the landscape is represented as the coupling of male and female elements." See Andrew March, "An Appreciation of Chinese Geomancy," *Journal of Asian Studies*, vol. 27, no. 2 (1968), 258.

35. A private discussion with Professor Wolfram Eberhard at the University of California, Berkeley, in fall quarter 1974.

36. A discussion with Wolfram Eberhard, as above.

37. For a comprehensive study of the story, see Wolfram Eberhard, *Studies in Taiwanese Folktales* (Taipei: The Oriental Cultural Service, 1970), 14–103.

38. The discussion in this section has developed from and is a modified version of my earlier article, Hong-key Yoon, "An Early Chinese Idea of a Dynamic Environmental Cycle", *GeoJournal*, vol. 10. no. 2, 211–212. I wish to thank my friend, Bikshu Hamwol, for discussion and comments on my manuscript for the GeoJournal version.

39. See Choi Changjo, trans., *Chong'okyong, Komnangkyong* (Seoul: Minumsa, 1993). 307 for the original Chinese statement in facsimile form and 17 for the Korean translation.

40. I read a copy of Qingwujing that is in Kyujanggak (the Choson dynasty Palace Library Collection, now a branch library of Seoul National Library). See Choi Changjo, trans., *Chong'okyong, Komnangkyong*, 23–24 for Korean translation and 303 for the original Chinese version in facsimile.

41. Wang Yude(1991), *Shenmide fengshui* [Mystic Geomancy] (Nanning: Guangxi renmin chubanshe, 1991), 127–129. Mr Wang's logical philological argument is translated into Korean in Choi Changjo, trans. *Chong'okyong, Komnangkyong*, 14–16.

42. Joseph Needham, History and Human Value: A Chinese Perspective for World Science and Technology. (Montreal: McGill University, 1975).

43. Joseph Needham, History and Human Value: A Chinese Perspective for World Science and Technology. (Montreal: McGill University, 1975).

44. The discussion in this section is a significantly revised version of my earlier paper printed in GeoJournal ; Yoon, Hong-key (1982), "Environmental Determinism and Geomancy: Two Cultures, Two Concepts", *GeoJournal,* vol. 8, no. 1, 77–80. I wish to

thank Professor Gordon R. Lewthwaite for his valuable comments and suggestions to improve on my original manuscript for the GeoJournal.

45. Gordon R. Lewthwaite, "Environmentalism and Determinism: A Search for Clarification," *Annals of the Association of American Geographers*, vol. 56 (1966), 1–23.

46. G. Taylor, Australia: A Study of Warm Environments and their Effect on British Settlement (London: Methuen & Co., 1947).

47. Clarence J. Glacken, *Traces on the Rhodian Shore* (Berkeley, University of California Press, 1967), vii.

48. Clarence J. Glacken, *Traces on the Rhodian Shore*, 80–82.

49. Hong-key Yoon, Geomantic Relationships Between Culture and Nature in Korea (Taipei: Orient Culture Service, 1976).

50. Hong-key Yoon, The Nature and Origin of Chinese Geomancy," Eratosthene-Sphragide, vol. 1 (1986), 94–98.

51. G. Taylor, *Australia*, 1.

52. Hong-key Yoon, *Geomantic Relationships*, 211–220.

53. Guo Pu, Zangshu, in *Dili zhengzong*.

54. Guo Pu, Zangshu, in *Dili zhengzong*.

55. Ellen C. Semple, *Influences of Geographic Environment*. (New York: Henry Holt, 1911).

56. A comprehensive study of these three ideas in the West from ancient times to the end of the eighteenth century is found in Glacken, *Traces on the Rhodian Shore*.

57. Hong-key Yoon, *Geomantic Relationships*, 131–151.

58. Rollin D. Salisbury, Harlan H. Barrows, Water S. Tower, *Modern Geography for High Schools*, American Science Series, (New York: Henry Holt, 1913), 1.

59. Carl O. Sauer, "The Morphology of Landscape," *University of California Publications in Geography*, vol. 2, 19–54.

Chapter 9
The Cartography of Geomancy

Throughout the long history of East Asia (China, Japan, and Korea), cartographers have produced numerous maps of various kinds, with the earliest extant Chinese topographic map dating as early as the first century B.C.[1] Although the rich Chinese cartographic tradition has been well documented, the contribution of geomancy maps to the history of Chinese cartography has been overlooked by modern scholars.[2]

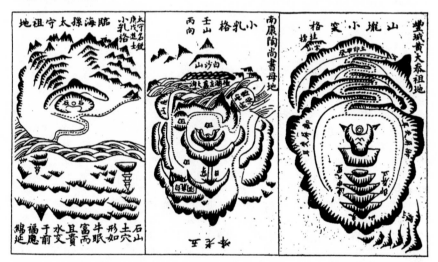

Figure 9.1 Three examples of geomancy maps, compiled from *Dili-Renzixuezhi (The Fact That All Humanity Must Know)* by Xu Shanji and Xu Shanshu (Ming dynasty), vol. 3, parts 1 and 2.

The geomancy map is a traditional map of East Asia that indicates an auspicious site and its facing direction as well as its surrounding environment, especially the mountains and watercourses (Figure 9.1). The topographic mapping skills employed in Chinese geomancy maps may well represent the most elaborate form of presenting land relief in the history of Chinese cartography until modern Western cartographic skills were introduced. This chapter introduces the unique characteristics of relief expressions in geomancy maps in China and Korea and argues that geomancy maps strongly influenced traditional Korean cartography in general. It attempts to document and explain how the traditional geomancy maps might have influenced the Korean topographic mapping techniques represented by Kim Chongho's Taedong yojido (The Whole Map of the Great Eastern Nation). Kim's map was the most developed form of traditional Korean maps using cartographic techniques adopted before the introduction of modern Western mapping techniques with contour lines.

To date only a few published works are devoted to the study of geomancy maps, especially those of Korea. My 1992 article in the *Cartographical Journal* must be one of the earliest works on geomancy maps in China.[3] I also wrote three articles on Korean geomancy maps and traditional Korean maps.[4] David Nemeth wrote several articles on geomancy maps from Cheju Island, Korea, and his article in *Cartographica* may be the most substantial report on Korean geomancy maps in the English language today.[5] Gari Ledyard's well-known 1994 work on the history of cartography in Korea may represent the most comprehensive account of Korean cartography to date in English.[6] But he discussed geomancy maps only briefly, and did not discuss the geomantic cartographic methods of relief expressions.

A Geomancer's Survey of an Auspicious Place and Geomancy Maps

Geomancy maps portray the surrounding landscape conditions of an auspicious site. By applying geomantic principles, geomancers carry out field surveys to determine such a site (see Figure 9.2). They use a geomantic compass to ascertain a favorable direction and sometimes rulers to measure length, though they normally only use rulers when placing a house in a section or a gravesite in an auspicious location. A draft survey that results in a geomancy map drawing is mainly based on eye measurement and impressionistic sketches of important landscape features. This is why the expression of landform patterns and scales are more accurate near the auspicious place and the accuracy diminishes quickly in places distant from a geomancy cave (the most auspicious site) on the map. The main purpose of presenting landforms (mountain ranges in particular) beyond the immediate one is to demonstrate how the auspicious location is situated in the surrounding landscape and how it relates to the ancestral mountain. Traditional geomancy maps in China and Korea are not based on a scientific survey in the sense in which a modern survey team would conduct one with sophisticated surveying equipment. They are generally sketch maps based on crude measurements with simple instruments. However, with a sophisticated Chinese magnetic compass the determination of orientation (direction) is accurate and the description of the shapes of mountains and hill as seen from the auspicious site is reliable.

The search for auspicious gravesites requires extensive field excursions, for gravesites can be in fields as well as mountainous areas. Often they are on foothills with background hills. The geomancers' field surveys were often

Figure 9.2 A geomantic survey team in action. This is a late Qing dynasty (1936–1912) illustration of selecting an ancient Chinese capital, Loyang, as recorded in Shujing, The Zhaogao section. In the illustration, the use of the magnetic compass by the master geomancer of the survey team is incorrect as the scene occurred more than a thousand years before the magnetic compass was originally invented by the Chinese. This illustration originally appeared in Ch'in-ting shu-ching t'ushuo (1905), and is quoted in a number of publications in English, including J. Needham, *Science and Civilization in China,* vol. 3, p. 362, and P. Wheatley, *The Pivot of the Four Quarters,* p. 422.

recorded in map form, many of which have survived. During the Choson
dynasty (1392–1910) there was much litigation among people over geomantically auspicious sites, especially gravesites.[7] Anyone who filed such litigation in
court would document the case in detail. The documents filed may have
included one or more geomancy maps describing the location and landscape of
the gravesites (see Figure 9.3). Court documents relating to propitious gravesites
were only some of the documents that employed geomancy maps. Others
included sales documents, genealogical books documenting gravesites of
important ancestors, and geomancy manuals and atlases of auspicious places
that were widely circulated in Korean society.[8]

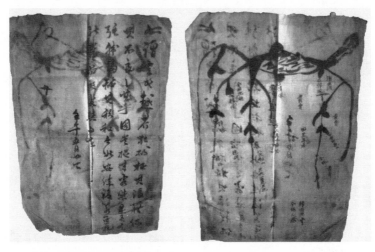

Figure 9.3 An example of Korean geomancy maps accompanied by litigation documents
in court.

Most geomancy maps, whether Chinese or Korean, adopted common symbols for mountain ranges, rivers, and geomancy caves. Geomancy maps in
general are in fact large scale maps that focus on auspicious grave or house sites
and their surrounding landforms. In most cases, professional geomancers were
the surveyors and cartographers. Some high-ranking geomancers were trained in
the royal institutes of geomancy in China and Korea, though most geomancers
became professionals through private tutorial lessons taken from a well-known
local master. Most extant geomancy maps in China and Korea are dated no
earlier than the Ming dynasty (1368–1644) and the Qing dynasty (1636–1912)
in China and the Choson dynasty (1392–1910) in Korea. For example, *Dili-
Renzixuezhi (The Fact that All Humanity Must Know)*, an important and popular
geomantic manual of China that includes a number of geomancy maps and
illustrations, was written by twin brothers, Xu Shanji and Xu Shanshu, during
the Ming dynasty.[9] Since the fifteenth century, many geomancy maps were

reproduced in different editions of various geomantic manuals as well as in atlases of auspicious places.

The Composition of a Geomancy Map

Chinese geomancy maps always mark the auspicious site (normally a gravesite or house site) with a small circle. Mountain ranges are usually most conspicuously featured and presented in the greatest detail, because they are considered the arteries of vital energy. They are symbolized by a solid black line marking the end of foothills and the beginning of flat land, while a serrated (zigzag) demarcation line represents slopes along the edge of mountain ridges, which are also black (Table 9.1). The mountain ridges and peaks are presented in more realistic shapes, but are mostly stylized to indicate one of the five mountain shapes a peak may belong to.[10]

Table 9.1 Symbols and their meanings in geomantic maps

SYMBOL	MEANING	REMARKS
◎ ○	Geomancy Cave	The auspicious site: sometimes the type of geomancy cave is commented in writing on the map.
	Peaks and Ridges	The shape of mountains, which often represents any one of the five categories (earth, fire, water, wood and metal types), as seen from the auspicious place.
	Upper Mountain Slopes	Slope pattern: the thicker the black area, the higher the upper mountain ridges.
	Shape of Foothills	The wider the white area, the gentler the lower slopes.
	End of Foothills	Transition between mountain and flat land.
	Small Water Courses	Smaller water courses including streams, creeks and small rivers.
	Big Rivers	Any sizeable river.
	Big Water Features	Indicating waves, or the scales of the water dragon. (River was sometimes referred to as the water dragon.) Great rivers, such as the Yangste and Yellow Rivers; wider river mouths, big lakes, and seas.

Source: This table of Geomantic Map symbols is compiled and interpreted by the author.

Geomancy maps usually present streams or smaller watercourses by the symbol of broken lines. However, bigger rivers are represented by a broken line with a solid line on one side or a broken line between two solid lines. Seas, lakes, and wide riverbeds like the Yangtse River are often represented by the symbol of fish scales, which can also be seen as the icon for waves. In geomancy, water is important for the preservation of vital energy in an auspicious place, as it is believed that the vital energy cannot cross water.

Besides mountains and water, some geomancy maps record the existence of boulders with Chinese characters for stone (石), and fields for agriculture with Chinese characters for farmland (田).

Geomancy Maps in Contrast With Modern Topographic Maps

To understand the characteristics of geomantic topographic maps, it is useful to compare and contrast them with modern Western topographic maps.

Center-oriented map

The geomantic topographic map is a center-oriented map. The focus of the map is the auspicious site and only the relief formations of the mountain slopes facing the center (the auspicious site) are presented. All map symbols and even Chinese characters that are inserted in such maps are positioned toward the center. This sometimes requires that the map be turned around to read these details. The nonvisible side of the slope is assumed to be similar to the visible slope in its shape (as shown in the cross-sectional diagram of a geomancy map in Figure 9.4).

Map symbol for direction

In modern Western topographic maps, there is normally a map symbol indicating cardinal directions, and it is assumed that the top of a map is the north and the bottom is the south. However, in a geomancy map, unless stated otherwise, the top of the map is assumed to be the front of the auspicious site, which normally faces southward (including southeast and southwest). Naturally, the bottom of the map represents the back of the auspicious site, indicating northward (including northwest and northeast). There is no map symbol indicating cardinal directions on the geomancy map. However, the specific direction that an auspicious place faces is sometimes noted in writing.

Points of perspective

In modern Western topographic maps using contour lines, the point of perspective is in the sky directly above the concerned landform. In the geomancy map it is on the ground at the auspicious site, which, again, is normally the approximate center of the map (see Figure 9.4). However, the point of perspective for watercourses is in the sky directly above the concerned watercourses, giving a modern orthogonal view.

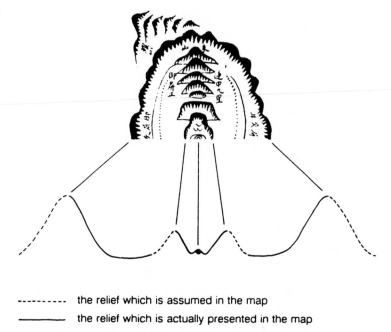

--------- the relief which is assumed in the map

——————— the relief which is actually presented in the map

Figure 9.4 A cross section of landform expressions (not to scale).

Map scale

Most geomancy maps are large-scale maps focusing on a specific location. This location usually covers a small catchment area or a small basin surrounded by sheltering mountains. No other traditions in Chinese or Korean culture may claim a richer heritage of large-scale mapping than geomancy.

The importance of mountain ranges

In geomancy maps, mountain peaks feature prominently, but their relationship to other prominent peaks or other mountain ranges is more important. Geomancers are so obsessed with the connections of mountain ranges that they sometimes slightly edit the weak connections or gaps between mountain ranges to make them look as if they are soundly joined together.[11] This is because the mountain ranges are considered dragons through which the auspicious vital energy flows. When the connection of two mountain ranges (or peaks) is not real, a geomancer might justify the weak connections or gaps by saying that the two mountain ranges are connected by a hidden dragon, which implies that a mountain range is hidden under the flat land. Therefore, geomancy maps often give the impression of being maps of mountain ranges encircling an auspicious place.

The origins of geomancy mapping techniques
    The origins of the mapping techniques of Chinese geomancy maps are yet to
be traced, but ancient China is certainly their source. We do not clearly know
when or how these unique mapping techniques evolved to the level presented in
the Ming dynasty geomantic manual *Dili-Renzixuezhi (The Fact that All
Humanity Must Know),* which may be the earliest work that includes a fully
developed geomancy map. These techniques may have developed from the early
Chinese topographic mapping techniques as seen in the Han maps during the
first to second century B.C. This is because of the sophisticated landform
presentation in the geomancy maps of mountain ranges (which specified the
peaks, slopes, and the end of foothills), which seems to be related to the crude
presentation of mountain ranges in the Han topographic maps.[12] However, the
relationship between geomancy maps and early Chinese cartography is yet to be
ascertained.

Korean Geomancy Maps and Traditional Korean Cartography

The geomancy map's important contributions to East Asian cartography need to
be re-evaluated. Korean geomancy maps originated from Chinese ones. That is
why most geomancy maps included in Korean geomantic manuals or litigation
documents are more or less the same as Chinese ones in terms of relief
expressions and other cartographical techniques. In terms of the cartographic
techniques, some Korean geomancy maps often represent simplified versions of
Chinese geomancy maps, such as the ones in *Dili-Renzixuezhi.* However, other
Korean geomancy maps deviate significantly from those in *Dili-Renzixuezhi.*
For instance, David Nemeth reports on three geomancy maps from "Yongju
sallokdo (Maps of Propitious Mountains on the Blessed Isle) used in Cheju
Island, Korea.[13] In these maps, all parts of the mountain ranges are colored black
without distinguishing mountain peaks from slopes and the ends of foothills,
although the types of some mountain peaks are shaped according to the five
mountain shapes in five elements theory. These Korean geomancy maps
represent simplified versions of their Chinese counterparts. In one of these three
maps, mountain peaks, especially those of fire mountain types, are clearly
described with pointed pyramid or flame shapes.[14] However, others generally
indicate the locations and situations of the mountain ranges surrounding the
auspicious places. Korean geomancy maps were very popularly used as a
method of documenting auspicious places and they stimulated the development
of unique Korean traditional cartographic techniques.
    The nongeomantic traditional Korean maps covering large areas (ranging
from a province to the whole of Korea) can be classified into two types: a
picture-style map featuring mountain peaks and rivers, but not mountain ranges;
and the traditional map with mountain ranges as its most prominent feature.[15]
The latter was more sophisticated than the former and held more practical values

for Koreans until modern surveyed topographic maps became available in the first two decades of the twentieth century. This type of map (referred to here as a standard traditional map of Korea) is more accurate and reliable than picture-style maps. An example of the standard traditional map is Taedong yojido (1965), which is so reliable that it is known to have been used by the Japanese army during the Sino-Japanese conflict in the Korean Peninsula toward the end of the nineteenth century.

The way that mountain and river patterns are treated in standard traditional Korean maps probably represents the influence of Korean geomantic ideas and geomancy maps. Although both types of traditional Korean maps described above are influenced by the geomantic worldview, those that feature mountain ranges are more strongly influenced by geomantic ideas and geomancy maps than those that don't. The influence of geomantic ideas and geomancy mapping techniques on traditional standard maps of Korea can be conjectured from the following points:

1. Mountain ranges as the main feature of relief in the map

Throughout much of Korean history, geomantic ideas have played a major role in conceptualizing landform features of places. As we have seen, mountain ranges are called dragons in geomancy because of their undulation. The features and directions of these dragons are critically important in geomancers' inspections because of the vital energy that is assumed to flow through the dragons. In their field surveys, geomancers give more attention to mountain ranges than to any other aspects of the landscape. As geomancers record their survey results by drawing a sketch map, their main concerns are the configurations and orientations of mountain ranges surrounding an auspicious site. Therefore, geomancy maps are naturally topographic maps with a special emphasis on mountain ranges.

The traditional standard Korean maps are also topographic maps with a special emphasis on the mountain ranges. As in geomancy, which argues that vital energy stops where a mountain range is disjointed or terminated, Korean standard maps have given special attention to the linking of mountain ranges. Where important mountains are not well connected, Korean standard maps often exaggerated the proximity—evidence, perhaps, of the influence of geomancy.

The importance of mountain ranges in a geomancer's field survey is clearly reflected in most geomancy maps that describe auspicious sites in Korea. These maps clearly describe how well the mountain ranges behind an auspicious site are connected. Taedong yojido (Map of the Great Eastern Nation) is the most famous traditional standard Korean map of all ages. When we compare this traditional map and geomancy maps, we find that there are crucial similarities in their emphases on mountain ranges and in the cartographic technique of representing those mountain ranges (compare Figure 9.1 with Figure 13.1). These similarities strongly suggest the influence of geomancy maps and the geomantic mentality on the cartographer, Kim Chongho, and on Taedong yojido. Taedong yojido exaggerated the key geomantic mountain ranges to give the impression of a sound connection between them. A Korean old map researcher, Yi Uhyong, commented that Taedong yojido boldly represented the key mountain ranges, even in a plain area, by exaggerating the height and feature of the range.[16]

2. Presenting Mount Paiktu as the ancestral mountain

According to the traditional geomantic worldview, the backbone of the world is Kunlun Mountains, which is in the western part of China. From this mountain range, several branch ranges spread out to the different corners of the world.[17] Among them, the eastern branch came into Korea, coming around Mongolia, to form Mount Paiktu, which is the ancestral mountain of all Korean mountain ranges. So to speak, all Korean mountain ranges have branched out from Mount Paiktu, and the vital energy of all auspicious places in the Korean Peninsula originally flowed out of this mountain. This geomantic view of the Korean mountain systems is well reflected in traditional standard Korean maps, including Taedong yojido. In them the features and running directions of the main mountain ranges are particularly emphasized. This type of map editing and map arrangement is quite conspicuous in traditional Korean maps showing the whole Korean Peninsula. This too suggests that traditional Korean maps were shaped by geomancy.

Not only geomancers but the public believe that Mount Paektu is the patriarch of the whole Korean mountain system. The main mountain range dispatched from Mount Paiktu to the southern part of South Korea is known as Paektu Taegan (literally, the Great Trunk Line of Mount Paektu). In this sense, geomantic perspectives permeated the general Korean mentality of cognizing landforms of their country and played a critical role in the conceptualization of their country's topography in general. The traditional standard Korean maps closely reflect this geomantic perspective of the Korean mountain system.

3. Crescent-shaped mountain ranges around townships

As noted, an ideal place for a propitious site is surrounded by a horseshoe-shaped range of hills or mountains. The most auspicious site (a geomancy cave) is at the foot of a hill in the central point of a surrounding horseshoe-shaped range. While many Korean settlements and royal tombs are located in geomantically auspicious sites chosen by professional geomancers, most are not sited in an ideal horseshoe-shaped landform, although they may have background hills. In traditional Korean standard maps, geomantically important sites of settlements and tombs were often edited and idealized to show a more perfect horseshoe shape for an auspicious site than the site actually had. This also suggests that the traditional standard maps of Korea were influenced by geomantic perspectives.

4. Changes in mountain range expression techniques in traditional Korean maps

In geomancy maps, the techniques of presenting mountain ranges are most sophisticated in the East Asian cartographic traditions. In the most important traditional Korean standard map, Taedong yojio, these techniques resemble those for presenting mountain ridges in geomancy maps. As in Figure 3.1, solid black-colored drawings of mountain ranges reflect the features (mainly height) of a mountain range through the varied thickness of the line. The portion of a mountain range that becomes the background for an important settlement is often marked with a serrated edge and the prominent peak of an important mountain range is rendered in a more detailed manner. The traditional Korean cartographic evolution and revolution reached its peak with the famous Korean cartographer-geographer Kim Chongho. He published several famous maps of Korea. Among them are the Chongkudo (Map of Green Hill) and the Tae-dongyojido (Map of the Great Eastern Nation); the former represented mountain ranges with repeated mountain peak shapes, while the later did so with a continuous black line of varying thicknesses to express different mountain heights. The technique of expressing a mountain range with repeating mountain peak shapes is a commonly used traditional Korean map technique of nongeo-mantic purpose. Using a continuous black line of different thicknesses is a much more sophisticated and advanced technique. In fact, the relief expression techniques used in Taedong yojido by Kim Chongho must have been the most sophisticated mapping techniques not only in Korea but in the whole of East Asia (including China and Japan) until modern Western cartographical skills were introduced. However, these new techniques may not necessarily be Kim Chongho's own original development but an adaptation of the traditional geomancy map technique, as a similar method of relief expression had long been used in geomancy maps to indicate height differences of mountain peaks in a mountain range. The oldest geomancy maps that used this relief expression method seem to be those in the famous Ming dynasty geomancy manual *Dili-Renzixuezhi,* which was widely circulated and extremely popular among Koreans. Geomancy maps in this and similar geomantic manuals perhaps drew Kim Chongho's attention and improved his relief technique as used in his Taedong yojido.

Concluding Remarks

Geomancers surveyed geomantically propitious sites and recorded their locations and surrounding environment as maps. These are traditional geomancy maps that often accompanied lawsuits arising from disputes over auspicious sites. Geomantic manuals and atlases of auspicious sites include numerous geomancy maps.

Geomancy maps show the development of unique and sophisticated mapping techniques. These techniques were originally developed from China, and Koreans adopted these methods with little modification, although some Korean maps show considerable variation from those of China.

Based on the close similarities between the Korean standard maps and geo-mantic maps, it is reasonable to assume that Korean maps were influenced by geomantic ideas and geomancy mapping techniques. The similarities are centered around the way mountain ranges are presented and the emphasis on mountain ranges and geomantically propitious places in traditional Korean standard maps.

A principal reason geomancy maps were ignored by East Asian scholars may be that they were not proud of the practice of geomancy, for it is generally considered a superstition not worthy of serious study.

Notes

1. China Pictorial (1974), no. 11, 40–41, and 1975, no. 9, 34–37; M. Hsu, "The Han Maps and Early Chinese Cartography," Annals of the Association of the American Geographers, vol. 68, no. 1(1978): 45–60.

2. For instance, the following works overlooked geomancy maps when they discussed the cartographical tradition in China: Zhongguo Kesueyuan Zirankexueshi Yanjiusuo Dixueshizu, *Zhogguo gudai Dilixueshi* [History of Ancient Chinese Geography] (Beijing: Kesue Chubianshe, 1984); Wang Yong, *Zhongguo dilixueshi* [History of Chinese geography] (Taipei: Shangwu Yinshuguan, 1968); and Joseph Needham, 1959), *Science and Civilisation in China*, vol. 2–4. (Cambridge: Cambridge University Press, (1959), 525–590.

3. Hong-key Yoon, "The Expression of Landforms in Chinese Geomantic Maps", The Cartographic Journal, vol 29 (June 1992), 12–15; Hong-key Yoon, "Chinese Geomantic Maps," in *Encyclopaedia of the History of Science, Technology and Medicine in Non-Western Cultures* (Dordrecht: Kluwer Academic Publishers, 1997), 570-571.

4. Hong-key Yoon, "The Expression of Landforms," 3-9; Hong-key Yoon, "Taedong yojidoui Chido chokboronjokin yongu (A Carto-Genealogical Study of Taedong yojido)", in Korean with English Abstracts, *Yoksa Munhwa Chiri (Journal of Cultural and Historical Geography)*, vol. 3 (1991), 37-47; Hong-key Yoon, " Taedongyojichondo Somunetaehan Yepikochal" [A Preliminary Study of 'The Preface' to The Whole Map of Korea]. *Yoksa Munhwa Chiri* [Journal of Cultural and Historical Geography] vol. 4 (1992), 97-107.

5. David J. Nemeth, "Bright Yard, Maps from Cheju Island, *Landscape*, vol. 25, no. 2 (1981) 20-21; David J. Nemeth, "Fengshui as Terrestrial Astrology in Traditional China and Korea", in James A. Swan, ed., *The power of Place: Sacred Ground in Natural and Human Environments* (Wheaton, Ill: Quest Books, 1991), 215-234; David J. Nemeth, "A Cross-Cultural Cosmographic Interpretation of Some Korean Geomancy Maps," *Cartographica*, vol.30, no.1(1993), 85-97.

6. Gari Ledyard, "Cartography in Korea," in J.B. Harley and David Woodward (eds), *The History of Cartography*: vol. two, Book two, Cartography in the Traditional East and southeast Asian Societies (Chicago: University of Chicago Press, 1994), 235–345.

7. Chong Yakyong, *Kukyok Mokmin-simso* [Criticisms and Advice on Governing the People, A Modern Korean Translation] (Seoul: Minjok Munhwa Chujinhoe, 1969), vol. 2, 628. For quotation, see chapter one.

8. A large number of such litigation documents are kept in the old Korean Palace Library, Kyujanggak Archive at Seoul National University, and I confirmed that many of such litigation documents accompany geomancy maps. According to a study, about half of the litigation documents kept at Kyujanggak Archive are cases relating to disputes over auspicious gravesites. See Choi Sunghi, *Hankuk Komunso Yongu* [A Study of Old Korean Documents] (Seoul: Hankkuk chongsin munhwa yonguwon, 1982), 20; Hong-

key Yoon, Hankukjok Geomentality e taehayo [On the Korean Geomentality. *Chirihak Nonchong* [Journal of Geography] vol. 14 (1987), 189.

9. Xu Shanji and Xu Shanshu, *Dili-Renzixuezhi* [The Fact that All Humanity Must Know] (Hsin-chu: Chulin Shu-chu, 1969).

10. For the shapes of the five mountain types, see chapter 5, Figure 5.5.

11. A good example of this case is seen in the Korean map of Taedong yojido, re-printed by Yi Uhyong (Seoul: Kwang'udang, 1990).

12. China Pictorial, no. 11 (19784), 40–41.

13. David J. Nemeth, "A Cross-Cultural Cosmographic Interpretation," 85–97.

14. David J. Nemet, "A Cross-Cultural Cosmographic Interpretation," 87.

15. Hong-key Yoon, "The Traditional Standard Korean Maps and Geomancy," *New Zealand Map Society Journal*, no. 6, (1992), 3.

16. Yi Uhyong, *Taedong jojido ui Tokdo* [Reading the Map of the Great Eastern Nation] (Seoul: Kwang'udang, 1990), 31 and 44.

17. Yang I, *Han lung ching*, in *Dili Zhengzhong* [Authentic Collection of Geomantic Principles]. Commentary by Jiang Guo, (Hsin-chu: Chu-lin Shu-chu, 1967), 1.

PART III:
GEOMANCY AND RELIGION

Chapter 10
Geomancy's Interaction with Buddhism

The basic doctrines of Buddhism and the principles of geomancy have developed separately without influencing each other. Buddhism developed from the Indian subcontinent and later spread to China. Key Chinese classical geomantic literature of geomancy before the introduction of Buddhism to China such as *Qingwujing* and *Jiangjing* (*Jingnangjin*) do not show signs of Buddhist influence. However, it seems that Buddhism and geomancy adapted to each other on the consumer level, forming a symbiotic relationship, as reflected in geomancy tales and in some geomancy manuals or textbooks written after Buddhism had spread widely in East Asia after the Tang dynasty (618–907). But even in the geomantic manuals that show signs of Buddhist influence on the practice of geomancy—for example, by commenting on the virtues of people seeking geomantically auspicious sites—there are no signs of Buddhist influence on basic geomantic principles, in terms of evaluating landforms, water, or cosmic direction. The general importance of the moral conduct of those who seek geomantically auspicious sites is only mentioned in the introductory and concluding material of these geomantic manuals. For instance, *Dilili-Renzixuezhi* (*The Fact That All Humanity Must Know*), written by the famous twin geomancers of the Ming dynasty, Xu Shanji and Xu Shanshu, lists charitable deeds as only one of ten general points of advice to those seeking auspicious sites through the practice of geomancy. These ten points are:

1. One should know (study) geomantic principles.
2. One should not keep a coffin without a burial underground for a long time.
3. One should not invade (interfere with) existing graves of ancestors.
4. One should not bury in a former gravesite.
5. One should not be involved in a sibling feud over the types of auspiciousness to be manifested (who will benefit the most) from the grave.
6. One should not shift a grave without careful consideration.
7. One should not indulge in finding an extraordinary quality of an auspicious site.

8. One should observe the qualities of earlier auspicious sites.
9. One should choose a good quality geomancer.
10. One should build up the virtuous deeds of charity (benevolence).[1]

The twin geomancers did not list charitable deeds as part of basic geomantic techniques. The author of *Dilili-Renzixuezhi* cited geomancer Choi's argument that accumulating charitable deeds is a basic condition for seeking an auspicious site.[2] However, this ethical consideration never entered these authors' discussions on the geomantic principles for the evaluation of landforms, water, and cosmic directions.[3]

In traditional Korean society the two key religions, Buddhism and Confucianism, have both had a significant impact on the art of geomancy. And geomancy, in turn, has had a considerable influence on them. The interrelationships between geomancy and these two religions are reflected in the religious landscapes of Korea. For example, in the process of constructing Buddhist temples and Confucian shrines, the art of geomancy was commonly employed from the initial stage of site selection to the final stage of building completion. Geomancy also adopted some of these religious institutions as a means of reinforcing or correcting the shortcomings of the geomantic landscape. The ethical values of these religions are also reflected in geomancy tales.

The interrelationships between Korean shamanism and geomancy have been significant and are perhaps best reflected in muga, the recitative epic chant of Korean shamans. In their muga, Korean shamans sometimes refer to the power of geomantically auspicious sites and often suggest that their clients shift their houses or graves to more auspicious sites to cure sickness or avoid misfortune. Sometimes people employed shamans to exorcize the shortcomings of their local geomantic landscape. Geomancy and shamanism in Korea influenced each other and embraced some aspects of each other's belief system.

The relationship between geomancy and Buddhism was more intimate and significant than that between geomancy and Confucianism. Many Buddhist monks came to be experts in the art of geomancy and were known as geomancer-monks. Most Buddhist temples built during the traditional period of Korea until the end of the Choson dynasty (1392–1910) were sited according to geomantic principles. Geomancers built Buddhist temples as a means of correcting or making up for shortcomings in the geomantic landscape, while a key Buddhistic precept such as charitable behavior was often considered in geomancy tales to be the necessary condition for finding an auspicious place.

Until recently there has been little attempt to examine the overall relationship between Korean geomancy and Korean Buddhism, although some works have investigated specific aspects of the relationship.[4] These aspects include the influence of geomancy on Korean politics, Buddhist temples and pagodas that were used for the reinforcement of local geomantic harmony, and Buddhist monks who were experts on geomancy.[5] However, scholars have generally evaluated specific aspects of the geomancy-Buddhism relationship separately, without considering either the overall relationship or how the specific relationships contributed to that overall relationship. This may be due to the fact that Korean scholars took the intimate relationship between geomancy and Buddhism for granted. I believe that understanding the overall relationship between geomancy and Buddhism is critically important in explaining specific aspects of the relationship, such as the placement of Buddhist temples in geomantically auspicious sites.

The conceptual framework for my research is represented in the following diagram (Figure 10.1).

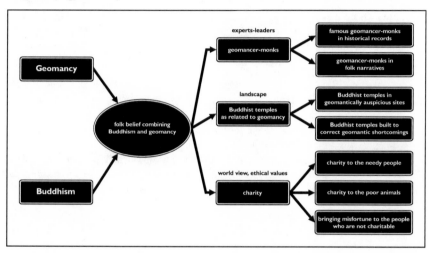

Figure 10.1 The conceptual framework representing the relationships between geomancy and Buddhism in Korea

This chapter aims to discuss the three most important aspects of the geomancy-Buddhism relationship. First, it looks at the relationships between the experts and leaders in the profession of geomancy (geomancers) and those in Buddhism (priest-monks), focusing particularly on the Pungsusung, a geomancer-monk who has practiced geomancy as a Buddhist monk. Second, it examines the relationships as expressed in the landscapes of Buddhist temples and pagodas that are associated with geomancy. Third, the chapter examines the relationships as expressed in their worldviews and ethos, focusing on the ethical value of charity as represented in geomancy tales. The overall relationship between geomancy and Buddhism is not limited to these three aspects, but it is my view that they form the fundamental elements of the relationship.

In addition to field trips to Buddhist temples and library work investigating historical records, I used folk narratives relating to geomancy as the main tools for researching this chapter. Because of their anonymity, the authors of folklore freely express their feelings and thoughts, while the authors of scholarly works do not have this freedom. The folklore material contains some of the best unedited raw information on people's behavior. Therefore, Korean folklore can be an efficient tool for learning about the relationship between geomancy and Buddhism in Korea.

The Geomancer-Monk: a New Profession
Combining Geomancy and Buddhism

Although many Korean Buddhist monks have also been experts on geomancy, the most famous was Toson (827–898), who is considered the father of Korean geomancy and the person who introduced geomantic re-enforcement techniques to improve the auspiciousness of landscape to Korea. Another prominent geomancer-monk was Muhak, who helped the first king of the Choson dynasty to shift the capital from Songdo to Seoul in 1394.

Master Toson, the First Korean Geomancer-Monk

Master Toson has often been quoted and his life discussed in various books of geomantic prophecies in Korea over the last thousand years or so. He became the catalyst in the blending of geomancy with Buddhism in Korea and the first well-known geomancer-monk. Since his time there have been numerous geomancer-monks, but no one can claim to be more important than Master Toson in blending geomancy with Buddhism in Korea.

There is no extant biography of Toson. Much of what is known about him is based on the stele of Toson-Sonkakkuksa (Sonkakkuksa-pimyong), *Annals of Toson (Toson kuksa sillok),* and orally transmitted legends about his life and work. Much of the information in these sources dates long after his death and is thought to have been heavily edited to present many of his deeds as mysterious and supernatural. These sources are not necessarily reliable or accurate. Among them, academics consider the stele of Master Toson-Ongyongja (Ongyongja-pimyong) the most reliable; it contains a relatively detailed account of his life.

According to the stele of Master Toson, Toson was born in present-day Yong'am, South Cholla Province, in 827 during the second year of King Hungduk's reign in the last period of the Silla dynasty. It is believed that he died in 898 during the second year of King Hyogong of the Silla dynasty.

There are several legends about the birth of Master Toson. According to one, one night in her dream his mother (from the Kang family) received a marvel, which is a jewel, from a person and swallowed it. [6] After this, she became pregnant and gave birth to Master Toson. When he grew up, he showed a strong interest in Buddhism and his parents allowed him to become a Buddhist monk.

According to another legend, a girl in Yongam found an unusually big cucumber in the vegetable garden and ate it. She then became pregnant and gave birth to Master Toson. This second legend is more widely distributed in Korea, but has two different versions: one from Yong'am, one from Hwasun (although the two versions share the same story plot). Here is an example from Yong'am:

Once upon a time Mr Choi had a fairly large farmland. In his vegetable garden, there was a cucumber, longer than 1 ja [about 30 centimetres]. People thought this was an extraordinary phenomenon. One day the daughter of Mr Choi ate the cucumber. [Some people say that the daughter of Mr Choi ate a cucumber that was floating down the stream, while she was washing clothes there.] After this, she became pregnant and in 10 lunar months time gave birth to a boy. However, the parents of the girl abandoned the baby in the woods in fear of neighbours discovering that their not-yet-married daughter had given birth to a baby. Seven days after that event, when the daughter of Mr Choi went to the forest to see what had happened to the baby, she found that the pigeons were protecting the baby under their wings. She reported what she saw to her parents. Her parents thought that this was an extraordinary phenomenon and they took the baby back and raised him. The baby became the Buddhist monk, Master Toson.[7]

In this legend, the birth of Master Toson is mythologized to a level similar to that in tales of some of the founders of Korean kingdoms. This type of mythical legend is usually found in accounts of heroes, suggesting that Toson was treated as a hero in Korean folk society. We know little that is definite about his life and work, but what is certain is that his life has been mythicised and his work has been exaggerated and glorified.

According to the stele of Master Toson-Ongyongja (Ongyongja pimyong), Toson left home to join the Hwaomsa Monastery in Wolyu Mountain at the age of fifteen and was ordained as a Buddhist monk at the age of twenty-three by the Zen Master Hejol.[8] The stele of Master Toson also informs us that he met a sage (a supernatural being) at Chiri Mountain before the age of twenty-nine, and that from him he learned about the principles of geomantic landscapes. Although this mythicised information is highly unreliable, it may nonetheless be true that he became an expert in geomancy before the age of twenty-nine. It is almost certain that he exercised an enormous influence over the building of Buddhist temples in geomantically critical places of Korea to correct the shortcomings of local geomantic conditions. This is supported by the numerous temples in Korea that are claimed to have been built (or whose sites are believed to have been selected) by Master Toson, as well as by the ten injunctions of the first king of the Koryo dynasty, Taejo Wanggon.

Geomancer-Monks Who Feature in Geomancy Tales

In geomancy tales, many Buddhist monks who were also experts in geomancy often selected auspicious sites for people. Geomancer-monks feature in legends in several ways. One is as a traveling monk who knows geomancy well, passes by a certain place, and mutters to himself about an auspicious site in that place. Then local people who overhear him appeal to him to let them know the location of the site, and give various reasons why they need and deserve such a site. The following legend about Chonghwa nung is an example of this type of tale:

While the First King of the Choson Dynasty [before enthronement], Yi songge, was looking for an auspicious grave site for his father who had just passed away, an older monk and a younger monk were passing by the mountain where he was thinking of burying his father's corpse. While in conversation, the older monk told the younger monk that the lower site was good enough to produce high government ministers, but that the upper site was bound to produce a king.

A little boy who overheard the conversation told Yi Songge, who immediately chased the two monks and requested them to instruct him where those sites were. The two monks went back to the mountain with Yi Songge and told him the upper of the two sites would produce a king, while the lower would produce ministers. Taking the monks' advice, Yi Songge took the upper site for the burial of his father. The grave is the Chonghwa nung in Hamung District and Yi became the First King of the Choson dynasty.[9]

Buddhist monks during the Choson period mainly lived in remote mountainous areas and frequently came down to villages and towns for the collecting of alms. When they visited other temples, they had to walk long distances. The traveling monk was the rural people's image of Buddhist monks during the Choson dynasty. When monks who were knowledgeable about geomancy traveled and passed by certain places, they naturally may have talked about the conditions of the auspicious sites they passed. They also often evaluated landscapes geomantically and commented on the existence of auspicious sites. It is easy to believe that people who overheard such comments asked the monks for help in finding an auspicious site. The above legend probably reflects the social environment of Korea during the Choson dynasty.

The second type of Buddhist monk to feature in geomancy tales are those who were helped by good persons. A typical story of such a tale is that when a hungry monk was well fed and looked after by a good person, he then selected an auspicious site for the person as repayment. The following tale from South Cholla Province is an example:

To the west of Sajaam, the Temple of the Lion in Miruk-san Mountain, there is Changkun-bong, the Army General Peak. To the south of this peak there is Kwe dung, the prominently convex hill. This hill was an extraordinarily auspicious site. In the Temple of the Lion, there was a Chief Monk, Minil who was knowledgeable about geomancy. One day he went down to a village where he was well treated by a poor farmer.

As a reward for the good deeds of the poor farmer, the monk chose the auspicious site at Kwedung and told him that he should lay a coffin not too deep from the ground surface and make an earthen mound over the burial. A rich man overheard this conversation and decided to bury his ancestor in that auspicious site. However, he only heard that he should make a mound over the burial, and missed the instruction that the grave pit should be shallow. The rich man dug the grave pit deep and laid a coffin there, and he did not receive any benefit from the auspicious site and lost his fortune. The poor man made a shallow grave pit as the monk instructed in the same site and became a rich man.[10]

This type of legend is very widely spread throughout Korea. It seems to manifest the Buddhist virtue of charity by conveying that an ethical person will be rewarded with an auspicious site. This type of legend clearly demonstrates that ethical values are incorporated into the practice of geomancy in Korea. That the geomancer-monk repaid a charitable person by finding an auspicious site indicates that geomancy and Buddhism are blended into one folk belief system in Korea. Many Buddhist monks were also experts in geomancy and Buddhism embraced the practice of geomancy in Korea. This may indicate that geomancy had a significance influence on Buddhism.

The Location and Natural Environment of Buddhist Temples

The intimate relationships between geomancy and Buddhism are clearly demonstrated in Buddhist pagoda and temple sites. Surviving Buddhist temples and pagodas that were built during or before the Choson dynasty were either built geomantically on auspicious sites or on geomantically important sites to improve the shortcomings of the local landscapes. In Korea the first written record of placing Buddhist temples on auspicious sites is the stele of Sungbok Temple written by Choi Chiwon.[11] In it many special geomantic terms as well as the early Chinese geomancer's name appeared. According to these engravings, in the year 798, when King Wonsong passed away, they removed the Buddhist temple called Koksa to build the royal tomb on that site, despite many objections. As there was conflict between Buddhist temples and royal tomb makers over geomantically auspicious sites, geomancy must have been introduced to Korea long before the eighth century of the Silla dynasty. Many temples during that time were located on sites chosen by applying geomantic principles. The first record of placing temples to make up for geomantic shortcomings is in the ten injunctions given by the first king of the Koryo dynasty.

Koryo Taejo's Faith in Geomancy and the Construction of Buddhist Temples

The second article of the ten injunctions by the first king of the Koryo dynasty clearly indicates that Korean temple sites were chosen according to geomantic principles. During the summer of 943 the first king dictated these ten injunctions, the second article of which states:

> Secondly, all temples were built by evaluating the auspiciousness and inauspiciousness of the landscape of Korea according to Master Toson's view. He said that if more [Buddhist] temples were built thoughtlessly in addition to the temple sites he had chosen, the dynasty would not last long. I feel that future kings, royal family members, queens and high government officers may desire their own private temples and that is what I am greatly worried about. During the last period of the Silla Dynasty many temples were built and damaged the land energy of the

nation. As such activities caused the dynasty to collapse eventually, how can we afford not to guard against this affair?[12]

King Taejo ordered his descendants not to build Buddhist temples without serious consideration of where to build them. That most temples had been placed in geomantically important sites according to Master Toson's advice meant that there was already an adequate number of temples for the given size and characteristics of the landscape in Korea at the time. But Taejo nevertheless constructed many Buddhist temples himself during his reign. According to *Koryosa (History of the Koryo Dynasty),* in December 936 during the nineteenth year of his reign, he completed Kwanghungsa Temple, Hyonsongsa Temple, Miruksa Temple, and Sachonwangsa Temple.[13]

Although the king clearly constructed temples and pagodas on geomantically auspicious sites, we should not automatically assume Taejo's behavior to be a result of his indulgence in geomancy. It is reasonable to conjecture that Taejo had some faith in geomancy, but there are indications that he might have used the art of geomancy and Buddhism for political gains by shaping the public attitude toward his newly established kingdom, for these two belief systems were very popular. Attracting the people's support must have been a priority for him in order to wage war against his rival states. During the time when he was unifying Korea, the whole of society was in turmoil, and many prophecies or rumors were circulating. Many were related to geomancy or Buddhism. King Taejo knew this well and attempted to influence public opinion by constructing temples and pagodas in geomantically auspicious sites that were frequently mentioned in prophecies and rumors. A record in Pohanjip by Choi Ja states:

> Taejo was interested in geomancy and Buddhism when he was to establish the Kingdom, while carrying out the war [against his rivals]. His officer Choi Ung told him an old saying that one gains people's support by governing them with civility during times of instability and confusion. A person in the position of the king of a nation must practise and keep improving his own (Confucian) virtue of literati even during the warfare. I have not heard of any one who was able to establish a dynasty by relying on Buddhism and geomancy.

> Taejo replied like this to Choi Ung's suggestion: "How can I not know such a saying? However, the mystic power of our nation's landscape (land energy) is in a ruinous state and the natural tendency of the people is to rely on Buddhist gods blessing their life. Now the war has not finished and the future (of our nation) can not be predicted (planned) for certain. I do not know how to deal with fear and overwhelming events that arise every morning and evening. Therefore, I was hoping that the blessings of Buddhist gods and the mysterious power of the land energy might be effective even temporarily. How can I adopt the art of geomancy and faith in Buddhism as a means of governing the nation and winning the people's support? When the war is over and the nation is in peace, the people's customs [ways of doing things] will have to be corrected and educated to the degree of beauty.[14]

Taejo was effectively saying that his main motivation for practicing geomancy and Buddhism was to identify with the people and gain support from them. He insisted that he was not indulging in geomancy or Buddhism, only that he was hoping that his faith in them might have some beneficial effect on his military campaign against his enemies. However, when we consider that he included and emphasized geomancy in his ten injunctions for his descendants and that he built many temples by consulting geomancers, we cannot deny that his faith in geomancy was very strong. When he asked, "How can I adopt the art of geomancy and faith in Buddhism as a means of governing the nation and winning the people's support?" he might have intended to avoid confrontation with Choi Ung, who was a Confucian scholar. Confucian scholars were generally rationalists and often opposed Buddhism and geomancy, which they considered superstitious beliefs.

The first king of the Koryo dynasty might be one of the best-known persons to have a strong faith in both geomancy and Buddhism. His attempt to use geomancy and Buddhism for political purposes is an indication that geomancy and Buddhism were already closely associated at the beginning of the Koryo dynasty.

Temples for Reinforcement of Geomantic Landscapes

Many legends about the choice of Korean Buddhist temple sites have geomantic elements. Anyone who has a basic knowledge of the principles of geomancy can easily confirm, even through field observation, that Buddhist temple sites are actually geomantically important locations. There are numerous records indicating that many Korean temples are located in auspicious sites. As shown in the ten injunctions of King Taejo, there are also many legends suggesting that Buddhist temples were built on geomantically important sites (rather than auspicious sites of local landscapes), especially in response to Master Toson's advice to make up for shortcomings in the local geomantic harmony. One of these legends, "The Temple of Tiger Protuberance (Hogapsa) of Tiger Rock Mountain (Hoamsan)," is included in *Sinjung Tongkuk Yojisungnam*, the official geography of Korea published by the government in 1531 during the Choson dynasty:

> Hoam-san: It is located in the place 5 *ri* from the county office. The mountain was so named because there is a rock shaped like a tiger. Yun Cha said, "Because the mountain in the east of Kumchon is shaped like a walking tiger as well as being rugged and dangerous looking, it is called Tiger Rock or Hoam." A geomancer examined this rock and built a Buddhist temple on the Northern corner of the mountain and named it Hogap [literally, Temple of Tiger Protuberance]. People named a bridge in 7 *ri* to the north of the mountain, "Bow Bridge or Kungkyo," and the Buddhist temple in 10 ri from the mountain, "Sajaam or Temple of Lion." All of these structures were made and named so to control and suppress the mountain shape of a walking tiger. When I was transferred from the position of government inspector and became the governor of this county, the custom of the locals were rather foolish and so was I. All natives said that the foolishness of the people was due to the rock [which has the shape of a walking tiger]. They say that all efforts

of such landscape modification were done in order to save the locals from foolishness.[15]

One can assume from this that the author of the book, Ro Sasin, did not
believe in geomancy, especially the geomantic art of modifying the landscape to
improve the local geomantic harmony. The author effectively conveyed the local
people's remedy of ameliorating the shortcomings of the local landscape—
building and naming temples and bridges. That locals built Buddhist temples to
counter the threatening features of the geomantic landscape is evidence of the
close relationship between geomancy and Buddhism.

Besides building temples, Koreans often tried to correct and improve the
geomantic harmony of the local landscape by planting trees, building pagodas,
creating artificial hills and dunes, or naming places and buildings to reinforce
geomantic harmony or to correct geomantic shortcomings. One of the most
common methods was building Buddhist temples and pagodas in appropriate
places—evidence that geomancy employed Buddhism in facilitating geomantic
harmony. According to *Yonggaji,* the local gazetteer of Andong County
published in 1608, four pagodas and nine Buddhist temples were built then to
correct and improve the shortcomings of the local geomantic landscape.

Buddhist Temples That Were Built in Auspicious Sites to Extract Auspiciousness

Many Buddhist temples were built in auspicious sites to extract auspiciousness from these places, unlike temples that were built to correct local geomantic
harmony. This is evidenced by temples located in geomantically auspicious sites
surrounded by hills in a horseshoe shape. The famous Korean temples such as
Haeinsa, Tongdosa, Songkwangsa, Woljongsa, and Chilbosa are all located in
such geomantically auspicious sites.

According to recent research on the locations of nine key Zen temples established during the early part of the tenth century (the end of the Silla dynasty and
the beginning of the Koryo dynasty), eight out of nine are located in the current
territory of South Korea and in geomantically auspicious sites.[16] The other one,
which is in North Korea, is known to be in a geomantically auspicious site as
well.

Quite clearly, the temples built before the end of the Choson dynasty (1910)
were often located in geomantically auspicious sites, and this is reflected in
legends. For instance, according to the legend of the temple site of Songrimsa
(Temple of Pine Forest) of Chilgok County, North Kyongsang Province, it is
located in an auspicious site that was the source of intense competition between
Buddhist monks and Confucian scholars. The story of "The Locale of Songrimsa Buddhist Temple" is as follows:

> During the Choson Dynasty, a geomancer-monk was passing through a site in
> Chilgok County, North Kyongsang Province, which later became the site for the

present day Songrimsa, or the Temple of Pine Forest. The monk found an auspicious place and decided to build a Buddhist temple there. At the same time a professional geomancer also discovered this auspicious place and advised a Yangban [Korean scholar-gentry] to move his father's grave there because the place would produce ministers for ten generations.

The Yangban was very pleased with this advice and asked his people to move the grave there. While they were making preparations to move the tomb, the Buddhist monk started to build his temple there.

When the Yangban realised what the Buddhist monk was doing, he was very disappointed and consulted the geomancer. Because the monk had polluted the site already, the geomancer advised the Yangban to beat the monk until the monk had cried out three times, in order to drive away the polluting spirit.

The Yangban decided to carry out the geomancer's instructions by force and went there. When he arrived at the place, the old Buddhist monk had already finished his temple and several dozen monks were in worship service with him. So the Yangban had to give up the temple site. The location of the Temple of Pine Forest is said to be a very auspicious site in terms of geomancy.[17]

Another geomancy legend that explains how a temple was built at an auspicious site is "The Story of Namwon Temple":

A small Buddhist temple called Namwon-sa is located to the east of Yonghwa-Mountain. There is also a small, ruined three-story pagoda on the temple grounds.

Once upon a time a newly appointed governor of Namwon County slept at the location of the temple [before it was built] for a night on his way down to the county. That night, in his dream, an old man appeared to him and said that in order to administer the county well and to bring glory to his future, he should build a Buddhist temple where he had slept because the location was exceptionally auspicious. After saying this, the old man disappeared.

After such an extraordinary dream, the governor awoke the next morning to see a strange pagoda. The governor then realised that the old man's saying was not groundless. After his starting his duty as the new governor of Namwon County, he completed building the Buddhist temple by sending workers and building materials there and called it Namwon-sa or the Temple of Namwon.[18]

These are only two examples of a large number of such Korean legends. I remember one geomancer saying that most of the auspicious places of Korea have been occupied by Buddhist temples. His comment is not groundless. In fact, most Korean Buddhist temples are located in auspicious spots to extract auspiciousness or on geomantically critical sites to improve the geomantic harmony of the local landscape. In this way, Korean Buddhism adopted geomancy in choosing Buddhist temple sites and Korean geomancy adopted Buddhism in improving the geomantic landscape.

The building of temples in geomantically auspicious sites is mainly the result of the impact of geomancy on Korean Buddhism. Buddhist monks accepted and believed in geomancy and chose to build temples in geomantically auspicious places to benefit from auspicious land energy.

Charity: the Buddhist Worldview and the
Principle of Ethics

The ethical principle most emphasized in geomantic tales is charity to all poor living things, such as suffering animals or traveling monks. This may be considered a reflection of Buddhist influence on Korean geomancy, since extending charity to poor and needy people and animals is an important precept in Buddhism. The plots of many folk narratives dealing with geomantic issues involve the offering of charity to poor people or animals who in gratitude choose an auspicious place for their benefactor.

The idea that an auspicious place can be found only by an ethical person is deeply rooted in Korean geomancy. Ethical values, however, can be grouped into several categories, some of which are emphasized more than others both in the geomancy tales and by present-day geomancers. The ethical values discussed here mainly derive from an analysis of Korean folk narratives. Since geomancers usually cite folk narratives to elaborate on the relationship between geomancy and ethical values, such tales are the best source. Also, as Wolfram Eberhard said, since the Chinese and Korean tales are "essentially educational,"[19] we can regard all ethical principles that appear in geomantic tales as expressing real ethical values of Koreans of the time.

An important aspect of geomancy in folk narratives is that a good person will somehow be given an auspicious place. A local scholarly geomancer told me that to obtain an auspicious site and receive benefits from it, both the person to be buried and the descendants who bury the corpse should not have accumulated evil deeds during their lives.[20] Only a family that has accumulated good deeds for several generations can find an auspicious site, it is believed. Another geomancer told me the story of "Mr Nam Sago and His Mother's Grave," in which even the most famous and prominent geomancer of Korea was not able to find an auspicious place for his mother's grave due to his mother's sin.[21]

Ideas on bringing ethical values into the art of geomancy are not found in mainstream classical geomantic literature, despite their presence in geomancy tales. This suggests that the authors of geomantic literature did not consider ethical values since geomantic principles are objective, similar to natural laws. However, the practitioners and believers of geomantic principles incorporated ethical values into the art of geomancy by subjectifying those principles.

In geomancy tales, several types of ethical values are reflected, but the most important are from Buddhism and Confucianism. Charity, the most recommended ethical value, is an important Buddhist principle. In geomancy tales charity can be grouped into three categories: charity to needy people, especially to traveling monks; charity to suffering animals; and noncharitable people who suffer misfortune.

Charity for Needy People

In geomancy tales, a charitable person is often rewarded with auspicious sites. This popular moral is in accord with the Buddhist principle of causality, or cause and effect (good or bad). There are numerous folk narratives concerning good people's attainment of auspicious places and receipt of benefits from them. This idea is firmly rooted both among geomancers and the people who use their services. The following folktale from North Cholla Province, called "A Site for a Man of Charity (Hwalin chokdukjiji)," is a good example of tales reflecting the Buddhist principle of charity:

Once upon a time when a woman was collecting wild herbs on a mountain, two monks, a master monk and his disciple, were passing by. The disciple told the master monk that there was a good site nearby. The master listened to him then rebuked the younger monk by saying, "Don't mention this site." Nevertheless, the disciple asked him whether the site would produce high government officers. The master replied, "I told you not to mention that . . ." The woman heard the conversation, went over to the monks and asked the master to show her the auspicious site. The master said that there was such a site. When the woman told him that she had overheard their conversation, the monk replied that he was only rebuking his disciple for his irresponsible sayings. Still the woman appealed for the monk's instruction as to the site. The monk could not avoid telling her about the auspicious site, but he added that the site was so auspicious that it would produce high government officers but could only be used by a charitable person, and that if an uncharitable person buried an ancestor there all auspiciousness would be rendered void. Therefore, one could not easily attempt to bury a dead person there.

After the woman heard the monk's comment about the site, she asked the monk if one who has been as charitable as to have provided a room for a beggar to give birth to a baby and to have supported them for three years could be qualified to bury a corpse at the location. The monk replied that such a charitable person would be qualified to make his or her ancestor's grave there. Then the old woman said that she was such a person. She also told the monk that her husband's father had died and that her family was looking for a good site to bury the corpse. She asked the monk for his help by pointing out the location. Then the monk drew a map of the auspicious site and gave it to her. He did not tell her of an auspicious date to bury the corpse but said that the proper day could only be determined by Mr Yi Chinsa. Then the monks suddenly disappeared. As soon as the woman returned home, she reported to her husband what had happened in the mountain. The husband went out to find Mr Yi Chinsa who knew geomancy well enough to determine the auspicious date to bury his father. However, he was not able to find Mr Yi Chinsa. After a painful search, he eventually met a person called Yi Chinsa. Although this person did not have the noble appearance of a Chinsa [Chinsa is a noble title that was given to scholarly persons], the husband noticed that he appeared to be very intelligent. Therefore, he realised that this was the person he was looking for and he knelt down before him and begged him to tell the auspicious date for burying his father's corpse. The Chinsa, however, refused to select the date for him, pretending that he knew nothing about geomancy. Then the husband told him about the story of his wife's meeting the two monks. Yi Chinsa then selected an auspicious date for him.

When the husband returned home they buried the corpse at the auspicious site on the proper day and later had many high government officers among their descendants.[22]

In this story, the charitable person was able to obtain a good site in a mysterious way and received benefits from the grave. Through it we can appreciate how importantly the Buddhist precept of charitable behavior is treated in geomancy. And while a charitable person benefits from an auspicious site, an evil person may experience misfortune instead.

In classical geomantic literature, there is no hint of requiring ethical conduct of either the buried persons or their descendants for the manifestation of benefits from auspicious burial sites. As in the principles of the natural world, an auspicious site will manifest its benefits to the descendants of the buried person regardless of the extent of good behavior. As reflected in folk tales, the geomantic belief that the quality of an auspicious site or the kinds of benefits manifested can vary depending on the degree of ethical conduct may suggest that the classical Chinese geomantic principles have been reinterpreted to accommodate the Korean Buddhist worldview.[23]

There are many other Korean geomancy tales that reflect the idea that a charitable person will somehow be given an auspicious site from which many blessings will be received. The theme of charity to traveling monks is an especially popular theme in such tales. The following short legend, "The Grave of Mr Yun of Haepyong," is an example.

Yun Ungyol was very poor during his boyhood. His mother, however, was well known to the people as a charitable lady. One day a poor monk was fed well at her house. As a reward, the monk selected an auspicious place for her. At that time, however, the place was located in a mountain which belonged to a rich man of the area. Mr Yun's family secretly moved an ancestor's grave to this place, but they did not make a dome above the ground so that no one could tell the place was a grave. After this, the descendants became prosperous.[24]

The theme of charity to needy people other than monks is also often seen in geomantic tales. Needy people who appear in them mainly beg from strangers or wandering geomancers. In the story of Taekgul-Rock, this idea is well demonstrated:

Taekgul-Rock, which has the shape of a ring, is where General Yim exercised in his boyhood. General Yim's parents were so poor that they had to beg for food and lived in a simple shelter outside the village.

One day a stranger was treated well by General Yim's parents. The stranger asked the parents what their wishes were. They answered that they wanted to be a rich family in the village. Then the stranger selected an auspicious place which would bring wealth to their sons.

After they buried their ancestor at the site, they gave birth to a boy who exercised at the rock and eventually became a general.[25]

Geomancy tales about the acquisition of auspicious sites by charitable persons are very widely spread in Korea and found in all of its provincial districts. In these tales, the theme of charity to poor Buddhist monks is more common than charity to other needy people.

Charity to Suffering Animals

Animal tales are not common in Chinese folk narratives. In Korean folklore, however, animal tales are popular. Charity to suffering animals—in fact, any animal—and a respect for life are basic precepts of the Buddhist creed. In geomancy tales, a popular theme is that when a person is charitable to a suffering animal, the animal somehow returns the favor by finding an auspicious site for the person. This idea is reflected in the following story of "The Grave of Mr Yu":

> Long ago, in a certain county of Hamkyong Province, there lived a strong man called Mr Yu. One day while passing through a mountain trail, he came across a tiger which was having trouble with its mouth. Mr Yu realised that the tiger was asking for his help. Upon examining the tiger's mouth, he found a *pinyo* [a woman's hairdressing stick] and removed it. When the tiger was relieved from its pain, it bowed its head several times as if expressing its gratitude toward Mr Yu, before running away to the mountain. Judging from the hairdressing stick he took out from the tiger, Mr Yu assumed that the tiger had gotten it stuck in its throat after eating a woman.

> Years after, when Mr Yu died of a sickness, the tiger appeared before the funeral procession and led the funeral cart to an auspicious place. Mr Yu's sons buried the corpse of their father at the site the tiger indicated. After that, Mr Yu's descendants became high government officers for 9 generations.[26]

In this tale, the animal and person communicate and are friendly to each other. The person graciously eases the tiger's pain even though the tiger ate another human being. The person treats the animal as if it was another person, and the tiger expresses gratitude and repays the good deed as human beings often do. And the tiger has a mysterious power to find an auspicious site; it even knew the funeral day of its benefactor. In such tales, the differences between human beings and the natural world are minimized and the boundaries between them are blurred.

Even in this tale the idea that one's good deed will be rewarded with an auspicious site is clearly conveyed. Charity, which is not primarily a Confucian but a Buddhist ethic, has certainly been one of the most emphasized ethical values of Korean folk narratives in general, not just geomancy tales.

Uncharitable Persons Will Suffer Misfortune, Even if They Have Occupied an Auspicious Site

In geomancy tales a cruel and uncharitable person will not find an auspicious site. Even if such a person found an auspicious site and occupied it, somehow the person would come to mismanage and damage the site, which would result in great misfortune. These types of ideas are based on the Buddhist concept of causality, which advocates that good people will be blessed while evil people will be punished. In the following geomancy tale, "Dotgoge Hill," a person who was uncharitable to a monk suffered a terrible misfortune:

> According to geomancy, Dotgoge Hill is in the geomantic landscape of a mouse. A man made a grave on the hill. A travelling monk who saw the grave went to the house of the man who had made the grave to request an almsgiving (donation). The man beat the monk badly and asked him, "What do you know about the grave site?" After the monk had been beaten, he told the owner of the house that "although you beat me, if you turn the direction of the grave to the left and lower the hill a little bit, your descendants will be prosperous for generations." Then the monk went away. In spite of having beaten the monk, he did as the monk recommended hoping that he might gain such benefits. Soon after that, the family collapsed. Misleading the man was the monk's revenge for having been beaten.[27]

Judging from the house owner's question, "What do you know about the grave site?" the monk must have previously said to him that there was something geomantically wrong with the grave. That the owner lowered the hill and changed the direction of the grave may suggest that he was a rather rich person. Perhaps that is why the monk asked for a donation.

"The Story of Master Toson" included the idea that if one has an ancestor who committed a great sin, one may not be able to benefit from an auspicious site even if the person who made the grave was not such a person. This type of legend emphasizes the importance of accumulating charitable deeds. That the ethical quality of a person who occupies the site is more important than the geomantic conditions of the site contradicts the notion that geomantic principles are objective. "The Story of Master Toson" states:

> Once upon a time there were three poor brothers who plotted to ask Master Toson for an auspicious site (so they could be rich by taking advantage of the land energy from the site), when and if their father died. The children starved their father to death. The children went to Master Toson and asked him to choose a grave site that could bless them with riches. Master Toson chose such a site for them. Then an old man (the mountain god) appeared and told them that the site would bless them to be rich, but it would also cause them blindness. As proof, the mountain god showed them 3 gold fish in the spring below which went blind by his magic power. Then the three brothers started beating Master Toson who quickly ran away from them.

> Master Toson was about to destroy his geomantic compass thinking it had misled him in his site selection and was not only of no use, but could also bring him fatal misfortune. Then the old man came to him and told him not to destroy it. When Toson asked him why, he said that the three evil brothers had killed their father by starving him and did not deserve the auspicious site he chose. Only the filial son Mr Shim who lived elsewhere was worthy of having the site. The old man told Master Toson that he caused the three gold fish to go temporarily blind as to not waste the site on the three evil children. He told Master Toson, "You are a skillful

geomancer who can choose auspicious sites well. When you choose such a site, you should firstly consider the client's past (moral worthiness)."[28]

The following is another legend about the famous geomancer-monk Toson. It explains why he chose an auspicious site for a poor couple and why the site did not manifest blessings to the couple. "The Famous Geomancer Toson's Mistake" goes:

Once upon a time there was a poor couple in a remote mountainous area who had prayed for one hundred days to meet Toson. Toson happened to pass through the couple's house where he was well looked after. In his appreciation for their hospitality, Toson chose a site that would bless them with wealth and children within three years. He promised to come back in three years time to check the degree of blessings manifested from the site.

After three years when Toson returned to the place, he found that the couple had vanished. Toson was surprised to see such unexpected results, for he had chosen an auspicious site with good intentions. He thought he may have made a mistake and rechecked the site, which confirmed that he had chosen the auspicious site correctly. On his way out from the place Toson heard a voice from the sky advising him that the site was auspicious, but the couple's ancestor of 7 generations ago committed a crime of murdering someone, which was why the couple had perished. The moral behind the story is that one should never commit an evil deed.[29]

The above two legends about Toson may have evolved from the original legend due to the story being handed down through generations in different places. When we combine these two stories, their key elements are as follows:

1) Master Toson chose an auspicious site that would enable the poor couple in the mountain to become rich within three years.

2) When Master Toson returned to the place after three years, the man who had made his parent's grave in the auspicious site that was chosen by him had perished due to misfortune.

3) Master Toson wondered whether he had made a mistake when he chose the site. He re-examined the site, which proved to be auspicious. However, the owner of the grave in the site had perished.

4) Master Toson attempted to punish himself for this misjudgment of the quality of the place by destroying his geomantic compass. At that time the mountain god appeared and asked him not to destroy it, saying that the reason auspiciousness did not manifest itself was that an ancestor of the couple of seven generations ago had committed a great sin.

These two legends suggest that even an auspicious site chosen by the most qualified geomancer may not manifest its benefits to the descendants of the grave if the person who was buried there were evil or had evil descendants.

I collected another legend about Toson during my fieldwork in Korea from a knowledgeable rural geomancer in 1974. It effectively combined the previous two tales about Toson, though the story was set up differently. The geomancer who recounted "Master Toson and the Spoiling of an Auspicious Place" was answering my question on the relationship between geomancy and ethics.[30] This story, along with the previous one, certainly supports the Korean belief that if one has accumulated sinful deeds, it will more adversely influence one's descendants than oneself.[31]

That idea explains a person's relationship to their family in the traditional Korean society. Regardless of what people achieved in their life, their destiny (especially social status) could not be separated from that of their family. One's glory, failure, prestige, or responsibility to society were not just one's own but affected one's entire extended family. Therefore, when one achieved something, the entire family shared the glory, while if one committed a crime, the responsibility and punishment was extended to the entire family. Whenever one did something while away from one's family, one was, in effect, a representative of the family. Traditional Koreans probably understood themselves not as independent individuals but as members of a family. This idea is well illustrated in geomancy tales, as we have seen in the above examples.

There are many other geomancy tales that advise us that an evil or uncharitable person will perish by suffering misfortune. They seem to express the Buddhist message that people have to be merciful and charitable to be blessed. Showing how an evil person was punished can be an effective way of emphasizing the importance of being good. As a Korean saying goes, promoting goodness and discouraging evil go hand in hand and serve the same purpose.

Korean geomancy as practiced by commoners seems to have emphasized the Buddhist precept of charity more than orthodox geomantic principles. Auspicious sites are reserved only for charitable people, it is believed, and the benefits from them will only be manifested to a good person. Thus, there may be no need to look for an auspicious site unless one is ethically qualified to do so. On the other hand, one may also not need to search for such a site if one is a good person because it will be given to him somehow. According to this logic, the practice of geomantic art becomes unnecessary since what is needed is to accumulate good deeds by being charitable to needy people and poor animals. This may eventually lead to the idea that there is no need for the practice of geomancy to exist. However, whether one was a good or evil person, many Koreans eagerly searched for auspicious sites during traditional Korean society. One can say that Buddhism was only able to moderate the objectivity of geomantic principles. Of course, geomancy tales that showed that only charitable people can benefit from an auspicious site provided an excuse for geomancers when their prophecies about sites proved false—prophecies that were offered after receiving hefty fees from their clients.

Concluding Remarks

The authors of geomantic literature and Buddhist doctrines were not related and have not seemed to have influenced each other. However, the consumers of these two belief systems in Korean folk society *have* influenced each other. Thus, the two systems were merged to some degree, whereby their practitioners adopted each other's theories and doctrines. They had a symbiotic relationship in the site selection of Buddhist temples and the practice of geomancy by some Buddhist monks. In understanding their relationship, the question of who practiced what belief system seems to be more important than the doctrines of the two systems. This is due to the fact that the occupations of Buddhist monk and geomancer were merged to form geomancer-monk, while geomantically auspicious sites and Buddhist temples were combined to become "Buddhist temples in geomantically auspicious sites."

Further research is needed on why, when, and how relationships between geomancy and Buddhism were initiated and how they developed into their present forms. Data needs to be collected more widely through the examination of historical records, folklore materials, and field surveys of geomantically important sites and Buddhist installations. Then we may be able to understand the relationships between the two belief systems more fully.

Notes

1. Xu Shanji and Xu Shanshu, *Dili-Renzixuezhi* [The Fact that All Humanity Must Know] (Hsin-chu: Chulin Shu-chu, 1969), 2–4.

2. Xu Shanji and Xu Shanshu, *Dili-Renzixuezhi*, 4.

3. For example, see *Qingwujing* or *Jiangjing (Jingnangjin)* as well as Xu Shanji and Xu Shanshu, *Dili-Renzixuezhi*.

4. In my view the first attempt in Korean to appreciate the overall relationships between geomancy in terms of the geomancer-monk, geomantically considered temple sites, and the Buddhistic worldview and ethical values as reflected in geomancy tales was Hong-key Yoon, "Hankuk pungsuchrisolkwa pulkyosinangkwui kwange [The Relationships between Geomancy and Buddhism in Korea]," *Yoksa Minsokhak* [Journal of Korean Historical-folklife], vol. 13 (2001), 125–158.

5. See Yi Pyongdo, *Koryo Sidaeui Yongu* [A Study of the Koryo Period], revised edition. (Seoul: Asea Munhwasa, 1980); Choi Byong-hon, "Tosonui Saengaewa Rmalyochoui Pungsuchirisol [The Life of Toson and Geomancy during the Period of the End of Silla and the Beginning of Koryo]," in *Hankuksa Yongu [A Study of Korean History]*, vol. 11 (1975), 101–146; Sung Dong Hwan, "*Ramalyocho Sonjongkeyol sachalui ilji yongu*" [A Study on the location of Zen Buddhist temples during the Late Silla dynasty in Korea]," PhD dissertation, Taegu Hyosong Catholic University, 1999; Choi Won-Suk, "Yongnamui Bibo [Bibo of the Yongnam Region]," PhD dissertation, Korea Universit, 2000.

6. Yi Kwangjun, "Toson Kuksa wa Tosonsa" [The National Master Toson and the Toson Temple]. *Proceedings, 12th International Buddhism Conference, Toson Kuksawa Hankuk* [The National Master Toson and Korea], 31 July 1996, Kwangju, 55–95. It is a commonly known theme in Korean and Manchurian folklore for the mother of a folk hero or the founder of a dynasty at their conception to dream of "swallowing marble, the Sun or mysterious fruits."

7. Hankuk Munhwa Inryuhakhoe, ed., *Hankuk minsok chonghap chosapogoso, Cholla Namdo pyon* [A Comprehensive Report on Korean folklore and folk custom, South Cholla Province Part] (Seoul: Ministry of Culture and Information, 1969), 749.

8. Choi Chang-jo, Choi Changjo (1996) Han'guk Pungsu Chiri ui Kujowa wonri [The Structure and Principles of the Korean Buddhism), *Proceedings, The Twelfth*

International Buddhism Studies Conference, Tosonkusawa Hankuk [National Master Toson and Korea], (Kwangju: Korea, 31 July 1996), 284–287.

9. Choi Sangsu, *Hankuk Mingan Chonsoljip* [Collection of Korean Legends] (Seoul: Tongmunkwan, 1958), 453–454.

10. Hankuk Munhwa Inryuhakhoe, Hankuk Munhwa Illyu Hakhoe, ed., *Hankuk minsok chonghap chosapogoso, Cholla Pukdo pyon* [A Comprehensive Report on Korean folklore and folk custom, North Cholla Province Part] (Seoul: Ministry of Culture and Information, 1971), 594.

11. Yi Pyongdo, *Koryo Sidaeui Yongu* [A Study of the Koryo Period], revised edition. (Seoul: Asea Munhwasa, 1980), 29; Lee Ki-baek (Yi Kibaek), "Han'guk pungsu-chirisol ui kiwon" [The Origin of Korean Geomancy]. *Han'guksa siminkangchoa,* vol. 14 (1994), 7–8.

12. Chong Inji and others (1992), trans. by Pak Sihyong and Hong Hwoiyu, *Pukyok Koryosa* [the North Korean translation of Koryosa into modern Korean], vol. 1, Sega 2, Taejo 2 (Pyongyang: Kwahakwon Chulpansa, 1962: reprinted in Seoul: Sinsowon, 1992), 115.

13. Chong Inji and others , *Pukyok Koryosa*, 112.

14. Choi Ja, *Pohanjip*, trans. into modern Korean by Yi Sangpyo, *Pohanjip, Nakongpisol, Hankuk Myongjo Taejonjip* [Series in Great Korean Classics] (Seoul: Taeyang sojok, 1975), 134.

15. No Sasin et el., *Sinjung Tongkuk Yoji Sungnam* [Newly Augmented Survey of the Geography of Korea] (Seoul: Minjok munhwa chujinhoe, 1969), vol. 10, 221.

16. Sung, Dong Hwan, "Ramalyocho Sonjongkeyol sachalui ilji yongu".

17. Choi Sangsu, *Hankuk Mingan Chonsoljip*, 274–275.

18. Hankuk Munhwa Inryuhakhoe, *Hankuk minsok, Cholla Pukdo pyon*, 587.

19. Private discussions with Professor Wolfram Eberhard at the University of California, Berkeley, during the spring of 1972.

20. An interview with Mr Chong Changsop at Mikimi, Modong-myon, Sangju County, North Kyongsang Province, 23 November 1973.

21. An interview with Mr Chong Changsop as above. For the story, see my discussion of "the personified image" in chapter eight.

22. Hankuk Munhwa Inryuhakhoe, *Hankuk minsok, Cholla Pukdo pyon*, 613–614.

23. A comment made by the story teller of "A Site for a Man of Charity (Hwalin chokdukjiji)," Mr Ha Pyoksu of Hyunpung, Muju County, North Cholla Province, as reported in Hankuk Munhwa Inryuhakhoe, *Hankuk minsok, Cholla Pukdo pyon*, 614.

24. Chugan Choson, *"Pungsu Sipgang"* [Ten Lectures on Geomancy], 24 October 1971.

25. Translated and abridged from Songgyunkwan Taehakgyo Kuko Kukmunhakgwa, *Andong Munhwakwon Haksul Chosa Pogo* [Report of Academic Survey of Andong Culture Region] Volume I &II, (Seoul: Songgyunkwan Taehakgyo, 1967), vol.1, 110.

26. Translated and abridged from Choi Sangsu, *Hankuk Mingan Chonsoljip*, 464.

27. Translated and abridged from Songgyunkwan Taehakkyo Kuko Kumunhakkwa, *Andong Munhwakwon*.

28. Translated and abridged from Hankuk chongsin munhwa yonguwon, *Hankuk Kubi Munhak taege* [Grand Collection of Korean Oral Literature] (Seoul: Hankuk Chongsin Munhwa Yonguwon, 1980), vols. 1–2, 65–67.

29. Translated and abridged from Hankuk chongsin munhwa yonguwon, *Hankuk Kubi Munhak taege*, vols. 2.2, 739–743.

30. From an interview with Mr Kim Songchan at Usijang (the cattle market), Andong City, North Kyongsang Province, on 16 February 1974.

31. An interview with Mr Chong Changsop at Mikimi, Modong-myon, Sangju County, North Kyongsang Province, 23 November 1973.

Chapter 11
Confucian Ethos and Geomancy[1]

Ever since geomancy was introduced to Korea from China, it significantly affected Korean religious creeds. The impact of geomancy on the main religions of Korea, such as Buddhism, Confucianism, and Shamanism, is plainly visible in temples, shrines, and religious prose. Folk narratives also demonstrate the incorporation of geomancy into the practice of these religions. Geomancy and traditional Korean religions thus have symbiotic relationships.

Many Korean tales tell about the way Koreans practice geomancy in pursuit of an auspicious site. These tales, which include the folk narrative genres of myths, legends, and folktales, will be called Korean geomancy tales in this chapter. They reveal important aspects of traditional Korean worldviews, social values, and wishes. Generally, people do not know the author of a particular tale nor how much it has changed in the process of telling and retelling it to different audiences; the tales can be considered communally authored and owned. The anonymous authors freely expressed their wishes. Therefore, we can regard the ethical principles in geomancy tales as people's genuine expressions of their ethical values. Because geomancers often cite folk narratives in the process of practicing geomancy and these geomancy tales have some of the most popular story themes in the Korean folk tradition, they are probably the most important source for examining ethical values in geomancy as practiced in Korea.

Charity or compassion to humanity and animals is probably the most emphasized ethical value of Korean folk society and the most popular ethical value in Korean geomancy tales. As noted earlier, it is primarily a Buddhist rather than a Confucian ethic. Though Confucian ethics ruled the country for a long time, geomancy tales were much more influenced by Buddhist ethical values than by Confucian ones. This may indicate that Buddhist values survived among commoners in Korea long after neo-Confucianism replaced Buddhism as the dominant ideology.

Buddhism was probably introduced to Korea before the officially recognized year of 372 during the Three Kingdoms period. Neo-Confucianism was introduced to Korea much more recently, toward the end of the Koryo dynasty (918–1392). While Buddhism provided the dominant social and political ideology of Korea during the Koryo period, neo-Confucianism came to play that role only during the subsequent Choson dynasty (1392-1910). Neo-Confucian-ism, which is basically a scholarly tradition of China, was embraced first by the upper-class scholar-gentries (Yangban); it only later gradually penetrated downward to the commoners (Sangmin) during the Choson dynasty.

While matters of proper social ethics and political ideology were the neo-Confucians' main concerns, teaching people how to overcome suffering (especially by consoling the human mind) was the Buddhists' main concern. Buddhism as a religion exerted greater influence on Korean people's social psyche than did Confucianism, which is probably why Buddhist values are more commonly featured in Korean geomancy tales.

This chapter examines the relationships between Confucian ethical values and geomantic beliefs, especially in parent-child relationships as reflected in geomancy tales. As patrilineal heritage is an important principle of Confucian social ethics, the chapter briefly discusses a daughter's attitudes toward her husband's family and her birth family before examining relations between parents and children.

A Married Woman's Confucian Attitudes Toward Her Husband's Family

In geomancy tales, the influence of Confucian social values is readily apparent. Scholars often agree that Confucian social relationships have been dominated by patriarchal, patrilineal, and patrilocal relationships. Namely, family members submit to their father's authority and heed his leadership, and family inheritance passes from father to son rather than to daughters. Daughters become an integral part of their husband's family after their marriage and are excluded from their own birth family. They should live in the village or town where their husbands' families live. After she marries, a woman has the full privileges and responsibilities of belonging to her husband's family, which has become her own family. For a married woman to live with her birth family (except during brief visits) was frowned upon and thought shameful. Therefore, a Korean married woman would not go back to her own family even after death: her grave remained with her husband's place.

These Confucian values are reflected in Korean geomancy tales such as "The Grave of the Yu family of Andong":

> During the Choson Dynasty (1392-1910) in Korea, a girl of the Kim family of Andong District married into the Yu family, also in same region. On the very same day, the woman's father and father-in-law died. Therefore, both families came to look for a grave site each. Her father's family was rich and was able to search for and choose an auspicious grave site by hiring famous geomancers from all over Korea. However, her husband's family could not do that for they were poor and powerless.

> In the meantime, the woman who was married into the Yu family overheard a geomancer reporting to her brother that he had found an auspicious location and

prepared a grave site on it. The geomancer said that if water did not spring from the site by the next day at noon, the place (the descendants of the buried person there) would produce prime ministers of the nation for three generations. After overhearing this news, the woman secretly went to the grave site and poured water into it during the night.

Next day at noon, when the Kim family went to see the grave site, there was water in it. So they abandoned the place and chose another. At this point, the woman begged her mother to give her the abandoned grave site for her own father-in-law burial. The mother allowed her daughter to do so. After the grave was made, the Kim family gradually lost their fortune and the Yu family became prosperous. Indeed (the famous) prime minister Yu Songryong was born from the Yu family.[2]

In this tale Confucian values are apparent in the married woman's attitudes toward her husband's parents at the expense of her own parents.

The Confucian values about patriarchal, patrilineal, and patrilocal family relationships are perhaps best illustrated by the following three virtues that a woman should have: before marriage, a girl should be obedient to her father; after marriage, she should be obedient to her husband; in her old age, she should be obedient to her son. When we consider the Confucian precept that a girl belongs to her husband's family after marriage, it is understandable that the married woman in the above tale cheated her own parents and brothers for the benefit of her husband's family. All benefits, success, honor, failure, or shame caused by a married woman could be claimed only by her husband's family. After being buried in the graveyard of her husband's clan, the geomantic benefits from her own grave could go to her children (i.e., her husband's family), but not to her birth family. Slightly modified versions of "The Grave of the Yu Family of Andong" with the same Confucian ethos are found widely in different parts of Korea, perhaps signifying that this type of attitude by a woman toward her husband's family was considered not only acceptable but commendable.

The story of "The Grave of Mr Yun of Haepyong"[3] also conveys a married woman's attitude toward her father's family. Mrs. Yun, a poor lady who had obtained a good gravesite, buried one of her husband's ancestors there rather than holding it for her own father's ancestors. It is no wonder why Koreans often joke that married daughters are thieves of their father's home.

Confucian Ethics on Parent-Child Relationships Expressed in Korean Geomancy Tales

Next to the Buddhist value of charity, the Confucian notion of ideal interpersonal relationships is the most common ethic in geomancy tales. The essence of Confucian social ethics is encapsulated in the so-called Five Cardinal Articles of Morality (Oryun) on the relationships between a ruler and subjects, father and son, husband and wife, seniors and juniors, and between friends:

1) Between the ruler and subject there should be righteousness (loyalty to the ruler).

2) Between father and son there should be intimacy (filial piety to the parents).

3) Between husband and wife there should be difference (different roles—women should be domestic and accept the supremacy of their husbands).

4) Between the senior and junior, there should be order (respect toward elders).

5) Between friends, there should be faithfulness (trustworthiness).

Of these five principles, the most commonly represented in geomancy tales are the ones relating to parent-child relationships and a married woman's attitudes toward her husband's family.[4] The other ethical values play minor roles. That these values are less evident than the Buddhist concept of charity demonstrates that the relationship between Korean geomancy and Confucianism, though quite close, is not as close as that between geomancy and Buddhism.

Three of the Five Cardinal Articles of Morality lay the ground rules in a Confucian family: the relationships between father and son, husband and wife, and elder child and younger child. Of the three, the intimacy between father and son (i.e., parents and children) was the most important in a traditional Korean family and forms the basis of all Confucian ethical values. The parent-child relationship has emphasized the children's unconditional filial piety (*hyo* in Korean) toward their parents; the parents' unlimited love for their children was assumed. In examining the Korean parent-child relationship as reflected in traditional geomancy tales, I will argue that the emphasis on parental sacrifice for their descendants is in line with the geomantic principle of transmitting vital energy from auspicious sites to living descendants through buried parents.

Parents' Sacrifice For Their Descendants: Children's Inheritance

Confucian ethics concerning parent-child relationships require every son's total and unconditional sacrifice for his parents. No parental sacrifice for children is required. In the geomancy tales, however, there are stories about poor parents sacrificing themselves to acquire gravesites that will guarantee a prosperous future for their descendants. "The Grave of the Crop Keeper Old Lady" is one of the best examples of this type of legend:

> During the reign of King Sonjo lived Mr and Mrs Ho in the Pyongan Province. They were so poor that they had to work as servants in the house of a rich man, Mr Yi. They knew that there was an auspicious place in the mountain which their master owned. Mr Ho's family, which included three sons who could not yet marry, plotted to obtain this auspicious place.

> One day, as she did every day, Mrs Ho went to the bird-lookout in the fields. When the master appeared, she pretended to be asleep. On seeing this, the master became angry and shouted, "Why do you sleep without keeping the birds away?" Mrs Ho, feigning great surprise, fell from the bird-tower. After three or four days, she died.

This was all according to a plan which Mrs Ho's family had devised. Mrs Ho's sons went to the master accusing him of the murder. The sons threatened that they would sue at the regional court unless the master gave them the chosen place for their mother's burial. The master thought that giving up the site was better than being sued as a murderer, so he gave up the spot, albeit with great reluctance. After Mrs Ho's burial at the auspicious site, her descendants became rich.[5]

This is an extreme case of the extent to which a typical Korean parent, in particular the mother, would sacrifice for her children, although it would not happen today. In the story the mother was prepared to give her life for the sake of her children's prosperity. Mrs. Ho did not kill herself for her own happiness but for her family's prosperity. We can assume that Mrs. Ho's sons did not allow their mother's suicide for their own personal happiness either but for the future of the family. The wish reflected in the tale was for the prosperous future of their descendants, not themselves. This tale reveals the Korean mother's psyche toward her family quite well. Even nowadays, a mother's sacrifice for her children's success is virtually unlimited. Although they do not necessarily give their lives away, mothers still make enormous sacrifices for their children. A prime example is when they take university entrance examinations. For the whole year before the exams, the mothers' lives center around their children: preparing food for them, arranging tutors, and so on. Parents' fanatical enthusiasm for their children's education is, of course, fueled by their interest in their children's success. Thus, the spirit of Mrs. Ho's altruism continues. One can say that Koreans prepare for tomorrow rather than for today.

Another story, "An Auspicious Place of Yondok-san in Pukchong," also describes fairly well the idea of parents' sacrifice for their descendants.[6] In this tale, Mr Chin committed suicide, thereby tricking his friend to obtain an auspicious place to benefit his descendants. Chin, a geomancer, obviously did not kill himself for a blessed life after death, as neither the principles of geomancy nor the tale itself discuss the afterlives of those buried in an auspicious place. Therefore, it is quite probable that the geomancer committed suicide to obtain the place because he knew that it would guarantee a prosperous future for his descendants.

Koreans traditionally considered their descendants to be more important than themselves and thus were willing to sacrifice themselves for their children. The emphasis in these two stories on parental altruism for children could be considered a non-Confucian traditional Korean moral value, one that existed at the time of the stories. On the other hand, children's filial piety toward their parents is expected. Filial piety, which is the basic ethical value for the family system of both Korea and China, requires children's unlimited obedience and sacrifice for their parents.

The practice of parental sacrifice for the family's future is consistent with one of the three principles suggested by Wolfram Eberhard on the Chinese social structure. He argued that three principles have shaped the "Chinese" feature in Chinese society: every person is educable, people are not equal, and society cannot function unless the individual relinquishes some of his freedoms.[7] What Eberhard said may well be applied to Korea, for both countries share

Confucianism as the key guiding light of their society. Limiting individual freedom for the sake of the community one belongs to means that sacrificing individual rights and gains are needed for the well-being of one's group. In this sense, the story of parents' sacrifice for the well-being of their descendants is an elaboration of Eberhard's third principle.

Filial Piety Toward Parents

Filial piety may have been the most important ethical principle among traditional Koreans. In practice it is an important obligation of any child toward parents, in return for the love and other material items received from the parents. The act of filial piety *(hyodo)* includes an unconditional obligation to have respect for parents, no matter how poorly the children have been endowed by their parents. In traditional Korean society the concept of parents can be extended to include grandparents, great-grandparents, and other direct ancestors. In spite of its importance, geomancy tales with this ethical theme have not been popular in Korea. I have been able to find only several that emphasize filial piety. One of them, "Tiger Mountain," is as follows:

> About five hundred years ago, a Mr An lived in Hosan-ri, Hwanghae Province. He was so filial to his parents that after his father's death, he went to his grave with a bowl of rice and bowed to the grave every day.
>
> One day a tiger was in front of his father's grave. The tiger had been helped once by Mr An who had taken a stake out of its mouth. Mr An was surprised at seeing the tiger again. He pushed the tiger to make it go back to its cave, but it would not move. When the tiger started walking and looking back of him, Mr An realised that this was a sign for him to follow. At a certain place, the tiger stopped and dug in the soil with its paw. Mr An understood that the tiger was offering a good place for Mr An to bury his father. Thus, he moved his father's grave to that place.
>
> After that, Mr An's family came to be prosperous, and eventually became the richest family of the region. This is why the people call the mountain "Bomme" or "Hosan," both of which literally mean "Tiger Mountain."[8]

Many unfilial sons who did not care for their parents while they were alive suddenly became filial after the death of their parents when it came to searching for an auspicious gravesite. This clearly was selfish and not an expression of filial piety. Even in such cases, however, the well-being of the deceased ancestor was taken into consideration, as offspring take better care of their graves and offer worship when they become prosperous. Still, the Korean practice of grave geomancy is mainly for the benefit of living descendants and future generations.

Two Explanations For Koreans' Fanatic Quest For Auspicious Gravesites from A Confucian Point of View

The following two points are important in explaining Koreans' use of geomancy as a way of gaining family prosperity and their fanatic quest for auspicious gravesites.

a) Parents' sacrifice for their descendants in geomancy tales is supported by the principles of geomancy

The geomantic principles stated in classical geomancy textbooks are mainly concerned with how to extract benefits through the bones of ancestors placed at auspicious grave locations.[9] The principles explained in the single most important geomancy textbook, *Zangshu (Book of Burial)*, are rather materialistic. This book does not mention anything about life after death. Therefore, the enthusiasm of Koreans for grave geomancy was for the sake of their living descendants rather than their deceased ancestors, although they pretended that their primary motivation was filial piety to their deceased parents.

The key geomantic principle expressed in *Zhangshu* is responsible for Koreans' belief that blessings from an auspicious place can be transmitted to descendants through the buried ancestors. *Zhangshu*, it will be recalled, argued that when the buried corpse is influenced by the vital energy under the ground, the energy is conveyed to the living descendants, because the children are the branches of the trunk (the parents).[10] There are no discussions in geomantic textbooks on the mechanism of the flow of auspicious energy from the deceased ancestor to living descendants; believers accept this idea on faith rather than logical grounds.

The corollary idea that if a dead ancestor's body suffers in its grave the living descendants will suffer as well is effectively described in the following legend:

On his way down from a remote mountain after completing his ten-year study of geomancy, a geomancer found an extremely auspicious gravesite worthy of producing a prime minister. On the site an exposed skull was lying there and so he poked a stick through an eye of the skull to see what would happen.

At that very moment, the prime minister of the nation suddenly came to suffer a severe pain in his eye. No medicine was effective for his pain and he went searching for a doctor who could cure it. The same geomancer went to the prime minister and promised to cure his sickness within three days, and told him that he needed to see his ancestor's graves. When the geomancer examined the graves of the prime minister's family, he realised that all had been well maintained but were not located in geomantically good places. Therefore, the geomancer went to the mountain where the auspicious site with the exposed skull was lying. He pulled out the stick from the skull, and the pain in the prime minister's eye suddenly went away.

The geomancer then told all that he did to the prime minister and advised him that the grave that was originally thought to be his father's was not his real father's grave; the exposed skull in the auspicious site was his real father's. With great surprise the prime minister asked his mother for an explanation. Then his mother told him her secret and shameful story that the prime minister was born out of wedlock between her and a male slave in the family. After this incident the slave ran away from the family and she did not know what happened to him. The prime minister then made a decent grave for the skull and maintained it well.[11]

According to the logic of *Zangshu* and this tale, the following paradox is possible: people never die; rather, they always live in the world through their descendants even after their death. Thus, expecting prosperous descendants is also a hope for ancestors. Even a filial son who moves his parents' graves with the sincere hope of securing their peaceful rest at an auspicious site can also hope for blessings from the grave for the descendants, including him. This hope, of course, would not contradict the principles of filial piety, but would support the importance of patrilineal continuity in the Confucian family structure.

b) Koreans' identity comes from family lineage

Koreans' fanatic interest in obtaining an auspicious site for the well-being of living descendants may be due to their strong family identity that blurred the boundary between oneself and one's family. Often, traditionally minded Koreans thought their duty to their family was greater than their duty to anything else, including themselves. This idea is consistent with Eberhard's third principle on Chinese society: An individual should sacrifice some of his freedom for his community.

The most important aspect of a person's identity always came from his or her family in traditional Korea. A person did not always make clear distinctions between "I," "my ancestors," and "my descendants." The destiny of "I" could hardly have been separated from that of the family line. Thus "I" could be sacrificed for ancestors or descendants. To a Korean, the existence of "I" may not terminate with his or her death but continues through the descendants. One's ancestors could know nothing more pitiable than to see the discontinuance of the family line, it is believed. Although a person may have enjoyed a prosperous and glorious life before death, if the person did not have a son he would not be considered a blessed man, because he would not have descendants who would take care of his grave and perform worship ceremonies for him through the following generations. The wish to have prosperous descendants can be seen as the desire for a guarantee that they, as ancestors, will be served and honored even after their deaths. To receive good worship ceremonies and have a well-maintained grave were two of the greatest concerns. Therefore, the prosperity of one's children was no less important than one's own prosperity. If one had an honorable descendant, the ancestors could be glorified by him even after their death. Yi Songge, who became the first king of the Choson dynasty, is the best example of this. He glorified his ancestors by conferring posthumous kingships on them up to the fourth generation. This type of family relationship may explain why a person might choose his own gravesite in terms of its effect on the prosperity of his descendants.

Confucian Scholars' Adoption and Criticisms of Geomancy

Many Confucian scholars of the Choson dynasty were experts on geomancy and accepted the practice of it to varying degrees, sometimes claiming that the great Confucian scholars of China such as Confucius and Chu Hsi accepted geomantic ideas. The founder of neo-Confucianism, Chu Hsi (1130–1200), seemed to have embraced geomancy. He was interested in searching for auspicious gravesites for his family and wrote the geomantic *Discourse on Royal Tombs (Shanling yizhuang)*, which was presented to the Chinese emperor in 1194.[12]

A Korean Confucian scholar–court officer, Ha Ryun, was an expert on geomancy and played an important role in searching for the new capital site during the first king of the Choson dynasty (1392–1910). Another Confucian scholar–court officer of the early Choson dynasty, Chong Inji, also had a good knowledge of geomancy and was involved in determining King Sejong's original tomb site. The *Annals of King Sejong* includes Chong Inji's letter reporting his geomantic fieldwork to examine an auspicious tomb site for the king.[13] The beginning part of his letter is translated here:

This officer [Chong Inji] together with other [officers] went to the auspicious site in the West of The Honrung Royal Tomb and surveyed the orientation and shapes of the main mountain and other surrounding hills and waters of the place. With the reference to a report prepared by a person, I will discuss [the geomantic quality of the site] one by one as below:

First, [the geomantic manual of] Supyu stated: "In a place with a gentle and flat shape embracing a geomantic vein, the auspicious spot is located in the centre. In such a case, blessings will be gathered in the central site, while the fringe sites will cause the family [occupier] to perish." [The geomantic manual of] Chihyunron also stated that "the auspiciousness is in the centre, not in the fringe." In Supyu, the subsequent paragraph stated that the flat site on high ground is the concave site surrounded by projected mountains that are extensions of low lying landforms, while a projected spot in a hollow land is the convex site in low land." A commentary to this statement declared that "The centre of a place is the precious [the most auspicious] spot, but it does not need to be the [physical] centre of the place. The centre means the concave of the high ground and the convex of the low land. The qi [chi: vital energy] expresses itself depending on the feature [of the landscape]." The distance from the main auspicious site of the Royal Tomb of Hunrung to the white tiger [the mountain on the right side], the slope of Kuryong [Nine Dragon] Mountain, is 3,264 chuk; to the slope of chongryong [the mountain on the left side] is 1,873 chuk. The distance from the west auspicious site to the outer white tiger is 2,328 chuk; to the slope of the azure dragon [the mountain on the right side] is 2,817 chuk; to the inner peace mountain, 2,751 chuk. The distance between the eastern and western auspicious sites is 944 chuk. Therefore the both eastern and the western auspicious sites are located in the centre of geomantic landscape, not on the edge of the landscape.[14]

Chong Inji's letter was based on a field survey at the proposed royal tomb site by a group of court officers including himself. In his letter he listed eleven geomantic reasons (including ten other reasons than the one quoted above) why the royal tomb should be made on a site in the present-day eastern outskirts of Seoul. His letter is a good example of the degree of geomantic knowledge held by the then-highly esteemed Korean Confucian scholar–court officers, as it evaluated the geomantic quality of the proposed site using technical geomantic terms and citing specialized geomantic manuals. Many Confucian scholars of the Choson dynasty acquired some knowledge in geomancy and herbal medicine as a matter of common sense.

As Korean geomancy came from China, the principles that were applied in the search for an auspicious site were more or less identical to those of the Chinese. Geomantic classics and manuals used in Korea are generally either directly from China or are edited and translated versions of the Chinese texts. However, Koreans sometimes interpreted and applied the Chinese geomantic principles in a Korean context. One of the most important geomantic discourses in Korea is by Yi Chung-hwan (1690–1756), a Shirhak scholar during the Choson dynasty. His book, *Taengniji,* is a widely read Korean classic on choosing auspicious settlements and sometimes treated by geomancers as secret geomantic literature.

The close relationships between geomancy and Korean Confucianism are also reflected in the locations of Confucian academies throughout Korea. For instance, Songgyunkwan, the Korean National Academy of Confucianism, in Seoul is located in an obviously auspicious site: between Korean palaces with appropriate background hills and an open front. Various regional Confucian academies *(hyanggyo)* throughout Korea are also generally located in geomantically chosen sites. For example, the site of Tosansowon, the Confucian academy in Andong commemorating Yi Hwang, the famous Confucian scholar of the Choson dynasty, is known to be auspicious.

While many Koreans during the Choson dynasty were preoccupied with practicing geomancy, a number of Confucian scholars came to criticize the practice of grave geomancy. These Confucian scholars were often Sirhak, or Practical Learning School, scholars, including the well-known Yi Ik, Chong Yakyong, Pak Chaga, and Chong Son. Chong Yakyong (1762–1836) severely criticized the practice of grave geomancy and lamented its tragic social conse- quences leading to serious litigation.[15] Chong Son even more vividly described the crimes and litigation that resulted from the people's fanatic practice of geomancy. To quote Chong Yakyong's *Mokminsimso*:

Chong Son said, "People in the world are brainwashed and seduced by Guo Pu's art of geomancy and do not bury their deceased parents for several years by covet- ously looking for auspicious gravesites. Some people, even after burying the de- ceased, doubt the quality of the gravesite and shift the corpse to different places for 3 or even 4 times. Some families quarrel over gravesites and cannot decide where to bury their ancestor's corpse, turning family relationships sour. In some cases, brothers, taking different geomantic advices have disputes and become enemies." He also said, "people who bury their parents and indulged in the art of geomancy end up illegally invading gravesites in mountains belonging to other people. In some cases they illegally dig out other peoples graves and throw bones away (in order to bury their ancestors there). This kind of behaviour leads to the ultimate animosity among the people and ends up in serious litigations to which people are determined to win the case at all costs. Therefore some people waste their wealth and ruin their businesses in such manner while not being able to secure an auspicious site. Such behaviour brings misfortune instead of the blessings they seek (through an auspicious gravesite). How has the people's foolishness reached this degree?"[16]

During the Choson dynasty, the practice of grave geomancy became very popular among the people. This had considerable negative impact on the Korean culture. Another Shirhak scholar during the later Choson dynasty, Pak Chega, lamented in his book:

> The idea of geomancy has had a more adverse influence [on Korean society] than Buddhism or Taoism. Even the scholar-gentry class followed this idea and made it a custom. It is said that moving an ancestor's grave to a better location is an act of filial piety. Since the scholar-gentry class considered the making of its ancestor's graves as important, the common people imitated their behaviour. . . Generally, it is a bad intention to depend upon one's fortune through one's deceased parents. Moreover, occupying others' mountains illegally and destroying others' funeral biers are not right things to do. To have more splendid worship ceremonies at graves than at home during special occasions is against proper principles. It is not possible to list all the stories about people who perform deeds against proper principles by wasting all of their wealth [in finding auspicious places] but do not take care of their ancestral bones, and yet expect blessings [good fortune].[17]

As Pak Chega argued, many Koreans of his time indulged in the selfish pursuit of blessings from an ancestor's grave in an auspicious site rather than caring about the well-being of their ancestors. Moving one's ancestral grave to a geomantically better place is mainly motivated by hope for blessings to one's descendants rather than by feelings for one's ancestors. The Chinese practice of geomancy was no different from the Korean situation. Maurice Freedman, a British anthropologist, once commented on the Chinese practice of grave geomancy:

> Indeed, we may say that, in the traditional Chinese setting, there is more involved than a mere desire to procure good fortune; there is a moral obligation to seek a future of happiness for those for whom one is responsible. If I select my grave site in anticipation of my death, it is for the benefit of my sons and remoter agnatic issue. If my sons choose my grave, they are intent not only on their own prosperity but also on that of their descendants.[18]

Freedman understood the purpose of practising grave geomancy in China quite accurately and pointed out a critically important aspect of the theory of geomancy. His comment is applicable to the practice of geomancy in Korea. Several centuries before Freedman's observation on the motivation for practicing grave geomancy in China, the same issue was debated in Korean courts in the case of relocating King Sejong's tomb, as documented in *Chungbo Munhon Pigo*:

> In the first year of King Yejong [A.D. 1469], Yongnung [the name of King Sejong's tomb] was moved to Yoju. Originally the tomb was nearby Honrung [the name of King Taejong's tomb]. During King Sejo's reign, there was discussion that Yongnung should be moved, since it was not located at an auspicious place. Therefore, King Sejo summoned So Kojong [a famous scholar-officer] and asked him about the matter. Mr So said that "the art of geomancy is used for receiving blessings and for avoiding misfortune to the descendants. I, your officer, do not know much about the art, but the moving of the ancestor's graves by the people [to a better place] is an attempt to seek and acquire fortune [for the descendants]. As a king, what more fortune do you expect [by moving the tomb of the king]." Then, the king said, "I no longer wish to move the tomb."[19]

In geomancy legends the concern of people for their descendants extends several generations. Usually descendants living at the time that a grave was made expected the benefits to come several generations later. For instance, there is the story of "The Ancestor's Grave of the Yi Family of Hansan":

> The gravesite used to be the location of the local administration office of Hansan County, Kyongsang-do Province.

> Mr Yi was working as a low-level clerk at the local office. One day he noticed that the floor where the governor's seat was located was in a process of decay. He judged that the decay occurred because of the power of the earth (vital energy) of the site. He concluded that it was an auspicious place, and secretly buried his father's body under the floor.

> This was the top secret of his family, and three generations later, the merit of the grave came to be available to the descendants and many great men were produced among the descendants.[20]

In this tale, the blessings from the grave were manifested three generations after the grave was made. This meant that the descendants had to wait about 100 years to experience the benefits.

In traditional Korean society wishes for family prosperity typically centered around bringing material wealth to the family, having many children, or gaining appointments of descendants as high governmental officials. Such wishes may have reflected the average short life expectancy and high mortality, poverty, and envy of government officers who wielded power.

Concluding Remarks

Korean geomancy is closely related to Buddhism and Confucianism. Although Buddhism is more strongly tied to geomancy than Confucianism, the relationships between geomancy and Confucianism are well developed and clearly evidenced in the locations of Confucian shrines and schools, Confucian scholars' interest in and criticisms of geomancy, and the expression of Confucian values in geomancy tales. In these tales, the Confucian ethical values regarding the relationships between parents and descendants are the most commonly expressed.

Notes

1. A portion of this chapter is based on and has developed from my PhD dissertation, University of California at Berkeley, 1976: Hong-key Yoon, *Geomantic Relationships Between Culture and Nature in Korea* (Taipei: The Orient Culture Service, 1976), 181–188, and my recent conference paper that was presented at the 1st World Congress of Korean Studies, Seoul, July, 2002: Hong-key Yoon, "Confucian ethical values regarding the parents-children relationships in Korean geomancy tales," *Proceedings of the 1st World Congress of Korean Studies*, July 2002, 554–564.

2. Choi Sangsu, *Hankuk Mingan Chonsoljip* [Collection of Korean Legends] (Seoul: Tongmunkwan, 1958), 256–257; Hong-key Yoon, *Geomantic Relationships*, 28

3. For the story of the legend, see page 192.

4. For an earlier discussion of this issue, see Hong-key Yoon, *Geomantic Relationships*, 181–182.

5. Translated and abridged from Chugan Choson (Seoul), 12 September 1971.

6. For the story, see my discussion of "cheating and tricks" in chapter eight, 140–141.

7. Wolfram Eberhard, "On Three Principles in Chinese Social Structure," *Journal of Sociology*, National Taiwan University, no. 6 (1970), 13.

8. Choi Sangsu, *Hankuk Mingan Chonsoljip* [Collection of Korean Legends] (Seoul: Tongmunkwan, 1958), 353.

9. From interviews with geomancers and other villagers in Sangju and Sonsan Counties during November 1973. All benefits to be manifest from auspicious gravesites, which are reflected in folk narratives and geomantic textbooks, are solely concerned with blessings to the descendants of the dead.

10. Guo Pu, Zangshu, in *Dili zhengzong* [The Cardinal Principles of Geomancy] commentary by Jiang Guo, (Shinchu: Chulin shuchu, 1967),1.

11. Translated from Shin Wolgyun, *Pungsu Solhwa* [Folk Narratives of Geomancy] (Seoul: Miral, 1994), 42–43. Different versions of this tale are found in Hankuk Chongsin Munhwa Yonguwon (Academy of Korean Studies), *Hankuk Kubi Munhak taege* [Grand Collection of Korean Oral Literature] (Seoul: Hankuk Chongsin Munhwa Yonguwon, 1980–1983), vol. 3.2, 449; vol. 7.7, 793; vol. 8.1, 105; vol. 8.3, 36.

12. Kim Dukyu, *Choson Pungsuhakin ui taegna wa Nonjaeng* [Discourse and Life of Scholarly Geomancers of the Choson Dynasty], (Seoul: Kungni, 2000), 18 and 439.

13. Annals of King Sejong (Sejong Sillok), the day of Ulchuk, the Fourth Moon, twenty-seventh year of the king's reign.

14. Translated from Annals of King Sejong (Sejong Sillok), the day of chongmi, the Fourth Moon, 27th year of his reign; Quoted in Kim Dukyu, *Choson Pungsuhakin*, 140–157.

15. Chong Yakyong, *Kukyok Mokmin-simso* [Criticisms and Advice on Governing the People, A Modern Korean Translation] (Seoul: Minjok Munhwa Chujinhoe, 1969), vol. 2, 390.

16. Chong Yakyong, *Kukyok Mokmin-simso*, 393.

17. Pak Chega, *Pukhakui* [Discourse on Northern Studies], Translated into modern Korean by Yi Sokho (Seoul: Taeyang Sojok, 1972) 402.

18. Maurice Freedman, "Geomancy," Proceedings of the Royal Anthropological Institute of Great Britain and Ireland, (1968), 12.

19. Hongmunkwan, *Chungbo Munhon Pigo* [The Revised and Enlarged Edition of the Comparative Review of Records and Documents] (Seoul: Hongmun-kwan, 1908), vol. 71, the section of Yego, 5.

20. Translated and abridged from *Chugan Choson* (Seoul), 31 October 1971, 28.

PART IV: GEOMANCY AND SETTLEMENT

Chapter 12
The Use of Geomantic Ideas in Chinese, Japanese, and Korean Cities[1]

Geomancy has played a vital role in city planning in East Asia. It has been a key factor in determining urban locations and planning urban landscapes there. An auspicious city site is typically a flat basin with protective hills in the background. A useful watercourse such as a river, stream, or lake is situated in front. The watercourse should not form a straight line but flow slowly in a meandering shape, giving the impression that it loves the auspicious site and is reluctant to flow away from it. The site should face an auspicious cosmological direction, which is normally south, as it allows the maximum amount of sunshine. This direction can only be determined with the aid of a geomantic compass by a geomancer. In the construction of palaces and other city structures, the choice of an auspicious direction is considered critically important. Geomancers say that no matter how auspicious the surrounding landforms and watercourses may be, a wrong choice of direction can bring great misfortune to the place. The hills in back of the site should form the end of an undulating mountain range called the main mountain. They should be shaped like a horseshoe and have arms extending forwards on either side, as if to protect the site. The most auspicious site at the foothill of the main mountain is known as the geomancy cave (xue). It is not literally a cave but an auspicious site where the palace or administrative headquarters should be built. The front of an auspicious site should be an open space. And the size of the site should be suitable for its purpose.

Of course, vital energy is believed to accumulate in such a site. It flows under the ground and can give birth to and invigorate living creatures, including humans. Thus, the aim of finding an auspicious site for a city is to utilize the vital energy that is there.

The evaluation of the site for a city is based on complicated geomantic principles recorded in various geomantic manuals and carried out by professional
geomancers who may employ mystic and vague jargon to justify their choice of
site. However, the traditional geomancers and geomancy textbooks generally
agree that the three important factors in determining an auspicious site are the
landform conditions, the availability of water, and the cosmic orientation. The
obvious question now is, how were these principles for evaluating a site
developed into the art of geomancy?

Tracing the Use of Geomantic Ideas in Ancient Chinese Cities

A prominent Korean historian of geomancy, Yi Pyongdo, once wrote: "As a new
dynasty succeeds the existing one, the change of the dynasty name and the
moving of the capital to a new site were often practiced in China and other East
Asian countries. The Koryo and Choson dynasties of Korea were no exceptions
from this."[2] Yi Pyongdo pointed out that East Asian capital city sites have in
most cases been selected for their geomantic conditions by their rulers and
builders. In the movement of capitals to new places in East Asia, city builders in
the past carefully considered various factors, as recorded in ancient Chinese
historical documents. For example, *The Book of Historical Documents (The
Shoo King),* discusses the following historical event that led to the early Chou
dynasty's selection of a new capital site:

> Thence the Grand-guardian went before the duke of Chow to inspect the localities,
> and in the third month, on the day Mow-shin, the third day after the first appear-
> ance of the new moon on Ping-woo, came in the morning to Lo. He consulted the
> tortoise about the localities, and having obtained favourable indications, he set
> about laying out the plans. On Kang-suh, the third day after, he led the people of
> Yin to prepare the various sites on the North of the Lo; and this work was com-
> pleted on the fifth day, Kea-yin.

> The day following, being the day Yi-maou, the duke of Chow came in the
> morning to Lo and thoroughly surveyed the plans for the new city.[3]

The book also records, "In the third month when the moon began to wane,
the duke of Chow commenced the foundations and proceeded to build the new
city at Lo of the eastern States."[4] The duke of Chow seems to have gone through
the following process before the selection of the new capital site:

> On the day Yih-maou, in the morning, I came to the city of Lo. I first divined con-
> cerning the country about the Le water on the North of the Ho. I then divined con-
> cerning the east of the keen water and the West of the Chien water, when the
> ground near the Lo was indicated. Again I divined concerning the east of the Chen
> water, and the ground near the Lo was likewise indicated. I now send a messenger
> with a map, and to present the divinations.[5]

The following verse from The Book of Poetry (The She King) also suggests the practice of geomantic art when the ancient Chinese were to choose a new capital city:

> He examined and divined, did the king,
> About settling in the capital of Haou.
> The tortoise-shell decided the site,
> And king Woo completed the city.
> A sovereign true was king Woo![6]

These records do not indicate what types of landforms and facing directions were preferred by the ancient capital builders. They do, however, suggest that they chose auspicious capital locations through a form of divining sites that may have developed into Chinese geomancy as we know it today. Before the invention of the compass for divining sites, the tortoise shell was used. From ancient times, geomancy has played a critically important role in the formation of city landscapes in East Asia

Dili-Renzixuezhi (*The Fact that All Humanity Must Know*): A Ming Dynasty Geomantic Manual's Interpretations of China's Past Capitals

The ancient Chinese classics on geomancy such as *Qingwujing* and *Jiangjing* do not discuss the geomantic qualities of any particular city locations in China or elsewhere. However, the popular geomantic textbook *Dili-Renzixuezhi* does.[7] According to it, Kunlun Mountain in western China was considered the origin of the world mountain system and the backbone of the world. From Kunlun, the four branch dragons, or mountain systems, were developed and stretched out into the four directions of the world.[8] The branch that came into China was known as the southern dragon of Kunlun. China's mountain system is also divided into three main trunk lines: the north, south and middle dragons. Along these three mountain ranges, China's important past capitals are located. Between the land divided by these three main mountain systems, the two major river systems, the Yellow River and the Yangtse River, flow and collect water from their catchments.

Dili-Renzixuezhi argues that choosing an imperial capital in an auspicious site is of the utmost importance, for it is the greatest place on earth, the pivot of all directions, and where all subjects are governed by officers of various ranks and the outlying barbarians are managed.[9] The book also states that an imperial city should be built on a place where its landscape reflects the constellations above and which has the royal energy of the proper dragons (mountain ranges) gathered below on earth.[10] The emperor is the Son of Heaven, and the imperial capital should be in a central location which mirrors the imperial constellations from the center of heaven.

All this represents the Chinese view on the function of the imperial capital. It also reflects the well-known Chinese view that the world is divided into two parts: China and its surrounding barbarian lands. China proper was civilized and governed by Chinese officers who were appointed by the emperor. The non-Chinese who were barbarians had to be controlled effectively so that they would not cause disruption. The commanding headquarters for this important task was the imperial capital, and so finding an ideal capital site corresponding to the heavenly one was the paramount geomantic task.

As geomancers reviewed the geomantic qualities of China's capital locations through time, they found that imperial capital sites were located along the three main Chinese mountain ranges. Those capitals that were located in the correct vein of the proper dragon with the geomantic landscape corresponding to the heavenly one would rule the world for many generations, while those that were not so located perished quickly: the fate of capital cities in history were clear evidence of the effectiveness of geomancy.[11]

Now, let us review *Dili-Renzixuezhi*'s evaluations of China's imperial city locations along the three Chinese mountain ranges: the northern dragon, the central dragon, and the southern dragon.

a) The imperial capital cities located in the northern dragon

Dili-Renzixuezhi comments on the northern dragon first, probably because Beijing, the capital of China, was in the territory of the northern dragon. The manual states that the northern dragon has Yanshan (Swallow Mountain), an ancestral mountain of Beijing (see Figure 12.1). It is called Yanshan because a mountain range that is shaped like a swallow ends there.[12] The main points of the manual's description and justification of the geomantic landforms of Beijing are summarized as follows:

> Geomancer Yang said that Yanshan has the geomantic configuration of the supreme heavenly city. This is the proper auspicious site of the northern dragon. This mountain range started from the middle part of the Kunlun Mountain [of West China] and ran several thousand ri [1ri=1/2km] to reach the gate [The First Eastern Gate of the Great Wall of China ?]. It crossed the Pohai Sea and stretched out first in a zigzag shape to the Eastern barbarian land and then stretched out about 10 thousand ri to reach Yanranshan. After the mountain range entered into China, it formed Yanyun [Beijing and Datong]. It extended itself again several hundred ri and formed Tianshoushan Mountain before dropping its height to the level of a plain that is a thousand ri wide. . . . The Yellow River forms the [waist] belt [for Beijing] and the Yalu River flows around the back of Yanranshan Range. . . . Evaluating the geomantic quality of Beijing, the mountain range [dragon] behind the city stretches out long and the beautiful geomantic landscape reaches its zenith at the main dragon. It becomes the meeting point of mountains and rivers. The Yellow river became its waist belt and Tianshoushan became the background folding screen where the Yalu River stepping behind it and Heshi

locked its gate securely. Therefore, it is the best place in accordance with geomantic principles.[13]

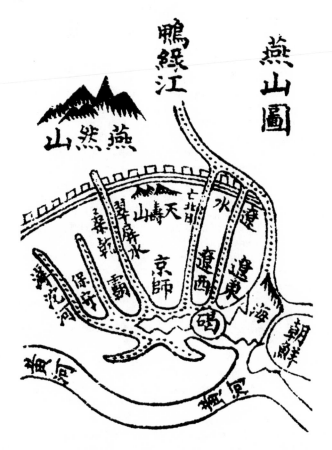

Figure 12.1 A geomantic map of the city of Beijing and its surroundings (from Xu Shanji and Xu Shanshu, Dili-Renzixuezhi, vol. 1, part 2, p. 7).

Despite the manual's praise and justification of the geomantic quality of the landforms around the Beijing district, the city is located on flat land, not on a basin surrounded by hills on three sides. The background mountains of Beijing are too far from the city, and with no surrounding mountains shaped like a horseshoe, its landform is not geomantically ideal. One may wonder whether this is related to the fact that the city site was chosen by the Manchu and Mongol conquerors who were nomads, not by the Hans who were sedentary farmers. To the nomads, the flat grassland was perhaps most desired, and their choice of present-day Beijing as their capital might reflect their nomadic origin more than geomantic considerations. The geomantic model suggested above does not seem to have been applied in the selection and planning of Beijing. In my view, the site of Beijing was later arbitrarily justified geomantically by the Han-Chinese geomancers.

The geomantic landform condition of Beijing has been artificially enforced by creating a background hill. Behind the imperial palace, the Forbidden City, there is an artificially created mountain, the Jingshan. This mountain seems to have been created to function as the protective main mountain or placenta hill for the geomancy cave, which is the palace and the city itself.

The creation of Jingshan Mountain was initiated by the Jing (a Manchurian dynasty) during the twelfth century by piling up the soil that resulted from the creation of an artificial lake near their palace.[14] In the thirteenth century, during Emperor Kubilai Khan of the Yuan (a Mongol) dynasty, this area became the center of the city and the back garden of the palace. During the fifteenth century, when the Ming dynasty rebuilt Beijing as its capital, this artificial mountain was greatly enlarged to its present size and shape.[15] Presently the mountain is 43 meters high with a hiking route to its peak from all four directions; it has five pavilions, with Wanchunting the central and largest one.[16] The well-balanced and symmetrical shape of this artificial mountain with the highest peak in its center is obviously a geomantic arrangement, and it was placed directly behind the palace. The Ming dynasty's enlargement of this artificial mountain to its present size and the building of the palace right in front of it were clearly products of geomantic consideration. For the Ming dynasty rulers, their original capital, Nanjing, had a natural mountain behind its palace. The Ming rulers who moved the capital from Nanjing to Beijing knew well that an auspicious site (palace) needed to back onto a hill behind it. In Beijing the flat land with no mountains behind the palace perhaps compelled them to build up the artificial background hill.

The geomantic manual Dili-Renzixuezhi presents a map of the surrounding environs, with the key mountains and rivers of Beijing, to illustrate that Beijing is a geomantically auspicious capital site. When we compare this geomantic map with a contemporary map, which shows the surrounding landform of the city, with Tianshoushan Mountain and Yanranshan Mountain in the background and three rivers each on the left and right of Beijing, we can see that the geomantic map presents a distorted and exaggerated view. In reality, Beijing is situated on a plain and does not have the geomantically required landforms to be an auspicious capital site.

b) The imperial capital cities located in the middle dragon

Dili-Renzixuezhi discussed the ancient capital cities along the middle dragon in two sections of the book: the first section was on Changan and other ancient capital cities in the Guanzhong Basin, and the second was on Luoyang in the south of the dragon (i.e., south of the Chinling mountain range). In the book's discussion on Changan and other cities in the Guanzhong Basin, it states:

The middle dragon is in Guanzhong which has Feng, Hao, Hanyang and Changan . . . Geomancer Yang commented that Changan is the best site of the middle range dragon. Its dragon originated from the Kunlun Mountain and passed through the Black River and joined the Western River. The mountain range then rose to form Hengshan as its ancestral mountain and eventually reached Yongzhou [which means Guanzhong] where early Chinese capitals were located . . . Guanzhong is enclosed by rugged mountains in four directions . . . Guiwen xianggong said "Guanzhong is protected by [fence like] mountains in four directions and it is the supreme location of the world."[17]

From this summary, we can see that the flat basin of Guanzhong is an exceptionally auspicious place, with a proper dragon (mountain range) originating from the proper source. The mountain ranges surrounding the basin originated from the backbone of the world, Kunlun Mountain, and protected the basin by encircling it with rugged mountains. Among the locations of past capitals in the basin, Changan, which had been the capital of China for more than 500 years, was considered the most auspicious in the region.

The book then described Luoyang as the next best place for a capital in the middle dragon region as follows:

The next best place of the middle dragon is [the city site of] Luoyang. This place encounters Yiguan in the front and backs toward Mangshan Mountain in the background. To the left of the city is Chanshui River; to the right Jianshui River; and to the center the Luoshui River flows through the middle in the shape of the Hehan River This auspicious landscape corresponds to the heavenly constellation of Ziweiyuan.[18]

The above description of Luoyang's geomantic quality is much more reasonable and realistic than those of Beijing and Changan. In my view, Luoyang in the south of the lofty Chinling Mountain is, in fact, better in terms of the geomantic qualities of the surrounding landforms than the Guanzhong Basin (see Figure 12.2). The authors of *Dili-Renzixuezhi* argued that Luoyang is located in the central part of the world and thus is in the belly of the great dragon.[19] This comment represents the authors' rationalistic understanding of the geopolitical position of Luoyang as the center of China's territory during the Ming dynasty. Geomancer Zhang Ziwei praised Luoyang as an auspicious location having the landscape of a flying dragon.[20]

c) The Imperial Capital Cities Located in the Southern Dragon

The southern dragon was the last of the three main dragons in China and its most important capital site is Nanjing. The following is a summary of some important points on Nanjing's geomantic quality as discussed in *Dili-Renzixuezhi*:

Jinling [present-day Nanjing] is in the southern dragon range. Earlier geomancers commented that the geomantic landscape of Nanjing is of the same quality as that of Luoyang. Geomancer Liaostated that Nanjing will become the Bell Land [important land] of royal energy. Xiao Peheng commented that the earthly vein [mountain range] of Jingling extends several hundred ri along the Jiangjang [Yangtze River] to the opposite direction of its water flow from the southeast direction before stopping itself. The landscape of the end of the mountain range is like a harmoniously crawling centipede.[21]

Only Nanjing fits comfortably into the geomantic model suggested above by having horseshoe-shaped mountains around the city. Even with a geomancer's elaborate justification, the other cities such as Beijing and Changan do not fit comfortably into the model. These cities are river-centered locations and don't have protective hills in the background (i.e., the northwest direction).

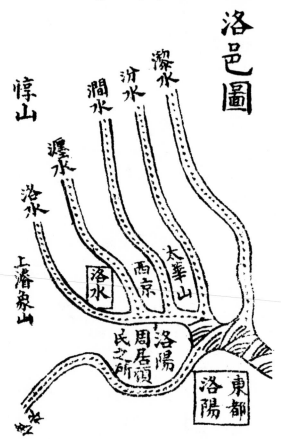

Figure 12.2 A geomantic map of the city of Luoyang and its surroundings (from Xu Shanji and Xu Shanshu, *Dili-Renzixuezhi*, vol. 1, part 2, p. 9).

An Appreciation of East Asian City Sites in Terms of Geomantic Principles

Cities That Fit the Ideal Geomancy Model: Seoul, Kyoto, and Nanjing

The original site of Seoul was obviously located in a geomantically auspicious site. Kyongbok Palace is located in the geomancy cave of the city. The original city is surrounded by mountain ranges, especially its northern end (see Figure 12.3). Pukak Mountain is the main mountain or the black turtle of the city. From there a mountain range extends in an arch flanking both sides of the city. The Inwang mountain range encircles Seoul on the right side of the main mountain, becoming the white tiger of the city. Naksan is the hill that encircles Seoul to the left, hence it's the azure dragon. Namsan, the south mountain, is the peace mountain of Seoul, and Kwanak Mountain is the homage mountain; these two mountains thus become the red bird of Seoul. A long mountain range behind Pukak Mountain represents the ancestral mountains of the main mountain. Seoul has a relatively large basin that becomes the bright yard of the city located between the main mountain, azure dragon, white tiger, and peace mountain. Small streams from the nearby main mountain flow into the center of Seoul, while the large Han River flows in front of the city.

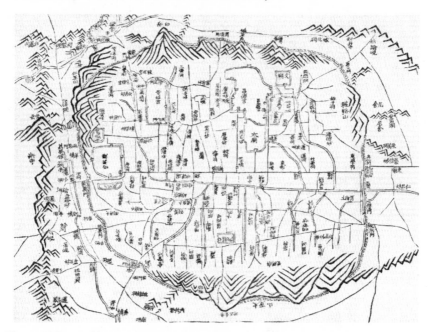

Figure 12.3   A Choson dynasty topographic map of the city of Seoul (from Kim Chongho, Taedong Yojido, 1861)

   Seoul thus has highly auspicious geomantic harmony. As many geomancers have noted, it is one of the most qualified capital sites of Korea. Within the naturally formed geomantically harmonious landscape, the Choson dynasty developed a city of balanced size that fits well into the basin. On the ridges of the mountain range that surround Seoul, the city wall was built to define the city boundary and complete the city landscape.

   The city of Kyoto is in a large basin surrounded by mountain ranges shaped in a horseshoe (see Figure 12.4). In my view the Kyoto Basin is almost a textbook example of an auspicious site. In fact, we know that before the construction of the new capital in the Kyoto Basin in 793, the court consulted geomancers and the minister for home affairs, Wake no Kiyomaro, made sure Kyoto was in accordance with geomantic requirements for an auspicious site.[22]

Figure 12.4 An aerial photographic mosaic of the Kyoto Basin

However, I have not seen any literature evaluating the geomantic quality of the landforms around Kyoto using geomantic concepts and the model of an auspicious place. In my view, the ancient Japanese geomancers and the city builders of Kyoto must have taken the lofty Hiei Mountain as either an ancestral mountain or the main mountain for the capital city and Funaokayama Hill as its entrance head. The Higashiyama mountain range that encircles the Kyoto Basin is definitely the azure dragon for the city, while the Nishiyama mountain range is the white tiger. The Kamo River and the Katsura River are the bright yard watercourses that fed into Ohokura ike Marsh, which has now disappeared. To the south of the swampland there were mountains in the distance that functioned as the red bird, namely the peace mountain or the homage mountain.

The palace in Kyoto is located in town somewhat further down from the geomancy cave. In my view the locations of some Buddhist temples along the northern edge of the city might, in fact, be more auspicious geomantically than the present palace site. According to geomantic principles, it is not desirable to have any architectural structures in the vein of vital energy that runs from the main mountain to the palace.

Nanjing was a capital city for several dynasties, the most important ones in terms of its planning being the Wu kingdom during the third century and the Ming dynasty during the fourteenth century (see Figure 12.5). The Wu kingdom's palace site and city planning became the basis for the later kingdoms of the Six Dynasties period. The palace site backs onto a hill on the northern side and occupies the middle of the basin. The geomancers who advised the city planning must have taken the hilly land of Jilongshan Mountain or Fuzhoushan Mountain as the main mountain in the north, Zijingshan, also known as Zhongshan, as the azure dragon in the east, and Qinliangshan Hill, also known as Shitoucheng Hill, which extended to the Tiger Mountain or Hushan, as the white tiger in the west.[23] Indeed, the protective arms on the eastern and western edges of Nanjing were so conspicuous and auspicious that the famous prime minister and military strategist of the Three Kingdoms period, Zhugeliang, commented that the (azure) dragon "is hidden and crouching in Zhongshan, while (white) tiger is poised and crouching in Shitoucheng."[24]

The authors of *Dili-Renzixuezhi* commented that Nanjing is truly a place deserving to be an imperial capital.[25] Geomantically speaking, the central locations of palaces during the Wu kingdom and others during the Six Dynasties period are better than the location of the later Ming palace in the fourteenth century that was built at the eastern end of the city. While the Ming palace also backs onto a hill, geomancers of the Ming Court obviously interpreted the surrounding landforms of the Nanjing Basin differently than did the previous kingdoms. The Wu and other kingdoms during the Six Dynasties period took the western slope of Zhongshan, which is located on the eastern edge of the basin, as the azure dragon of the city and palace. However, the Ming geomancers must have interpreted Fuquishan Hill on the western slope of Zhongshan or the Zhongshan Mountain itself as the main mountain of the city, and thus the Ming palace was built backing toward it, although it is on the eastern edge of the city (and the basin). This interpretation might have been caused by the majestic position of Zhongshan in the region and the ill fates of the Wu and other kingdoms that had their palaces in the central location of the northern part of the

Nanjing Basin. In my view, the Ming interpretation was a rather unorthodox view of the surrounding landforms of Nanjing and did not really match the geomantic model of an auspicious site that was commonly accepted during the time.

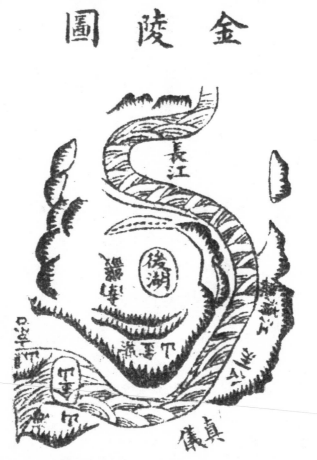

Figure 12.5 A geomantic map of the Nanjing Basin (from Xu Shanji and Xu Shanshu, *Dili-Renzixuezhi*, vol. 1, part 2, p. 9).

Cities That Do Not Fit the Classical Model: Beijing and Changan

Although geomancers justified Beijing's location and a popular geomantic manual claimed it was an auspicious site, it does not fit the model. Indeed, it has a modified landform; i.e., the creation of an artificial mountain behind the palace was an attempt to make up for the geomantic shortcomings of the city.

On a grand scale Changan is naturally quite a good site, as it is on a large flat basin. However, the immediate surroundings of the city are not good, as the protective mountains are too distant from the city site, the river is on flat land, and there are no immediate surrounding hills visible from the palace site.

Concluding Remarks

Geomantic principles for city locations seem to have developed from the art of identifying favorable cave dwelling sites in the Loess Plateau. When one observes the landforms surrounding traditional cities in China, Japan and Korea, it becomes apparent that numerous traditional cities in East Asia are located in geomantically auspicious places, but some are not. Nanjing, Seoul, and Kyoto fit well the geomantic model of an auspicious site, while Beijing and Changan don't. There may be no simple way to interpret this. However, the following conjectures need to be considered to explore this mystery further:

a) The principles of Chinese city planning and those of geomancy may have separate origins. The ancient cities that were developed before the formulation of geomantic principles were not chosen and planned in terms of geomancy. Geomantic principles were only applied in selecting and planning cities of later development, say, after the Han dynasty or even the Tang dynasty.

b) Although the site selection techniques for ancient Chinese cities were developed from geomancy, these principles may not have been applied universally. Geomantic principles regarding an auspicious site are basically for sedentary people like the northern Chinese cave-dwelling builders and farmers to whom a basin that is protected from the cold northwesterlies was of critical importance. Therefore, cities that were built by the people of nomadic herder origin did not comply with the geomantic principles of landforms. Cities in East Asia have diverse origins and those built applying geomantic principles may represent only one type.

c) The geomantic principles as we know them now are a product of evolution. There were many different types of geomantic principles earlier with emphases on different aspects of places. These principles often contradicted each other, and different geomantic conditions of cities in East Asia may represent these variant forms of geomancy practiced during different times and in different places.

Notes

1. This chapter is based on and has developed from a part of my conference paper, presented at International Research Center for Japanese Studies 21st International Research Symposium, Urban Morphology and the History of Civilization in East Asia, Kyoto, December 2002: Hong-key Yoon, Yoon, "Geomancy and Cities: A Preliminary Inquiry into the Origin of Chinese Geomancy and Its Application on City Locations in East Asia," *Urban Morphology and the History of Civilization in East Asia*, International Research Centre for Japanese Studies 21st International Research Symposium, edited by

Minoru Senda, (Kyoto: International Research Centre for Japanese Studies, 2002), 371–389.

2. Yi Pyongdo, *Koryo Sidaeui Yongu* [A Study of the Koryo Period], revised edition. (Seoul: Asea Munhwasa, 1980), 361

3. James Legge, trans., *The Shoo King* (Hong Kong: Hong Kong University Press, 1960) The Book of Chow: Book XII. The Announcement of the Duke of shaou. 420-423.

4. James Legge (1960), *The Shoo King*, 434.

5. James Legge (1960), *The Shoo King*, 436–437.

6. James Legge (1960), *The She King*, p 463.

7. This book was written by twin brothers, Xu Shanji and Xu Shanshu, who started studying geomancy for more than forty years after their father's death.

8. Yang I (1967), *Han lung ching*, in *Dili Zhengzhong* [Authentic Collection of Geomantic Principles]. Commentary by Jiang Guo, (Hsin-chu: Chu-lin Shu-chu, 1967) 1.

9. Xu Shanji and Xu Shanshu, *Dili-Renzixuezhi* [The Fact that All Humanity Must Know] (Hsin-chu: Chulin Shuchu, 1969), vol. 1, part 2, 5.

10. Xu Shanji and Xu Shanshu, *Dili-Renzixuezhi*, vol. 1, part 2, 5.

11. Xu Shanji and Xu Shanshu, *Dili-Renzixuezhi*, vol. 1, part 2, 4.

12. Xu Shanji and Xu Shanshu, *Dili-Renzixuezhi*, vol. 1, part 2, 7.

13. Xu Shanji and Xu Shanshu, *Dili-Renzixuezhi*, vol. 1, part 2, 7.

14. Anon. *Beijing Lvyou shouce* (Travel guide to Beijing), 56.

15. Anon. *Beijing Lvyou shouce* (Travel guide to Beijing), 57.

16. Anon. Beijing Lvyou shouce (Travel guide to Beijing), 59.

17. Xu Shanji and Xu Shanshu, *Dili-Renzixuezhi*, 1, part 2, 8

18. Xu Shanji and Xu Shanshu, *Dili-Renzixuezhi*, 1, part 2, 8–9.

19. Xu Shanji and Xu Shanshu, *Dili-Renzixuezhi*, 1, part 2, 9.

20. Xu Shanji and Xu Shanshu, *Dili-Renzixuezhi*, 1, part 2, 9.

21. Xu Shanji and Xu Shanshu, *Dili-Renzixuezhi*, 1, part 2, 9.

22. George Sansom, *A History of Japan to 1334* (Stanford: Stanford University Press, 1958), 99–100.

23. Tongjidaxue Chengshiguihua Yanjiushi, ed. (1982), *Zhongguo Chengshi Jianshesh* [History of Chinese City Construction], (Beijing: Zhongguo Jianshegongye chubanshe, 1982), 24.

24. Xu Shanji and Xu Shanshu, *Dili-Renzixuezhi*, vol. 1, part 2, 9.

25. Xu Shanji and Xu Shanshu, *Dili-Renzixuezhi*, vol. 1, part 2, 9.

Chapter 13
Seoul: A New Dynasty's Search for an Auspicious Site

Many kings and officials in China, Japan, and Korea were keen to shift their capital cities to auspicious sites. The process of making Seoul the capital of the Choson dynasty shows how eager rulers of a new dynasty in East Asia could be in their search for a new capital site.

For Taejo, the first king of the Choson dynasty, geomancy was critically influential in his choice of Seoul as the capital. The city was laid out according to geomantic principles and Kyongbok Palace was built in the city's most auspicious location. The *Annals of King Taejo* vividly trace the story of the impact of geomancy on the selection and laying out of Seoul.

This chapter is almost totally based on the historical records from the *Annals of King Taejo* and Yi Pyongdo's comprehensive and meticulous historical investigation into this topic.[1] Yi's work is considered in Korea to be the authoritative work on the topic and my discussion benefited much from it.

On the seventeenth day of the seventh moon in 1392, Yi Songge, a general of the Koryo dynasty, took power and established the Chonson dynasty.[2] Within one month of his coronation, the king ordered his officers to select a new capital site. He and his officers had serious discussions on this matter, which was too important to be decided without careful deliberation. The king himself undertook several field surveys of newly proposed capital sites (Figure 13.1). These discussions and field surveys were primarily based on geomancy.

According to the *Annals of King Taejo*, or the *Taejo Sillok*, on the thirteenth day of the eighth moon in 1392 the king ordered the Supreme Policy Council, or *Topyonguisasa*, to move the capital to Hanyang, which is present-day Seoul.[3] This decree was pronounced within one month of his coronation. Two days after the order went out, on the fourteenth day of the same moon, the king sent Yi Yom, an officer of the Finance Commission, or *Samsawupokya*, to Seoul to make preparations.[4] The king was going to move the capital for the first time from Songdo, the former dynasty's capital, to Hangyang. His great interest in moving the capital to Seoul was a result of geomantic prophesies about that city that were made during the Koryo dynasty.[5] Throughout the Koryo dynasty, especially during its last period, there was a popular geomantic prophecy that

Tree-Son, which means Mr Yi, would be king at Seoul.[6] Yi Songge, the new king whose family name was Yi, apparently tried to have his coronation coincide with the prophecy.

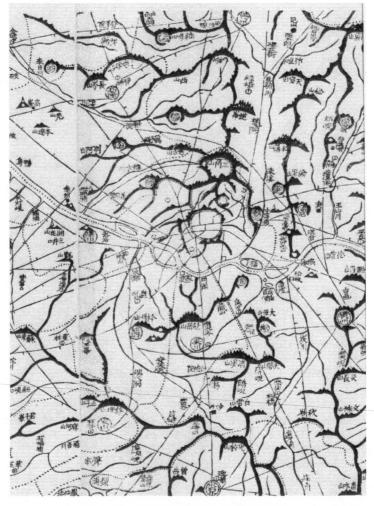

Figure 13.1 Locations of administration centers around Seoul. From Kim Chongho, *Taedong Yoji-do*. The circles with Chinese characters inside represent local administration centers. Notice that most local administration centers are surrounded by mountain ranges.

The king, however, suddenly ordered his officials to prepare for his journey to Keryongsan, and on the nineteenth day of the first moon in 1393 he left for Keryongsan with his officials to examine the geomantic qualities of a possible new capital site.[7] It is unknown why the king changed his mind and suddenly made a trip to the distant area of Keryongsan. But the following two events must be considered: on the twenty-seventh day of the eleventh moon in 1392 the king sent Kwon Chunghwa, the assistant executive of letters, or *Chongdang-munhak*, to Yangkwang, Kyongsang, and Cholla Provinces to select an auspicious site for burying the placenta of (probably) a prince;[8] and on the second day of the first moon in 1393 the king received the report from the officer. According to the *Annals of King Taejo,*[9] when Kwon Chunghwa returned he reported to the king that he had found an auspicious site in Chindong-hyon, Cholla Province. He also presented a landform map of the auspicious site and a map of Keryongsan, a possible capital site in Yangkwang Province.

From the above we may speculate, as has Yi Pyongdo, that the reason the king made a sudden trip to Keryongsan was Kwon Chunghwa's special report on the new capital site.[10]

The king's company arrived at Keryongsan on the eighth day of the second moon in 1393 and the next day started surveying the new capital site. On the eleventh day of the same moon, after the court geomancers examined the possibilities of the site as the new capital, the king himself climbed up to the highest peak in the center of the area accompanied by the geomancer-monk Muhak to consult about the overall geomantic auspiciousness of the place.[11] In response to the king's questions about this, the geomancer-monk answered that he was at a loss to understand its auspiciousness. Despite this reply, the king chose the place as the new capital site. After five days of examining it, King Taejo left for Songdo, leaving some of his officials to supervise the construction of the new capital. Thus the first plan, which was to build the new capital at Seoul, was dropped by the king.

The construction work at the Keryongsan site progressed for about a year (see Figure 13.2). We do not know how much of the construction was actually done, but judging from the unprocessed foundation stones that remain we can assume that the work included only the preparation of construction materials and building sites.[12]

All work on the Keryongsan site was suspended by order of the king, who sent the grand general, or *Taejanggun*, whose name was Shim Hyosaeng, to stop all work on the eleventh day of the twelfth moon in 1393.[13] The reason the king suspended the construction work is found in the record of the eleventh day of the *Annals*. The governor of Kyonggi Province, Ha Yun, informed the king as follows:

> While the capital is supposed to be located in the middle of the country, the Kery-ongsan site is located far south in the nation. The other day, when my father passed away, I looked through geomantic literature [to find an auspicious place to bury him]. Today, when I heard about the landforms of Keryongsan, and that the mountains run in the northwest direction and that the water flows in a southeast-ward direction, I remembered what Hu Shun-chen stated during the Sung dynasty: "It is a location where water destroys long lives and bad elements are fostered

such as dwindling and perishing." Therefore, the Keryongsan area is not an appropriate place to build a capital.[14]

Figure 13.2 The remains of foundation rocks that were partly processed for the construction of the royal palace in the Keryongsan site.

The king then ordered that the geomantic literature Ha Yun consulted, probably Dili xinfa (New Principles of geomancy) written by Hu Shunshen, be brought forward and that his officers examine the correctness of the geomantic principles contained in the book by applying them to the royal tombs of the former dynasty. The principles were found to be correct; the landforms and water direction of the royal tombs coincided with Hu Shun-chen's theory of auspiciousness and inauspiciousness concerning the direction of watercourses and the positions of the mountains. The king then sent Shim Hyosaeng to stop the work on the new capital site in Keryongsan. The *Annals* state that Hu Shun-chen's geomantic writings henceforth became popular in Korea.[15]

On the same eleventh day of the twelfth moon in 1393, the king decreed that all geomantic literature stored in the Bureau of Writings and Clouds, or *Sowunkwan* (the Bureau of Geomancy, Astronomy and Divination), be sent to Ha Yun for review. The king also asked Ha Yun to select another auspicious capital site.[16] Thus, within one year, work was begun and dropped on two possible new capital sites.

After acceptance of Governor Ha Yun's proposal and the abandonment of the Keryongsan site, the king ordered his officers to search for better capital sites. Some officers proposed Muak, situated near the present-day western outskirts of Seoul (around Yonsei University). The land was surveyed by the royal officers.[17] After the king personally examined the area, it was rejected both by himself and the royal officers because of its small size and many geomantic deficiencies. After rejecting the Muak site (on the eleventh day of the eighth moon in 1394), the king again ordered the selection of a new capital site. The officers of geomancy recommended to the king a location that is today Seoul as the new capital site.[18] On the twelfth day of the same moon, King Taejo and his officers went to the area of present-day Seoul to survey, and on the thirteenth day they observed, for possible geomantic harmony, the landforms in the area. When King Taejo asked geomancer Yun Sindal about the qualifications of Seoul as a new capital site, the geomancer replied that Songdo (present-day Kaesong) was a better place and that Seoul should be considered only as a secondary site. He also said that the deficiencies of geomantic harmony in Seoul were the depressed landform of the northwestern area and the lack of water. The king was pleased because he felt that these were not critical geomantic shortcomings, and perhaps because the place had a geomantic prophecy that predicted that Mr Yi would be the new king of Seoul. When King Taejo asked the royal preceptor, a geomancer-monk named Muhak, about the geomantic conditions of Seoul, the monk replied that although he thought the place was qualified in terms of geomantic harmony, the king should discuss this matter with his officers before making a final decision. Again the king was pleased and ordered his officers to present their opinions on the relocation of the capital from Songdo to Seoul. All the officers except one, Ha Yun, informed the king that Seoul would be the best-qualified place.[19] Therefore, King Taejo again decided to select present-day Seoul as the new capital site (Figure 13.3).

Later, on the first day of the ninth moon in 1394, the king established the Bureau of Palace Construction in the New Capital (*Sindo Kungkwol Togam*),[20] and on the ninth day of the same moon he sent Kwon Chunghwa, Chong Tojon, and four other officers to Seoul to lay out the locations of the Royal Ancestral Temple, the palace, the market, and the city streets. The officers chose the present Kyongbok Palace area as the palace site. Having completed their duties, the officers reported to the king on the completion of the layout. According to the *Taejo Sillok*, on the twenty-third day of the ninth moon, the officers returned to Songdo, the capital of that time, but two officers, Shim Tokpu and Kim Chu, remained in Hanyang, the new capital site, for the further supervision of the planning and construction of the city.

After present-day Seoul was again chosen as the new capital site, the king decided to move the capital there even before construction of the city had begun. On the twenty-fifth day of the tenth moon in 1394, he left Songdo, the old capital, for Hanyang, the new capital site.[21] While moving to the new capital, he ordered every department of the central government to leave two officers in the old capital. This hasty movement of the capital by the resolute king may have been due to a strong belief in geomancy. Perhaps the king thought that to be auspiciously influenced by the land he had to leave immediately the old capital, where the former dynasty had collapsed by his hand, and settle in the new capital that was geomantically auspicious and had perhaps a favorable geomantic prophecy. The king arrived in the new capital, Hanyang, on the twenty-eighth day of the same moon and stayed at the visitor's house (*Kaegsa*) of the old Hanyang town, now the new capital site.[22] It is assumed that the king stayed there until the new palace was prepared.

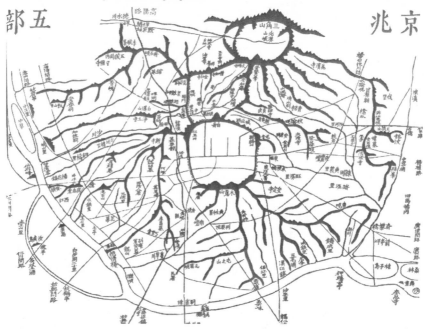

Figure 13.3 A Choson dynasty map of the landforms around Seoul. From Kim Chongho, *Taedong Yoji-do.* The thick lines represent mountain ranges and the thin and curved lines are watercourses.

On the third day of the twelfth moon in 1394, the king ordered Chong Tojon, his faithful officer, to perform a ground-breaking ceremony to the gods, and then the real construction work began.[23] On the fourth day of the same moon, to eliminate the heavy workload for the common people, the government drafted Buddhist monks and assigned them to various construction sites to help with the building work. The first stages of work were, of course, preparing the sites for palaces, royal family temples, and so on; and by leveling the land, transporting construction materials, and the like. However, more laborers were needed, and so on the twelfth day of the eighth moon in 1395 (the fourth year of the king's reign), the government drafted 15,000 laborers from the middle part of Korea (4,500 from the Left Province, 5,000 from the Right Province, and 5,500 from Chungchong Province).[24] These laborers were assigned to the construction work of the palace (see Figure 13.4). On the twenty-ninth day of the ninth moon, about one and a half months from the draft of workers, the palace and the Great (Royal Family) Temple were finally completed. On the fifth day of the tenth moon in 1395, the first royal ancestral worship ceremony was performed in the newly completed temple, and the first royal banquet was held with court officers in the new palace.

Figure 13.4 The throne hall of Kyongbok Palace

The king selected the location for the city walls of the capital, and on the ninth day of the first moon in 1396 he drafted about 118,070 laborers from Kyongsang-do, Cholla-do, and Kangwon-do Provinces, and from the southern part of the northwestern and northeastern territories.[25] The great construction project continued until the end of the second moon of the same year, at which time the laborers were sent back to their homes to work on their farms, as the sowing season was approaching. On the sixth day of the eighth moon of 1396, as soon as the autumn harvesting was completed, the king again drafted 79,400 laborers from the provinces of Kyongsang-do, Cholla-do, and Kangwon-do to complete the construction work of the city wall.[26] After about two months' work, the city wall with its gates and the other city buildings were completed.[27] Thus the long search and the laborious construction of a new capital had come to an end.

This hard-earned new capital was abandoned temporarily during the reign of the next king, who returned to the capital of the former dynasty. King Taejong (a son of Taejo who founded the dynasty) did, however, return to Seoul not long after. His return was due to geomantic reasons and respect for his father's will. Seoul has been the capital of Korea ever since.

The above account was summarized from the *Annals of King Taejo (Taejo Sillok)*. Now, let us consider a legend about the selection of Seoul to show how the real history has been distorted. "Castle of Seoul" goes:

> In the middle years of the Koryo dynasty, the government sent an officer to plant plum trees in Seoul and to prune them ruthlessly when they grew large. This work was done because To Son, the famous geomancer-monk, had inscribed on a stone of one of the peaks of Paekak-san in Seoul, "The next king shall be Yi [which means plum], and the capital shall be transferred to Han Yang [the name of Seoul]."

> As predicted, a general named Yi deposed the king and took over his place. He sent a noted Buddhist monk-geomancer named Muhak to select a site for his new capital.

> Muhak set out and, when he came near Seoul, stood there pondering where he should go. At that moment, Muhak heard a ploughing farmer shout at his ox, "You are as stupid as Muhak!" The monk, Muhak pricked up his ears when he heard this. He told the farmer about himself and asked where he should go to find a new capital site. The farmer advised him to go ten ri (two and a half miles) northwards.

> Muhak followed the farmer's advice and found a suitable site for the new capital. The field where this site is now located is called Wang Sim Ni, which means "go ten ri."

> It was decided that the new capital should be built there; they could not make up their minds, however, about the location of the city wall. One night it snowed and in the morning they found a circle of snow around the site. They decided, therefore, to build the wall along this circle of snow.[28]

Comparing this legend with the official history, we see that the complicated story behind the selection of Seoul has been omitted. This omission, perhaps, was caused either by the author's lack of information or by his desire to simplify the story in order to make it more interesting or easier to tell.

Another difference between the official history and the legend is seen in the role of the geomancer-monk, Muhak. In the legend, his role is exaggerated and glorified; he is helped by a supernatural man who appears to him as a simple farmer.

The legend shows us how official history is preserved, reflected, simplified, and distorted in folk narratives.

Let us now briefly reiterate the auspicious geomantic qualities of Seoul. As seen in Figures 31 and 32, the original city is encircled by a mountain range from the north, east and south, and the main palace of the city is located at the foothill of the southern slope of the encircling hills.[29] At a somewhat distant location south of this palace, a lower hill fences the city, and further south from the hill a river flows from east to west. Within the landmarks of the four directions, a relatively large basin developed, and the original city of Seoul was built on this flat land. With such a situation, Seoul has highly auspicious geomantic harmony. As many geomancers have noted, it is certainly one of the most qualified capital sites of Korea.

Within the existing geomantic harmony, the Choson dynasty developed a city of balanced size that fits well into the surrounding environment. The important mountains around the city have been carefully protected from denudation. Presently, however, the geomantic balance of Seoul is being ignored and destroyed by the developments of a large metropolitan area. The downtown area is now filled with tall buildings, the small streams inside the old city are covered with concrete, and the sacred mountains and hills are covered with houses and apartments.

When one observes the landforms surrounding traditional Korean cities, including Seoul, one can usually see the geomantic reasons for their sites. But traditional city sites are now becoming indistinguishable in appearance from modern ones, for the modern areas have generally expanded in size and have replaced the buildings of the older areas with Western-style buildings. Almost all administrative cities of Korea built before 1910 have their main offices, such as the royal palace and the local government offices, in the most auspicious area of town.[30] These cities are located where all the necessary geomantic objects (such as the main mountain, azure dragon, and white tiger) are found. *Shinjung Tongkuk Yoji Sungnam*, the standard geography of the Choson dynasty that was prepared by the government, shows the locations of the main mountains of cities and of every local county administration center in Korea. The county offices or city halls during the Choson dynasty were located at the foothills of these main mountains. The places where local county offices were considered as administrative urban centers were usually enclosed by city walls. A significant portion of the population inside the walls were people who had non-agricultural occupations such as civil servants, merchants, artisans, and entertainers. The location of the main mountain of every county indicated in the geography book is evidence that each administrative urban center of Korea was placed in a geomantically auspicious site.

Notes

1. Yi Pyongdo, *Koryo Sidaeui Yongu* [A Study of the Koryo Period], revised edition. (Seoul: Asea Munhwasa, 1980), 348–411.
2. Taejo Sillok, vol. 1, 37.
3. Taejo Sillok, vol. 1, 52.
4. Taejo Sillok, vol.1, 52.
5. Professor Yi Pyongdo has said that the king's order concerning the movement of the capital to Hanyang was probably based on the evaluation of the place as an auspicious capital site by the Koryo regime. See Yi Pyongdo, *Koryo Sidaeui Yongu*, 358–359.
6. According to Koryosa, a folk song with the lyrics "Tree-son, which means Mr Yi, will be the king," was very popular among soldiers and civilians, including minors and adults. See Chong Inji and et al. Chong Inji and others, *Koryosa* [History of Koryo] (Seoul: Yonhi Taehakgyo Chulpanbu, 1955), vol. 54, 34.
7. Taejo Sillok, vol. 3, 2.
8. Taejo Sillok, vol. 2, 15.
9. Taejo Sillok, vol. 3, 4.

10. Yi Pyongdo, *Koryo Sidaeui Yongu*, 360.

11. Taejo Sillok, vol. 3, 3.

12. Yi Pyongdo, *Koryo Sidaeui Yongu*, 363

13. Taejo Sillok, vol. 4, 13–14.

14. Taejo Sillok, vol. 4, 14.

15. Taejo Sillok. vol. 4, 14

16. Taejo Sillok. vol. 4, 14

17. Taejo Sillok, vol. 5, 5–6.

18. Taejo Sillok, vol. 6, 10–11.

19. Taejo Sillok, vol. 6, 13.

20. Taejo Sillok, vol. 6, 14.

21. Taejo Sillok, vol.6, 16.

22. Taejo Sillok, vol. 6, 16.

23. Taejo Sillok, vol.6, 18.

24. Taejo Sillok, vol. 8, 4.

25. Taejo Sillok, vol. 9, 1.

26. Taejo Sillok, vol. 9, 5.

27. Taejo Sillok. vol. 9, 5.

28. Abridged from Zong In-sob (1953), 68–69.

29. The spatial geomantic organization of Seoul is well known to the public and especially by geomancers in Korea.

30. This is common knowledge among geomancers and historians in Korea. Local gazetteers as well as the standard Korean geography of the Choson dynasty, Sinjung Tongkuk Yoji Sungnam, support the statement.

Chapter 14
The Social Construction of Kaesong[1]

Kaesong is one of the most talked-about geomantic cities in Korea. This capital city of the Koryo dynasty (918–1392) has probably been in more geomantic tales than any other capital city in Korean history. It was also the only capital city in which the house site of the founder of a Korean dynasty became the palace site.

Historically, Kaesong City and its adjacent district were originally Pusokap County and Tongbihol County of Koguryo. But they were renamed Song'ak County and Kaesong County after Silla conquered the territory in the seventh century.[2] During the second year of, the first king of the Koryo dynasty, King Taejo-Wang Kon moved the capital from Cholwon to the south of Mount Song'ak. It was called Kaeju City after combining the above two counties, and its district was divided into five wards.[3] During the twentieth year of King Sejong's reign of the Choson dynasty, the city was renamed Kaesong, a name that remains today.[4]

Historical records, especially the *History of Koryo (Koryosa)*, and various geomancy tales describe Kaesong's geomantic landscape as sacred and auspicious: the city was destined to be the capital of the Koryo dynasty. The first king of the Koryo dynasty, Wang Kon, and his ancestors were presented as the rightful inheritors of Kaesong and were implied to have a heavenly mandate to unify Korea and rule the country. This interpretation of Kaesong's landscape and the presentation of the folklorized family history of Wang Kon are probably both the result of the social construction of Kaesong as a sacred place. Wang Kon's family history was folklorized and fabricated while Kaesong's geomantic conditions were interpreted and modified to serve the Wang family in establishing, legitimizing, and maintaining their power.

Social Construction

The popular belief system of geomancy provided the ideological support for the social construction of Kaesong as a worthy capital site and the Wang family as the destined rulers of the Koryo dynasty. A place is a product of social construction, or the social processes involving the interpretation, choices, and

241

use of it by people. According to a social constructivist view, social and cultural phenomena and even natural facts do not represent the natural conditions of things but rather are socially constructed and relative to social circumstances. On this issue, David Harvey once commented, "So those measures of space and time which we now treat as natural conditions of our existence were in fact the historical product of a very specific set of historical social processes achieved within a specific kind of society."[5] Trevor Barnes aptly pointed out that the way the social construction perspective views knowledge is always relative to its social setting and the outcome of an active process of fabrication rather than the discovery of a reality.[6]

Karl Marx provided one of the most important intellectual sources of the social construction approach. It was, of course, Marx who made the famous statement, "It is not the consciousness of man [sic] that determines their social being, but, on the contrary, their social being that determines their consciousness."[7] On the intellectual background of social constructivism, W. Detel pointed out that this approach is based on ideas derived from three sources: the Marxist sociology of science, the historical turn of twentieth-century philosophy of science, and the program of naturalizing epistemology initiated by Quine.[8]

It is my view that the geomantic interpretation of Kaesong and its surrounding environment and the mythologized presentation of Wang Kon and his family history can be explained best by taking a social construction approach. The geomantic interpretation of the Kaesong district and the artificial reinforcement of the landscape to achieve geomantic harmony were social constructions intended to make people believe that the place was destined to be the capital of Koryo. The folklorized version of Wang Kon's family history as presented by Kim Kwanui (as cited in *Koryosa segye*) was another social construction to make people accept Wang Kon and his descendants as the legitimated rulers of Korea. Cultural geographers have sometimes suggested that people's relationships with place become important elements in the construction of their individual and collective identities.[9] Certainly Wang Kon and his ancestors' relationship to Kaesong was probably one of the most important elements in constructing their social identity.

The Geomantic Interpretation of Kaesong According to Geomantic Principles

Now we will examine the quality of the geomantic landscape of Kaesong and attempt to trace the way the surrounding landscape was interpreted and implemented by the Koryo government (see Figure 14.1). An auspicious site, whether for a grave, house, or settlement, requires the same basic conditions of landforms and cosmological direction. If a site is qualified in terms of landform conditions, the availability of water, and the cosmic orientation, it will, of course, be facing south with horseshoe-shaped background hills and water nearby. But while a gravesite does not require much space, a village or a town site requires a much larger area of flat land. In order to be an auspicious site for a large city, especially that for the capital of a nation, the site is normally a big flat basin with protective hills in the background and a useful watercourse (a river or lake) in front.

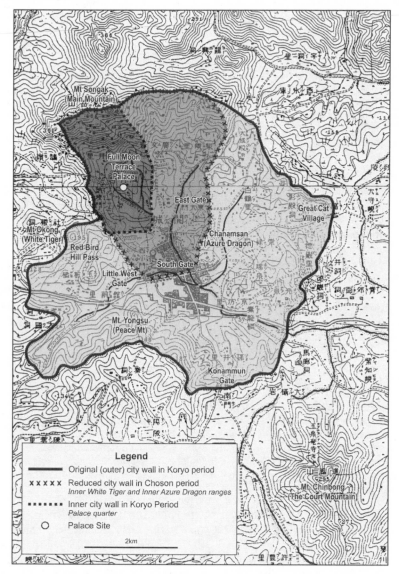

Figure 14.1 Locations of City Walls and Key Geomantic Landmarks of Kaesong

How do these place evaluation principles apply to the landforms and other environmental conditions of Kaesong? Yi Pyongdo probably described the geomantic conditions of Kaesong the most authoritatively and comprehensively based on his rich knowledge of Koryo history and Korean geomancy along with his own fieldwork in the city.[10] My discussion below thus relies substantially on his work.

Surrounding Landforms

Kaesong does not have extensive flat land, for it is on undulating hilly land. Its immediate surroundings are low-lying hills. However, it qualifies as an auspicious site because it has all the necessary geomantic landforms around the city: the oncoming dragon, the main mountain, the azure dragon, the white tiger, the geomancy cave, the peace mountain, and the homage mountain.

a) The oncoming dragon
The oncoming dragon is the background mountain range behind the main mountain of an auspicious place. It extends from the ancestral mountain in the distance and ends at the main mountain. As mentioned, geomancers call this type of mountain range a dragon because it resembles the Chinese dragon, which is thought to have an undulating snake-like form.[11] It is desirable for a mountain range to be long without being disjointed and shaped as if alive by having many folds and a pleasing appearance.

The origin of Kaesong's oncoming dragon that ends at the main mountain, Mount Song'ak, is said to be distant and the range is long and continuous, which is highly desirable in geomancy. Many geomancers have commented that the range started from Mount Paektu, which is the patriarch of all mountains in Korea. It is the source of Korean vital energy that is delivered to auspicious places in various parts of Korea. Kaesong is known to have excellent background mountains, as discussed by Yi Pyongdo:

> Reviewing the geomantic conditions of Kaesong, one can say that its geomantic landscape is majestic and grand in scale by having the auspicious Song'ak Mountain as the main mountain of the city and Mt Ogwan as the mountain behind the main mountain. Mt Ogwan has its origin in the mountain range dispatched from the Great Trunk Mountain Range of Paektu that has run to the South west direction to become the Mashik mountain range. Mt Songak is connected to and arises from there.[12]

Yi Pyongdo's view is in accordance with *Taengniji*, the famous writing of Yi Chung-hwan of the seventeenth century, and with Murayama Chijun's comprehensive work on Korean geomancy in 1931.[13] A recent study by Kim Ki-duk argued that Mount Ogwan is not part of the main line of the mountain range dispatched from Mount Paektu, but is connected to an offshoot branch line of the range.[14] In my view, whether Mount Ogwan belongs to the main line or the branch is not important. What is important is the public sentiment that Mount Ogwan is an important part of Kaesong's background mountains and that its origin can be traced back to the Korean patriarch mountain, Mount Paektu. In geomancy manuals, Mount Paektu is considered to have formed from the eastern branch of Mount Kunlun, which is considered the backbone of the world, in the middle of the world, and with four branches into the world.[15] Therefore, it is believed that the oncoming dragon of Kaesong's Songak Mountain is auspicious and that its "glorious" geomantic genealogy can be traced to the source of the world's vital energy.

b) The main mountain

An auspicious site should have its back toward a hill that forms the end of an undulating mountain range of distant origin called the main mountain. Mount Songak is the main mountain overlooking the city of Kaesong. Although this mountain is well shaped and auspiciously located at the end of the "long and majestic" dragon emanating from Mount Paektu, it is a "child mountain (tongsan)" in geomancy. This means that it is a poorly vegetated hill with exposed boulders and bedrock. This type of mountain was considered to be one of the five most inauspicious mountains in geomancy. That is the reason Wang Kon's ancestor Kangchung was advised by the geomancer Parwon to plant pines to hide the boulders and thicken the vegetation cover. Mount Songak embraces the city. Yi Pyongdo wrote:

> The landform of Songak Mountain is like a majestic folding screen on display. Its shape is called 'The earth mountain that is gathered in heaven' [chuchonto] by geomancers. The mountain sits in the Northwest behind an auspicious place [Kaesong] in the Southeast [Eastwest direction in Yi Pyongdo's book must be a typographical error direction].[16]

This praise of Mount Songak by Yi Pyongdo is directly based on the seventeenth-century Korean geographer Yi Chung-hwan's evaluation of the mountain in his book *Taengniji*.[17] There has been much praise of the geomantic quality of Mount Songak, most of it based on Yi Chung-hwan's comments.

c) The azure dragon and white tiger

An auspicious site must have hill ranges on its left and right that can act as an azure dragon and white tiger. Ideally, the white tiger emanates from the main mountain to the right side of the auspicious site (palace site or city site), and the azure dragon emanates from the mountain to the left. The azure dragon and white tiger should be like two arms stretching from the main mountain and embracing the auspicious site. According to *Zangshu*, the classic geomancy textbook of ancient China, a range that becomes the azure dragon should be undulating, as if a living dragon, with the desire to embrace the site, while the white tiger should sit well tamed to embrace and protect the site.[18] Kaesong has a suitable azure dragon and white tiger. The hill range that descends to the left (east) from the main mountain, Mount Songak, to Mount Chanam is the azure dragon. This range is in accordance with geomantic principles and appears to embrace the palace. It is, however, a somewhat smaller and lower range than the white tiger on the other side. This weakness of the azure dragon was popularly believed to be one of the shortcomings of Kaesong's geomantic conditions.

The hill range that descends to the right of Mount Songak to Mount Okong (Centipede Mountain) is the white tiger of the city. It is the main extension of Mount Songak. Because the hill range on the right side of the city (the white tiger) is stronger than that on its left side (the azure dragon), we have what is called a "right turn" geomantic landscape (wusonkuk) here. In geomancy the dominant white tiger represents women against men and military power against civil and literati power. Because of these geomantic attributes, people often believed that the capital city's women were strong or that the Koryo government was plagued with military revolts and dictatorships.[19] These beliefs were handed down through the generations. Yi Chung-hwan commented that the Koryo dynasty had no distinguished ministers of literati origin but it experienced several military upheavals because the white tiger of Kaesong City was strong while its azure dragon was weak.[20] Yi Pyongdo wrote based on his own field observation:

> The hill ranges dispatched to the left and right from the Songak Mountain: the branch to the western side passes the ruins of Neri Gate and bends toward the Southeast direction in a bow shape, embracing the front of the Full Moon Terrace [Palace]. It runs further to form the red bird hill [chujak hyon] that becomes the inner peace mountain. The branch to the right reaches to form Mt Chanam [inner azure dragon]. The right side of the range is called the inner white tiger by geomancers; the left side, the inner azure dragon.[21]

d) Geomancy cave

The most auspicious site at the foothill of the main mountain is known as the geomancy cave (xue). This is where the vital energy accumulates that is available for people who occupy the site properly by building a house or grave. A geomancy cave is where the palace or administrative headquarters should be built. Kaesong City's geomancy cave is the site of the palace of the Koryo dynasty and is called the "Full Moon Terrace" (Manwoldae) because it is encircled by hills resembling the full moon.

e) The peace mountain and the homage mountain

The first and most important landform condition for an auspicious geomantic landscape is a desirable main mountain that can deliver vital energy to the geomancy cave. The next most important condition is an azure dragon and white tiger that can protect the auspicious site from both sides. It is then desirable to have mountains at the end of the open land (the opposite side of the main mountain) that can act as the peace mountain and the homage mountain. The peace mountain is nearer to the main mountain and the homage mountain is always behind the peace mountain, in the distance. These two mountains together are called the "red bird." *Zangshu* declared that the mountains acting as the red bird should be shaped as if entertaining the main mountain by dancing.[22]

This geomantic principle suggests that the function of the red bird is an auxiliary and complementary one in a geomantic landscape. The peace mountain and the homage mountain are to the gate of a house what the main mountain and geomancy cave are to the house and its resident. The red bird should not dominate the surrounding landscape but contribute to the geomantic harmony of the place by serving the main mountain. Therefore, the red bird should be somewhat smaller than the main mountain and look as if embracing the auspicious site with two arms.

For the city of Kaesong, there are hills and mountains in the southern end of the flat land that can act as the peace mountain and the homage mountain. In fact, there are more than the geomantically required number of such hills. Two peace mountains are identified, although only one is needed. They are classified as the front peace mountain, or Chujakhyon (red bird hill pass), and the back peace mountain, or Yongsusan (mountain of dragon cave).[23] Behind these two peace mountains in the distance, Mount Chinbong (Mountain of Advancing Phoenix) acts as the homage mountain.

Kaesong is said to qualify as an auspicious city site by having all necessary geomantic landforms surrounding it. In my estimation, it has more than enough hills and mountains to meet geomantic requirements, but it does not have enough flat land for a national capital. Still, it was considered the most auspicious and appropriate site for the national capital at the time of the Koryo dynasty by scholars and geomancers, perhaps because it was Wang Kon's hometown and his power base. Yi Pyongdo described the geomantic conditions of the red bird of Kaesong this way:

> It [the hill range dispatched from Mt Songak] runs further to form the Red Bird Hill [Chuchak-hyon] that becomes the inner peace mountain.
>
> In the outer district in the west, Mt Ogong, the point where the inner city wall and the outer city wall are split, extends a branch range in a long bow shape to Mt Yongsu. This hill range becomes the outer peace mountain.
>
> The remaining three mountains, Mt Yongsu, Mt Chinbon and Mt Tukchok, form three rows as the so-called peace mountain [ansan] and homage mountain [chosen].[24]

Through Yi Chung-hwan's remarks on the peace mountain and homage mountain of Kaesong, we can appreciate their geomantic images as well as how people related them to social phenomena of the Koryo period:

> Geomancers labelled Mt Chinbong as the geomantic landscape of a woman sitting in front of a dressing table. For this reason, the kings of the Koryo dynasty came to marry the princesses from China [during the Mongol rule] and because of Mt Pilsan [the Mountain of the Writing Brush], many Koreans passed the Chinese Civil Servant Examinations with excellent results.[25]

Here Mount Chinbong is the homage mountain of Kaesong, and Mount Pilsan is one of the two peace mountains and the nickname for Mount Yongsu because it is a "fire" type of mountain. A fire mountain has a sharp pointed peak and is often known as a "mountain of the writing brush," because its pointed peak resembles a writing brush.

Water Conditions

Kaesong has the streams and rivers required for an auspicious site; two small streams join to form a large stream and two large streams join to form a river. All these patterns are formed in the Kaesong area in accordance with geomantic principles. These watercourses eventually flow southward to form a big river in the south of Kaesong. Yi Pyongdo described the water conditions of Kaesong's geomancy as follows:

> Inside the geomantic landscape of Kaesong [the land surrounded by the main mountain, the azure dragon and white tiger], the watercourse that flows from the left and right of the Full Moon Terrace joins in a letter 'Y' shape at the ruin site of Hungkuksa Temple [The Temple of the Prospering Nation] with that from the district of the Standing Rock [Ipamdong]. After this the water flows further southward and absorbs the watercourse from the direction of Kaesong Station. Then this water flows east to join with the watercourse from Sunjukkyo [Virtuous Bamboo Bridge] in a great 'Y" shape for the second time. After this, the water flows to the southeast to cross the outer azure dragon range before joining the Imjin River.[26]

These watercourses were thought to flow too rapidly and sometimes violently. Yi Pyongdo has correctly argued that their rapid flows were even noted by the first king of the Koryo dynasty who moved the capital to Kaesong.[27] His conjecture is based on Taejo's statement in his ten injunctions for his descendants that "the feature of water in Sokyong (present day Pyongyang) is gentle and concurrent. Therefore, the place is the foundation of all Korean land veins and is the land to deliver great work to the posterity of ten thousand generations."[28] The citizens of Kaesong have suffered from frequent flooding after heavy rains, for much of the water floods into the inner city district.

Flooding in a place was considered an indication of geomantic shortcomings. Building a Buddhist temple in such a place was a popular way of improving its auspiciousness. This type of action reflects the blending of Buddhism and geomancy in practice. That many famous geomancers were prominent Buddhist monks demonstrates the intimate relationship between the two institutions. In geomancy it was understood that building a temple or pagoda in a geomantically weak spot would be similar to applying medicine on a wound or curing the weakness of the human body with acupuncture.

To avoid these flooding problems in the city of Kaesong, several Buddhist temples were established along the critically weak points of the flood-prone watercourses. For instance, Popwang Temple was built on the middle part of Chungdaechon Creek. Hungkuksa Temple was built on the junction where several watercourses merge. Kaekuksa Temple was built on the "inner water outlet of Kaesong," a geomantically important "Y" junction where two large streams merged.[29] Judging from the locations of critical points of Kaesong's drainage pattern in terms of geomancy and flooding problems, it is reasonable to assume that these temples were built for the control of flooding by making up for the shortcomings of Kaesong's geomantic conditions. In particular, the written record on the Kaekuksa (Establishing New Dynasty) Temple is proof that the temples were built on the site to make up for local geomantic short-comings.[30] Building temples and monasteries in such flood-prone places could also be seen as having some practical advantages, as Choi Changjo commented, because such institutions can act as water-watching stations and also provide labor for the resident monks for work projects to prevent and manage flooding, when necessary.[31]

To avoid the inconvenience of flooding almost every year during the Japanese domination of 1910–1945, Yi Pyongdo wrote, these watercourse channels were altered by cutting through the low part of the eastern range (azure dragon) to empty the water outside of the city wall.[32] Although the people and government of Kaesong knew about the shortcomings of Kaesong's watercourses, they did not alter the channels through artificial means until this time. That was because disturbing the auspicious nature of the place was an unthinkable geomantic act, as it would invite misfortune to Kaesong.[33] People simply adjusted to the given environmental conditions and endured the annual flooding problems through acceptable geomantic means, such as building a temple. Recent research on Kaesong's water conditions from a geomantic point of view argues that the general pattern of watercourses there, whether inside or outside the city district, was in straight lines. Kim Ki-duk believes that this drainage pattern is the fatal geomantic shortcoming of Kaesong, because the principle for water conditions recommends that water should not flow in a straight line but in meandering curves.[34] However, in my view the general pattern of watercourses, which the locals did not dare to change, was in accordance with geomantic principles and was not completely straight (although it had no meandering curves).

Cosmological Direction

As we have seen, an auspicious site should also face an auspicious cosmological direction, normally south, which can only be determined with the aid of a geomantic compass. Geomancers say that no matter how auspicious the surrounding landforms and watercourses may be, a wrong choice of direction can bring great misfortune to a palace or other city structure. Kaesong's palace faces south and the city was built to the south of Mount Songak. Geomancers generally agree that both the palace and the city as a whole properly face the auspicious direction, which is why Kaesong is sometimes called "The Auspicious Place of Horse Head (Madu-myongdang)."[35] The term "direction of horse head" was a geomantic one indicating "directly facing south," but it is not commonly used among geomancers today.

Concluding Remarks on the Geomantic Conditions of Kaesong

By examining the surrounding landforms of Kaesong and the building sites for the palace and city wall, it becomes plainly clear how Koryo geomancers interpreted the city's geomantic conditions. A classic description of those conditions is by Yi Chung-hwan in his *Book of Choosing Settlements (Taeng-niji)*, a monumental work in Korean Studies of the seventeenth century:

> A mountain only looks magnificent and has clear water springs, if a mountain's peaks are formed of splendid looking rocks. If a mountain lies where rivers and the sea meet, it has powerful energies. There are four such mountains in the country. One is Mt Ogwan in Kaesong City, another is Mt Samgak in Hanyang [Seoul], another is Mt Kyeryong in Chinjam County and the last is Mt Kuwol in Munhwa County.
>
> Monk Toson said that Mt Ogwan consisted of a summit of the water mountain type with a main body of the wood mountain type (*sumomokkan*) and that its energy reaches far and lasts long. It then ends abruptly and forms Mt Song'ak, which geomancers call an earth-mountain reaching towards the sky (*chuch'ont'o*).
>
> Mt Ogwan is grand and majestic and its spirit seems as if willing to embrace the whole area. There is Majon River to the east, Huso River to the west, and Sung-ch'onp'o Harbour in the front. The two big islands of Kyodong and Kanghwa form a line which blocks both the sea to the south and the lower stream of Han River to the north. They look like guards standing quietly outside the mountain. The whole area is so deep and wide that Tongwol said the landscape here is better formed than that of Pyongyang City. There are many valleys around Mt Ogwan. To the west are the Pagyon Falls and to the east is Hwadam Pond. All the other springs and waterfalls are extremely beautiful as well.[36]

The influential Yi Chung-hwan here praised Kaesong as one of four auspicious places with powerful vital energy in Korea. These places have either been capital cities or been considered as possible capital sites. Mount Ogwan does not appear on a modern topographic map, but it is considered to be the mountain directly behind Mount Songak or even Mount Songak itself. Yi Chung-hwan described Kaesong as an auspicious place having suitable geomantic landforms. His description of the geomantic conditions of Kaesong has been accepted and repeatedly quoted by later scholars.[37]

My own view is that the landforms of Kaesong meet the general requirements for an auspicious capital site, although those landforms are no better than those at some other well-known cities worthy of being capitals, such as Seoul or Keryongsan. By being located in a hilly area, Kaesong does not have as much flat land as Seoul or Pyongyang. One could even say that it is not as good geomantically as the other two cities. The weak background mountain range behind the main mountain of the city and the low-lying eastern side range of the city, the azure dragon, were widespread concerns during the Koryo period.[38] But Koryo rulers and geomancers of the time may not agree with my evaluation of Kaesong, as geomantic principles are relative and landforms can be interpreted from different perspectives, depending on what aspect of geomantic principles one chooses to emphasize.

As of water conditions, it seems that the Koryo rulers and the geomancers of the time agreed that those at Kaesong were not as good as conditions at Pyongyang. In my view, Kaesong's water conditions were certainly not as good as those of Seoul. It seems certain that the water flow was rather rapid, collected in the lowlands of the inner city, and caused flooding. Although Kaesong had the required water, its flow was not as gentle as desired.

But, of course, Kaesong has desirable cosmic directions, and its overall geomantic conditions are suitable for the capital city of Korea. Several other places such as Seoul and Pyongyang are as qualified. Kaesong's choice and promotion as the capital site during the Koryo dynasty were results of the social construction of Kaesong, as it was the hometown and power base of Wang Kon, the founder and first king of the dynasty.

The Personification of Geomantic Landscape and the Reinforcement of Geomantic Harmony

Only a geomantic landscape that has achieved harmony between the various landscape elements can conserve vital energy and make it available to the occupant of the place. Geomantic landscapes are considered to be sort of functioning systems and are compared with functioning systems of living organisms, including people.[39] They are perceived and evaluated as personified objects. The types of blessings to be manifested by auspicious sites are determined by the type of the landscape.[40] Now let us examine how the surrounding landscape of Kaesong was personified in geomantic terms. The landscape, especially the district around the Palace of the Full Moon Terrace, is considered to be the geomantic landscape of an old mouse descending to the field (Noso hajonhyong). This interpretation is perhaps best recounted by Murayama Chijun, who introduced the story in his book based on the *Gazetteer of Kaesong County*.[41] According to the story, the analogy was formed by using the symbols of a mother mouse and her baby to explain the landscape of Kaesong. The story is about controlling "the old mouse" descending to the field with its "baby mouse." The site of the Palace of the Full Moon Terrace is the old mouse and Mount Chanam, a small mountain to the left of the front of the palace site, is a baby mouse. The geomantic reasoning was that if the baby mouse ran away to play, the old mouse would not be happy and would also leave the place to find its baby. This would mean that the auspiciousness of the palace site would disappear and thus the power of the throne would not be stable. To make the old mouse settle in the palace site, they had to keep the baby mouse where it was. To do that, a cat, dog, tiger, and elephant were made on Mount Chanam. The cat controlled the mouse, the dog controlled the cat, the tiger controlled the dog, and the elephant controlled the tiger. The elephant, in return, was believed to have a friendly relationship with the mouse. In this manner, the chain of landscape control was established and ensured the stability of the old mouse in the Palace of the Full Moon Terrace.

Murayama Chijun reports that places such as Cat Well (Myojong), Dog Rock (Kuam), Elephant Rock (Sang'am), Tiger Spring (Hochon), and Boy-Child Mountain (Chanamsan) are said to be the remains of the chain of control of the five animals (which are geomantic personifications).[42] He also reports based on the *Gazetteer of Kaesong County* that a stone cat was placed at the foot of the mountain before the palace, a stone dog was placed at "The Bridge of Sitting Dog (Choakyonkyo)," another stone dog was placed at the foot of Mount Chanam, and a stone tiger was placed at the foot of Mount Nabok.[43] According to his report, all of these stone statues were meant to form a chain of control to establish the stability of the palace site. Settlement names such as the Village of the Sitting Dog (Choakyon-ri) and the District of Tiger Well (Hojong-dong) are said to have originated from the Koryo period and are the relics of a geomantic endeavor to stabilize the geomantic energy of the palace site in the geomantic landscape of the old mouse descending to the field.

To view the landscape of Kaesong is to read the geomantic meanings as reflected in it. To read Kaesong's landscape is to read an allegorical folktale, the story of an old mouse descending to the field. Each part of the landscape has a geomantic message and participates in the story by playing its designated role. In fact, the landscape of Kaesong is a concrete transformation of the geomantic folk narrative of the old mouse and its little mouse and the people's plot to keep them there. No other geomantic landscape in Korea may have such an interesting narrative, which was for those who could read the geomantic landscape of Kaesong.

Mythical Legends From *Koryosa Segye* Relating to the Social Construction of Kaesong and the Wang Family

Koryosa Segye (The Genealogy of Wang Kon, the Founder of Koryo in the History of the Koryo Dynasty) includes stories relating to Kaesong and the ancestors of Wang Kon, the founder of the Koryo dynasty. These stories are from the *Abridged Chronological History (Pyonnyon tongnok)* by Kim Kwanui, which was written during the reign of King Uijong (1146–1170) and is no longer available.[44] Kim Kwanui's work was the main source for *Koryosa Segye* in this regard, while the *Classified Chronological History (Pyonnyon gangmok)* by Min Ji (1248–1326) became a complementary and auxiliary reference.

The Main Points of the Narratives as Quoted from *Pyonnyon Tongonk* in *Koryosa Segye*

Once upon a time a person named Hogyong (Tiger Scenery) called himself Songgol changgun (Hallowed-bone: highest bone rank of Silla general). He traveled from Mount Paektu through various mountains in Korea and arrived at the left valley of Mount Puso (another name for Mount Songak), where he settled and married a local woman.

He was rich and often went hunting, but he had no sons. One day he went hunting to Mount Pyongna with nine other villagers and happened to stay overnight in a cave. A tiger appeared in front of the cave and roared ferociously. The ten men were all scared that the tiger would eat them. They decided to throw their hats in front of the tiger and whoever's hat was bitten first had to confront it. Once they had thrown their hats, the tiger bit Hogyong's hat and he went out to fight it. However, once he got out of the cave, the tiger had disappeared and the cave collapsed, killing all nine villagers. At the funeral of the nine victims he prepared sacrificial offerings to the mountain guardian spirit. Then the mountain spirit, who identified herself as a widow, appeared to him and told him that she wanted him to be her husband. She consecrated him as the king of the mountain. No sooner had she spoken when both Hogyong and the mountain spirit disappeared. After this episode, Pyongna County folks worshiped him as the king of the mountain and made a shrine for him.

Hogyong missed his first wife and appeared to her every night in a dream and slept with her. Soon after, she gave birth to a clever and noble-looking son, Kangchung. He lived in Mahagap of Mount Ogwan in Puso County.[45] At that time a well-known geomancer named Parwon came to Puso County, which was on the northern side of Puso Mountain.[46] The geomancer advised Kangchung to move his residence to the south of Puso Mountain and plant pines to hide boulders on the mountain shape. If he did so, a son would be born there who would unify Korea. After hearing this, Kangchung, together with fellow county people, shifted the county settlement to the south of the mountain and planted pines all over the mountain. He changed the county name to Songak (Pine Hill) and became the county commander. Afterwards he resided in both the new house and the old one at Mahagap by traveling between the two places. He became rich and had two sons; the second was Poyuk, a man of wisdom, who became a monk. While he lived in Mahagap, he dreamed one night that when he urinated from the Kongnyong Hill pass toward the south, his urine flooded Korea and the whole land changed to a silver sea. A geomancer of Silla came to tell him that one day he would have the emperor of the Tang dynasty of China as his son-in-law if he continued to live there.

Poyuk had two daughters. Chinui, the second daughter, was beautiful and clever. One day her elder sister had a dream of her urinating at the peak of Mount Ogwan, which caused flooding everywhere. This was an auspicious dream and Chinui bought her elder sister's dream with her silk skirt.[47]

At this time Emperor Suzhong of the Tang dynasty came to the Kongnyong Mountain Pass of Songak County before his enthronement, and while looking toward the south he announced the place as worthy of being the capital city. Then an assistant told him that this was the place where eight *shinson* (Taoist supernatural beings) lived. Suzhong stayed at Poyuk's house in Mahagap for one month and made Chinui pregnant. Chinui gave birth to a son, Chakchegon, who was clever and brave. Chakchegon boarded a merchant ship bound for China at the age of sixteen to meet his father. Due to bad weather, he was left on the bank where the dragon king of the West Sea lived. The dragon king asked Chakchegon to kill a wicked fox that had been the cause of a severe headache.

Chakchegon killed the disguised evil fox with a bow and arrow and the dragon king granted him a wish as a reward. Chakchegon told him that he wanted to become the king of Korea. The dragon king told him that he was not yet qualified to be so and asked him to wish for something else. Chakchegon told him that he wanted to marry his daughter. The dragon king agreed and as a wedding gift gave seven treasures and a sacred pig to Chakchegon. When the newly wed couple arrived home, people from the four districts of Kaeju, Chongju, Yomchu, and Paekju, as well as the three counties of Kanghwa, Kyodong, and Haum, built Yongansong Palace and a defence wall around it for them.

When the dragon lady, Chakchegon's wife, arrived at Kaesong, she dug a well at the northeastern slope of the mountain and collected water from it with a silver container. This place is now the Great Well of Kaesong. One day, after they had been living at Yongansong for a year, the pig refused to get into its pigsty. The owner told the pig that if it was not a suitable place to live, he would follow it to a better place. The next morning the pig went to a site on the southern slope of Mount Song'ak. Because of this, Chakchegon and his wife moved to the site and built a new house there. This happened to be the place where Kangchung used to live. Chakchegon lived there for thirty years, commuting between his new home and Yongansong.

The eldest son of Chakchegon and the dragon lady was Yonggon, whose name was changed to Ryung. He was the father of Wang Kon. He lived in the old house on the southern slope of Mount Song'ak for many years, but later he built a new house further south. This was the site of Pongwonjon of the Yonkyong Palace. At this point in time Master Toson returned to Korea, having studied geomancy from Master Ilhaeng of the Tang dynasty in China. He traveled from Mount Paektu to Kongnyong of Kaesong observing geomantic conditions. He arrived at Wang Kon's father's house and uttered, "Flax is planted in the place where the millet should be planted."

After Wang Kon's father and Master Toson had been up to Kongnyong Hill and had discussed the geomantic conditions of the Kaesong area, Master Toson said to Wang Kon's father: "The geomantic vein of this place is from the north, Mount Paektu, which has the 'water' element (root) and the 'wood' element (trunk) and forms the auspicious place of the 'Horse Head.' Since your cosmological characteristics also belong to the 'water' element, you should build a house of thirty-six compartments, six-times-six, which is the number representing the 'water' element. Then it will correspond to the cosmological characteristics of heaven and earth, and a son will be born to you next year who shall be named Wang Kon."

On the site, Master Toson wrote on a piece of paper: "While humbly bowing a hundred times, I present this to you, the great man who will unify the whole of Korea." Wang Kon's father built his house as Master Toson had directed and in the very first month his wife became pregnant and later gave birth to Wang Kon, the first king of Koryo. *Koryosa Segye* also quotes the following from the *Classified Chronological History (Pyonnyon Gangmok)* by Min Ji:

> When Wang Kon was 17 years old, Master Toson came back to see him and told him that because he was born on this extraordinarily auspicious site, appropriate for the time of confusion, the people were waiting for him to rescue them at this time of internal strife. Toson taught him at that place about battle formation tactics, methods of choosing advantageous time and place as well as the skill of drawing strength from nature.[48]

An Analysis and Interpretation of the Legends

Now I would like to analyze and explain how these stories reflect the social construction of Kaesong as a worthy capital site and Wang Kon and his family as worthy rulers of the country.

Among the studies of these tales, Yi Pyongdo's is probably the most important, and it is the most relevant for my inquiry here.[49] Murayama Chijun's work on this topic is extensive and perceptive but focused on interpreting the importance of geomantic values as a folk belief in Korea.[50] Unlike Yi Pyongdo, he did not attempt to divide the tales into different units, but pointed out that Hogyong becoming the mountain god of Mount Song'ak and the Chinese Emperor Suzhong's siring of Chakchegon in the tale are merely attempts to demonstrate the dignity and sacredness of the Koryo royal line.[51] He also commented that geomantic values and principles are well expressed in Hogyong's journey from Mount Paektu to settle in Songdo and in geomancer Parwon's advice to move Kangchung's house to the south of Mount Song'ak and to plant pines to hide boulders.[52]

Two other recent studies on the tales by Choi Pyong-hon and Kim Ki-duk are both based on Yi Pyongdo's work.[53] Two additional works by Na Kyongsu and You In Soo examine these tales as oral literature and analyze their literary style and structure.[54] I will now introduce Yi Pyongdo's study before presenting my own. Yi Pyongdo summarized and divided the above tales into four units:

1) Hogyong's settling in Pususan (Mount Song'ak), becoming a mountain deity, and having a son, Kangchung.

2) The movement of Song'ak County to the south of Mount Song'ak by Kangchung as advised by the geomancer Parwon.

3) Suzhong of Tang's staying at Poyuk's house and making his second daughter, Chinui, pregnant. She gave birth to Chakchegon, the grandfather of Wang Kon.

4) Sejo (Yonggon), the father of the first king of Koryo, meeting the geomancer-monk Toson while building a new house. Toson commented that he
   was planting flax in the location where millet should have been planted and
   advised him to build a house of thirty-six compartments. After building his
   house according to Toson's advice, he became the father of a new son,
   Wang Kon.[55]

Yi Pyongdo believed the tales had little value as reliable historical records,
but that they attempted to demonstrate three things: Mount Song'ak, the
hereditary home of the Wang family, as a mystic and sacred place; Wang Kon's
birth and his family line as sacred and divine; and Wang Kon as the person
having the heavenly mandate to establish a new dynasty by unifying Korea.[56]
Among all studies on the tales, his seems to me the most perceptive and
enlightening; he suggests that the tales indicate a kind of social construction of
Kaesong as a sacred place and Wang Kon as the legitimate ruler of Korea.
However, he did not analyse the process of social construction as reflected in the
narratives and present evidence to substantiate his views.

Kim Ki-duk, following Yi Pyongdo's study, divided the tales in *Koryosa
Segye* into six units, each representing one of the five generations of Wang
Kon's ancestors plus Wong Kon himself. These were Hogyong, Kangchung,
Poyuk, Chakchegon, Yonggon (Sejo), and Wang Kon.[57] He then listed information related to geomancy from the tales. Kim agreed with Yi Pyongdo's
interpretation of the tales, saying that the geomantic elements in them must
represent the attempt to consecrate Kaesong as a sacred place and to present
Wang Kon as the one having the heavenly mandate to unify Korea.[58] However,
he argued that the main point indicated by the geomantic elements in the tales
was the question of "which mountain should be the main mountain" of Kaesong.[59] His argument is based on his assumption that these tales reflect the
geomantic principles for the main mountain of an auspicious place as understood by the people of the time. I think that Kim's assertion is somewhat
unreasonable and implausible, for it is difficult to see the tales as a reflection
and documentation of the early Koryo people's debate on where the main
mountain should be. Murayama Chijun correctly pointed out that the stories are
geomantic and intended to mask Wang Kon's birth and his family lineage in
mystery, although he did not point out that the tales were ultimately intended to
legitimize Wang Kon's unification of Korea and establishment of a new
dynasty. Previous research on the geomantic aspects of the *Koryosa Segye* tales
mainly focused on the documentation of the mysteriously auspicious nature of
Kaesong, and of how, by occupying such a site, Wang Kon's family was
consecrated to be the rulers of Korea.

In 1982 Michael C. Rogers published a substantial article on the parts of
Kim Kwanui's *Abridged Chronological History (Pyonnyon tongnok)* quoted in
Koryosa Segye. In this article, he accepted that a prime purpose of the narratives
by Kim Kwanui was "the glorification, indeed the sacralization, of the dynastic
line."[60] However, he presented an ingenious and rather unorthodox view that the

folklorized genealogy of Wang Kon was written by Kim Kwanui by selectively drawing from the material transmitted from the time of Wang Kon. Rogers argued that this was done to meet the pressing need for strengthening the legitimacy of the Koryo government in Kaesong during the reign of King Uijong after the rebellion of the western capital (1135–1136) by Myochong and the establishment of the Jurchin (Chin) state in Manchuria.[61] Although his view is noteworthy, a noticeable shortcoming of it is his consideration of Kim Kwanui's quoted version alone and failure to examine it in a wider context as a part of *Koryosa Segye* utilizing readily available material. The compilers of *Koryosa Segye* included the relevant narratives and comments in the *Classified Chronological History* by Minji as well as their own comments. An example is the comment that these tales were known to China and were treated as a historical record of the Koryo history as implied in the story of King Chungson's conversation with a royal archivist in Beijing.[62] The validity of Rogers' view on the narratives is further cast into doubt when we consider that King Uijong's time was more than 200 years after the establishment of the Koryo dynasty and long after the establishment of the legitimacy of Wang Kon's descendants as the rulers of the Koryo dynasty. It is difficult to believe that Moyochong's short-lived rebellion or the rise of the Jurchin state seriously challenged the legitimacy of the Wang family as the rulers of Korea. It is more reasonable to conclude that the legends were meant to promote and justify Kaesong as a sacred place and Wang Kon as the legitimate ruler of the unified Korea.

I will now analyse the social construction of Kaesong as the capital and Wang Kon and his successors as the legitimate rulers by focusing on three issues relevant to the process of construction:

(i) The geomantic quality of Kaesong: the social construction process of presenting Kaesong as the sacred capital in the narratives. Wang Kon's folklorized genealogy promotes the idea of the Wang family as the inheritor of Kaesong through a divine and mysterious association with the place.

(ii) The mysterious lineage of the Wang family: this aspect of the narratives is about the process of deifying and glorifying Wang Kon's family heritage and his birth. The narratives promote Wang Kon's family lineage as having divine and Chinese imperial heritage. They also promote Wang Kon himself as the one who Toson prophesied would unify Korea. In my opinion, the story is arranged in a logical sequence. The first part is about deifying the earliest ancestor of Wang Kon in Kaesong as the mountain deity (king) of Mount Songgak. The narratives concluded with Wang Kon being the person predicted to unify Korea, which was in tripartite states. As early as 1947, Yi Pyongdo perceptively read the *Koryosa Segye* tales and declared that "they are seen to mystify Song'ak (Kaesong) as the origin of the Wang family and sanctify Wang Kon's birth and his family line. They also glorify Wang Kon as having a heavenly mandate to unify Korea and establish the Koryo dynasty."[63] He pointed out the essence of the hidden text of the *Koryosa Segye*, although without analysis and supporting evidence.

(iii) Analogy to the stages of the geomantic survey: I suggest here that the narratives in *Koryosa Segye* were roughly arranged in sequence analogous to the process of a geomancer's field survey to find an auspicious site and to eventually construct an appropriate structure in the geomancy cave. In my view, the narratives reflect a geomancer's field survey by identifying the main mountain first, examining its root from Mount Paekdu, and concluding with finding an auspicious site.

I have divided the legends of Wang Kon and his ancestors into six parts. My analysis considers how each of the above three issues are reflected in these parts.

Part one: The mythical legend relating to Hogyong. The story begins with Hogyong, the first ancestor of Wang Kon who settled in Kaesong

(i) The geomantic quality of Kaesong

According to the story, Hogyong traveled from Mount Paektu through different parts of Korea and eventually arrived at the left valley of Mount Puso (Song'ak) of Kaekyong. Mount Paektu is the highest mountain in Korea, the patriarch of all Korean mountains, and thus the source of vital energy. Therefore, this part of the story implies that Kaesong's background mountain range, namely its oncoming dragon, extends from Mount Paektu in the northern end of the Korean Peninsula. This makes Kaesong an auspicious place of exceptional quality, and the city can claim geomantic authenticity and legitimacy.

(ii) The mysterious lineage of the Wang family

Hogyong (which literally means "Tiger Scenery") is described as an immigrant from the north, probably near Mount Paektu. This might imply that he was a descendant of the Koguryo people. Wang Kon's Koryo dynasty wished to be the successors of Koguryo, as evident in its name: Koryo is the abridged name of Koguryo.[64] The fact that Hogyong married a local woman may signify the marriage between the northern immigrants and the local inhabitants.

Hogyong is presented in the tale as a divinely chosen man who became a mountain deity. When Hogyong went hunting and stayed overnight with nine villagers, a tiger singled him out and rescued him from the cave before its mysterious collapse, while the others were left to perish in it. In Korean folk beliefs, the tiger is often considered an agent of a mountain deity or the transfiguration of the deity itself. This is clearly evident in the sacred paintings of mountain deities posing with tigers, which are worshiped in many Korean Buddhist temples. The tiger in the story may represent the female deity of the mountain itself. The tiger's rescue of Hogyong may demonstrate that he is divinely anointed.

In the story, Hogyong was consecrated by the mountain spirit whom he married as the king of the mountain. Afterwards the people built a shrine for him and worshiped him as the mountain king. In this way the first ancestor of Wang Kon was deified. This story implies that Wang Kon's family line came from the mountain god of Kaesong, which claims divine legacy of their genealogy over the district of Kaesong. It implies that the Wang family has divine power over Mount Song'ak, the main mountain of Kaesong, and effectively consecrates Hogyong, the first ancestor of Wang Kon in Kaesong, as the divine ruler of the district. This is the mythological stage of the Wang family genealogy.

(iii) Analogy to the stages of the geomantic survey

Hogyong's journey from Mount Paektu to Mount Puso (Song'ak), the main mountain of Kaesong, is comparable to a geomancer's initial stage of a field survey. The quality of the main mountain is of particular importance. The first step in a geomantic survey is to examine the root—the background mountain range—of the main mountain by following the range extending from the ancestral mountain to the auspicious site, where it ends. It is important for a geomancer to examine the background mountain as to whether it carries vital energy from the ancestral mountain. Hogyong's journey to Mount Song'ak is analogous to this initial stage of a geomancer's field survey of an auspicious site.

Part two: The legend relating to Kangchung. The next stage of the story of the Wang family is about Kangchung, the son of Hogyong.

(i) The geomantic quality of Kaesong

Mount Puso (Song'ak) is geomantically auspicious in its shape and formation, but is poorly vegetated with exposed boulders, hence inauspicious. Such mountains are to be avoided for use as sites for human settlements or graves, no matter how well shaped they may be. Their defects must be remedied by planting trees to hide the barren surface before they can be used as auspicious sites. Murayma Chijun thought that pines were preferential to other kinds of vegetation because pines were considered auspicious in Korean folk beliefs: They are evergreen and their leaves are bifurcated needle shapes in a balanced proportion, which symbolizes the harmony of yin and yang elements.[65] I feel his conjecture is reasonable; the pine symbolizes longevity, unbending will, and integrity, because it is constantly green even during the winter. By planting more pines in the mountain, one is making the mountain more auspicious and more sacred.

The event of Kangchung moving his house to the southern slope of Mount Song'ak and planting pines there should be viewed as the result of his geomantic consideration for two reasons. First, his action was advised and directed by the geomancer Parwon of the Silla dynasty. Second, it clearly reflects the geomantic principles for an auspicious site: one facing south is more desirable than one facing the opposite direction. The south side of a hill or mountain in East Asia always has more luxuriant vegetation than the north side since it is the area that enjoys maximum sunlight. By planting pines Kangchung converted the inauspicious "child mountain" into an auspicious one. The renaming of the county Song'akgun (Pine Hill) was geomantically appropriate because the name implies that pines are the main feature of the hill. Planting pines and changing the name of the hill strengthened the geomantic landscape by making up for its shortcomings. By moving their home to the southern slope of Mount Song'ak, Kangchung and his family were, in effect, proclaiming that their family residence was on the most auspicious site of the auspicious mountain.

But why did Kangchung retain his original residence at Mahagap after building the new one on the southern slope of Mount Song'ak, and why did he continue residing at his old house along with his new one? One cannot help but wonder whether he had moved to the new place for symbolic reasons, as it was said to be geomantically superior and politically more appropriate for the leader of the local community. That is probably why he moved the whole county settlement to the new place. However, his economic base may have remained in his old residence at Mahagap and he may have been more attached to his hereditary residence. In fact, he may have even spent more time in his old residence than in his new one.

(ii) The mysterious lineage of the Wang family

Kangchung married the daughter of a rich man. This story signifies the elevation of the Wang family's socioeconomic status as members of the leading local gentry and represents another step forward in the social construction of the family as the rulers of Korea.

(iii) Analogy to the stages of the geomantic survey

This part of the story is comparable to the second stage of the geomantic survey: examining the surrounding landscape of an auspicious site after arriving at the main mountain. This stage involves examining and enhancing the main mountain by planting pine trees and pine branches around an auspicious site after locating the approximate site of the geomancy cave.

Part three: Poyuk and Chinui.

In the legend Poyuk was the second son of Kangchung and Chinui was Poyuk's second daughter. They were posthumously honored as the national foundation king and the first queen of the dynasty by Wang Kon.[66] Yi Chehyon (1287–1367), an honored scholar of the Koryo dynasty, questioned the logic behind such posthumous royal honoring, but went no further.[67] The honoring could suggest that they were, in fact, husband and wife rather than father and daughter. The couple may have been folklorized as father and daughter to bring in the story of the Chinese emperor's visit to Chinui, who made her pregnant to sire Wang Kon's grandfather, Chakchegon. Perhaps fabricating such a story was a convenient means of imparting unimpeachable prestige to Wang Kon's family lineage. Such a claim to Chinese royal blood could have enabled the Wang family to be seen as having a unique genealogical heritage superior to any Korean families. Therefore, the story was useful in legitimising Wang Kon and his descendants as the royal family of Korea.

(1) The geomantic quality of Kaesong

This story of Poyuk's return to Mahagap may not be another step in the social construction of Kaesong as a sacred place, but it can be seen as consolidating the past progress made by earlier generations and reflecting on it. We can assume that his move back to his old home district provided an opportunity to reaffirm Kaesong as the sacred place. It also proved that his ancestor Chakchegon's move back to Kaesong (the site of Kangchung's old residence) was the correct one Poyuk practiced Buddhism and built a small temple in Mahagap, where his two daughters were born. This story lays a foundation for his son (or grandson) to move back to Kaesong and confirm its auspiciousness.

In the story, Suzhong of the Tang dynasty expressed his view that Kaesong was a place worthy of becoming a capital city. He uttered the statement while looking south from Kokyong (Mount Song'ak). The story describes the Chinese emperor as a geomancer or geomantic prophet who recognized the geomantic quality of Kaesong. This story carries much weight in promoting Kaesong as the capital city because it implies that even the Chinese emperor praised the geomantic landscape of Kaesong. In the story the emperor's assistant commented that eight supernatural beings (Taoist sages) were living there. This part of the *Koryosa Segye* tales seems to have aimed to add more prestige to Kaesong and present it as the place destined to be the capital of the Koryo dynasty.

Both Poyuk and Chinui are associated with dreams of flooding the world with their urine. Poyuk had such a dream and Chinui bought such a dream from her sister with a silk skirt. How are we to explain this? A flood is a common theme in folk narratives around the world, ranging from the well-known biblical story of Noah's ark to the less-known Maori story of the origin of the Gisborne River in New Zealand by the urination of the Maori kuia (old lady) from a hilltop. Flood myths are said to symbolize the new mana (power or authority) over the land, the renewal of the earth, or the baptism of the land, such as in the flood myth in Genesis. Similarly, one could interpret Poyuk's and Chinui's flood dreams as symbolising Korea being placed under the Wang family's authority. The location in their dreams was the hilltop in the Kaesong district, which could signify that Kaesong was destined to be the capital city where the Wang family would rule Korea.

(2) The mysterious lineage of the Wang family

Bringing the Chinese imperial heritage into the Wang family lineage is an important stage in molding the Wang family's social prestige. Glorification of a family line by making links to a famous person or prestigious family line was not uncommon in Korea, nor in the rest of the world.

China was the center of the known world to Koreans during the ninth and tenth centuries. The Chinese emperor and his royal family line were perhaps recognized as the most prestigious people in the world. That is why the authors of the folklorized Wang Kon family history fabricated the story of Suzhong of the Tang dynasty staying in Poyuk's house and making Chinui pregnant to give birth to Chakchegon. This part of the story is not particularly plausible and thus could be seen as an attempt by the Wang family and their followers to present Wang Kon and his descendants as prestigious and equal to the Chinese imperial family. It could also be seen as an attempt to convince the Korean people that the Wang family was special and worthy of ruling Korea, and that it was therefore untenable to challenge their legitimacy.

(3) Analogy to the stages of the geomantic survey

This part of the story is comparable to the stage of re-checking a new site and going back to the old place. It is the stage of reconfirming the auspicious site after rechecking it.

Part four: Chakchegon

(i) The geomantic quality of Kaesong

Chakchegon was born in Mahagap but moved back to Kangchung's old house in Kaesong, the future capital site. This implied that Kaesong was more auspicious than Mahagap or Yongansong castle. With the mysterious guidance of the "golden pig," Chakchegon returned to and reoccupied the most auspicious spot chosen by his grandfather. This story shares the same type of moral as the earlier story of Koguryo moving the capital to Kungnaesong.[68] That earlier story of moving the capital to Kungnaesong during the reign of the second king of Koguryo, King Yuri, is recorded in *Samkuksagi (History of the Three Kingdoms)* as follows:

> On the Third Moon of the 21st year of the reign of King Yuri [2A.D.], the pig chosen for sacrificial rites escaped and ran away. The king ordered Solji, the officer in charge of sacrificial rites, to chase it. He chased it and caught it at Kungnaewinaam and arranged a local resident to look after it. Then, Solji reported back to the king, "When I chased the pig to Kungnaewinaam, I found that the place was both well protected by mountain barriers and suitable for growing crops. It was also rich in game animals and fish. If you move the capital to this place, it will be advantageous for the people's economic well-being as well as defence from the enemy." During the 9th Moon of the same year, the king went to Kungnae to have a look at the place and in the 10th Moon of the following year [3A.D.], the king relocated the capital to this site.[69]

The story of Chakchegon finding an auspicious site on the southern slopes of Mount Song'ak is remarkably similar to the Koguryo story of Solji finding a new capital site. Chakchegon's "golden pig" story seems to be a rearranged story of Solji's placed in a different context, because in both cases the sacred pigs ran away and were caught at the auspicious site, which was to be the new capital. The finding of an auspicious site by animals is an important theme in Korean geomancy tales; tigers and other animals sometimes point out geomantically auspicious sites for charitable human beings. The idea of finding an auspicious site through a sacred pig may indicate the transmission of the Koguryo heritage to Koryo. Koguryo was sometimes called Koryo, and the founders of Koryo naming their kingdom Koryo was meant to claim that they were the successors of Koguryo. The recovery of the old Koguryo territory had always been an important national policy of Koryo.

Why does a sacred pig rather than a tiger or human being find an auspicious site in the story? What does the pig symbolize in Korean culture? Briefly, a pig symbolizes good luck or wealth and prosperity. Many Koreans still believe that dreaming of a pig on New Year's Eve is a good omen for the New Year.[70] Perhaps to a Korean finding the lost or escaped "lucky" pig was a sign of good luck and the location where it was found was a lucky place. Using an animal to find an auspicious site reflects the merging of traditional Korean symbolism and Chinese geomantic ideas.

On this issue, Choi Pyonghon drew our attention to a Chinese historical source, the Tung'i section of *The Book of Wei* in the *History of the Three Kingdoms (Sankuoji)*. The Upru people who are related to ancient Koreans favored rearing pigs and used pig meat for food, pig skin for cloth, and pig fat for protecting them from cold by applying it to their skin.[71] Choi conjectured that the belief in pigs as good finders of auspicious places might have been widely spread among the ancient Puyo people who were later incorporated into Koguryo.[72] Choi seemed to suggest that the moral of pigs finding auspicious sites was repeated in the story of Chakchegon, because the Koryo inherited the traditions of Koguryo. It is a reasonable conjecture, although it is unknown whether such a belief was widely spread among the ancient Korean people. For research on this issue, the analysis of Korean geomancy tales could provide some insight, for Korean folk narratives have a number of legends and folktales about animals finding auspicious sites for good people.

Even after moving from Yongansong on the West River of Kaesong to the new place on the southern slope of Mount Song'ak, Chakchegon, as noted above, did not abandon the old home but used it as another residence. He commuted between the two places. With Chakchegon's and Kangchung's way of living between the two places, we can perhaps see a precedent for, or even the origin of, Koryo's two capital system. From the beginning of the Koryo dynasty, Taejo attempted to maintain the two capital system, with Kaegyong (the main capital) and Sogyong (the western capital, presently Pyongyang) given equal importance.

With the story of Chakchegon moving to the southern slopes of Mount Song'ak by rediscovering and reoccupying his ancestor's old house site, the legend may have been intended to facilitate the social construction of Kaesong's palace site: namely, to convince the readers that the palace site was double-checked and reconfirmed as the most auspicious location in Kaesong.

(ii) The mysterious lineage of the Wang family

Claiming to be a son of a Chinese emperor who was married to the daughter of the dragon king of the West Sea represents a major elevation of the Wang family's prestige to the highest possible social and political level. How should we interpret Chakchegon meeting the dragon king and marrying his daughter? Here the *Koryosa Segye* quoted another source that stated that Chakchegon, in fact, may have married the daughter of a powerful family, the first ranking officer of the Silla dynasty in Hwanghae Province, which is to the west of Kaesong. [73] Based on the information in *Koryosa Segye*, it may be reasonable to interpret Chakchegon marrying the daughter of the dragon king as a folklorized version of his marriage to a powerful family in the west of his home district. Choi Byong-hon aptly interpreted this legend as embellishing the most humble background of the Wang clan of Kaesong. He suggested that it gave insight into the relationship that the Wang clan had with the maritime commercial powers of the West Sea. [74]

The legend, centering around Chakchegon landing on an island and the seven treasures there, implies that his wife's family was based in a harbor district, extending its influence over the islands on the west coast of Korea, which involved a considerable amount of trade and commercial power. Judging from the story of the dragon king fighting and asking Chakchegon to kill his arch rival, the magic-performing fox, one can conjecture that his wife's family was in conflict with another force or clan and sought help from Chakchegon. With the help of Chakchegon's military power, the dragon king was able to defeat the adversary and invited Chakchegon to marry his daughter. This tale of Chakchegon might be the folklorized version of the above conjectured "historical" event. The fact that his wife was presented as the daughter of the dragon king should be seen as an attempt to give prestige to his family by associating his family with the folk belief in dragons.

(iii) Analogy to the stages of the geomantic survey

This part of the story is comparable to the process of rediscovering and re-confirming the geomancy cave—the most auspicious spot where the pig went—and to double-checking the auspiciousness of the chosen site, which was done by Chakchegon's ancestor with the sacred pig.

Part five: Yonggon

(i) The geomantic quality of Kaesong

Yonggon lived for a long time in the house that was built by Chakchegon at the southern slope of Mount Song'ak and then built a new house further south. The new house site later became the Pongwonjon building site of Yon'gyong Palace, suggesting that the palace site needed a larger amount of flat land. This is the stage of the story when the building site was arranged to be in the most auspicious location in Kaesong.

(ii) The mysterious lineage of the Wang family

No major social elevation of the family occurred during Yonggon's time. Yonggon chose his wife as the one he saw in his dream. This may signify that he chose his bride for her own personal qualities, perhaps her beauty, with her family background, wealth, and social status having little influence on him.

(iii) Analogy to the stages of the geomantic survey

To extract maximum blessings from the auspicious site, Yonggon built his house as the geomancer-monk Toson suggested. This is the stage of adjusting the layout of the house after confirming an auspicious site. It is also the stage of considering how to use an auspicious site most effectively. Toson came to Yonggon's new house and commented that the house was not appropriate for the given land by saying that flax was planted in the place where millet should be planted. Accepting Toson's advice, Yonggon built a big mansion with thirty-six compartments (probably much bigger than the original plan for the house). By this stage, finding an auspicious site and building a suitable structure on it had been completed. Hence the whole geomantic process of inhabiting a place was completed and waiting for blessings to be manifested from the site could take place.

Part six: Wang Kon

(i) The geomantic quality of Kaesong

Before Wang Kon became king, Master Toson revisited the place and told Wang Kon that he was the special person who would unify Korea and save its people. Toson's revisit can be interpreted as a trip to confirm whether his geomantic survey was correct and whether his geomantic prophecy (the birth of Wang Kon) had materialized.

(ii) The mysterious lineage of the Wang family

Wang Kon himself is proof of the specially consecrated family to rule Korea by being the first king of Koryo. When Master Toson revisited Wang Kon's house in Mount Song'ak, he was said to have taught Wang Kon battle formation tactics, methods of choosing advantageous times and landforms, and the skill of drawing strength from nature. This story is meant to enhance and mystify Wang Kon's skills as a military strategist and to describe him as a person having supernatural powers. At the time Master Toson was the most famous geomancer and people must have revered him as having supernatural powers, as reflected in many Korean geomancy tales. The story of Toson's revisit and his teaching of Wang Kon may well have been fabricated, but it adds more prestige to Wang Kon as a person. It was a useful addition to the social construction of Wang Kon as the deserving ruler of Korea.

(iii) Analogy to the stages of the geomantic survey

This stage of the story is comparable to the manifestation of blessings from an auspicious site: Wang Kon becomes the first king of Koryo.

Overview of the Koryosa Segye

The tales in *Koryosa Segye* in each stage can be classified into one of three main types of folk narratives discussed in folklore scholarship: myths, legends, and folktales. Folklorists generally agree that a myth is a folk narrative about gods or one that explains the mystic origins of things and events; a legend is a narrative relating heroes to historical events; and folktales are stories relating to fantasy. Therefore, what myth is to religion, legend is to history, and folktale is to fiction. Our interpretation of the tales can be represented in Table 14.1.

Table 14.1 An analysis of the tales relating to Wang Kon's genealogy

Generations of ancestors	Sanctifying of Kaesong	Glorifying of Wang Kon's family lineage	Analogy to the geomantic process of surveying a place	Tale type
Hogyong	Identifying the main mountain through the ranges extending from Mount Paektu	Becoming the guardian spirit of Mount Song'ak and creating the legacy of divine power	Finding the main mountain by following its "root" ranges from Mount Paektu and arriving where it ends	Myth-legend
Kangchung	Moving to the south of Mount Song'ak and improving the geomantic landscape by planting pines	Marrying into a rich family resulting in a major elevation of economic power	Initially locating an auspicious site by checking the surrounding landforms	Legend
Poguk and Chinui	Moving back to Mahagap	Gaining the highest social status available by claiming connections to the Chinese emperor	Testing the auspicious site	Legend
Chakchegon	Using the sacred pig, he confirms that Kangchung's old place was the auspicious site	Claiming he was sired by Suzhong of Tang and marrying the daughter of the sea dragon (establishing political power)	Confirmation of Kangchung's old house site as the geomancy cave	Legen-dary folktale
Yonggon (Ryung: Sejo)	Building a house according to Toson's advice and moving further down toward the south, later the palace site	Finding dream woman of his choice (no need for further elevation of social status), and Wang Kon was born after building the new house	Building a suitable structure on the geomancy cave in the auspicious spot by consulting a professional geomancer	Legend
Wang Kon	Toson confirmed that Kaesong is the most auspicious place	Direct learning from Toson on geomancy and military skills	Manifestation of blessings from the auspicious site— Wang Kon was born	Legend–historic record

All of the tales in the *Koryosa Segye* are related to the geomancy of Kaesong and the Wang family. They were presented and put together with some logical sequence for the social construction of Kaesong as the capital city and Wang Kon as the ruler. In the narratives, the geomantic landscape of Kaesong and the history of Wang Kon's ancestors were interpreted and fabricated to promote

Kaesong (Songdo) as a sacred place destined to be the capital of Korea and Wang Kon as the person to unify and rule Korea. An overview of my analysis of the tales follows:

i) The process of sanctifying Kaesong as a sacred and geomantically auspicious place

According to the tales in *Koryosa Segye,* all aspects of the geomantic conditions of Kaesong are sacred and auspicious. The distant oncoming dragon—the root of the main mountain—is auspicious as it was dispatched from Mount Paektu, the patriarch of all Korean mountain systems. The surrounding landscape is auspicious as it has a well-shaped main mountain and faces south. Exposed boulders and bedrock of the main mountain were not good, but this defect was overcome by planting pines. The most auspicious spot of Kaesong, the geomancy cave, was located by the geomancer Parwon of the Silla dynasty and confirmed by the "golden pig." Wang Kon's father, Yonggon built his house on the most auspicious site following the advice of Toson, the most highly qualified geomancer in Korea of all time. Wang Kon was born in the house that was built to suit geomantic principles on the most auspicious site of Kaesong. Thus Kaesong was socially constructed and geomantically interpreted to be the capital of Korea at the beginning of the Koryo dynasty.

ii) The process of glorifying Wang Kon's birth and family line

Wang Kon and his ancestors were glorified in the tales by their claiming divine power from the mountain god, securing wealth by marrying into a rich family, and claiming Chinese royal blood. The glorification of the Wang family was also carried out by promoting Kaesong, their home district, as having the best geomantic landscape of Korea. By doing all this Wang Kon and his descendants secured and justified their geomantic mandate to unify and rule Korea from Kaesong. Choi Pyonghon pointed out that according to the tales presented in *Koryosa Segye,* geomantic ideas played an important role at every stage of the growth of Wang Kon's family.[75]

iii) Stages of the geomantic survey

The descriptions of geomantic principles and geomantic events in the tales of *Koryosa Segye* correspond well with a professional geomancer's survey of an auspicious site: examining the geomantic conditions of the main mountain by examining its root from the ancestral mountain; examining the surrounding landforms of the southern slope of the main mountain; identifying and confirming the geomancy cave. Then, the construction of the structure (house, palace, or grave) must be suited to the given geomantic landscape. Hogyong's journey to Kaesong from Mount Paektu corresponds to the first stage of a geomantic survey, while Yonggon's building of the house according to Toson's advice corresponds well with the last stage. The other parts of the story correspond with the other stages.

The folklorized version of Wang Kon's genealogy in *Koryosa Segye* is the result of turning Wang Kon's family history into myths and legends. The version is based on Kim Kwanui's *Abridged Chronological History (Pyonnyon tongnok),* which was written some 260 years after Wang Kon. However, evidence indicates that these stories were in existence by the time Kwanui recorded them in his book. It is difficult to accurately date orally transmitted folklore materials; a relative dating method of "the time before which concrete evidence exists" is often used. The concrete evidence of a tale's existence is often a written record. In the case of the stories of Wang Kon's ancestors, Kim Kwnaui's book is the *terminus antiquem* (the time before which), for it provides concrete evidence of the existence of these tales by the time he recorded them. The stories in his book may well represent edited and collated versions of tales that were retold by different people through the generations.[76]

If the *Koryosa Segye* tales represent the social construction of Kaesong as a geomantically sacred place and the Wang family as the royal family, we have to address the question of the identities of the authors of these tales. An inherent characteristic of folk narratives (including myths, legends, and folktales) is anonymous authorship. Folklore materials often have multiple authors, and unlike scholarly writings the authors are not documented due to the oral transmission of the tales. However, some of the well-known social functions of folklore are to support religious doctrines and the dominant ideology of society, including by instilling proper societal values in the young.[77] In the case of the *Koryosa* tales, religious doctrines and desirable social values are the "honorable" version of the family history of Wang Kon. The "politically correct" interpretation of Kaesong's geomantic quality was that it was the most suitable for the capital of Korea.

It is therefore not difficult to imagine who may have been responsible for the creation of these tales. The Wang family and their close associates were probably mainly responsible. During the Silla dynasty, Wang Kon's ancestors had a humble family background; they were not members of the royal or aristocratic family of Silla. They could have been the descendants of a shaman (mudang), since their first ancestor in Kaesong was claimed to have been deified as a mountain spirit and worshiped as a mountain king in a local shrine. The Wang family was from Kaesong, then a small rural settlement. They were probably the descendants of the Koguryo people defeated by Silla. When Wang Kon became the district leader and eventually the king of a new dynasty, his family history needed glorification and glamour. Therefore, I suspect that these *Koryosa Segye* stories of Wang Kon's ancestors and Kaesong were actively promoted and indeed originally fabricated by members of the Wang family themselves or their close associates, who would have benefited from such glorified narratives. While some parts of the stories may have existed before Wang Kon's time, many as we know them today were created after Wang Kon founded Koryo or were further embellished to justify the establishment of the new dynasty.

This folklorized version of the Wang family history and Kaesong's geomantic quality was seemingly accepted as the true and only available official version and was widely circulated among the people during the Koryo period (as the stories in the Book of Genesis were among Christians). This must be the reason these stories are presented in the *Koryosa Segye* without hint of the existence of other records of the Wang family's genealogy. Another possible piece of evidence that this folklorized version was the official version of the Wang family history is a conversation that supposedly happened between the Korean delegation (King Chungson and Min Ji) and an officer in the Mongol Court in Beijing, as recorded in *Koryosa Segye:*

> When King Chungson was in Yuan (Mongol) China before his enthronement, he was having a conversation with a royal archivist. He asked the king, "I heard that your ancestor was sired by Emperor Suzhong of Tang. On what ground is it said so? In fact Suzhong never went outside the palace during his younger years and was crowned at Lingwu during 'the An Lushan Rebellion.' How could he have gone to Korea and sired a child?"
>
> The king's face then flushed and he hesitated before answering the question. Min Ji, who was beside the king, answered on the King's behalf, "That is an inaccurate recording of our national history. In reality, it is not Suzhong, but Xuanzhong."
>
> Then the royal archivist agreed that such an instance could have happened, since Xuanzhong had suffered for a long time in the outer regions.[78]

If this indeed took place, it is clear evidence that the folklorized version of the Wang family was known not only in Korea but in China, at least to a Mongol court officer in Beijing at the beginning of the fourteenth century. If it did not take place, the story may have nonetheless been circulated as part of the Koryo ruling class's campaign of promoting the folklorized Wang Kon genealogy as the official history.

Concluding Remarks

If the tales in *Koryosa Segye* represent the Koryo royal family's and their associates' intentions, the family and their associates may have attempted to use the popular belief in geomancy to portray Wang Kon as the person designated to establish Koryo by unifying Korea and the Wang family as the family designated to rule Korea. They may have also used geomantic principles to portray Kaesong as the place designated to be the capital of Koryo. While the overall geomantic conditions of Kaesong are auspicious for a capital city and comparable to several other places such as Seoul, Kaeryongsan, and Pyongyang, the fact that Kaesong was chosen and promoted as the best capital site was the result of the social construction of the place, which was the hometown and power base of the first king of the Koryo dynasty.

Because Kaesong's natural landscape met the general requirements for an auspicious site, it was interpreted in a geomantic way, which became an important factor in determining the people-land relationship in Kaesong. It is impossible to understand the traditional cultural landscape in Kaesong without understanding both geomantic principles and the geomantic interpretation of its landscape during the Koryo period. Reading Kaesong's landscape is like reading an allegorical folktale, the story of an old mouse descending to the field. Many parts of its landscape, whether a hill, bridge, temple, or statue, have geomantic significance and contribute to the geomantic harmony of the place. Through this concrete association of people and places, the Koryo government justified Kaesong as the capital of Korea and maintained it accordingly. Its landscape represents the transformation in concrete form of geomantic ideas by Wang Kon and his people during the Koryo dynasty.

Notes

1. This chapter is based on and has developed from my conference paper, presented at Kaesong Workshop, Harvard University, 17 May 2003.

2. No Sashin and others, *Sinjung Tongkuk Yoji Sungnam* [Newly Augmented Survey of the Geography of Korea] (Seoul: Minjok munhwa chujinhoe, 1969), vol. 1, 435.

3. No Sashin and others, *Sinjung Tongkuk Yoji Sungnam*, vol. 1, 435.

4. No Sashin and others, *Sinjung Tongkuk Yoji Sungnam*, vol. 1, 436.

5. David Harvey, "The Social Construction of Space and Time: A Relational Theory", *Geographical Review of Japan,* series –B, vol.67, no.2 (1994), 127.

6. Trevor Barnes, "Social construction," in *The Dictionary of Human Geography*, 4th ed., edited by R.J. Johnston, Derek Gregory, Geraldine Pratt and Michael Watts (2000), 748.

7. Trevor Barnes, "Social construction," 748.

8. W. Detel, "Social Constructivism," in *International Encyclopaedia of the Social & Behavioural Sciences*, vol. 21, ed. Neil J. Smelser and Paul B. Baltes (Oxford: Elsevier Science, 2001.), 14264.

9. J. Nicholas Entrikin (1991), *The Betweenness of Place*, (Baltimore: Johns Hopkins University Press, 1991), 1.

10. Yi Pyongdo (1980), *Koryo Sidaeui Yongu* [A Study of the Koryo Period], revised edition. (Seoul: Asea Munhwasa, 1980), 90–92.

11. Xu Shanji and Xu Shanshu, *Dili-Renzixuezhi* [The Fact that All Humanity Must Know] (Hsin-chu: Chulin Shuchu, 1969), 5.

12. Yi Pyongdo, *Koryo Sidaeui Yongu*, 90.

13. Yi Chung-hwan, *Taengni-ji* [Book of Choosing Settlement] (Seoul: Choson kwangmunhoe, 1912), 65; Murayama Chijun, *Choson ui Pungsu* [Korean Geomancy], Translation of *Chosen no Fusui* into Korean by Choi Kilsong (Seoul: Minumsa, 1990), 602.

14. Kim Ki-duk, "Koryo sidae Kaegyong ui Pungsuchirijok Kochal" [Examining the Geographical Features of the Koryo Dynasty's Gaegyeong in Fengshui Theoretical Terms]. Hankuk Sasangsahak [Studies in Korean Thought] vol. 17 (2001), 79.

15. Yang I, *Han lung ching*, in *Dili Zhengzhong* [Authentic Collection of Geomantic Principles]. Commentary by Jiang Guo, (Hsin-chu: Chu-lin Shu-chu, 1967), 1.

16. Yi Pyongdo, *Koryo Sidaeui Yongu*, 90.

17. Yi Chung-hwan, *Taengni-ji*, 65.

18. Guo Pu, *Liujiangdong jiacang shanpen Zhangshu* (commentary by Zheng Mi) in Linlang Mishi Chongshu. Case 2. vol. 10, n.p. (1888), part 2, 36.

19. Yi Chung-hwan, *Taengni-ji*, 41; Murayama Chijun, *Choson ui Pungsu*, Translation into Korean by Choi Kilsong, 610; Kim Ki-duk, "Koryo sidae Kaegyong ui Pungsuchirijok Kochal," 97.

20. Yi Chung,-hwan, *Taengni-ji*, 41.

21. Yi Pyongdo, *Koryo Sidaeui Yongu*, 90.

22. Guo Pu, Liujiangdong jiacang shanpen Zhangshu, 36.

23. Yi Pyongdo, *Koryo Sidaeui Yongu*, 90–91.

24. Yi Pyongdo, *Koryo Sidaeui Yongu*, 90–92.

25. Yi Chung-hwan, *Taengni-ji*, 41.

26. Translated and abridged from Yi Chung-hwan, *Taengni-ji*, 92

27. Yi Pyongdo, *Koryo Sidaeui Yongu*, 96.

28. The quoted statement is included in the fifth article of Taejo's ten injunctions. See Chong Inji and others (1992), trans. by Pak Sihyong and Hong Hwoiyu, *Pukyok Koryosa* [the North Korean translation of Koryosa into modern Korean], vol. 1, Sega 2, Taejo 2 (Pyongyang: Kwahakwon Chulpansa, 1962: reprinted in Seoul: Sinsowon, 1992), the section on the fourth moon, twenty-sixth year of King Taejo's reign, 116.

29. Yi Pyongdo, *Koryo Sidaeui Yongu*, 97–98.

30. Yi Pyongdo, *Koryo Sidaeui Yongu*, 97–98.

31. Choi Changjo, *Hankuk ui Pungsusasang* [Geomantic Thought of Korea] (Seoul: Minumsa, 1984), 213.

32. Yi Pyongdo, *Koryo Sidaeui Yongu*, 96.

33. Yi Pyongdo, *Koryo Sidaeui Yongu*, 96.

34. Kim Ki-duk, "Koryo sidae Kaegyong ui Pungsuchirijok Kochal," 103.

35. Yi Pyongdo, *Koryo Sidaeui Yongu*, 90.

36. Yi Chung-hwan, *Taengni-ji*, 65. The translation quoted is from Inshil Choe Yoon, *Yi Chung-hwan's T'aengniji: The Korean Classic for Choosing Settlements* (Sydney: Wild Peony, 1998), 103–104.

37. Yi Pyongdo, *Koryo Sidaeui Yongu*, 90; Choi Changjo, *Hankuk ui Pungsusasang*, 204–210; Kim Kiduk, "Koryo sidae Kaegyong ui Pungsuchirijok Kochal," 77–78.

38. Yi Pyongdo, *Koryo Sidaeui Yongu*, 100.

39. Hong-key Yoon, "The Image of Nature in Geomancy," *GeoJournal,* vol. 4, no. 4 (1980), 345.

40. The origin of personifying the geomantic landscape is unclear, but it is well discussed in Dili-Renzixuezhi, which was published in 1564. However, Qingwujing and the inner volume of Jiangjing, which are known to be the ancient Chinese classics of geomancy but were written no earlier than the third century, do not discuss the personified geomantic landscapes of persons, animals, or flowers.

41. Murayama Chijun, *Choson ui Pungsu*, Translation into Korean by Choi Kilsong, 603–609.

42. Murayama Chijun, *Choson ui Pungsu*, Translation into Korean by Choi Kilsong, 607.

43. Murayama Chijun, *Choson ui Pungsu*, Translation into Korean by Choi Kilsong, 609.

44. For the abridged and translated version included here, I used the North Korean translation of Koryosa Segye into modern Korean: Chong Inji and others, *Pukyok Koryosa*. Michael C. Rogers translated the full text quoted from Pyonnon tongnok in Koryosa Segye and discussed the ideological, geomantic, and other religious background of the text in his article. Rogers' translation of the text includes the parts that seem to be the translation of literal meanings of each word, rather than the meaning of an entire sentence in context. For the full text of narratives quoted from Pyonnon tongnok, see Michael C. Rogers "Pyonnyon Tongnok: The Foundation Legend of the Koryo State," *Journal of Korean Studies*, vol. 4, (1982–83), 3–72.

45. According to the general usage of Chinese characters in Korea, Mahagap should be pronounced as Magaga However, the word written in Chinese characters is a

Buddhistic term and is pronounced "maha" in Korean Buddhism. See, Kim Kidok, "Koryo sidae Kaegyong ui Pungsuchirijok Kochal", 67.

46. Michael Rogers argued that "Parwon is undoubtedly to be identified with the Kim Parwon who flourished in the 870s. His title Kamgan has been linked with the Silla fortress of P'aegang,—Michael C. Rogers "Pyonnyon Tongnok," 37. Roger's assertion is based on Yi Kidong, "Silla hadae ui Paegangin" [The Paegang Fortress during the Late Silla Period]. *Hanguk Hakpo,* vol. 4, (1976), 2–21. Although it is likely, it is not yet certain whether Geomancer Parwon here is the same person as Kim Parwon.

47. A dream of inundating land with urine and selling the dream to another person is a well-known type of legend in Korean folklore. Samguk yusa records the story of Silla hero Kim Yusin's sister Munhui who became the wife of Kim Chunchu (later King Muyol) by buying her sister's dream of inundating the capital city (Kyongju) with her urine. See Ilyon, *Samguk yusa* [Memorabilia of the Three Kingdoms], Translated into modern Korean by Yi Cheho (Seoul: Kwangmunchulpansa, 1969), 156;Michael C. Rogers, "Pyonnyon Tongnok," 40.

48. Chong Inji and others, *Pukyok Koryosa*, 54.

49. Yi Pyongdo, *Koryo Sidaeui Yongu*, 85–89.

50. Murayama Chijin, *Choson ui Pungsu*, Translation into Korean by Choi Kilsong, 585–613.

51. Murayama Chijin, *Choson ui Pungsu*, Translation into Korean by Choi Kilsong, 592.

52. Murayama Chijun, *Choson ui Pungsu*, Translation into Korean by Choi Kilsong, 592–593.

53. Choi Byong-hon, "Toson's Geomantic Theories and the Foundation of the Koryo Dynasty," *Seoul Journal of Korean Studies*, vol. 2 (1989), 79–85; Kim Ki-duk, "Koryo sidae Kaegyong ui Pungsuchirijok Kochal", 66–75.

54. Na Kyongsu, "Konkuksinhwarosoui Koryosegye" [Koryo Segye as National Foundation Myths], *Mokpo omunhak*, vol. 2, 67–86; You In Soo, "Koryo Konkuk Solhwaui Yongu" [A Study of Koryo Dynasty Foundation Myth]. master's degree thesis, Hanyang University, 1989.

55. Yi Pyongdo, *Koryo Sidaeui Yongu*, 85–86.

56. Yi Pyongdo, *Koryo Sidaeui Yongu*, 87.

57. Kim Ki-duk, "Koryo sidae Kaegyong ui Pungsuchirijok Kochal", 67–69.

58. Kim Ki-duk, "Koryo sidae Kaegyong ui Pungsuchirijok Kochal", 69.

59. Kim Ki-duk, "Koryo sidae Kaegyong ui Pungsuchirijok Kochal", 70.

60. Michael C. Rogers, "Pyonnyon Tongnok," 19.

61. Michael C. Rogers, "Pyonnyon Tongnok," 50–51.

62. Chong Inji and others, *Pukyok Koryosa*, 47.

63. Yi Pyongdo, *Koryo Sidaeui Yongu*, 87.

64. For discussion of Koryo's state founding ideology being the succession of Koguryo, see Michael C. Rogers, "Pyonnyon Tongnok,", 17–19.

65. Murayama Chijin, *Choson ui Pungsu*, Translation into Korean by Choi Kilsong, 595.

66. Chong Inji and others, *Pukyok Koryosa*, 55

67. Chong Inji and others, *Pukyok Koryosa*, 54–55.

68. Michael Rogers claims that Kim Kwanui made use of this Koguryo-style story of the pig as a discoverer of an auspicious site because his basic purpose was "to proclaim the supremacy of Kaesong as the capital city, invalidating any claims that might be advanced by partisans of Pyongyang, the Western Capital." See Michael C. Rogers, "Pyonnyon Tongnok," 46–47. Rogers' thoughtful conjecture seems to be somewhat

illogical, because Kaesong is to Koguryo's Cholbon what Pyongyang is to Kuknaewi-naam. The story of the pig running way from Chakchegon's house and finding an auspicious house site (his ancestor's old house site) can be interpreted as an allegory advocating moving Koryo's capital from Kaesong to Pyongyang (the old capital of Koguryo, "the ancestral state") rather than proclaiming the supremacy of Kaesong as the capital city.

69. Kim Pusik, *Samkuk sagi* [history of the Three Kingdoms], translated into modern Korean by Yi Pyongdo (Seoul: Eul-yoo Publishing, 1987), 256–257. Here, I have abridged and translated the information relevant to Solji's finding of Kungnasong and moving capital to the place only.

70. In many tribal cultures, pigs are a highly valued commodity. Pigs are considered to be one of the most valued items as a gift or the most important food for celebration in the festivals of many Pacific Island cultures.

71. Choi Byonghon, "Tosonui Saengaewa Ramalyochoui Pungsuchirisol [The Life of Toson and Geomancy during the Period of the End of Silla and the Beginning of Koryo]," in *Hankuksa Yongu [A Study of Korean History]*, vol. 11 (1975), 127; Michael C. Rogers, "Pyonnyon Tongnok," 46.

72. Choi Byonghon, "Tosonui Saengaewa Ramalyochoui," 127.

73. Koryosa Segye stated that according to Songwonnok, Chakchegon's wife was the daughter of the first ranking officer of the Silla dynasty, Tuonjom kakgan of Pyongju (presently Pyongsan of Hwanghae Province). Yi Chaehyon, a famous scholar of the Koryo dynasty, criticized the story of the dragon king's daughter by quoting the above information in Songwonnok. See Chong Inji and others, *Pukyok Koryosa*, 56.

74. Choi Byong-hon, "Toson's Geomantic Theories," 81.

75. Choi Byong-hon, "Toson's Geomantic Theories," 80.

76. Na kyongsu, "Konkuksinhwarosoui Koryosegye," vol. 2, 84.

77. My view on the social function of folklore is derived from William R. Bascom. For a more comprehensive discussion on the subject, see William Bascom, "Four Functions of Folklore", in *The Study of Folklore*, Allan Dundes, ed., (Englewood Cliffs, NJ: Prentice-Hall,1965) 279–298.

78. Chong Inji and others, *Pukyok Koryosa*, 47.

PART V: GEOMANCY AND ICONOGRAPHY

Chapter 15
Iconographic Warfare and the
Geomantic Landscape of Seoul[1]

On 15 August 1995, exactly fifty years after the liberation of Korea from Japanese colonial rule, Koreans started dismantling the office building of the former Japanese colonial government. The building was a majestic five-story granite structure built by the Japanese as a showpiece at great cost, and was considered an important East Asian architectural monument. Public opinion had been divided over whether this majestic and imposing building should be demolished or preserved. Eventually some people took the Korean government to civil court to stop it from demolishing it, delaying the work for more than a year, until the court ruled that the Korean government had the right to demolish the building.

The divided public sentiment and the process leading to the demolition of the building demonstrate how important reading the landscape as a text is, and how important it is to understand the power of landscape interpretation. This episode also illustrates the process of naturalizing a monumental landscape and the subsequent denaturalization process.

In this chapter I look at the iconographical warfare between the Japanese and Koreans over Kyongbok Palace. Because the palace was interpreted as the icon of Korean sovereignty, the Japanese mutilated it by destroying many of its buildings and by constructing their Government-General Building on the palace ground. That act was an attempt to justify and naturalize the icon of their colonial rule. For the same reason, the Korean government, after liberation from Japanese colonial rule, demolished the Japanese colonial building to reconstruct the icon of Korean sovereignty, Kyongbok Palace, to its former glory.

Behind this war of icons between Japanese colonialism and Korean nationalism lies the age-old Korean art of geomancy. People often assert that geomancy was the main reason for the choice of Kyongbok Palace as the Royal Palace of the Choson dynasty, the Japanese construction of their government building, and the eventual removal of the building by the Korean government and the reconstruction of the palace.

Indeed, the first king of the Choson dynasty toward the end of fourteenth century carefully examined the geomantic conditions of Seoul through field trips with his government geomancers before deciding to move the capital to Seoul from Kaesong and to build Kyongbok Palace on the present site. The Japanese government studied Korean geomancy carefully, and it seems obvious that the Japanese attempted to cut off the geomantic vein to the main building of the palace to nullify the geomantic benefits to the palace. This was done by mutilating the palace and building the Government-General o Building in the front of the grounds. By such means the Japanese forced Koreans to accept Japanese colonial rule. In justifying the demolition of the Government-General Building, the Korean government listed as an important reason the uplifting of Korean morale by revitalizing the geomantic energy of Kyongbok Palace.[2]

Thus it is not surprising that a popular interpretation of this landscape is that geomancy was the key factor at every major stage of its transformation. From the new cultural-geographic point of view, however, especially that of landscape interpretation, such an explanation only taps the surface of the phenomena. The record stating that the first king of the Choson dynasty chose Seoul as the capital site because of his faith in geomancy does not consider more fundamental reasons behind moving the capital from Kaesong to Seoul. The more important reason for choosing the palace site was to express the icon of the newly established Choson dynasty and to demonstrate the mana of the new royal power. By doing so the new government attempted to encourage people to accept the new dynasty and minimize resistance. In other words, they tried to naturalize the icons of the new government and denaturalize Koryo palace in Kaesong, an icon of the former dynasty, by leaving it empty and in a ruinous state. The Japanese seemed to have used the same tactic by mutilating Kyongbok Palace. They denaturalized this icon of Korean sovereignty, and by building the majestic Japanese colonial government building they attempted to naturalize their own icon. The present Korean government then used the same methods: they denaturalized the Japanese icon by demolishing it and attempted to naturalize the Korean icon of sovereignty by reconstructing Kyongbok Palace.

Landscape as Text

The new cultural geography tradition of reading landscape as text was initiated by James Duncan.[3] However, reading the landscape as text must have originated in hexaemeral literature and in the idea of nature as a book in physico-theology. According to Clarence J. Glacken, hexaemeral literature is the literature of comment on and explanation of the six-day creation in Genesis, and "St. Basil's (ca. 331–379) is the most comprehensive of the early hexaemera."[4] St. Basil's interpretation of nature is expressed in his homilies that intended to show that the wisdom of the Creator was evident in the balance and harmony of nature.[5] One can say that the writers of early hexaemeral literature attempted to document and read (i.e., interpret) the natural landscape, including landforms and the biosphere, in light of the six-day creation story from Genesis. This must be an early practice of reading landscape as text and signifying system in the West.

In most cases cultural landscapes, which are transformations of nature by different cultural groups, have textual qualities and can reflect certain social and political ideologies, cultural values, or even social structures. The analysis and interpretation of landscapes for such information is called reading landscape. Indeed, reading landscape as a text is interpreting the cultural landscape as icons, symbols, meanings, and images.

Glacken also eloquently discussed the idea of nature as a book, which is based on the assumption that "God is revealed in the Scripture, but his works are also visible in the world."[6] According to Glacken, this idea originated in "pulpit eloquence" and St. Augustine expressed it fully and vigorously.[7] He quoted St. Augustine: "Some people, in order to discover God, read books. But there is a great book: the very appearance of created things. Look above you! Look below you! Note it; read it. God, whom you want to discover, never wrote that book with ink; instead He set before your eyes the things that He had made. Can you ask for a louder voice than that? Why, heaven and earth shout to you: God made me!"[8]

Thus, Glacken suggested that "the book of nature becomes a commentary, further substantiation of the truth of the revealed word [in the Bible]."[9] The early Christian church had an elegant tradition of reading landscape as text and signifying system in order to see God's work and existence in landscape. This metaphor of nature as a book can still be heard today, and its usage is not limited to Sunday sermons. It seems clear that hexaemeral literature and the idea of nature as a book were the ancient sources of the modern cultural geographers' treatment of landscape as text and signifying system. The early scholars of reading landscape as text or signifying system were the early church fathers and theologians rather than geographers.

The contemporary geographical ideas of reading landscape as text and signifying system are expressed in the works of Peirce Lewis and Donald Meinig. Lewis suggested seven axioms, or rules, for reading landscapes.[10] Meinig presented ten different "meanings," or interpretations, of the same landscape.[11] Meinig's ten different meanings represent an attempt to read ten different texts and ten different signifying systems from the same landscape. Meinig's interpretation of landscape as ideology and history is literally the practice of reading landscape as text and signifying system.[12] Although Lewis and Meinig explicitly attempted to read landscape and detect significations from it, James Duncan formally introduced and promoted reading landscape as a text in today's cultural geography by adapting and applying insights from linguistic and literary theories. James Duncan and Nancy Duncan suggested that "landscapes can be seen as texts which are transformations of ideologies into a concrete form."[13]

The landscape of Seoul can be read as a text. The surrounding landforms and city plan within the basin reflect the fact that the city site was chosen and planned in terms of geomancy. By examining the landscape of Seoul, including the surrounding hills, stream flows, and locations of important buildings and gates, we can determine how the city builders interpreted and applied geomantic principles in their selection of the site and construction of the city. Seoul is a clear example of the transformation of written geomantic text into landscape. Simply put, to view Seoul's landscape is to read the geomantic manual.

The city landscape of Seoul also reflects the social structure and political ideology of the Choson dynasty. The most auspicious site in the city was occupied by the main palace and the rest of the more auspicious sites were occupied by other royal families or families from the upper social strata. In this sense, we can read the landscape of Seoul as a social text of the Choson dynasty.

The authors (i.e., builders) of the landscape as well as the readers (i.e., viewers) of the landscape can clearly identify the geomantic text to which the landscape of Seoul refers: the well-established geomantic principles for landforms, watercourses, and cosmic directions. James Duncan and Nancy Duncan would classify Seoul as a typical example of "focused reading (transformation)," because "the authors and readers are able to identify the specific texts to which the landscape alludes."[14] According to them, unfocused transformation is where "the authors or readers of the landscape are only vaguely aware or perhaps even unaware of the textual basis of the landscape."[15] The new cultural-geographic approach of reading landscape as a text like a book, where one can learn about how ideologies and social structure are transformed into physical form, can enlighten us about the role of geomancy in fomenting iconographic warfare in Seoul.

Naturalizing and Denaturalizing Landscape: Three Different Types

People generally accept nature as it is and do not question why it is there. They take it for granted. However, today people modify the natural environment to a significant degree: for example, by changing water channels or building dams. Therefore, some of the natural environment is not as permanent as it was once assumed to be. Some cultural landscapes, especially of monuments, are more naturalized in people's minds and more unchallengeable than some natural landscapes. For example, the Eiffel tower in Paris and the historical townscapes of Florence and Venice are accepted in people's minds as they are. They are good examples of the naturalization of the cultural landscape. J. Duncan and N. Duncan first introduced the concepts of naturalizing and denaturalizing landscape in geographical literature. Subscribing to Eagleton's view that one of the functions of ideology is to naturalize social reality, Duncan and Duncan argued that "one of the most important roles that landscape plays in the social process is ideological, supporting a set of ideas and values, unquestioned assumptions about the way a society is, or should be organized."[16] This argument suggests that people accept unquestionably the way the landscape is read and interpreted. The naturalized landscape has the power of indoctrinating people in how society should be structured and operated.

When a challenge to the existence of a landscape or a refusal to accept the existing interpretation of the landscape succeeds, a naturalized landscape can be denaturalized: it can be removed, physically changed, or newly interpreted. An excellent example of the denaturalization of landscape is the removal of the former Japanese colonial government building in front of the main hall of the Korean palace, Kyongbok Palace. This Japanese icon was reinterpreted as a symbol of Japanese aggression and colonialism. The denaturalization process represents the process of changing the landscape physically or reinterpreting it "to reflect changes to the dominant value system."[17]

When the process of naturalizing and denaturalizing landscape occurs in a place due to a conflicting interpretation of the landscape by different sociocultural groups, we can call their conflict iconographical warfare. Adopting Stock's concept of "textual communities" as introduced by Duncan and Duncan, we can say that these different groups of people constitute different "textual communities" that share a common interpretation of a landscape.[18] Their iconographic warfare—the conflict between different textual communities—results in changing a landscape icon or its interpretation. The iconographic warfare that accompanies naturalizing and denaturalizing landscape can be grouped into three types:[19]

1. Complete replacement

An example is the construction of a Christian cathedral over a pre-Christian religious site. In this type of iconographic warfare, the dominant sociocultural group denaturalizes the conquered group's icon by removing it and replacing it with their own icon. This type of conflict occurred during the Christianization of Europe. As pagans were converted, the conquering Christian powers built their grand churches (often cathedrals) over the former pagan religious sites. For example, the site of the cathedral of Florence used to be a pre-Christian religious site. It is well known that many Christian churches were built over the old Roman temple sites, which was an effective way of retaining new converts and preventing them from returning to their former religion. This type of iconographic warfare is thought to have occurred widely elsewhere in the world, when old religions were replaced by new ones.

2. Palimpsest

This type of iconographic conflict, though not common, involves manipulating the art of palimpsest to enhance the conqueror's new icon. When conquering groups erect their icons, they deliberately build their monument juxtaposed to the icon of the conquered group to contrast their "superior" icon with the "poor" one of the conquered group. They may use the art of palimpsest by imperfectly erasing the icon of the conquered group so that the mana of their new icon can be more clearly and favorably contrasted with it. An example of this type of iconographical conflict was the Japanese dwarfing of the traditional Korean palace with their modern colonial government building in Seoul. Before constructing this icon of their colonial rule, the Japanese severely mutilated the Korean icon of sovereignty, Kyongbok Palace, by removing and clearing out many buildings on the palace grounds. After this the Japanese built their majestic Government-General Building to contrast it with the old Korean palace.

This was an effective method of demoralizing people by giving the impression that they had little chance to overcome their conquerors. It may have been used particularly by conquerors who needed to suppress the resistance of the conquered people.

3. Monument to a "dying race"

An example of this type of iconographic warfare is the One Tree Hill monument to the Maori people, the natives of New Zealand. The conquerors built a monument as a memorial to the conquered people because they felt no threat from the Maori, who were expected to die out soon. This type of monument may represent the conquerors' values and serve as an icon of their rule, even though it is meant to be a tribute to the conquered. The One Tree Hill domain in Auckland is probably one of the most important pre-European Maori settlement sites. As requested by the first mayor of Auckland City and the donor of the land, Logan Campbell, the One Tree Hill obelisk was built to commemorate the "conquered" Maori people.

The obelisk, a four-sided pillar that tapers as it rises and ends in a pyramid, originated in Egypt, an important source of European culture. It was often considered by Europeans an important war trophy, as shown in the Egyptian obelisk, which is now in Concorde, Paris (it was taken by Napoleon; the Ethiopian obelisk was taken by the Italian army). The obelisk on top of One Tree Hill can be seen as a war trophy erected for European New Zealanders. The Maori people, who are no longer thought to be a dying race, consider this monument an offensive symbol of European dominance and oppression.[20]

Reading Folk Geographic Ideas and Iconography of Landscape

J. K. Wright may be the first modern geographer to have advocated the study of folk geographic ideas.[21] To Wright, the history of geography was that of geographic ideas, of which unscientific folk geographic ideas and knowledge are integral parts. As Wright has argued, geographic thought is universal among people and in no sense a monopoly of professional geographers.[22] A student of geographic thought needs to study both the geographic ideas and knowledge of professional geographers (academic tradition) and those of non-professional geographers (folk tradition), because they are mutually dependent. The geomantic ideas reflected in the planning and development of Seoul are folk geographic ideas, for example, as are those evident in the iconographic warfare between the Koreans and Japanese.

Stephan Daniels and Denis Cosgrove wrote that "a landscape is a cultural image, a pictorial way of representing, structuring or symbolising surroundings."[23] By examining the changes in the landscape of Seoul, we can see that certain elements represent Korean nationalism and the Korean people's resistance to Japanese colonial rule, while others represent Japanese colonialism and an attempt to suppress Korean national pride. According to Panofsky, iconographical analysis is "the identification of conventional, consciously inscribed symbols," while iconology, or iconographical interpretation (synthesis), is excavating "the intrinsic meaning of a work of art by ascertaining those underlying principles which reveal the basic attitude of a nation, a period, a class, a religious or philosophical persuasion—unconsciously qualified by one personality and condensed into one work."[24] While the Korean palace carries traditional Korean symbols of sovereignty, the Japanese building consciously represented Japanese symbols, especially of colonialism. The iconographic conflict is plainly evident, for the Japanese icons and the Korean icons are easily identified.

As the Japanese invaded Korea, they deliberately destroyed symbols of Korean sovereignty and replaced them with symbols of their colonial rule. Their colonial government building was meant to be a permanent symbol of their rule. They also attempted to naturalize this Japanese work of art, i.e., to get Koreans to accept its presence as an unchallengeable part of nature. Koreans, in turn, attempted to recover their icon by restoring the palace and removing the Japanese building. This process of landscape change involved a fight over the most geomantically auspicious site in Seoul. Let us now consider some of its phases.

Phases of Iconographical War with Japanese Colonialism in Korea

Phase One: The Construction of the Symbol of the New Dynasty by the First King of the Choson Dynasty; From 1392, The Process of Choosing Seoul as its Capital and Constructing His Palace to 1865, The Time of the Major Reconstruction of the Palace Buildings

Many kings and officials of Korea were very enthusiastic about applying geomantic principles to the selection of auspicious sites on which to build new palaces or cities. The first king of the Choson dynasty, Yi Song-gye, was no exception. His obsession and sense of urgency over choosing a new capital site are reflected in his order to search for a new site within one month of his enthronement and before the beginning of the process of adopting a name for the new dynasty.[25] Seoul was chosen as the capital of the Choson dynasty through an exhaustive process of examining various sites by applying geomantic principles. Before Yi Song-gye chose Seoul, it was already the southern (an auxiliary) capital of the Koryo dynasty because of its geomantically auspicious conditions, which received much attention from the kings of the dynasty.

In selecting and developing Seoul, Yi Song-gye was attempting to naturalize the authority of his new dynasty while denaturalizing the power symbol of the former dynasty by letting its capital, Kaesong, decay. He used geomancy to help carry out this process, for the people deeply believed in it. The king attempted to build the new capital at an auspicious site according to geomantic principles. In doing so he seems to have been attempting to get Koreans to accept his new dynasty smoothly, with minimal resistance. In his search for the new capital site, he made field trips to Kaeyongsan and Muak for geomantic surveys. He even started building a new capital at Kaeryongsan, but for geomantic reasons he gave that up and eventually chose Seoul. Even before completing the construction of Kyongbok Palace, the king moved the capital to Seoul and abandoned the capital of the former dynasty. Yi Song-gye's hasty shift to Seoul must have had a lot to do with the then-popular geomantic prophecy that a Mr Yi would become the king of Korea.[26] Apparently this rumor-prophecy was widespread toward the end of the Koryo dynasty of the Wang family. It was probably the most effective way to present Yi Song-gye as destined to become the king of Korea. The prophecy implied that the people of Korea should accept the new dynasty and forget about the old one since the prophecy had been fulfilled. Yi Song-gye's desire for legitimacy and acceptance is probably the reason he was so keen to move the capital to Seoul.

His construction of Kyongbok Palace on the foothill of Mount Pugak, the most auspicious site of Seoul, could have been motivated by his genuine faith in geomancy and his desire to extract a blessing from the land. However, by moving the capital to Seoul and building his palace in the most auspicious site, he may have also wanted to demonstrate proof of the geomantic prophecy that a Mr Yi would become the new king of Korea. Arranging a city plan according to geomantic principles might have been a means of convincing people that Yi Song-gye, the new monarch, deserved to be king and was auspiciously influenced by the auspicious capital site. However, Yi Pyongdo argued that the king's hasty move was due to his genuine faith in geomancy:

> By assuming that the shifting the capital was due to renew the political and social conditions as well as the outlook [of the new government] suitable to the new dynasty, we won't be able to understand the real reason why he was in such a great hurry in arranging it. The First King's real motivation was lying in a certain mystic ideology, namely he desired to leave Kaekyong that lost land energy and became the capital of the collapsed dynasty. Namely, the reason was due to his belief in geomantic ideas.[27]

To support his argument, Yi Pyongdo listed a record from the *Annals of King Taejo,* dated the thirtieth day of the ninth moon in 1392. It reveals that when the king was searching for the new capital site, the Bureau of Books and Clouds (which dealt with geomancy and weather) advised him that no place in Korea was better than Kaesong in terms of geomancy. The king replied, "How can the capital of the collapsed dynasty be used again?"[28] Yi Pyongdo interpreted this as proof that the king moved the capital to Seoul because of his personal faith in geomancy.

In my view, this instance is part of the king's attempt to naturalize the icon of the new dynasty by denaturalizing the former dynasty. He wanted to ruin the icon (i.e. the palace) of the Koryo dynasty and establish the icon of the new dynasty to make people accept the authority of the new regime that destroyed the former one. The king intended to achieve this by building a majestic new palace in a geomantically superior place to the capital of the former dynasty. By leaving the former dynasty's palace unused, it would decay and signal that the former dynasty was finished. In building Kyongbok Palace in Seoul, the king's political use of geomancy to legitimize the new dynasty was much more important than his own faith in geomancy.

The crown prince's quarter of Kyongbok Palace was destroyed in a fire during the first moon in 1532 during the twenty-eighth year of the reign of King Chungjong. During the ninth moon of the eighth year of the reign of King Myongjong (1553), a more important part of the palace was lost to a fire.[29] During this time the whole country suffered from a poor harvest and experienced famine, but the king immediately started the reconstruction of the palace. Although the country was in a difficult situation, he could not tolerate the ruined state of the palace that was built by earlier kings.[30] Even if the nation was financially troubled and people were hungry, reconstructing this symbol of the monarchy and icon of central government authority was vital. The reconstruction demonstrates how important this icon for the Choson dynasty court was to its political power and legitimacy. King Myongjong's decree on the reconstruction stated that despite the poor harvest the palace had to be reconstructed using all the necessary resources.[31] The government, by conscripting people and investing funds, completed the reconstruction work in a little more than one year.[32]

One can argue that an important purpose of constructing Kyongbok Palace by the first king in 1394 was to naturalize the icon of the new dynasty and claim a mandate to replace the former dynasty. The reconstruction of the palace, 160 years after its first construction, by King Myongjong in 1554 was also to prove the continuity of the legitimate crown succession and to demonstrate the ever-strong authority of the king. But the Korean king's attempt to naturalize the icon of government power was opposed by the oppressed class, especially government and private slaves, during the Hideyoshi invasion of Korea in the summer of 1592.[33] Just before the arrival of the invading Japanese, the king hurriedly evacuated himself from Seoul. By the time he had passed the northern boundary of Seoul, Kyongbok Palace and the Ministry of Justice, where slave documents were kept, had been completely burned down by the slaves and others of the oppressed class.[34] This burning of the Korean palace and ministry by Koreans as the Japanese army advanced toward Seoul was rather ironic, but it demonstrates the anger and resentment the oppressed class of Korean society felt toward their rulers. The burning was a literal denaturalization of the landscape icon. However, it must have helped the Japanese army justify their invasion of Korea and occupation of Seoul. From the Japanese point of view, the burning could be read as the destruction of Korean sovereignty and royal power.

After the removal of Kyongbok Palace as the landscape icon of Korean sovereignty by the Koreans, the palace site was left in ruins for the next 270 years, until 1865. If Kyongbok Palace was indeed the symbol of Korean sovereignty, why didn't they rebuild it soon after the Hideyoshi invasion? First, one can assume that the Korean government after seven years of war against the Japanese had no resources to finance the reconstruction of the palace. However, King Sonjo reconstructed Changdok Palace, an auxiliary palace adjacent to the main Kyongbok Palace. Both palaces were completely burned down during the 1592 Japanese invasion, but King Sonjo, on his return to Seoul, decreed in 1606 the reconstruction of Changdok Palace.[35] Sonjo's action can be compared with the first king of the dynasty's decision to abandon Kaesong, the capital of the former dynasty, and move to Seoul. The most devastating and longest war ever experienced by Koreans was caused by the Japanese invasion. Yet Kyongbok Palace was burned by its own people, not by the Japanese during the war. Therefore, it is quite possible that King Sonjo thought that Kyongbok Palace had lost its value as the landscape icon of royal authority and Korean sovereignty. Also, the cost of reconstructing it would have been too great for the government to bear with little revenue and few reserves. Thus, I wonder whether King Sonjo in 1606 decreed that Changdok Palace, a smaller palace, was to be reconstructed instead of Kyongbok Palace so as not to remind people of the bitter war and the burning down of Kyongbok Palace by its own people. Moreover, it was believed that the main geomantic vein from the main mountain of Seoul came into Changdok Palace rather than Kyongbok Palace. Just as the first king moved the capital to Seoul, leaving the former capital to decay, King Sonjo after the Japanese invasion shifted the official palace to Changduk Palace, leaving Kyongbok Palace in ruins. Sonjo might have been attempting to naturalize Changdok Palace as the new landscape icon of royal power after the war.

However, the size and geomantic location of Changdok Palace were not very impressive compared with the main Kyongbok Palace and thus Changdok was inadequate for displaying central government power. Therefore, during the middle of the nineteenth century, Taewonkun, the regent of the king, started the reconstruction of the main palace despite its enormous cost. This project was designed once again to make people accept the authority of royal power through the majestic appearance and geomantic location of the palace. The project was aborted due to its exorbitant cost, however.

But Taewongun, who had been given increased authority and who had carried out major political and social reforms, decided to reconstruct Kyongbok Palace in 1865 to encourage people to accept his authority.[36] He encountered considerable opposition because of the cost but started the reconstruction anyway. The project suffered setbacks, such as two fires which burned large stacks of timber and the temporary building at the construction site, but Taewongun was unswayed and pushed the project forward forcefully.[37] (These fires are thought to have been deliberately lit by people who opposed the reconstruction project.) A large number of people were drafted from all parts of Korea for the project, and to supply the needed timber the government harvested any sizeable trees in Korea from areas that included grave sites and other religious sites. Such harsh government measures fueled resentment toward the reconstruction project. To meet construction expenses, the government raised the land surtax and even charged passage fees to anyone going through the Seoul city gates. Taewongun also sold government titles to people and circulated bad currency (worth only one-twentieth of the real value), which caused severe inflation.

Kyongbok Palace was finally completed after five years and seven months of hard work, despite major discontent with the extreme measures taken to finance the reconstruction.[38] Why did Taewongun carry out the project despite such difficulties, opposition, and risks? Once again, to display the majestic landscape icon of the ideology and power of the central government and to make people respect Korean royal power. At this time in-laws of past kings weakened the royal power and Taewongun wanted to increase the authority of the king and the central government. Lee Ki-Baek aptly commented that Taewongun set about to reconstruct Kyongbok Palace to enhance the dignity of the royal house.[39]

Taewongun seems to have used the reconstruction of Kyongbok Palace as a means of reclaiming the authority of the king and his royal house and of weakening the power of the in-laws of the royalty. The project signified the restoration of the powerful government of the first king of the Choson dynasty, with the royal house being the legitimate successor of the throne. Taewongun attempted to naturalize (i.e., get people to accept) his political ideology and the "mana" of the royal house while weakening the opposition.

Phase Two: Defacing the Korean Symbol of Sovereignty by the Japanese Colonial Government and Planting the Icon of Japanese Power and Authority

After the Japanese annexed Korea, for their effective ruling the colonial government carefully studied Korean ethos and belief systems, which it compiled in a long series of monographs. Korean geomancy was also surveyed and studied; the results of this research were compiled by Murayama Chijun in his book *Chosen no Fusui (Korean geomancy)*. The Japanese colonial government carefully examined the geomantically auspicious sites of Korea, and then ruined and occupied the sites by replacing Korean buildings with Shinto shrines or Japanese government buildings. Kyongbok Palace is a good example. This Japanese method could be compared with the early Christian actions of converting Pagans and then building Christian churches over old Pagan temple sites. The Japanese built their colonial government building symbolising Japanese sovereignty over Korea on the grounds of Kyongbok Palace, thereby mutilating the Korean landscape. By doing this the Japanese government was signifying the end of the Korean dynasty. It was an effective means of justifying (naturalizing) their colonial government and convincing the Korean people to accept their rule. The Japanese government created opportunities to demolish the Korean palace buildings. It dismantled the Kyongbok Palace buildings one by one and sold them to be reconstructed as Japanese restaurants, Japanese temples, and even private residences for the rich Japanese in Seoul or elsewhere in Korea.[40]

However, two events led the Japanese government to dismantle the majority of the buildings.[41] The first was the 1915 Fair for Korean Goods Mutual Progress, which was organized by the Japanese government to commemorate their successful colonial rule over Korea for the first five years. The Japanese decided to hold the fair on the main palace grounds and removed a large number of palace buildings from the foreground of the main mall of Kyongbok Palace. They said they needed space for the construction of large display rooms for the fair. The other event was a fire in November 1917 that burned down the inner court buildings of the auxiliary Changdok Palace. On this occasion the Japanese dismantled a number of buildings in the inner court of Kyongbok Palace. They said demolition of the buildings was necessary to provide the needed timber for the reconstruction of Changdok Palace.

In the end, most of the 330 buildings on the Kyongbok Palace grounds were demolished, leaving only 36 buildings.[42] By this time the Japanese colonial government had cleared all the buildings from the foreground of the main hall (Konjongjon) of the palace and secured enough space for the construction of the colonial government building. After mutilating Kyongbok Palace, the front part of the palace grounds was cleared of Korean buildings and the Japanese constructed the majestic building that dominated the main hall of the palace. This was obviously done to display the power and authority of the colonial government in a physical form in the hope that Koreans would see the altered landscape and accept their rule. They attempted to denaturalize the Korean palace and naturalize their own icon.

Let us now imagine that the Americans or British had lost a war and were subject to colonial rule by the occupying force. Let's also imagine that the occupying force mutilated the White House or Buckingham Palace by demolishing the front ground and then built majestic five-story colonial government buildings several times larger than the White House or Buckingham Palace, making those buildings look sad and shabby by comparison. How would the Americans or the Britons feel? How would they react? A Japanese historian and folklorist, Yanagi Muneyoshi, criticized the Japanese colonial government for committing such a cruel act against Koreans and made a special plea to the Japanese to imagine the following scene when the Japanese were going to demolish the main gate of Kyongbok Palace:

> Assuming Korea was strong and prosperous, while Japan was weak and backward, at last Japan was annexed by Korea as its colony and the Japanese imperial palace was ruined and on the palace ground, the Korean colonial government building was being built. Imagine the scene over the moat filled with blue water, the white walled Edo castle is being demolished. Otherwise imagine the day near to hear the noise of hammers demolishing (the Japanese castle). If that is so, I would lament the death of the monumental building in Edo that represents traditional Japanese architecture.[43]

Japan's planting of its icon was even crueler than the Christian church's building of its churches over pagan religious sites. By mutilating the icon of Korean sovereignty the Japanese attempted to demoralize the Koreans. No official Japanese colonial government document exists that acknowledges that the Japanese mutilated Kyongbok Palace and built their government building on the palace site to demonstrate the worthiness of their colonial rule and to encourage Koreans to accept it. However, there is plenty of other evidence. I will now attempt to document and highlight some important events, comments, and reports.

i) Choosing the site for the Japanese colonial government building
    The first governor-general, Terauchi Masatake, upon Mr Ito Chuta's recommendation, chose the foreground of the main palace as the site for the new Government-General Building, rejecting other options. He made his decision despite recommendations by Japanese architects that the sites of present-day Seoul City Hall and the former Seoul National University in Tongsungdong were suitable.[44] According to a Japanese colonial government report, the Japanese decided on the foreground of Kyongbok Palace's main hall, Kunchongjon, because of its strategic location and size: "The land that is suitable for this Government Building site should occupy the important (key) position of the downtown (of Seoul) and be vast in size."[45] This report does not indicate when and who made this decision, but there is no doubt it was made or approved by the highest colonial government authority, the Japanese governor-general. Judging from his choice, we can assume that the "important" position in the city of Seoul meant a location that could symbolize the end of the Korean dynasty and display the authority and strength of the new Japanese colonial government. Otherwise, one cannot explain why the colonial government rejected other big pieces of land in downtown Seoul and chose the foreground of the main palace of the Korean dynasty, even though it was not an empty area but inconveniently filled with Korean buildings that they had to demolish.
    The Japanese must have determined that constructing their imposing icon in place of Kyongbok Palace was an effective way of communicating their power and determination to rule Korea. By doing so they could also effectively show that the old Korean dynasty's geomantic blessings were ruined and that the dynasty had collapsed. Geomantic art provided the Japanese with the means to denaturalize the Korean icon and naturalize the Japanese one.

ii) The landscape of Palimpsest—exposing the mutilated parts of the palace and contrasting the new Western-style colonial government building with the old Korean-style building (see Figure 15.1)
    On top of attempting to demoralize Koreans by cutting off the main Korean palace's source of vital energy by mutilating it and contrasting it with the new colonial government building, the Japanese turned Changkyong Palace into a zoo. This was the ultimate humiliation. It equated the palace of Korean kings with an animal shed. Both steps could be described as political manipulation of the landscape of palimpsest—superimposing a new cultural landscape over the

previous one that has been imperfectly erased and is still visible. This method can demoralize colonized people by contrasting their "inferior" culture with the new and "superior" one. The Japanese seem to have adopted this method by building their new granite building over the imperfectly erased and still visible Korean palace. After clearing away the buildings in the foreground, the Japanese built a five-story stone building that contrasted starkly with the old Korean throne hall built of wood. Seeing these two buildings side by side, one cannot help but feel that the contrast was intentional.

Figure 15.1 The Colonial Government Building. Behind this five-story stone building the comparatively small and wooden Throne Hall of Korean Palace is seen (circled). Adapted from *Newsreview*, September 24, 1994.

Why did the Japanese not also demolish Kunchongjon, the throne hall? So they could practice the art of palimpsest. By imperfectly erasing the former culture and contrasting it with the new one, their strength and superiority could be highlighted. The Japanese seem to have used this method effectively. The Korean throne building is a traditional tile and timber structure and much smaller than the Western-style granite Japanese colonial government building. Any viewers of these two juxtaposed buildings would easily feel that the old Korean building was backward, traditional, and dominated by the modern Japanese one. The Korean dynasty was finished, the Japanese wished to convey, and Korea's backward and shabby past was not worthy of pride or continued attachment. The modernization and Westernization signaled by the new Japanese colonial government building were meant to represent the hope of Korea and indicate the future direction. With traditional Korean architecture and technology, Koreans could not modernize their own country. The Japanese building intended to signify that the Koreans should admire and accept the modern Japanese technology and Western ideology that had been introduced. Looking at the site of the old Kyongbok Palace—the formerly highest building of Seoul—from the main road, the throne hall of the palace is not visible at all; it is completely blocked off by the Japanese government building. From the main street one can only see the Japanese building. And from that building one can look down at the small and inferior Korean throne building, but from the Korean building one has to look up at the imposing and magnificent Japanese building. The contrast was obviously deliberate.

When one reads landscape as a text, the meaning of the text may depend more heavily on "the relations among signs, rather than upon any inherent, eternal, or essential features of concrete objects."[46] When we apply this relational concept of meaning, the real Japanese intention of contrasting the two buildings is even clearer: that Japan was the future for Koreans, here to modernize and rule Korea, and that the old backward Korea is to be abandoned and despised.

iii) The architectural style of the Japanese Government-General Building

The Government-General Building was Western rather than Japanese in style. Why? One suspects that the Japanese calculated that a Japanese-style building could reveal their political ambitions too clearly and offend the Koreans, and that traditional Japanese-style buildings would not look majestic enough to dwarf the Korean palace buildings. A German architect, George de Lanade, designed the Government-General Building in the neo-Renaissance style, and after his death Ichiro Nomura, a Japanese architect, completed the blueprints.[47] Mutilating and dwarfing the Korean palace with their Western-style building was a veiled expression by the Japanese of their political ambition in Korea and a signal that they were there to modernize rather than "Japanese" Korea. Their goal was to show that their government was mighty, modern, and unchallengeable.

iv) The size of the colonial government building

When the five-story colonial government building was built, it was the largest Western-style building not only in Japan and its colonies but in East Asia as a whole, with a total floor space of 31,300 square metres.[48] The Japanese had to invest a huge government fund of 6.69 million yen—the price of some 560,000 sacks of rice—for the construction. The building was claimed to be bigger than the British colonial government building in India and the Dutch colonial government building in Borneo.[49] Why did they invest such a huge fund? Why did they build the largest building in Korea at that time? Obviously to impress Koreans while expressing their political goal so Koreans would accept their colonial rule smoothly.

v) The floor plan of the colonial government building

The floor plan of the building, from a bird's eye view, represents the Chinese character "the sun" that forms the first syllable of the word *Nippon* (meaning

Japan, "the home of the sun"). This seems to symbolize that the Japanese occupation was permanent and that the Korean monarchy was finished.

vi) The location of the Japanese governor-general's residence

In 1939, the Japanese governor-general's residence was built behind the Korean palace grounds, right on the geomantic vein of vital energy that was believed to be delivered from Mount Pukak, Seoul's main mountain. Now the Korean palace was sandwiched between the governor-general's office and his residence. Anyone who knows about geomancy would realize that the vital energy that was to be delivered to the Korean palace was stolen by the governor-general's residence. The Japanese colonial power had taken over the auspicious palace site on both ends of the palace: the governor-general's residence was at the back and the governor-general's office was in the front. Geomantically speaking, the Korean palace was now starved of vital energy. This seemed to signify that Korea's future looked bleak: their geomantic fortune was all in the hands of the Japanese.

vii) The attempt to demolish Kwanghwamun, the main palace gate

In the year following the completion of the colonial government building, the Japanese government decided to remove the main Korean palace gate, Kwanghwamun, which was in front of the government building. It claimed that the traditional Korean palace gate did not match the modern Western style of the colonial government building. Again the Japanese conscience Yanagi Muneyoshi protested in writing the Japanese government's barbaric action. In his emotionally charged essay "Oh, Kwanghwmun Gate," Yanagi lamented:

> Oh! Kwanghwmun, Oh! Kwanghwmun, Your life [as the main palace gate] is about to be finished. Your existence in the world is about to disappear into oblivion. What can I do? I know not what to do. The day is near when the cruel chisels and emotionless hammers will destroy your body little by little. Thinking about such an event is heartache for many, but nobody can save you. Unfortunately, the people who can save you are not the people who are sadly lamenting you.[50]

This lament was of no use, however, and the Japanese colonial government cleared away the gate that year. In its place, a modern Western-style fence and entrance were made. However, in response to Yanagi's appeal and upon realization of Koreans' feelings, the gate was rebuilt on the old side wall of the palace. When Korea was liberated from Japan, the palace gate was returned to its original location.

viii) News media reports

The *Kyongsongilbo,* the official newspaper representing the Japanese colonial government's views, included an editorial essay upon completion of the Japanese colonial government building on 1 October 1926, the day that commemorated the annexation of Korea by Japan. The article stressed the need for accepting Japanese rule and cooperating with the colonial government at the auspicious time of completing the majestic government building:

> Today is the anniversary day commemorating the beginning of governing Korea. Coinciding with this anniversary, the construction of the new government-general building is completed and the completion ceremony will be held. On this anniversary day commemorating the beginning of governing Korea, all people of the peninsula should think about this event by holding the suits they wear properly.[51]

The message conveyed in the editorial was that Koreans should give up resistance to Japanese rule and accept it, for Japanese rule was successful and would be as permanent as the new colonial government building. The message for Koreans was to look at the building and naturalize Japanese colonial rule in Korea, because it was not negotiable and challengeable.

ix) Criticisms by Japanese and Western scholars

Several Japanese scholars asserted that the colonial government building went too far in offending the Korean palace and the Korean psyche. Yanagi Muneyoshi was one of them. A prominent Japanese scholar of architectural aesthetics, Kon Wajiro, gave a lecture entitled "The Government-General Building Is Too Nakedly Frank" at an Association of Architects meeting in Korea:

> I regret the original plan for the Government-General Building, because I thought that it would always cause ill feelings among the Korean people. I think that the choice of the site for the Government-General Building was wrong and it would be better to destroy the Government-General Building. However, the building is being erected that high now and it cannot be destroyed [too late to destroy it]. Wouldn't it be better to use the building for some kinds of social welfare activities? [52]

The Japanese scholar criticized the colonial government for the obvious symbolic violence that the building committed against the main palace of Korea. The building clearly expressed Japanese imperialism.

The Japanese humiliation of the Korean palace with their colonial government building was plainly evident even to more detached Western visitors. A Russian visitor to Korea wrote in his travelogue:

> The victorious people deliberately chose to construct this building on the compound of the former kings' palace. The building is a poor imitation of Washington's government building and a poor rendering in concrete of the American architectural style. This ridiculous building is oppressively standing and blocking the view of this light and elaborate palace. The building made it impossible to appreciate the palace as a whole.[53]

Considering the nine pieces of evidence discussed above, we can safely conclude that the Japanese attempted to display their colonial power in a concrete form of landscape by mutilating the Korean palace and erecting the

Japanese icon in its place. The Japanese wished to denaturalize the Korean icon of sovereignty and naturalize their icon of colonialism. They attempted to convince the Korean people with the landscape of the new colonial government building on the ruined Korean palace site that their colonial government had effectively replaced the old Korean dynasty. With this landscape icon they hoped to make Koreans feel that there was no other choice than to accept Japanese colonial rule. Their effort shows their understanding of Koreans' strong belief in geomancy and their effective manipulation of it. They attempted to demonstrate that they were taking full advantage of Seoul's geomantic blessings, and that the Korean palace was ruined. In the process of denaturalizing the Korean icons by demolishing the palace buildings, they did not obliterate the Korean landscape but left some key Korean features to contrast with the new majestic colonial government building. It was an effective palimpsest method— to highlight the modernity and grandeur of the Japanese government building in contrast to the old and inferior Korean buildings. After its completion, the Government-General Building was used as the power base of the Japanese colonial government and the seat of the governor-general until the end of Japanese colonial rule in 1945.

Phase Three: The Story of Kyongbok Palace and the Japanese Colonial Government Building after the Liberation of Korea From Japanese Colonial Rule

After Korea became independent, some sections of Korean society wished to remove the Japanese colonial government building.[54] When the building was badly damaged during the Korean War (1950–1953) that started soon after independence, President Syngman Rhee refused to repair it, as he wished to demolish it.[55] However, the removal cost was too much for the Korean government to bear at the time. During Syngman Rhee's presidency, the building was unused and abandoned. In 1962 it was repaired and used as the central government building, but debate about whether it should be removed or preserved continued.

The Korean government attempted to replace the minor icons and symbols of Japan in the building, but continued to use it as its central government building. However, it later housed a national museum in it instead. Its usage as a national museum was symbolic, in my view, for the museum housed only materials from the past that were no longer in use. This usage could have symbolized the end of Japanese colonialism, which now only remained in a museum.

However, the Korean people and government could not tolerate the Japanese icon, so the reconstruction of the Korean place was started. The Korean nationalistic reading (i.e., interpretation) of the landscape was, of course, radically different from that of the Japanese or Japan sympathizers. The process of changing the usage of, modifying, and demolishing the Japanese building may be summarized as follows:

The first stage: use of the building as the Korean parliament and central government building

After Korea's liberation from Japan in 1945 until 1950 when the Korean War started, the first Allied Occupation Forces (1945–1948) and later the Korean government (1948–1983) used this building as the central government building without any structural changes or modification. The first session of the Korean parliament that determined the Korean Constitution was held in the Grand Hall of the building. After this, the building functioned as it had for the Japanese colonial government—namely, the Japanese governor-general's office and residence became the Korean president's office and residence. The Japanese government's office blocks became the Korean government's office blocks for several government departments.

The second stage: damage during the Korean War (1950–1953)

During the Korean War, the former Japanese colonial government building was burned and severely damaged, except for the main concrete and granite framework. The building was left unused and in a ruinous state even after the war, because the nationalistic President Syngman Rhee refused either to repair the building or reoccupy it. Its ruinous state was partly symbolic of the end of the Japanese occupation.

The third stage: the return of the Kwanghwamun gate to its original site and the repair of the government building (1962–1983)

In 1962 during the Park Chunghee government, the Kwanghwamun gate was returned to its original site as the main palace gate and reconstructed using the original granite stones. During reconstruction, its orientation was slightly adjusted to directly face the main avenue, and the upper part of the gate was constructed with concrete instead of wood. This was the first stage of the removal of landscape icons of Japanese colonial rule and the resurrection of the Korean icon of sovereignty. To bring back the Kwanghwamun gate to its original site, the Korean government demolished the modern Western-style gate and fence built by the Japanese colonial government. By restoring the palace gate and palace wall to their original states, the original Korean-style gate and wall now surrounded the Japanese Government-General Building. However, this was visually ineffective, as the Japanese government building was simply too large and majestic for the low-lying front gate and the new wall. The five-story Renaissance-style buildings still made the Korean palace seem shoddy and poor in comparison, and there was much debate about how to deal with the Japanese buildings. The Korean government carried out extensive repair and refurbishing work on the Japanese colonial government building to use it as the much-needed offices for the central government. The building was used as such until 1983.

The fourth stage: use of the building as the National Museum building (1983–1995)

From 1983 until 1995 the colonial government building was used as the National Museum. The interior of the building was extensively remodeled for the exhibition of Korea's heritage and national treasures. However, some Koreans objected to housing treasures that their ancestors had left for them inside the former Japanese colonial government building. They interpreted it as another instance of humiliating Korea's identity and heritage. It was suggested that a new building be built to house Korea's national heritage.

The fifth stage: the demolition of the residence of the governor-general (1991)

The residence for the Japanese governor-general, which had been built behind Kyongbok Palace by the Japanese colonial government and which became the residence of Korean presidents after liberation, was removed in 1991. After the new residence of the Korean president, the Blue House, was built on higher ground, the governor-general's residence was demolished. Kyongbok Palace was no longer sandwiched between the old Japanese government buildings and the Japanese governor's residence. Now the source of the blockage of the vein of vital energy—the Japanese governor's residence—and Kyongbok Palace could enjoy the geomantic blessings of the vital energy delivered from Seoul's main mountain.

The sixth stage: the decision to demolish the colonial government building (1991)

In a government publication reporting the demolition of the colonial government building, the Korean government noted that ever since liberation from Japanese colonial rule in 1945, there had been discussions among Koreans about the demolition of the building.[56] Some argued that rather than demolishing the building it should be used as a monument and a reminder to Koreans of their suffering caused by the Japanese. Others insisted that the Renaissance-style granite building was the best example of its kind in East Asia and thus it should be preserved for its architectural value. Others wished to make it into a museum, to show that colonialism was over.

As soon as Korea was on its way to economic recovery after the Korean War, there were many serious discussions about the inevitability of removing the imposing Japanese buildings to allow for the full restoration of the Korean palace. Many people argued that removal would express the national wish to eradicate the remains of Japanese imperialism in Korea, help recover national spirit and morale, and improve the landscape geomantically.[57] An official justification for the Korean government's demolition of the former colonial government building was to recover the self-respect of the Korean people by revitalizing the vital energy in the ground and reconstructing the Korean palace as it was before being mutilated by the Japanese.[58] Since this view of the geomantic conditions of the Kyongbok Palace site and the demolition of the former Japanese government building is from an official government publication, we can take it as the official Korean government interpretation of the situation.

After careful consideration, President Kim Young-sam issued a special presidential order to his cabinet on 8 August 1993 to remove the former Japanese colonial government building. In his decree he stated, "I have reached the conclusion that the former Colonial Government Building has to be demolished as soon as possible in order to recover our national pride and the spirit of the Korean People."[59] It is obvious from its statements that the Korean government could not tolerate the icon of Japanese colonialism. So to speak, the Korean government challenged the existing (i.e., naturalized) interpretation of the landscape and denaturalized it by providing another interpretation of the building from the point of view of Korean nationalism. The ultimate denaturalization of the building was demolishing it. For many Koreans, the building was an icon of Japanese humiliation of Korea and a reminder of cruel Japanese colonialism.

Yet some sectors of Korean society, including architects and lawyers, argued that the building should be preserved as an architectural monument in East Asia. Some said it should serve as a reminder to the Korean people of the cruel Japanese colonial rule and that it should be utilized, along with the mutilated site of Kyongbok Palace, as a field education site on modern Korean history and Japanese colonialism. Others argued that the Japanese colonial building should be demolished or moved elsewhere to restore Kyongbok Palace, the symbol of Korea's sovereignty, to its former glory. Many Koreans, including some Korean historians, argued that Kyongbok Palace had to be reconstructed at all costs. Others felt that moving the Japanese building would be too difficult and costly.

A Korean opinion poll suggests that Koreans were divided on this issue. The Japanese were thus successful to some degree in their intention of naturalizing the building, i.e., making Koreans believe that it should remain. On 3 June 1991, the National Museum of Korea conducted an opinion poll on the removal of the colonial government building through Korea Research. The survey of 1,000 people comprising 600 professionals and 400 members of the general public shows that 77 percent of the former and 65 percent of the latter agreed to the removal of the building.[60] As the government of President Kim Young Sam decided to remove the building, it facilitated a series of symposia with journalists, scholars, and other professionals to justify and advocate the government plan and communicate national opinion on it.

The seventh stage: demolition of the colonial government building (1991–1996)

At the grand national ceremony commemorating the fiftieth anniversary of Korea's liberation from Japan, attended by the president of Korea and other important Korean dignitaries and foreign diplomatic representatives, the Korean government tore down the steeple on the dome of the former Japanese colonial government building. Fireworks went off and the crowd cheered (see Figure 15.2). Of course, the ceremony was broadcast live on television channels all over Korea. One newspaper described the removal of the steeple as "removing

Figure 15.2   The moment before decapitating the steeple from the building: a ring of fireworks

the nail from the heart of the Korean People."[61] At the ceremony, President Kim Young-sam addressed the crowd:

> Fellow citizens, History is a creative process in which what is wrong is liquidated and what is good is preserved.
>
> Today we have undertaken the historic task of beginning the removal of the former Government-General office building. Only by dismantling this building can we truly restore the appearance of Kyongbok Palace, the most important symbol of legitimacy in our national history. Manifest in the removal is the will and determination of our people to sweep away the remaining vestiges of the days of foreign colonial rule and fully revive the righteous spirit of the nation.
>
> It was for this very same reason that the erstwhile residence of the governor-general was dismantled shortly after I was inaugurated as President. Greater meaning, however, lies behind the removal of these buildings than is outwardly apparent. It signifies the genuine, complete liberation of all of us from any wrongs of the past that may have lingered in our national consciousness.[62]

After this address by the president, the minister of cultural affairs read a letter to the Souls of National Heroes and Patriots reporting that the independent Korean government was about to demolish the icon of Japanese colonialism. Then, amid several hundred rounds of fireworks, the steeple of the dome of the building was removed by a huge crane boom of the Hyundai Construction

Company and taken to the ground (see Figure 15.3). Thus began the physical process of dismantling the Japanese building.

Figure 15.3 A giant crane taking away the decapitated steeple from the building

Even after this ceremony, the body of the building could not be dismantled for about a year due to court litigation organized by a group of Koreans, including some prominent lawyers. To stop demolition of the building, the group had filed a court case for a civil trial in the Seoul District Court against the Korean government and the Hyundai Construction Company. The group's reason: the building should be designated a historical monument that could witness the modern history of Korea.[63] After the Seoul District Court rejected the group's request on 8 July 1996, they appealed to the high court in Seoul. However, they withdrew that appeal on 18 November 1996, and soon after the Korean government resumed the demolition work of the building after more than a year's delay.[64]

Both the divisions in Korean public opinion over the demolition of the building and the court case suggest that a considerable portion of Korean society had accepted the building's existence and location. Even after liberation, many Koreans felt that this majestic granite structure was a great building with value as an historic monument. This is proof that the building was naturalized in many Korean minds. Pierce Lewis once proclaimed that our human landscape is our unwitting autobiography and is "liable to be more truthful than most autobiographies."[65] However, people who do not know how to read the landscape do not catch the symbolic values and signals that the landscape expresses. Indeed, the Japanese colonial government building is an example of "landscape illiteracy" for some Koreans. It was a chapter of Seoul's unwitting autobiography, perhaps one of the most traumatic and humiliating chapters, more truthful than many written histories of Seoul of that period. However, people did not accurately remember who built the building and why Kyongbok Palace was mutilated. Some Koreans did not see what the landscape signified. Of course, some pro-Japanese Koreans would have never wanted to see the building demolished.

But the majority of Koreans read the landscape of the Japanese colonial government building and the mutilated Korean palace as one of national shame and believed that the icon of Korean sovereignty should be reconstructed. They challenged the naturalized state of the colonial government building in other Korean minds by reinterpreting the landscape from a nationalistic point of view. Theirs was a challenge to the pro-Japanese reading of the building and to the ostensibly neutral architectural-historical interpretation of it. The desire to reconstruct the national icon of sovereignty won over the desire to preserve the scene of iconographical warfare between Japanese and Koreans as a reminder for future generations. Thus, the building had to go and the government carried out the majority will of Koreans to demolish it and restore Kyongbok Palace to its former glory.

The eighth stage: the establishment of the park displaying the steeple (1998)

In 1998, within the Memorial Hall of National Independence compound, the Korean government constructed a park for displaying the steeple of the dome and other materials from the former colonial government building. In response to advocates for the building's preservation, the Korean government and nongovernment organizations had suggested that a miniature model of the building or a park displaying the demolished building materials could achieve the same goal of history education for the citizens and should not prevent the restoration of the main Korean palace. For educational purposes the Korean government constructed the park.[66]

The government first planned to provide a transitional zone in the park to indicate that the former Government-General Building had become a ruin. After this a display space was set up for the materials from different parts of the building, with the steeple at the center of the display.[67] The purpose of this was to inform viewers that Japanese colonialism had ended and that the building was ruined. Thus, viewers could "reflect on the colonial past, while looking down on the steeple, the symbol of the former Government-General Building."[68] The steeple that once demanded attention at the top of the highest building in Seoul was humiliated by being placed at the lowest spot of the display park; now it was the subject of ridicule (see Figure 15.4).

People can look down on the steeple from a seat on any of the staircases that ring the display on three levels. Now people can approach it freely, touching and even kicking it if they want: the situation has been totally reversed. It effectively displays that Korea has regained its sovereignty. Anyone who knows of Korea's and the steeple's pasts knows that the current display represents a landscape of revenge.

Figure 15.4 The steeple of the Japanese colonial government building, now placed at the foot of a concentric staircase at the Independence Hall Garden.

People can look down on the steeple from a seat on any of the staircases that ring the display on three levels. Now people can approach it freely, touching and even kicking it if they want: the situation has been totally reversed. It effectively displays that Korea has regained its sovereignty. Anyone who knows of Korea's and the steeple's pasts knows that the current display represents a landscape of revenge.

When I went to the park, I had ambivalent feelings about the display. As a Korean, I felt a sense of justice, but I could not help but think that it went too far. It was too blunt and cruel. True, the Japanese mutilation of the Korean palace had been excessively cruel and aggressive. And the humiliation caused by the Japanese with their mutilation of the palace and construction of their majestic colonial building went too far, as Kon Wajiro commented. But the Korean display of the remains of the colonial government building is no better than the Japanese mutilation and humiliation. It is the landscape of "an eye for an eye and a tooth for a tooth." This iconographic warfare between Korea and Japan is warfare that humiliates the opponent's icon of ruling power. It seems as naïve as children's fighting. Alas, the adult world resembles the child's world, but a fight between nations seems crueler and more naive than the fighting of little children.

The ninth stage: the planned complete recovery of the symbol of Korean sovereignty (1991–2009)

In January 1991, when President Rho Tae-woo announced the ten-year plan for the restoration of Kyongbok Palace, he said that the former Government-General Building would be removed to restore the Korean palace to its original state. On 6 June 1991 the ceremony to start the restoration of Kyongbok Palace was held and Roh Tae-woo initiated the groundbreaking work by moving earth with a shovel.[69] The reconstruction plan also included the removal of any other vestiges of Japanese defacement of the palace, as reported in *The Korea Times* on 6 June 1991: "Last year, the ministry removed pagodas which the Japanese colonial government had erected on the palace grounds and dug up trees brought from Japan in a step to remold the natural environment of the palace to the indigenous Korean gardening style."

The Japanese colonial government building and the Korean palace could not reasonably co-exist, as the former was built by mutilating the latter. The Japanese building occupying the palace ground had to be demolished for the full restoration of Kyongbok Palace. That is why the building was demolished and taken away. The site has now been returned to the Korean palace and used for the restoration of the palace buildings. Currently, the Korean government is in the process of rebuilding Kyongbok Palace, aiming to restore about 40 percent of the original palace buildings in terms of floor space.[70] The palace had about 330 building structures, and the total floor area was about 50,545 square metres or 15,600 pyong, during King Kojong's reign. The Korean government plans to restore 120 of the buildings, with total floor space of about 20,025 square metres or 6,180 pyong.[71] The restoration plan started in 1990 and will take twenty years, costing the government 178,900 million Korean won (US$1 equals about 1,000 won) for the restoration of 40 percent of the palace buildings. It is a long-term and costly project, but Koreans feel that it is needed to restore the icon of Korean sovereignty.

Since Kyongbok Palace was left in ruins for more than two hundred years and Changdok Palace was used as the substitute palace, Kyongbok Palace had not been kept vividly in Koreans' minds. However, the very act of Japanese mutilation of the palace and the construction of their colonial government building on the grounds reinforced its status as the symbol of Korean sovereignty. Now Kyongbok Palace and its main gate, Kwanghwamun, are more than ever icons of Korean independence. Ironically, the Japanese construction of their government building through such an aggressive and violent process reinforced the symbolic value of the palace landscape and eventually caused the demolition of the Japanese building.

The iconographical struggle between the Korean palace and the Japanese colonial government building should not be seen as a geomantic fight over the most auspicious site of Seoul. Rather, geomancy was used in the struggle as a means of asserting political legitimacy and building public support.

By 2009, Kyongbok Palace will be restored to its original fourteenth-century state. Kwanghwamun gate was restored on its original site in 1962. The Korean government's official interpretation of the Japanese Government-General Building and its justification for the demolition of the building can be summarized as follows: the building was an icon of Japanese imperialist aggression and colonialism and should be removed for the restoration of national pride and spirit; to restore Kyongbok Palace, the icon of Korean sovereignty, the Japanese building on the palace grounds had to be removed; as a reminder of Japanese colonialism and a source of education for Koreans, the building did not need to be preserved, because forming a display park of material from the building was sufficient.

With these justifications, the Koreans executed the ultimate blow to the building and decisively denaturalized this Japanese icon of colonial power and ideology.

Concluding Remarks and Research Agenda: The Landscape of Geomancy, Colonialism, and Nationalism

The story of Kyongbok Palace and other government buildings at the site is a story of an iconographical war. It is also a landscape biography of Korean sociopolitical processes. The Korean practice of geomancy set the stage for the battle. It is almost impossible to read the historical landscape of the Kyongbok Palace compound, the most auspicious part of Seoul, without understanding geomancy. By manipulating geomantic ideas, the Japanese colonial government attempted to symbolically destroy the most auspicious site of the Korean capital by mutilating the palace and surrounding the site with its office building and governor-general's residence. This was Japan's attempt to demonstrate its dominance and rule over Korea. But despite the huge expenses involved, Koreans removed the icons of Japanese rule and elected to restore Kyongbok Palace, the symbol of Korean independence and pride. The site of Kyongbok Palace was an iconographical battleground between Japanese colonialism and Korean nationalism.

This recent iconographical warfare should be understood in light of the historical development of Seoul during the last 600 years; the battle over the Japanese colonial government building and Kyongbok Palace represents only the most recent phase of a long process of naturalizing and denaturalizing the palace. After the first king of the Choson dynasty attempted to naturalize the icon of his ruling power by constructing Kyongbok Palace, there were several major attempts to denaturalize and denaturalize it prior to Japan's actions. The Japanese mutilation of the palace and the present Korean government's rebuilding of it may merely be the most recent phases of this iconographic warfare. Indeed, the landscape of Seoul might be one of the best examples of ongoing iconographic conflict. Table 15.1 summarizes the history of iconographic warfare on the site of Kyongbok Palace from 1394, when Seoul became the capital of Korea, through the Japanese colonial rule (1910–1945), and then to present-day Korea.

Table 15.1 Chronology of iconographic warfare on the site of Kyongbok Palace since 1394

Period	Naturalizing landscape	Denaturalizing landscape
King Taejo (1392–1394)	Building Kyongbok Palace on most auspicious site of Seoul	Leaving the palace of the former dynasty unused and derelict
King Chungjong (1532)		The crown prince quarters of Kyongbok Palace burn in a fire
King Myongjong (1553–1554)	Despite poor harvest, Kyongbok Palace is rebuilt	More palace buildings are lost in a fire
King Sonjo (1592, the Japanese invasion)	Changdok Palace is rebuilt instead of Kyongbok Palace	Disgruntled Koreans burn down the whole palace, which is left in ruins
Taewongun	Kyongbok Palace is reconstructed to its former glory	
Japanese colonial government	The colonial government building is built on the palace grounds	The Korean palace is mutilated severely
The present Korean government (1995–)	Reconstruction of Kyongbok Palace	Demolition of the colonial government building

This landscape battle was not due to geomancy. Geomantic ideas were merely manipulated by the authors of the landscape to achieve their political aims: denaturalizing their opponent's icon and naturalizing their own.

Notes

1. This chapter has developed from my conference paper, Hong-key Yoon, "An Interim Report on the Iconographic Warfare in the Geomantic Landscape of Seoul", *20th New Zealand Geography Conference Proceedings* (1999), 326–330. (1999) and my article published in Korean, Hong-key Yoon, "Kyongbokkung kwa ku Choson Chonggokpu kunmul kyongkwan ul tullussan sangjingmul Chonjaeng" [The iconographical warfare over Kyongbok Palace and the former Japanese Colonial Government Building], *Konggan kwa Sahwoi* [Space & Environment], vol. 15 (2001), 282–305

2. Munhwa Choiyukpu [Ministry of Culture and Sports] and Kungnip Chungang Pakmulkwan [National Museum], *Ku Choson Chongdokpu Konmul Silchuk mit Cholgo Pogoso* [Report on theActual Measurement of the Former Colonial Government Office Building and Its Removal] (Seoul: .Kungnip Chungang Pakmulkwan, 1997), vol. 1, 30 and 342.

3. J. Duncan and N. Duncan, "(Re) reading the landscape", Environment and Planning D: Society and Space, vol.9 (1988), 117–126; J. Duncan, The City as Text: The Politics of Landscape Interpretation in Nineteenth Century Kandy (Cambridge: Cambridge University, 1990).

4. Clarence J. Glacken, *Traces on the Rhodian Shore* (Berkeley, University of California Press, 1967), 190.

5. Clarence J. Glacken, *Traces on the Rhodian Shore*, 190.

6. Clarence J. Glacken, *Traces on the Rhodian Shore*, 203–204. I have changed Glacken's wording slightly in the quotation here. The original statement is "God is revealed in the Scripture; his works are also visible in the world."

7. Clarence J. Glacken, *Traces on the Rhodian Shore*, 204.

8. Clarence J. Glacken, *Traces on the Rhodian Shore*, 204. Glacken in footnote 97 of page 204 in his book stated that "I quote this because of its interest without being able to give the source. Hugh Pope, St. Augustine of Hippo, quotes it on 227, but the citation of De Civ Dei, Bk. XVI. viii, is not correct."

9. Clarence J. Glacken, *Traces on the Rhodian Shore*, 203.

10. Pierce Lewis, "Axioms for Reading the Landscape: Some Guides to the American Scene," in *The Interpretation of Ordinary Landscapes: Geographical essays*, ed. D. W. Meinig, (New York, Oxford University Press, 1979), 14–32.

11. D. W. Meinig, "The Beholding Eye: Ten Versions of the Same Scene," in *The Interpretation of Ordinary Landscape*, ed. D.W. Meinig (New York: Oxford University, 1979), 33–48.

12. D. W. Meinig, "The Beholding Eye," 42–45.

13. J. Duncan and N. Duncan, "(Re) reading the landscape," 117

14. J. Duncan and N. Duncan, "(Re) reading the landscape," 121.

15. J. Duncan and N. Duncan, "(Re) reading the landscape," 121.

16. J. Duncan and N.Duncan, "(Re) reading the landscape," 123. Duncan's citation is from T. Eagleton, Literary Theory (Minneapolis: University of Minnesota Press, 1983), 135.

17. J. Duncan and N. Duncan, "(Re) reading the landscape," 125.

18. J. Duncan and N. Duncan, "(Re) reading the landscape," 117.

19. These three types of iconographic warfare were initially discussed in Korean in Hong-key Yoon, "Kyongbokkung kwa ku Choson," 287–288.

20. "A Short History of the Pine," Auckland City Council; Hong-key Yoon, "Kyongbokkung kwa ku Choson," 282–305.

21. J. K. Wright, "A Plea for the History of Geography," in John K. Wright, *Human Nature in Geography* (Cambridge, MA.: Harvard University Press, 1966), 11–23.

22. J. K. Wright, "Terrae Incognitae: The Place of the Imagination in Geography," *Annals of the Association of the Association of American Geographers*, vol. 37 (1947), 13.

23. S. Daniels and D. Cosgrove, "Introduction: iconography and landscape" in, *The Iconography of Landscape*, ed. D. Cosgrove, and S. Daniels (Cambridge: Cambridge University, 1988), 1–10.

24. S. Daniels and D. Cosgrove, "Introduction: iconography and landscape," 2.

25. Yi Pyongdo, *Koryo Sidaeui Yongu* [A Study of the Koryo Period], revised edition. (Seoul: Asea Munhwasa, 1980), 361.

26. Yi Pyongdo, *Koryo Sidaeui Yongu*, 87 and 356.

27. Yi Pyongdo, *Koryo Sidaeui Yongu*, 364.

28. Yi Pyongdo, *Koryo Sidaeui Yongu*, 364.

29. Paek Namshin, *Seoul Taekwan* [Seoul Gazetteer] (Seoul: Chongchi Shinmunsa, 1955), 187.

30. Paek Namshin, *Seoul Taekwan*, 187.

31. Paek Namshin, *Seoul Taekwan*, 187.

32. Paek Namshin, *Seoul Taekwan*, 187.

33. Toyotomi Hideyoshi, who succeeded in unifying Japan, attempted to invade China through Korea. He invaded Korea in the spring of 1592, and the Japanese army was countered by Korean and Chinese armies. The war that was fought on Korean soil lasted for seven years ending in 1598. For a brief introduction to this historical incident

and its impact on Korea, see Lee Ki-baek, *A New History of Korea.* Translated by Edward W. Wagner with Edward J. Shultz, (Seoul: Ilchoka, 1984), 209–215.

34. Paek Namshin, *Seoul Taekwan,* 187–188.

35. Paek Namshin, *Seoul Taekwan,* 188–189.

36. Paek Namshin, *Seoul Taekwan,* 346.

37. Paek Namshin, *Seoul Taekwan,* 346–348.

38. Paek Namshin, *Seoul Taekwan,* 350–356.

39. Lee Ki-Paek, *A New History of Korea,* 261.

40. Son Chongmok, "Choson Chongdokpu Chongsa mit Kyongsongpu chongsa kollipe taehan yon'gu" [A Study on the Construction of the Colonial Government Building and Seoul City Hall]. *Hyangto Seoul* vol. 48 (1989), 65–66. Son Chongmok's discussion of this event is based on a book, Kinki chiho no meisho shiseki (Famous Historical Remains of the Kyonggi Province), compiled and published by Kyonggi Province, 1937, 81.

41. Son Chongmok, "Choson Chongdokpu Chongsa," 66–69.

42. Munhwa Choiyukpu [Ministry of Culture and Sports] and Kungnip Chungang Pakmulkwan [National Museum], *Ku Choson Chongdokpu Konmul,* 342, munso (document) 1.

43. Yanagi Muneyoshi, "A Kwanghwamun iyo" [Oh, the Kwanghwamun Gate], in Yanagi Muneyoshyi, Choson kwa Yesul [Korea and its Art]. Translated into Korean by Pak Chesam, (Seoul: Pomusa, 1989), 99–100. Yanagi first published this article in Kaizo, September 1924.

44. Munhwa Choiyukpu [Ministry of Culture and Sports] and Kungnip Chungang Pakmulkwan [National Museum], *Ku Choson Chongdokpu Konmul,* 341.

45. Munhwa Choiyukpu [Ministry of Culture and Sports] and Kungnip Chungang Pakmulkwan [National Museum], *Ku Choson Chongdokpu Konmul,* 257.

46. J. Duncan and N. Duncan, "(Re) reading the landscape,", 118.

47. Lee Man-hoon, "Dismantling the Former Colonial Government Building to Restore the National Spirit," *Koreana,* vol. 9, no.2 (1995), 80.

48. Son Chongmok, "Choson Chongdokpu Chongsa," 71; Munhwa Choiyukpu (Ministry of Culture and Sports) and Kungang Pakmulkwan (National Museum) (1997), 341; Lee Man-hoon (1995), 80.

49. Lee Man-hoon, "Dismantling the Former Colonial," 80.

50. Yanagi Muneyoshi, "A Kwanghwamun iyo," 100.

51. Munhwa Choiyukpu [Ministry of Culture and Sports] and Kungnip Chungang Pakmulkwan [National Museum], *Ku Choson Chongdokpu Konmul,* 47.

52. Son Chongmok, "Choson Chongdokpu Chongsa," 90.

53. These comments were probably made when the main concrete structure of the colonial government building was completed but before covering its outside with granite. I have requoted and translated into English from a Korean source: Kim Changdong, "Choson Chongdokpu Chongsa Chajondp kwanhan che'un" [A Thought on the Existence of the Choson Government-General Building]. *Konchuk [Review of Architecture and Building Science],* vol. 35, no. 3 (May 1991), 77. This Korean source stated that the quote is a travelogue written in 1923 by Blasko Ivannes (1867–1928). The spelling of the name Blasko Ivannes is the transliteration from the Korean alphabets Hangul.

54. Munhwa Choiyukpu [Ministry of Culture and Sports] and Kungnip Chungang Pakmulkwan [National Museum], *Ku Choson Chongdokpu Konmul,* 341.

55. Son Chongmok, "Choson Chongdokpu Chongsa," 104.

56. Munhwa Choiyukpu [Ministry of Culture and Sports] and Kungnip Chungang Pakmulkwan [National Museum], *Ku Choson Chongdokpu Konmul,* 341.

57. Munhwa Choiyukpu [Ministry of Culture and Sports] and Kungnip Chungang Pakmulkwan [National Museum], *Ku Choson Chongdokpu Konmul,* 341.

58. Munhwa Choiyukpu [Ministry of Culture and Sports] and Kungnip Chungang Pakmulkwan [National Museum], *Ku Choson Chongdokpu Konmul,* 30 and 342.

59. Munhwa Choiyukpu [Ministry of Culture and Sports] and Kungnip Chungang Pakmulkwan [National Museum], *Ku Choson Chongdokpu Konmul,* 344.

60. Munhwa Choiyukpu [Ministry of Culture and Sports] and Kungnip Chungang Pakmulkwan [National Museum], *Ku Choson Chongdokpu Konmul,* 341 and 344. According to the same Korean government report (344), another public opinion survey on the demolition issue was held by KBS (Korea Broadcasting Service) on 30 June 1991. The survey of 500 people showed an inconclusive result of only 49 percent in favor of demolition and 51 percent opposed to it.

61. The Han-Kyore Shinmun [Hankyore daily newspaper], 16 August 1995, 23.

62. Kim Young-sam, Address by President Kim Young Sam on the 50th Anniversary of National Liberation (15 August 1995), 5.

63. Munhwa Choiyukpu [Ministry of Culture and Sports] and Kungnip Chungang Pakmulkwan [National Museum], *Ku Choson Chongdokpu Konmul,* 368.

64. Munhwa Choiyukpu [Ministry of Culture and Sports] and Kungnip Chungang Pakmulkwan [National Museum], *Ku Choson Chongdokpu Konmul,* 366–375.

65. Pierce Lewis, "Axioms for Reading the Landscape," 12.

66. Munhwa Choiyukpu [Ministry of Culture and Sports] and Kungnip Chungang Pakmulkwan [National Museum], *Ku Choson Chongdokpu Konmul,* 385.

67. Munhwa Choiyukpu [Ministry of Culture and Sports] and Kungnip Chungang Pakmulkwan [National Museum], *Ku Choson Chongdokpu Konmul,* 386.

68. Munhwa Choiyukpu [Ministry of Culture and Sports] and Kungnip Chungang Pakmulkwan [National Museum], *Ku Choson Chongdokpu Konmul,* 386.

69. The Korea Times, 6 June 1994.

70. Kyongbokkung Pokwonjongbi [The Restoration Plan of Kyongbok Palace], a three-page typed script document (unpublished), 1.

71. Pyong is a traditional Korean measurement unit. One pyong equals 3.954 square yards or 3.24 square metres.

Chapter 16
Conclusion

Traditionally, geomancy strongly influenced site selection and environmental management in Korea by shaping people's attitudes toward the environment. When villages and cities were located along a river in a geomantic landscape of a sailing boat, people were discouraged from digging wells for drinking water. To dig a well on such a landscape was analogous to making a hole in the bottom of the sailing boat, causing the boat to sink. Sinking the boat meant damaging the harmony of the landscape and bringing misfortune to the place.

Kangchong village, which is across the Nakdong River from my home village, Haepyong of Sonsan County, Kyongbuk Province, did not have any wells for drinking water during my boyhood. Instead, the villagers carried it in buckets from the Nakdong River and drank it without treating it, because they believed that digging a well would hurt the geomancy of the local landscape and bring misfortune to their village.

Even the people of Pyongyang, the present-day capital of North Korea, apparently refrained from digging wells during the Choson dynasty (1392–1910) because of geomantic ideas. According to *Taengni-ji (Book of Selecting Settlements)* by Yi Chunghwan (1690–1756), Pyongyang is a geomantic landscape of a "sailing boat," hence people were not allowed to dig wells. The book states that

> The geomantic condition [of Pyongyang] is considered to be auspicious. It is said that Pyongyang is located in the geomantic landscape of a sailing boat and thus people avoided digging wells. In the past, when they dug wells, there were many fires in the city. Therefore, people refilled the wells. Now all citizens of the town use river water for both official and private use.[1]

Indeed, the people of Pyongyang believed that digging wells brought misfortune and used river water for a long time. This geomantic interpretation of the city generated a famous Korean pun-fable, "The Story of Mr Pongi Kim Sondal Selling Water in the Taedong River of Pyongyang City."[2] Everyone in the city knew that the water in the river was public property and free to everyone, but in the story a covetous rich merchant from Seoul was fooled into buying ownership of the water. The merchant was ignorant about local geomantic conditions and customs. After seeing a set-up scene of Mr Pongi Kim Sondal collecting coins from everyone who took a bucketful of water from the river, the merchant bought the water from him. But when he attempted to collect coins from people fetching water from the river, they told him that the river belonged to everybody and that the water was free. When he realized that he had been fooled, it was too late to recover his money. Without knowing what the geomantic landscape of a sailing boat is, one cannot appreciate fully why Pyongyang citizens fetched water from the Taedong River.

Such stories are a testimony to traditional Korean geomantic attitudes toward nature, habitat, and home. The stories exemplify the traditional culture-nature relationship in Korea. Koreans were often fanatically enthusiastic in their efforts to find an auspicious place. In the process of finding and occupying such a site, they were prepared to put up with a huge financial burden (that is, if they could afford it) and suffer quarrels and physical aggression. Koreans' obsession with the practice of geomancy became an important cause of crimes, disputes, and litigation. But once they found a propitious place, they attempted to take good care of the site and lived there by themselves or buried their dead there in a harmonious way. Since the people perceived such landscapes as animate or inanimate objects, they were very careful not to disturb their geomantic harmony. Moreover, when people found minor shortcomings in the places, they often made the necessary corrections by building temples and pagodas, planting trees, making artificial hills and dikes, or even by making stone sculptures.

Since the 1960s and 1970s, traditional geomantic customs such as forbidding wells have now largely been abolished even in villages. It is clear, however, that without an understanding of geomantic ideas, it is almost impossible to understand earlier Korean behavior relating to environmental management. When Korea achieved economic success during the 1970s and 1980s, people came to be relatively well off and could afford to reconsider traditional cultural values, including the practice of geomancy. Before this they had given little thought and possessed few means to conserve their cultural heritage. But there occurred a kind of "cultural rebound," similar to the way some Irish and German immigrants to America revived their cultural heritage after establishing themselves in their American homes.[3] When Koreans achieved a living standard that allowed them to seek their cultural roots, traditional geomancy was revived, especially in decorating their ancestral graves and searching for auspicious sites.

Throughout this book, I have tried to examine the principles and practice of geomancy in Korea and the traditional culture-nature relationship expressed in Koreans' mindsets, cultural landscape, and social behavior. I have used narrative folklore in my analysis. Folklore is a living tradition reflecting the insights and perceptions of people, from which a student can learn the genuine relationship between people and their environment.[4] Folklore can be a very valuable tool in cultural geography. However, cultural geographers have only made slight use of it. It may even be necessary to develop a subdivision of cultural geography that is especially devoted to the study of the culture-nature relationship as revealed in folklore.

I would like to conclude this book by remarking once more on the nature of geomancy. After studying it, one is likely to ask whether it is a superstition, a religion, or a science. My conclusion is that geomancy is none of these things. There is no concept equivalent to geomancy in the West, nor can it be understood in terms of any Western notion. Geomancy is a unique and comprehensive system of conceptualizing the physical environment that regulates human ecology by influencing man to select auspicious environments and to build harmonious structures such as graves, houses, and cities on them.

Notes

1. Yi Chunghwan, *Taengni-ji* [Book of Choosing Settlement] (Seoul: Choson kwangmunhoe, 1912), 72.
2. Hankuk Chongsin Munhwa Yonguwon [Academy of Korean Studies], *Hankuk Kubi Munhak taege* [Grand Collection of Korean Oral Literature] (Seoul: Hankuk Chongsin Munhwa Yonguwon, 1982), vol. 1.7, 748–749 & vol. 2.5, 827–831.
3. Terry G. Jordan & Lester Rowntree, *The Human Mosaic: A Thematic Introduction to Cultural Geography*, *5th* Edition (New York: Harper & Row, 1990), 309–310.
4. Compare this with W. Bascom's statement, "The recording of folklore, in itself, is a useful field technique for the anthropologist. It gives further leads for the investigation of the content of culture, insuring that important cultural details are not overlooked; it provides a non-ethnocentric approach to the ways of life of a people, emphasising, as Boas pointed out, the things which are important in their own minds; it may offer clues to past events and to archaic customs no longer in actual practice, although not to the degree assumed by the Cultural Evolutionists; it may provide a means of getting at esoteric features of culture which cannot be approached in any other ways . . ." For further study, see William R. Bascom, Bascom, "Four Functions of Folklore", in *The Study of Folklore*, Allan Dundes, ed., (Englewood Cliffs, NJ: Prentice-Hall, 1965), 284.

References

Choson Wangjo Sillok [Annals of Choson Dynast] (Fascism. reproduction of Taebaek-san copy, except *Kojong Sillok*). Seoul: Kuksa Pyonchan Woi-wonhoe, 1955–58. The following annals of kings are cited from the above series of *Choson Wangjo Sillok:*

Taejo Sillok	[The Annals of King Taejo]
Taejong Sillok	[The Annals of King Taejong]
Sejong Sillok	[The Annals of King Sejong]
Tanjong Sillok	[The Annals of King Tanjong]
Sejo Sillok	[The Annals of King Sejo]
Songjong Sillok	[The Annals of King Songjong]
Yonsankun Ilgi	[The Annals of King Yonsankun]
Sonjo Sillok	[The Annals of King Sonjo]
Choljong Sillok	[The Annals of King Choljong]
Kojong Sillok	[The Annals of King Kojong]: *the copy used here is Tamgu-dang edition.* Seoul: Tamgu-dang, 1970.

Handwritten manuals of geomancy in Korea (no place and date of publication are indicated.). These manuscript editions were acquired through second-hand bookstores during the 1970s:

Anonymous. *Chiri-chongjong* [Ultra Correct Geomancy]
Anonymous. *Chiri-yogyol* [Necessary Decisions of Geomancy]
Anonymous. *Pak-ok* [Pearls of Guo Pu]
Anonymous. *Sanpop-chonso* [Complete Set of Books on Grave Geomancy]
Anonymous. *Sanga-yoram* [Required Reading of Geomancers]
Anonymous. *Yangtaek* [House Geomancy]

Ahern, Emily M. *The Cult of the Dead in a Chinese Village.* Stanford, CA: Stanford University Press, 1973.
An, Yongbae. "Rho Muhyon dangson Ddak machotta" [Correctly Predicted the Successful Election of Rho Muhyon]. *Chugandonga* [Weekly Donga] 365 (December 2002) cover story.
Anderson, Edgar. *Plants, Man and Life.* Berkeley and Los Angeles: University of California Press, 1969.

Anonymous. *Huangdi Zhaijing* [The Book of the Yellow Emperor's Discourse on House Geomancy]. 5th case, vol. 49 of Chongwen shuju huikeshu. Wuch'ang City: Hubei Ch'ung-wen Shu-chu, 1877.

Anonymous. *Tongkuk Yoji Pigo* [Reference Compilation of Geogrpahical Survey of Korea], vol. I of Soul Saryo Chongso. Edited by Soul Tukpyolsisa Pyonchan Wiwenhoe. Seoul: Soul Tukpyolsisa yonchan Wiwonhoe, 1956.

Anonymous. *Beijing Lvyou Shouce* [Travel Guide of Beijing]. Beijing: Beijing chubanshe, 1980.

Anonymous. *Kyongbokkung Pokwonjongbi* [Restoration Plan of the Kyongbok Palace], a three page typed script document (unpublished).

Aono, Yoshio and Kim Song-yol. *Chosen Bosei Ippan* [Burial Systems in Korea]. Seoul: Iwa Matsudo Shoten, 1924.

Barnes, Trevor. "Social construction." In *The Dictionary of Human Geography*, 4th ed., edited by R.J. Johnston, Derek Gregory, Geraldine Pratt and Michael Watts, 747–748. Oxford: Blackwell Publishers, 2000.

Bascom, William R. "Four Functions of Folklore." In *The Study of Folklore*, edited by Allan Dundes, 279–298. Englewood Cliffs, NJ: Prentice-Hall, 1965.

Bruun, Ole. *Fengshui in China: Geomantic Divination Between State Orthodoxy and Popular Religion*. Copenhagen: NIAS Press, 2003.

Chan, Wing-tsit, trans. and comp. (1973), A *Source Book in Chinese Philosophy*. Princeton: Princeton University Press, 1973.

Chang, Duksun. *Hankuk Solhwa Munhak Yongu* [A Study of Korean Folk Narratives]. Seoul: Seoul Taehakgyo Chulpanbu, 1971.

Chang, Yongduk. *Myongdang-non* [On Auspicious Sites]. Seoul: Emille Misulkwan, 1973.

Chang, Yongduk. "Myongdang Chapki" [Essays on Auspicious Sites]. *Hankuk I Ibo*. 19 February 1974–21 March 1974.

Chen, Mengjia. *Yinxu buci zongshu* [Comprehensive Discourse on the Divinational Phrases from Yin Ruins]. Beijing: Kexue Chubanshe, 1956.

Chen, Huaizhen. "Fengshui yu zhangmai" [Geomancy and Burial]. *Shehui Yenjiu* [Studies on Society]. vol.1, no. 3 (1937): 1–12.

Chi, Chong-o. "Myongdang Chaja Samchonri" [Searching for Auspicious Places over the Three Thousands Ri]. *Chugan Chung-ang* [Weekly Chung-ang]. 27 October 1974–2 March 1975.

Chi, Yongha. Hankuk Imjong-sa [History of Forestry Policy in Korea]. Seoul: Myongsu-sa, 1964.

Chindan-hakhoe. *Hankuk-sa* [History of Korea]. Seoul: Ulyu Munhwa-sa, 1959.

Cho, Dusun and others (1960), *Taejon Hoetong* [Comprehensive Update of Administrative Code]. Trans. into modern Korean of 1865 ed. Seoul: Koryo Taehakgyo Chulpan-bu, 1960.

Cho, Hiung, comp. *Han'guk Kubimunhak Taege* [Grand Collection of Korean Oral Literature]. Songnam City: Han'guk Chongsin Munhwa Yon'guwon Omun Yongusil, 1978-1985.

Cho, Songkyo, ed. *Namwon-ji* [Gazetteer of Namwon County]. Namwon: Namwon Gongnip Kungmin Hakgyo, 1950.

Choi, Byong-hon. "Tosonui Saengaewa Ramalyochoui Pungsuchirisol" [The Life of Toson and Geomancy during the Period of the End of Silla and the Beginning of Koryo]. In *Hankuksa Yongu [A Study of Korean History]*. 11 (1975): 101–146.

Choi, Byong-hon (1989), "Toson's Geomantic Theories and the Foundation of the Koryo Dynasty," *Seoul Journal of Korean Studies*. 2 (1989): 65–92.

Choi, Changjo. *Hankuk ui Pungsusasang* [Geomantic Thought of Korea]. Seoul: Minumsa, 1984.

Choi, Changjo. *Choun Ttang iran Udirum malhaminga* [Where Do We Mean by Good Land]. Seoul: Sohaemunjip, 1990.

Choi, Changjo. (1992), "Choson hugi sirhakja turui pungsusasang" [Geomantic thought of Sirhak Scholars during the later Choson Dynasty], *Hankuk Munhwa* [Korean Culture]. 11 (1992): 469–504.

Choi, Changjo. "Han'guk Pungsu Chiri ui Kujowa wonri" [The Structure and Principles of the Korean Buddhism]. *Proceedings, The Twelfth International Buddhism Studies Conference, Tosonkusawa Hankuk* [National Master Toson and Korea], Kwangju, Korea, (July 1996): 269–528.

Choi. Changjo. "Palmun." In *Hosunshin ui chirishinpop* [The New Geomantic Principles by Hosunshin], trans. and commentary by Kim dukyu, 5–7. Seoul: Changnak, 2001.

Choi, Changjo, trans. *Chong'okyong, Komnangkyong*. Seoul: Minumsa, 1993.

Choi Hang and others. *Kyongkuk Taejon* [National Code],. Seoul: Popje-cho, 1962.

Choi, Ja. *Pohanjip*, trans. into modern Korean by Yi Sangpyo, *Pohanjip, Nakongpisol, Hankuk Myongjo Taejonjip* [Series in Great Korean Classics]. Seoul: Taeyang sojok, 1975.

Choi, Kunhak. *Sokdam Sajon* [Dictionary of Proverbs]. Seoul: Kyonghak-sa, 1968.

Choi Sangsu. *Hankuk Mingan Chonsoljip* [Collection of Korean Legends]. Seoul: Tongmunkwan, 1958.

Choi Sunghi. *Hankuk Komunso Yongu* [A Study of Old Korean Documents]. Seoul: Hankkuk chongsin munhwa yonguwon, 1982.

Choi Won-Suk. "Yongnamui Bibo [Bibo of the Yongnam Region]," PhD dissertation, Korea University, 2000.

Choi Won-Suk. *Hankuk ui Pungsu wa Pibo* [Geomancy and Pibo in Korea]. Seoul: Minsokwon, 2004.

Chon Kwan-u. "Kijago" [A Study of Qizhi]. *Tongbang Hakji* 15 (1974): 1–72.

Chong Chisu. *Chiri-yocho* [Geomancy in Brief]. Taegu: Chinmun Chulpansa, 1968.

Chong Inji and others. *Koryosa* [History of Koryo]. Seoul: Yonhi Taehakgyo Chulpanbu, 1955.

Chong Inji and others. translated by Pak Sihyong and Hong Hwoiyu. *Pukyok Koryosa* [the North Korean translation of Koryosa into modern Korean].

vol. 1, Sega 2, Taejo 2. Pyongyang: Kwahakwon Chulpansa, 1962: re-printed in Seoul: Sinsowon, 1992.

Chong Yakyong. *Kukyok Mokmin-simso* [Criticisms and Advice on Governing the People, A Modern Korean Translation]. Seoul: Minjok Munhwa Chu-jinhoe, 1969.

Chugan Choson (Seoul). *"Pungsu Sipgang"* [Ten Lectures on Geomancy]. August 29, 1971 –December 26, 1971.

Dallet, Ch. *Histoire de L'église de Corée.* Paris: Librairie Victor Palme', E'diteur, 1874.

Daniels, S and Cosgrove D. "Introduction: iconography and landscape" In *The Iconography of Landscape*, edited by D. Cosgrove, and S. Daniels, 1–10. Cambridge: Cambridge University, 1988.

De Groot, J. J. M. *The Religious System of China.* Leiden: Librairie et Im-primerie, 1897.

Detel, W. "Social Constructivism." *International Encyclopaedia of the Social & Behavioural Sciences*, vol. 21, edited by Neil J. Smelser and Paul B. Baltes, 14264–7. Oxford: Elsevier Science, 2001.

Duncan, J and N. Duncan. "(Re) reading the landscape", *Environment and Planning D: Society and Space* 9 (1988), 117–126.

Duncan, J., *The City as Text: The Politics of Landscape Interpretation in Nineteenth Century Kandy.* Cambridge: Cambridge University, 1990.

Eberhard, Wolfram. "On Three Principles in Chinese Social Structure," *Journal of Sociology, National Taiwan University* 6 (1970): 13.

Eberhard, Wolfram. *Studies in Taiwanese Folktales.* Taipei: The Oriental Cultural Service, 1970.

Eitel, E.J. *Fengshui: Or the Rudiments of Natural Science in China.* Hong Kong: Lane, Crawford & Co., 1873.

Entrikin, J. Nicholas. *The Betweenness of Place.* Baltimore: Johns Hopkins University Press, 1991.

Feuchatwang, Stephan D.R. *An Anthropological Analysis of Chinese Geomancy.* Bangkok: White Lotus, 2002.

Feuchtwang, Stephan D.R. *An Anthropological Analysis of Chinese Geomancy.* Vientianne: Editions Vithangna, 1974.

Forke, Alfred. The World Conception of the Chinese: Their Astronomical, Cosmological and Physico-philosophical Speculations. London: Arthur Probsthain, 1925.

Freedman, Maurice. *Chinese Lineage and Society: Fukien and Kwangtune.* London School of Economics Monographs on Social Anthropology, No. 33. London: the Athlone Press, 1966.

Freedman, Maurice. "Geomancy," *Proceedings of the Royal Anthropological Institute of Great Britain and Ireland.* (London, 1968), 5–15.

Freedman, Maurice., *The Study of Chinese Society.* Stanford, CA: Stanford University Press, 1979.

Fu Sheng. *Shangshu dachuan.* Shanghai: Shangwu Yinshuguan, 1937.

Fung, Yu-lan. *A Short History of Chinese Philosophy.* New York: The Macmillan Co., 1948.

Glacken, Clarence J. *Traces on the Rhodian Shore.* Berkeley, University of California Press, 1967.

Guo, Pu. *Zangjing, neipian* [The Book of Burial, the inner volume]. In Chongwen Shuju Heikeshu. Wuhan: Hubei Chongwen Shuju, 1875.

Guo, Pu. *Liujiangdong jiacang shanpen Zhangshu.* (commentary by Zheng Mi). In Linlang Mishi Chongshu. Case 2. vol. 10, n.p., 1888.

Guo, Pu (1967), Zangshu, in *Dili zhengzong* [The Cardinal Principles of Geomancy]. (commentary by Jiang Guo). Shinchu: Chulin shuchu, 1967.

Hankuk Chongsin Munhwa Yonguwon [Academy of Korean Studies]. *Hankuk Kubi Munhak taege* [Grand Collection of Korean Oral Literature]. Seoul: Hankuk Chongsin Munhwa Yonguwon, 1980–1983.

Hankuk Munhwa Illyu Hakhoe, ed. *Hankuk minsok chonghap chosapogoso, Cholla Namdo pyon* [A Comprehensive Report on Korean folklore and folk custom, South Cholla Province Part]. Seoul: Ministry of Culture and Information, 1969.

Hankuk Munhwa Illyu Hakhoe, ed. *Hankuk minsok chonghap chosapogoso, Cholla Pukdo pyon* [A Comprehensive Report on Korean folklore and folk custom, North Cholla Province Part]. Seoul: Ministry of Culture and Information, 1971.

Han-Kyoreh Shinmun [a daily newspaper in Seoul], 16 August 1995, p. 23.

Harvey, David. "The Social Construction of Space and Time: A Relational Theory", *Geographical Review of Japan,* series –B, vol.67, no.2 (1994), 126–135.

Hong, Manson. *Sallim-kyongje.* Handwritten manuscript: copy in the East Asiatic Library, University of California, Berkeley.

Hongmun-kwan, comp. *Chungbo Munhon Pigo* [The Revised and Enlarged Edition of the Comparative Review of Records and Documents]. (Seoul: Hongmun-kwan, 1908.

Hsu, M. "The Han Maps and Early Chinese Cartography", *Annals of the Association of the American Geographers,* 68 (1978): 45–60.

Hu, Shunshen (n.d.). *Dili xinfa* [New Principles of Geomancy]. (The edition in the Kyujang-gak Collection at Seoul National University Library).

Hwang, Ilsun. *Pungsu Chiri-hak Kaeyo* [An Overview of Geomancy]. Seoul: Pakmun-gak, 1968.

Hyon, Yongjun. "Ammaejang ui Kaeson," *Chejudo* [Cheju Province], vol. 27 (1966), 79–86.

Ilyon (1969), *Samguk yusa* [Memorabilia of the Three Kingdoms]. Translated into modern Korean by Yi Cheho. Seoul: Kwangmunchulpansa, 1969.

Im, Kyong-il. "Chonggam-noke Taehayo," *Shinchonji* [New World], vol. 1, no. 6 (1946), 98–103.

Immannishi, Ryu. *Shiragi shi Kenkyu* [A Study of Silla History]. Seoul: Chikasawa shoten, 1933.

Jordan, Terry G. and Lester Rowntree. *The Human Mosaic: A Thematic Introduction to Cultural Geography*, *5th Edition*. New York: Harper & Row, 1990.

Kamura, Kunoi, comp. *Nagasaki Kohanga* [Old Print-Picture of Nagasaki]. Nagasaki bitutsu dokokai, 1964.

Keown, Jeong-hee. "*Pungsusolhwa Yongu* [A Study of Geomancy Tales], " Master's thesis, Ewha Women's University, 1986.

Kim, Changdong. "Choson Chongdokpu Chongsa Chajondp kwanhan che'un" [A Thought on the Existence of the Choson Government-General Building]. *Konchuk [Review of Architecture and Building Science]*. 35(3) (1991): 77.

Kim, Chongho. *Taedong Yoji-do* [Map of Korea, the Great East]. Seoul: Keijo Teikoku Daigaku, 1936.

Kim, Chunho, ed. *Sonsankun-ji* [Gazetteer of Sonsan County]. Sonsan: Sonsankun-ji pyonchan wiwonhoe, 1968.

Kim, Dukyu. *Hankuk Pungsu ui ho wa sil* [Truth and False of Korean Geomancy]. Seoul: Tonghaksa, 1995.

Kim, Dukyu. *Uri Ttang, Uri Pungsu* [Our Land, Our Geomancy]. Seoul: Tonghaksa, 1998.

Kim Dukyu. *Choson Pungsuhakin ui taegna wa Nonjaeng* [Discourse and Life of Scholarly Geomancers of the Choson Dynasty]. Seoul: Kungni, 2000.

Kim, Dukyu and An Yongbae. "Myongdang chja Nammolle Ijanghago Taekwon tojon" [Running for the Presidency after Secretly Moving Their Ancestral Graves to Auspicious Sites]. *Shindonga* [New East Asia]. 45–2 (2002): 180–193.

Kim, Dukyu and An Yongbae. *Kwonryok kwa Pungsu* [Political Power and Geomancy]. Seoul: Changnak, 2002.

Kim, Dukyu, trans. *Hosunsin ui Chiri Shinpop* [The New Geomantic Principles by Hosunsin]. Seoul: Changnak, 2001.

Kim, Hangbai. *Silyong Pungsuchiri* [Practical Geomancy]. Seoul: Ilsan Chulpansa, 1997.

Kim, Ki-duk. "Koryo sidae Kaegyong ui Pungsuchirijok Kochal" [Examining the Geographical Features of the Koryo Dynasty's Gaegyeong in Fengshui Theoretical Terms]. *Hankuk Sasangsahak* [Studies in Korean Thought]. 17 (2001): 63–119.

Kim, Myongje. *Chiri Palsip Pal-hyang Chinkyol* [True Discourse on Eighty-Eight Geomantic directions]. Seoul: Samsin sojok, 1971.

Kim, Myongjin. "Umyang Ohaengnonkwa Tongyang Jongchi Sasang," *Konkuk Haksul-ji* [Konkuk University Collection of Academic Essays] 12 (1971): 247–268.

Kim, Pusik. *Samkuk Sagi* [History of the Three Kingdoms], Translated into modern Korean by Kim Chong-won. Seoul: Sonjin Munhwa-sa, 1960.

Kim, Pusik. *Samkuk sagi* [history of the Three Kingdoms]. Translated into modern Korean by Yi Pyongdo. Seoul: Eul-yoo Publishing, 1987.

Kim, So-kyong, ed. *Kasang ui Kwahak* [The Science of House Geomancy]. Seoul: Hyonam-sa, 1972.

Kim, Susan. *Wonbon Chonggam-nok* [The Original Version of Mr Chong's Prophecy]. Seoul: Myongmundang, 1972.

Kim, Ugyong, Tong Kichun and Kim Chongsok. *Kumsusan Kinyom Kungjon Chonsoljip (1)*[Legends of Kumsusan Memorial Palace](1). Pyongyang: Munhak Yesul Chonghap Chulpansa, 1999.

Kim, Yongbin. "Pungsu sasang eso pon Choson wangnungwonmyo chosong kipop e kwanhan yongu [A Study from Geomantic Perspectives on the Construction Method of the Royal Tombs during the Choson Dynasty] sang, part 1. *Hankuk Chontong munhwa yongu* [Studies on the traditional Korean culture]. Hyosong Women's University 4 (1988): 1–89.

Kim, Yongbin. "Pungsu sasang eso pon Choson wangnungwonmyo chosong kipop e kwanhan yongu [A Study from Geomantic Perspectives on the Construction Method of the Royal Tombs during the Choson Dynasty] chung, part 2, *Hankuk Chontong munhwa yongu* [Studies on the traditional Korean culture]. Hyosong Women's University 5 (1989): 1–100.

Kim, Yonsu, ed. *Changbon Chunhyang-ga*. Seoul: Kukak yesul hakgyo chulpanbu, 1967.

Kim, Young-sam. *Address by President Kim Young Sam on the 50ᵗʰ Anniversary of National Liberation*, 15 August 1995. 5.

Kwon, Ki. *Yongga-ji* [Gazetteer of Andong County], 1899?.

Kyongsang namdo-ji pyonchan woiwonhoe. *Kyongsang Namdo-ji* [Gazetteer of South Kyongsang Province], 1960.

Ledyard, Gari, "Cartography in Korea," In *The History of Cartography*, vol. two, Book two, J.B. Harley and David Woodward, 235–345. Cartography in the Traditional East and southeast Asian Societies. Chicago: University of Chicago Press, 1994.

Lee, Ki-baek. *A New History of Korea*. Translated by Edward W. Wagner with Edward J. Shultz. Seoul: Ilchokak, 1984.

Lee, Ki-baek (Yi Kibaek). Hanguksa *Sillon* [A New History of Korea]. Seoul: Ilchokak, 1984.

Lee, Ki-baek (Yi Kibaek). "Han'guk pungsuchirisol ui kiwon" [The Origin of Korean Geomancy]. *Han'guksa siminkangchoa* 14 (1994): 1–17.

Lee, Man-hun (1995), "Dismantling the Former Colonial Government Building to Restore the National Spirit," *Koreana*, vol. 9, no.2, 79–80.

Lee, Mong-il, (1992), "Kyongbokgungkwa Choson chongdokbu chognsaui Pungsuchirijok kwanke" [The P'ungsu Relationship between the Kyongpok Palace and the Old Government-General Building in Seoul, Korea], *Chong kwan Yi Pyongkon Kyosu Hwagap Kinyum Nonmunjip* [Festschrift, in Honour of Professor Yi Pyongkon on his 60th Birthday], 333–363.

Legge, James, trans. *The She King*. Hong Kong: Hong Kong University Press, 1960.

Lemoine, Jacques. "Forward," In *An Anthropological Analysis of Chinese Geomancy*, by Stephan D. R. Feuchtwang, I–III. Vientiane: Vithangna, 1974.

Lewis, Pierce (1979), "Axioms for Reading the Landscape: Some Guides to the American Scene," In *The Interpretation of Ordinary Landscapes: Geographical essays*, edited by D. W. Meinig, 11–32. New York, Oxford University Press, 1979.

Lewthwaite, G.R. "Environmentalism and Determinism: A Search for Clarification," *Annals of the Association of American Geographers* 56 (1966): 1–23.

Maeng, Uisop. *"Sabon Sokjokchong Tapsagi"* Handwritten report of a stone-piled tomb in Chochiwon, on the author's personal field survey in the middle of October 1964), written on 15 December 1964, 4–5.

March, Andrew. "An Appreciation of Chinese Geomancy," *Journal of Asian Studies* 27 (1968): 252–267.

Marshall, Archibald. *The Dragon*. Illustrated by Edward Ardippone. New York: E.P. Dutton & Co., 1967.

McCune, G.M. and E.O. Reischauer. "Romanisation of the Korean Language". *Transactions of the Korean Branch of the Royal Asiatic Society* 29 (1934): 1–55.

Meinig, D. W. "The Beholding Eye: Ten Versions of the Same Scene," In *The Interpretation of Ordinary Landscape*, edited by D.W. Meinig, 33–48. New York: Oxford University, 1979.

Meinig, D.W. "Reading the landscape: An Appreciation of W. G. Hoskings and J. B. Jackson," In *The Interpretation of Ordinary Landscape*, edited by D.W. Meinig, 195–244. New York: Oxford University, 1979.

Munhwa Choiyukpu [Ministry of Culture and Sports] and Kungnip Chungang Pakmulkwan [National Museum of Korea]. *Ku Choson Chongdokpu Konmul Silchuk mit Cholgo Pogoso* [Report on theActual Measurement of the Former Colonial Government Office Building and Its Removal]. Seoul: . Kungnip Chungang Pakmulkwan, 1997.

Murayama, Chijun. *Chosen no Fusui* [Korean Geomancy] (Seoul: Chosen Shotofu, 1931.

Murayama, Chijun. *Choson ui Pungsu* [Korean Geomancy], Translation of *Chosen no Fusui* into Korean by Choi Kilsong. Seoul: Minumsa, 1990.

Myrdal, Jan. *Report from a Chinese Village*. London: Heinemann, 1965.

Na, Kyongsu, "Konkuksinhwarosoui Koryosegye" [Koryo Segye as National Foundation Myths], *Mokpo omunhak*, vol. 2, 67–86.

Nakamura, Kinjo. *Chosen Fuzoku Gafu* [Pictures of Korean Folk Life]. Tokyo: Tomisato Shoshindo, 1910.

Needham, Joseph. *Science and Civilisation in China*. Cambridge: Cambridge University Press, 1959.

Needham, Joseph. *History and Human Value: A Chinese Perspective for World Science and Technology*. Montreal: McGill University, 1975.

Nemeth, David J. "Bright Yard, Maps from Cheju Island, *Landscape* 25 (1981): 20–21.

Nemeth, David J. "Graven Images and Cosmic Landscape on Cheju Island," *Korean Culture* 4 (1983): 5–19.

Nemeth, David J. *The Architecture of Ideology: Neo-Confucian Imprinting on Cheju Island, Korea*, University of California Publications, Geography, vol. 26. Berkeley, University of California Press, 1987.

Nemeth, David J. "Fengshui as Terrestrial Astrology in Traditional China and Korea", In *The power of Place: Sacred Ground in Natural and Human Environment, edited by* James A. Swan, 215–234. Wheaton, Ill: Quest Books, 1991.

Nemeth, David J. "A Cross-Cultural Cosmographic Interpretation of Some Korean Geomancy Maps," *Cartographica* 30 (1993): 85–97.

No, Sasin and others. *Sinjung Tongkuk Yoji Sungnam* [Newly Augmented Survey of the Geography of Korea]. Seoul: Minjok munhwa chujinhoe, 1969.

Paek Namshin. *Seoul Taekwan* [Seoul Gazetteer]. Seoul: Chongchi Shinmunsa, 1955.

Pak, Chega, *Pukhakui* [Discourse on Northern Studies]. Translated into modern Korean by Yi Sokho. Seoul: Taeyang Sojok, 1972.

Park, Sea-ik. *"Pungsuchirisol Palsaeng Paekuyong e kwanhan punsok yon'gu"* [A Study on the Background and Origin of Fengshui Theory], PhD dissertation, Korea University, 1987.

Park, Sea-ik. Pungsuschriri wa konchuk [Geomancy and Architecture]. Seoul: Kyonghyang Shinmunsa, 1997.

Rogers, Michael C. "Pyonnyon Tongnok: The Foundation Legend of the Koryo State," *Journal of Korean Studies* 4 (1982–83): 3–72.

Rossbach, Sarah. *Feng Shui: The Chinese Art of Placement*. New York: E.P. Dutton, 1983.

Salisbury, Rollin D., Harlan H. Barrows and Water S. Tower. *Modern Geography for High Schools*, American Science Series. New York: Henry Holt, 1913.

Sansom, George. *A History of Japan to 1334*. Stanford: Stanford University Press, 1958.

Sauer, Carl O., "The Morphology of Landscape," *University of California Publications in Geography*. 2 (1925), 19–54.

Sauer, Carl O., *Agricultural Origins and Dispersals*. New York: The American Geographical Society, 1952.

Seike, Kiyoshi. *Kaso no Kagaku* [The Science of House Geomancy]. Tokyo: Kobunsha, 1969.

Semple, Ellen. C. *Influences of Geographic Environment*. New York: Henry Holt, 1911.

Shin, Wolgyun. *Pungsu Solhwa* [Folk Narratives of Geomancy]. Seoul: Miral, 1994.

Shinjo, Shinzo. *Zhongguo shanggu tianwen.* Chinese translation by Shen Xuan. Shanghai: Shangwu Yinshuguan, 1936.

Son, Chongmok. "Choson Chongdokpu Chongsa mit Kyongsongpu chongsa kollipe taehan yon'gu" [A Study on the Construction of the Colonial Government Building and Seoul City Hall]. *Hyangto Seoul* 48 (1989): 59–135.

Songgyunkwan Taehakgyo Kuko Kukmunhakgwa. *Andong Munhwakwon Haksul Chosa Pogo* [Report of Academic Survey of Andong Culture Region] Volume I &II. Seoul: Songgyunkwan Taehakgyo, 1967–1969.

Sung, Dong Hwan. "*Ramalyocho Sonjongkeyol sachalui ilji yongu*" [A Study on the location of Zen Buddhist temples during the Late Silla dynasty in Korea]," PhD dissertation, Taegu Hyosong Catholic University, 1999.

Taylor, G. *Australia: A Study of Warm Environments and their Effect on British Settlement*. London: Methuen & Co., 1947.

Tongjidaxue Chengshiguihua Yanjiushi, ed. *Zhongguo Chengshi Jianshesh* [History of Chinese City Construction]. Beijing: Zhongguo Jianshegongye chubanshe, 1982.

Wang, Yude. *Shenmide fengshui* [Mystic Geomancy]. Nanning: Guangxi renmin chubanshe, 1991.

Wang, Yong. *Zhongguo dilixueshi* [History of Chinese geography]. Taipei: Shangwu Yinshuguan, 1968.

Webster's New World Dictionary of the American Language, college edition. Cleveland and New York: The World Publishing Company, 1966.

Wheatley, Paul. *The Pivot of the Four Quarters*. Chicago: Aldine Publishing Company, 1971.

Wilhelm, Richard, trans. *I-ching*. The Richard Wilhelm translation rendered into English by Cary F. Baynes. Princeton: Princeton University Press, 1967.

Wright, J.K. "Terrae Incognitae: The Place of the Imagination in Geography," *Annals of the Association of the Association of American Geographers* 37 (1947): 1–15.

Wright, J.K. "A Plea for the History of Geography." In *Human Nature in Geography,* by John K. Wright, 11–23. Cambridge, MA.: Harvard University Press, 1966.

Xu, Jing. *Xuanhe fengshi Gaoli tujing* [Picture Book of Koryo by the Xuanhe Envoy]. Seoul, 1932.

Xu, Shanji and Xu Shanshu. *Dili-Renzixuezhi* [The Fact that All Humanity Must Know]. Hsin-chu: Chulin Shuchu, 1969.

Xu, Shen. Shuowen Jiezi [Etymology of Chinese Characters]. Beijing: Zhonghua Shuju, 1963.

Yanagi, Muneyoshi. "A Kwanghwamun iyo" [Oh, the Kwanghwamun Gate]. In *Choson kwa Yesul* [Korea and its Art]. By Yanagi Muneyoshyi, translated into Korean by Pak Chesam. Seoul: Pomusa, 1989.

Yang, I. *Han lung ching*, in *Dili Zhengzhong* [Authentic Collection of Geomantic Principles]. Commentary by Jiang Guo, (Hsin-chu: Chu-lin Shu-chu, 1967.

Yi, Chonghang (Lee, Joung Hang). "Pungsu Chirisol ui Songhaenggwa Kugosi uri Minjoksonge Michin Ak-yonghyange Kwanhan Ilkochal [A Study of the Practice of Geomancy and its Adverse Impact on Korean Characteristics]," *Kyongbuk Taehakkyo Nonmunijip* 5 (1962): 483–504.

Yi, Chung-hwan. *Taengni-ji* [Book of Choosing Settlement]. Seoul: Choson kwangmunhoe, 1912.

Yi, Hidok. "Pungsu Chiri." In *Hankuk Sasangui Wonchon* [Sources of Korean Thought], edited by Yi Sang-il and others, 174–213. Seoul: Yangyong-gak, 1973.

Yi, Hongjik, comp. *Kuksa Taesajon* [Grand Dictionary of Korean History]. Seoul: Paekman-sa, 1972.

Yi, Kidong. "Silla hadae ui Paegangin" [The Paegang Fortress during the Late Silla Period]. *Hanguk Hakpo* 4 (1976): 2–21.

Yi, Kwangjun. "Toson Kuksa wa Tosonsa" [The National Master Toson and the Toson Temple]. *Proceedings, 12th International Buddhism Conference, Toson Kuksawa Hankuk* [The National Master Toson and Korea]. Kwangju, (July 1996): 55–95.

Yi, Kyutae. *Kaehwa Paekkyong* [Hundred Scenes of the Enlightenment Period]. Seoul: Shintaeyang-sa, 1969.

Yi, Minsu, trans. *Oryun Haengsil-do* [Illustration of Five Virtuous Deeds]. Seoul: Ulyu Munhwa-sa, 1972.

Yi, Pyongdo. "Yijo chogiui kondo munjae" [Issues Relating to the New Capital during the Early the Choson Dynasty]. *Jindan Hakpo* 9 (1938): 30–85.

Yi, Pyongdo. *Koryo Sidae ui Yongu* [A Study of the Koryo Period]. Seoul: Ulyu munhwa-sa, 1948.

Yi, Pyongdo. *Hankuk Kodae Sahoewa ku Munhwa* [The Society of Ancient Korea and Its Culture]. Seoul: Somundang, 1973.

Yi, Pyongdo. *Koryo Sidaeui Yongu* [A Study of the Koryo Period], revised edition. Seoul: Asea Munhwasa, 1980.

Yi, Pyongmo. *Oryun Haengsil-do* [Illustration of Five Virtuous Deeds]. 1797 & 1859 Wood block print editions, The Jangseo-gak Collection, Academy of Korean Studies.

Yi, Sungnyong. "Sejong Taewang ui Kaesong ui kochal." [A Study of King Sejong's Personality]. *Taedong Munhwa Yongu* [Studies in Great Eastern Culture] 3 (1966): 19–88.

Yi, Uhyong. *Taedong jojido ui Tokdo* [Reading the Map of the Great Eastern Nation]. Seoul: Kwang'udang, 1990.

Yoon, Hong-key. "An Analysis of Korean Geomancy Tales." *Asian Folklore Studies* 34 (1975): 21–34.

Yoon, Hong-key. *Geomantic Relationships Between Culture and Nature in Korea*. Taipei: The Orient Culture Service, 1976.

Yoon, Hong-key. "The Image of Nature in Geomancy." *GeoJournal* 4 (1980): 341–348.

Yoon, Hong-key. "Environmental Determinism and Geomancy: Two Cultures, Two Concepts." *GeoJournal* 8 (1982): 1, 77–80.

Yoon, Hong-key. "An Early Chinese Idea of a Dynamic Environmental Cycle." *GeoJournal* 10 (1985): 211–212.

Yoon, Hong-key. *Maori Mind, Maori Land*. Berne: Peter Lang, 1986.

Yoon, Hong-key. "The Nature and Origin of Chinese Geomancy." *Eratosthene-Sphragide*. 1 (1986): 88–102.

Yoon, Hong-key. Hankukjok Geomentality e taehayo [On the Korean Geomentality]. *Chirihak Nonchong* [Journal of Geography] 14 (1987) 185–191.

Yoon, Hong-key. "Lun Zhongguo Gudai Fengshui de Qiyan he Fazhang" [A Theory on the Origin and Development of Ancient Chinese Geomancy]. *Ziran Kexueshi Yanjiu* [Studies in the History of Natural Sciences] (Beijing, China) 8 (1989): 84–89.

Yoon, Hong-key. "Loess Cave-Dwellings in Shaanxi Province, China," *GeoJournal* 21 (1990): 95–102.

Yoon, Hong-key. "Taedong yojidoui Chido chokboronjokin yongu" (A Carto-Genealogical Study of Taedong yojido). *Yoksa Munhwa Chiri (Journal of Cultural and Historical Geography)* 3 (1991): 37-47.

Yoon, Hong-key. "Taedongyojichondo Somunetaehan Yepikochal" [A Preliminary Study of 'The Preface' to The Whole Map of Korea]. *Yoksa Munhwa Chiri* [Journal of Cultural and Historical Geography] 4 (1992): 97–107.

Yoon, Hong-key. "The Traditional Standard Korean Maps and Geomancy." *New Zealand Map Society Journal* 6 (1992): 3–9

Yoon, Hong-key. "The Expression of Landforms in Chinese Geomantic Maps." *The Cartographic Journal* 29 (1992): 12–15.

Yoon, Hong-key. "Towards a Theory on the Origin of Geomancy." *Environment and Quality of Life in Central Europe: Problems of Transition: Proceedings, International Geographical Union, Regional Conference* (CD-ROM, ISBN 80–7184–153–6), Prague, 22–26 August 1994.

Yoon, Hong-key: " Pungsu Chirisol ui Ponjilkwa kiwon mit ku Chayonkwan" [The Principles and Origin of Korean Geomancy and Its Attitudes toward Nature]. *Hanguksa Shimin kangjoa* [Lectures on the History of Korea for Citizens]. 14 (1994): 187–204.

Yoon, Hong-key. "On the Origin of Geomancy and Its Diffusion to Korea" [Pungsu Chirisolui Kiwonkwa Hanbandoe Toipsigirul Otoke Pol Kossinka]. *Han'guk Hakpo* [Journal of Korean Studies] 21 (1995), 229–239.

Yoon, Hong-key. "Chinese Geomantic Maps," In *Encyclopaedia of the History of Science, Technology and Medicine in Non-Western Cultures*, 570–571. Dordrecht: Kluwer Academic Publishers.

Yoon, Hong-key. "An Interim Report on the Iconographic Warfare in the Geomantic Landscape of Seoul." *20th New Zealand Geography Conference Proceedings*(1999), 326–330.

Yoon, Hong-key. "Kyongbokkung kwa ku Choson Chonggokpu kunmul kyongkwan ul tullussan sangjingmul Chonjaeng" [The iconographical warfare over Kyongbok Palace and the former Japanese Colonial Government Building]. *Konggan kwa Sahwoi* [Space & Environment] 15 (2001): 282–305

Yoon, Hong-key. "Hankuk pungsuchrisolkwa pulkyosinangkwui kwange [The Relationships between Geomancy and Buddhism in Korea]," *Yoksa Minsokhak* [Journal of Korean Historical-folklife] 13 (2001): 125–158.

Yoon, Hong-key. "Hankuk pungsuchiri yonguui hoigowa chonmang" [Prospect and Retrospect of Research into Geomancy in Korea]. *Hankuk Sasangsahak* [History of Korean Thought] 17 (2001): 11–61.

Yoon, Hong-key. "Geomancy and Cities: A Preliminary Inquiry into the Origin of Chinese Geomancy and Its Application on City Locations in East Asia," In *Urban Morphology and the History of Civilization in East Asia*, International Research Centre for Japanese Studies 21st International Research Symposium, edited by Minoru Senda, 385–409. Kyoto: International Research Centre for Japanese Studies, 2002.

Yoon, Hong-key. "Confucian ethical values regarding the parents-children relationships in Korean geomancy tales," *Proceedings of the 1st World Congress of Korean Studies*, July 2002, 554–564.

Yoon, Inshil Choe, *Yi Chung-hwan's T'aengniji: The Korean Classic for Choosing Settlement.* Sydney: Wild Peony, 1998.

You, In Soo "Koryo Konkuk Solhwaui Yongu" [A Study of Koryo Dynasty Foundation Myth]. master's degree thesis, Hanyang University, 1989.

Yu, Chungson. *Yongnam ui Chonsol* [Legends of the Yongnam District]. Taegu: Hyongsol chulpan-sa, 1971.

Yu, Chungson (Ryu, Jeung Seon). "Andong ui Pibo Pungsu Sinang Chonsolkwa ku Paegyong [Geomantic Legends in Andong and their Background]" *Andong Munhwa [Andong Culture]*. 4 (1973): 3–23.

Yun, Chonkun. *Pungsu ui cholhak* [Philosophy of Geomancy]. Seoul: Norumto, 2001.

Zhongguo Kesueyuan Zirankexueshi Yanjiusuo Dixueshizu. *Zhogguo gudai Dilixueshi* [History of Ancient Chinese Geography]. Beijing: Kesue Chubianshe, 1984.

Zong, In-sob. *Folktales from Korea*. New York: The Grove Press, 1953.

Index

Anderson, Edgar, xiii
architecture: geomantic principles, 51; Japanese Government-General Building, 291; Kyongbok Palace, 289

Bruun, Ole, 8; defining geomancy, 9; Fengshui in China, xv
Buddhism: basic doctrines, 179; charity, 190; concept of charity, 143, 145; geomancer-monk, 182; and geomancy, 188, 197; geomancy relationship, 180, 181; impact on geomancy, 180; introduction to Korea, 201; Korean, 11, 33
Buddhist temple sites: geomancy of, 185; geomantic elements, 187

cartography of geomancy, 163
cave dwellers, 10, 15, 21, 24, 26, 29, 30
cave dwelling, 21, 24, 25, 26, 28, 109, 229
Changdok Palace, 288; compared with Kyongbok Palace, 286; reconstruction, 286
Changkyong Palace: turned into zoo, 289
charity: for needy people, 191; to suffering animals, 193
Cheju Island, 49
Chinese culture, 30; influence on, 57; origins of diffusion to Korea, 35; spreading to Korea, 10
Choi Chang jo, 49
Choi Chiwon, 39

Choi Pyonghon, 49
Choi Won-Suk, 50
Chon Kiung, 48
Chong Yakyong, 4, 42; disputes over gravesites, 126
Choson dynasty, 48; tombs, 121
Chu Hsi, 209
Chujak (red bird), 77
chusan, xiv
Confucian ethics: children's inheritance, 204; a married woman and her husband's family, 202; a married woman's attitudes, 145; parent-child relationships, 145, 204
Confucianism: ethical values, 190; impact on geomancy, 180; Korean, 11, 33; Neo-Confucianism, 201
cultural behavior, Koreans, 4
cultural landscape: naturalization of, 280

Dallet, C.H., 126
de Groot, J.J.M., 9, 15, 22, 30, 90; grave geomancy evolution, 16; theory of grave geomancy, 16
Dili-Renzixuezhi (geomantic textbook), 219
directions: in geomancy, 61
dragon: ancient cities along middle dragon, 222; azure, 77; in geomancy, 71; imperial cities in northern dragon, 220; Nanjing in southern dragon, 223; types of, 74
Duncan, James, 278

About the Author

Hong-key Yoon is an associate professor in the School of Geography and Environmental Science at the University of Auckland. He was born and brought up in a South Korean village, Haepyong of Sonsan County, North Kyongsang Province. He obtained a Ph.D. degree at Berkeley where he studied cultural Geography. He is the author of two books, *Geomantic Relationships Between Culture and Nature in Korea* and *Maori Mind, Maori Land* as well as a number of articles in the field of cultural geography, especially fengshui (geomancy) in Korea, Maori culture in New Zealand and environmental ideas in folklore. He lives in Auckland, New Zealand, with his wife and five children.